INDIVIDUAL CRIMINAL LIABILITY FOR THE
INTERNATIONAL CRIME OF AGGRESSION

Series Supranational Criminal Law: Capita Selecta, Volume 19

Published in the series:
1. *Supranational Criminal Law: a System Sui Generis,* Roelof Haveman, Olga Kavran and Julian Nichols (eds.)
2. *Double Jeopardy Without Parameters: Re-characterization in International Criminal Law,* Olaoluwa Olusanya
3. *Harmonization of Criminal Law in Europe*, Erling Johannes Husabø and Asbjørn Strandbakken (eds.)
4. *Sentencing and Sanctioning in Supranational Criminal Law,* Roelof Haveman and Olaoluwa Olusanya (eds.)
5. *Application of International Humanitarian and Human Rights Law to the Armed Conflicts of the Sudan: Complementary or Mutually Exclusive Regimes?,* Mohamed Abdelsalam Babiker
6. *Supranational Criminology: Towards a Criminology of International Crimes,* Alette Smeulers and Roelof Haveman (eds.)
7. *Individual Criminal Liability for the International Crime of Aggression,* Gerhard Kemp
8. *Collective Violence and International Criminal Justice – An Interdisciplinary Approach,* Alette Smeulers (ed.)
9. *International Criminal Law from a Swedish Perspective*, Iain Cameron, Malin Thunberg Schunke, Karin Påle Bartes, Christoffer Wong and Petter Asp
10. *The Implementation of the European Arrest Warrant in the European Union: Law, Policy and Practice*, Massimo Fichera
11. *The Principle of Mutual Recognition in Cooperation in Criminal Matters,* Annika Suominen
12. *The European Public Prosecutor's Office*, Martijn Willem Zwiers
13. *Victimological Approaches to International Crimes: Africa,* Rianne Letschert, Roelof Haveman, Anne-Marie de Brouwer, Antony Pemberton (eds.)
14. *The United States and International Criminal Tribunals*, Harry M. Rhea
15. *EU Sanctions: Law and Policy Issues Concerning Restrictive Measures,* Iain Cameron (ed.)
16. *Whose Responsibility?* Malin Thunberg Schunke
17. *Genocidal Gender and Sexual Violence*, Usta Kaitesi
18. *Addressing the Intentional Destruction of the Environment during Warfare under the Rome Statute of the International Criminal Court*, Steven Freeland

INDIVIDUAL CRIMINAL LIABILITY FOR THE INTERNATIONAL CRIME OF AGGRESSION

Gerhard KEMP

2nd edition

intersentia
Cambridge – Antwerp – Portland

Intersentia Ltd
Sheraton House | Castle Park
Cambridge | CB3 0AX | United Kingdom
Tel.: +44 1223 370 170 | Fax: +44 1223 370 169
Email: mail@intersentia.co.uk
www.intersentia.com | www.intersentia.co.uk

Distribution for the UK and Ireland:
NBN International
Airport Business Centre, 10 Thornbury Road
Plymouth, PL6 7 PP
United Kingdom
Tel.: +44 1752 202 301 | Fax: +44 1752 202 331
Email: orders@nbninternational.com

Distribution for Europe and all other countries:
Intersentia Publishing nv
Groenstraat 31
2640 Mortsel
Belgium
Tel.: +32 3 680 15 50 | Fax: +32 3 658 71 21
Email: mail@intersentia.be

Distribution for the USA and Canada:
International Specialized Book Services
920 NE 58th Ave. Suite 300
Portland, OR 97213
USA
Tel.: +1 800 944 6190 (toll free) | Fax: +1 503 280 8832
Email: info@isbs.com

Individual Criminal Liability for the International Crime of Aggression

Cover illustration: Francisco de Goya (1746–1828), Etching, Plate 6 from 'The Disparates (Foolish Fury)'

ISBN 978-1-78068-350-8
D/2016/7849/6
NUR 824

British Library Cataloguing in Publication Data. A catalogue record for this book is available from the British Library.

FOREWORD TO THE SECOND EDITION

The crime of aggression is the criminalisation of the unlawful use of force. This is conduct that has a political dimension by definition and triggers sensitivity in the sense that even the slightest suggestion that the crime has been committed will be hotly debated and may lead to angry reactions. This will certainly be even more the case if it comes to an investigation or prosecution. It is therefore not an easy exercise to embark on writing a monograph on the crime of aggression. Very few books have been published on the extraordinary case of the crime of aggression, which is at the same time an international crime of particular relevance currently and one for which no prosecution has yet taken place. The crime was inserted into the Statute of the International Criminal Court in 2010.

The first edition of this book appeared in 2010 just before the Kampala review conference. The book was well received and frequently used. It played a role in the formulation of the definition of the crime. Gerhard Kemp now surprises the reader with a second edition. This second edition fully incorporates the results of the Kampala conference. It has kept the structure of the first edition to a large extent, but expanded on the newly inserted Articles 8*bis*, 15*bis* and 15*ter* ICC Statute. In addition, the author has included a new Part V on the national and regional prosecution of the crime of aggression. That chapter provides case studies of the two European states that have been the most active in applying universal jurisdiction: Spain and Belgium. These examples demonstrate how disputed the use of universal jurisdiction is. States that do prosecute international crimes do not receive only applause, but must anticipate damage to their international relations or even fear reprisals. As may be expected, this risk is even greater where one state passes judgment on the conduct of another in the crime of aggression.

Gerhard Kemp acknowledges this in Chapter VIII, Concluding remarks: "The complementarity imperative is supposed to make the application of international criminal law before domestic courts the default option of the international criminal justice project. The crime of aggression poses legal and political complexities that put it in a different category than the other core crimes. Its nature as a leadership crime, and the conduct element that is reliant on state conduct, invoke rules and principles of international law that makes prosecution of the crime of aggression before domestic courts difficult. The lack of actual prosecutions at the national level is proof of this."

Another welcome extension to the first edition is the discussion of the criminal jurisdiction of the African Court on Justice and Human Rights. The 2014 Protocol on Amendments to the Protocol on the Statute of the African Court of Justice and Human Rights copied the crimes of the ICC Statute, including aggression, into the competence of the African Court. However, this was accompanied by certain immunities for heads of state. The author discusses the consequences of that protocol for the jurisdiction of the ICC.

Professor Gerhard Kemp is a leading South African criminal lawyer who publishes both on South African criminal law and procedure (i.e. *Criminal Law in South Africa* (2012) Oxford University Press, Cape Town) and on international criminal law (i.e. "The Implementation of the Rome Statute in Africa" in Werle, G, Fernandez, L & Vormbaum, M (eds) *Africa and the International Criminal Court – International Criminal Justice Series* Vol I (2014) Asser Press: The Hague & Springer Verlag: Berlin, and as a frequent commentator to the Annotated Leading Cases of International Criminal Tribunals).

The book is most informative in the sense that it provides the reader with the state of affairs of the crime of aggression. But it offers more. The author leads us through the opportunities and risks with the application of the definition of this new crime. The book provides us with an eloquent analysis of the foundations of the crime of aggression. It is critical in the sense that it also identifies the shortcomings of the choices made by the drafters.

The timing of the book is excellent as it appears the year before the ICC obtains jurisdiction over the crime of aggression. I strongly recommend the book as a thoughtful and thought-provoking study which raises important issues for our time.

André Klip
Professor of criminal law, criminal procedure and the transnational aspects of crime, Maastricht University, the Netherlands
October 2015

FOREWORD TO THE FIRST EDITION

Aggression has been a hot topic ever since it entered the realm of international criminal justice at the Nuremberg and Tokyo trials aft er the Second World War. It now belongs to the category of "the international core crimes", together with war crimes, crimes against humanity and genocide. A – provisional – point of culmination in the legal status of aggression as an international crime is its inclusion in the list of crimes that come within the jurisdiction of the International Criminal Court.

Despite its status as the "supreme international crime", suggesting that aggression is more serious than the other international crimes, aggression is not an uncontroversial crime. Ever since its appearance, there has been disagreement over its actual meaning. Unlike for war crimes and genocide, no specialised convention for aggression has been adopted after the Second World War. Whereas there seems to be a growing consensus that aggression is prohibited under customary international law, and while it is even an international crime giving rise to individual criminal responsibility, no generally accepted definition of aggression exists as yet.

Professor Kemp's book is the first comprehensive study of the subject with a focus on individual criminal responsibility. He starts by looking at aggression within the general framework of the collective security system of the United Nations set up after the Second World War, offering a detailed analysis of the various developments leading to the prohibition of the use of force in its normative and institutional perspective. Then follows an indepth study of various steps leading to the criminalisation of aggression, comprising the transition from a State responsibility-oriented approach towards a greater emphasis on individual criminal responsibility. Hardly any progress has been made after Nuremberg and Tokyo as far as individual criminal responsibility is concerned. While the 1974 General Assembly Resolution defining aggression has a clear focus on State Responsibility, projects oriented towards introducing individual criminal responsibility for this crime did not materialise. None of the International Law Commission's drafts defining aggression as an international crime made it into a treaty, and very little, if any, national legislation and jurisprudence exist on the "supreme international crime". The latter is hardly surprising, as there are many legal obstacles and, perhaps more importantly, as it is highly questionable whether national criminal courts are the adequate forum to try crimes of this nature. As a result, the only possible chance for such crimes to be brought to justice would be before an international criminal court or tribunal. Yet, the fusion of political and criminal justice responses to mass atrocities after the end of the Cold War, as evidenced by the creation of the *ad hoc* tribunals for the former Yugoslavia and Rwanda, have not, as yet, comprised aggression. The Rome Statute for an International Criminal Court may look like a big step forward, yet the drafters fell short of defining the concept. Professor Kemp's study describes in great detail how the question of aggression was treated at Rome and how the drafters came to include aggression in the list of crimes subject to the jurisdiction of the Court, but deferred the definition to a later stage. The last Chapter, offers a number of interesting suggestions and submissions for a framework on individual criminal liability for the crime of aggression.

Professor Kemp, whom I have known as one of my very bright students at the University of Antwerp not so long ago, is a quickly rising star in the firmament of solid young publicists in the field of international criminal law. This study on individual criminal liability for the international crime of aggression shows the author at his best. It offers the reader an excellent guide through the labyrinth of various sources of law that are relevant to comprehend this extremely complex notion on the borderline between public international law and criminal law. Critical observations and constructive suggestions figure throughout the work. The book strikes the right balance between an in-depth analysis and a clear synthesis of the complex issues that are relevant to this very thorny subject, while at the same time presenting them in a format that is pleasant to read. This study on aggression deserves its place on the shelves of academics, practitioners, lawmakers, treatymakers and all those who are committed to the cause of international criminal justice.

Professor Christine Van den Wyngaert
Judge at the ICC
15 January 2010

PREFACE

At the time of writing the crises in Syria and Ukraine have gripped the attention of the international media. Both crises caused extensive instability and human misery in some of the most volatile regions of the world. In neither of the two situations the 'international community' seemed to be able to find any real solutions. In both situations the use of armed force under international law formed part of the narrative. In Syria's case some presented the use of force as a *solution* (or at least as part of the solution) in order to stop an immoral and criminal regime from murdering its own people. Others objected to the use of force as a simplistic and prima facie unlawful way to solve a complex situation.[1] In the case of Ukraine the unlawful use of force (including a powerful neighbour's use of armed force by proxy) was presented as the root *cause of the conflict*.[2]

The UN Charter-based collective security system provides for a strict framework on the prohibition of the use of force. Self-defence and the use of force as per Security Council authorisation are lawful. Other claims to lawfulness, including humanitarian intervention, pre-emptive self-defence and modern versions of the Just War doctrine are not lawful. Thus provides the modern *jus contra bellum* which emerged in the aftermath of the Second World War.

The crime of aggression is the criminalisation of the unlawful use of force. The quest to find a suitable definition for this most opaque of the so-called core crimes resulted in the Kampala Resolution on the Crime of Aggression, which provides for a definition of aggression and for conditions for the exercise of International Criminal Court jurisdiction over the crime of aggression. The drafting, diplomacy and eventual adoption of the package of proposals constituted an achievement in its own right and a worthy monument to the legacy of Nuremberg; the birthplace of modern international criminal law. But there are significant substantive and jurisdictional limitations that render the Kampala Resolution on the Crime of Aggression perhaps more of a sentimental achievement than any real tool in the quest to end impunity for the most serious

1 See submissions by Carsten Stahn 'Syria and the semantics of intervention, aggression and punishment' 11 *Journal of International Criminal Justice* (2013) 955–977.

2 For background and analysis see Ireneusz Kaminski 'International law aspects of the situation in Ukraine' in Klaus Bachmann and Igor Lyubashenko (eds) *The Maidan Uprising, separatism and foreign intervention* (2014) Peter Lang, Frankfurt am Main, 379–404.

crimes under international law. Having said that, it is also prudent to note that any small measure to end impunity is better than nothing. The open question is whether the ICC will be able to adjudicate the crime of aggression, which is the most political of the core crimes.

National and regional efforts to criminalise and prosecute aggression are part of the legal landscape. The ICC, arguably the single most important player in the international criminal justice project, is not the only player. It should not be, not by legal design and not in terms of good policy. It is however clear that the national and regional efforts to criminalise aggression are even more constrained than the regime provided for in terms of the amendments to the Rome Statute of the International Criminal Court, adopted at Kampala in 2010.

This book describes and analyse pertinent aspects of the complex crime of aggression; a crime for which individuals, in particular individuals in political and military leadership positions, can be held criminally liable. The crime is also rooted in state conduct which is the domain of policy and politics. The inherent tension and awkward co-existence of the *criminal justice response* and the *political response* to the unlawful use of force inform the various chapters in this book. The topic is addressed from an international, regional and comparative perspective with the author's native South Africa as the vantage point.

Gerhard Kemp
Cape Town
August 2015

CONTENTS

PART IV.
THE INTERNATIONAL CRIMINAL COURT AND THE CRIME OF AGGRESSION

PART V. NATIONAL AND REGIONAL CRIMINALISATION AND PROSECUTION OF THE CRIME OF AGGRESSION

LIST OF ABBREVIATIONS

AIDP	Association Internationale de Droit Penal
AJIL	The American Journal of International Law
All ER	All England Law Reports
ASIL	American Society of International Law
AU	African Union
BC Int'l & Comp L Rev	Boston College International and Comparative Law Review
ECC	Extraordinary Chambers of Cambodia
ECOWAS	Economic Community of West African States
EJIL	European Journal on International Law
EU	European Union
Fordham Int'l LJ	Fordham International Law Journal
GA	(United Nations) General Assembly
GG	Government Gazette (South Africa)
ICC	International Criminal Court
ICJ	International Court of Justice
ICLQ	The International and Comparative Law Quarterly
ICLR	International Criminal Law Review
ICTR	International Criminal Tribunal for Rwanda
ICTY	International Criminal Tribunal for the Former Yugoslavia
ILA	International Law Association
ILC	International Law Commission
ILM	International Legal Materials
IMT	International Military Tribunal at Nuremberg
IMTFE	International Military Tribunal for the Far East at Tokyo
ILR	Israel Law Reports
IST	Iraqi Special Tribunal
JICJ	Journal of International Criminal Justice
LJIL	Leiden Journal of International Law
NAM	Non-Alignment Movement
NATO	North Atlantic Treaty Organization
NILR	Netherlands International Law Review
NLR	New Left Review

NYIL	Netherlands Yearbook of International Law
OAU	Organisation for African Unity
PrepCom	Preparatory Committee on the Establishment of an International Criminal Court
SACJ	South African Journal of Criminal Justice
SAJHR	South African Journal on Human Rights
SALJ	South African Law Journal
SAYIL	South African Yearbook of International Law
SC/UNSC	United Nations Security Council
SLSC	Sierra Leone Special Court
Stell LR	Stellenbosch Law Review
THRHR	Tydskrif vir Hedendaags Romeins-Hollandse Reg
UBLJ	University of Botswana Law Journal
UK	United Kingdom
UN	United Nations
UNHCR	United Nations High Commissioner for Refugees
UNTS	United Nations Treaty Series
USA	United States of America

PART I

INTRODUCTION AND FRAMEWORK OF ANALYSIS

INTRODUCTION

1. RESEARCH PROBLEM, RATIONALE, AND DEMARCATION

1.1. RESEARCH PROBLEM AND RATIONALE

This book critically assesses the most important components of the framework for individual criminal liability for the crime of aggression. Aggression is regarded as one of the core crimes under customary international law. The definition of aggression and the conditions for the exercise of International Criminal Court jurisdiction over the crime of aggression as adopted at the Kampala Review Conference on the Rome Statute of the International Criminal Court are yet to enter into force. National and regional legislative frameworks for the criminalisation of aggression complete the legal landscape.

It is argued that the creation of the ICC provides the international community with an historic opportunity to establish effective jurisdiction over the crime of aggression. This criminal justice response to aggression has implications for the collective security system (embodied by the UN).[1] Consequently, the latter aspect forms the first substantive part of the book, where some of the implications of aggression for the collective security system are highlighted and examined.

This book provides an historical account of the development of the notion of aggression. It identifies the important debates affecting the attempts to define the crime of aggression; puts the legal debates in normative and international political context; and examines the conditions necessary for the prosecution of the crime of aggression at national, regional and international level.

Special consideration is given to the different elements of the crime of aggression as adopted at the Kampala Review Conference. The reason for this is that the 'Kampala definition' constitutes arguably the most realistic and legally sound basis for the eventual prosecution of the crime of aggression before the ICC. An important regional instrument on individual criminal liability for the

---

1 This issue is presumably going to get more attention from international lawyers in future. See discussions in the Committee on the International Criminal Court of the ILA, Working Session, 7 Jun 2006, Report of the Seventy-Second Conference of the ILA (Toronto 2006), ILA, London, 594–599.

crime of aggression – the Malabo Protocol of 2014 – provides for a definition of aggression adapted to the relevant regional collective security regime. Domestic incorporation of the crime of aggression takes on different forms. In this book special attention is given to the possibility to prosecute the crime of aggression under customary international law before domestic courts. This choice is informed by the assumption that many states would resist incorporation of the 'Kampala definition' of aggression. Furthermore, many important states are not states party to the Rome Statute of the ICC. For them the crime of aggression in its customary international law form might have more relevance.

The *essential premise* of this book is that aggression is a not only a serious threat to international peace and security, but also threatens the stability of the international legal order. And, of course, on a micro-level it also affects the lives of individuals in a very real sense.

1.2. *JUS AD BELLUM* AND *JUS IN BELLO*

The crime of aggression has its normative roots in the historical developments towards the regulation of the use of armed force by states – the *jus ad bellum*. The UN Charter embodies the modern *jus ad bellum*, and provides for the legitimate use of force by states in two instances: Self-defence[2] and collective security operations as instituted by the Security Council under Chapter VII of the Charter. Historically, the *jus in bello* (the rules on the conduct of armed forces in armed conflicts) developed as a distinct branch of law. The modern *jus in bello* is collectively known as international humanitarian law. At the core of the *jus in bello* is the principle that, regardless of the legality of the armed conflict (as determined by the *jus ad bellum*), all combatants have the same rights and duties in warfare. Thus, regardless of the legal status of the use of force, the combatants participating in the conflict have equal protection under international humanitarian law, and the combatants have equal responsibility to uphold the rules of international humanitarian law. Violations of some of the rules of international humanitarian law (notably 'grave breaches of the Geneva Conventions of 1949') are treated as war crimes and can lead to individual criminal liability.[3] Customary international humanitarian law provides that serious violations of international humanitarian law (in both international

---

2 Art 51 UN Charter.

3 See Art 8 ('War crimes') of the Rome Statute of the ICC; Art 3 ('Violations of Art 3 common to the Geneva Conventions and of Additional Protocol II) and Art 4 ('Other serious violations of international humanitarian law') of the Statute of the Special Court for Sierra Leone (2002) (available at www.sc-sl.org); Art 4 ('Violations of Art 3 Common to the Geneva Conventions and of Additional Protocol II') Statute of the International Tribunal for Rwanda (1994) *ILM*, 1994, 1598; Art 2 ('Grave breaches of the Geneva Conventions of 1949'), Art 3 ('Violations of the laws or customs of war') Statute of the International Tribunal for the Former Yugoslavia (1993) *ILM*, 1993, 1192.

and non-international armed conflicts) constitute war crimes.[4] States also have the right (under customary international humanitarian law) to 'vest universal jurisdiction in their national courts over war crimes.'[5]

The most concrete distinction between the *jus ad bellum* and the *jus in bello* can be found in the Statutes of the Nuremberg and Tokyo Tribunals.[6] In both statutes a clear distinction is drawn between violations of the *jus ad bellum* (or 'crimes against peace'[7]) and violations of the *jus in bello* (or 'war crimes'[8]).

This book analyses the crime of aggression. Aggression is in a sense a criminalisation of the *jus ad bellum*. Insofar as the distinction between the *jus ad bellum* and the *jus in bello* is challenged (due to developments in international politics and law[9]), this book briefly addresses some of these debates where relevant. These developments include the notions of 'humanitarian intervention' and the so-called 'war on terror'.[10]

1.3. THE CRIMINALISATION OF INTERNATIONAL AGGRESSION

The International Military Tribunal (IMT) at Nuremberg that tried the major Nazi war criminals after the end of the Second World War, described the crime of aggression (or 'crimes against peace') as the 'supreme international crime'.[11] However, it is shown in this book that since the post-Second World War trials in Germany and Japan, there has been no prosecution of an individual for *this supreme international crime*.[12] This state of affairs prevails despite the fact that aggression is regarded as a crime under customary international law. In Chapter VIII the implications of this status of aggression for domestic legal systems are explored. It is argued that the crime of aggression (as it was prosecuted at

4 Jean-Marie Henckaerts and Louise Doswald-Beck *Customary International Humanitarian Law Vol I: Rules* (2005) Cambridge University Press, Cambridge, 568–603.

5 Jean-Marie Henckaerts and Louise Doswald-Beck (Customary International Humanitarian Law) (*supra*) 604–607.

6 See in general Yoram Dinstein 'The distinctions between war crimes and crimes against peace' in Yoram Dinstein and Mala Tabory *War crimes in International Law* (1996) Kluwer Law International, The Hague, 1–18.

7 Nuremberg Charter art 6(a); Tokyo Charter art 5(a).

8 Nuremberg Charter art 6(b); Tokyo Charter art 5(b).

9 See Antoine Bouvier 'Assessing the relationship between jus in bello and jus ad bellum: An "Orthodox" view' *ASIL Proceedings* (2006) 109–112; Julie Mertus 'The danger of conflating jus ad bellum and jus in bello' *ASIL Proceedings* (2006) 114–117; Carsten Stahn '"Jus ad bellum," "Jus in bello," "Jus post bellum?" Rethinking the conception of the law of armed force' *ASIL Proceedings* (2006) 158–160.

10 See Ch II section 5, and in particular section 2, *infra*.

11 Judgment of Oct 1, 1946, International Military Tribunal Judgment and Sentences, 41 *AJIL* 172, 186 (1947).

12 See discussion in Ch III of the trials at Nuremberg and Tokyo of the major war criminals.

Nuremberg and Tokyo) constitutes a narrow concept of *waging of an aggressive war.* This is the crime that has customary international law status.

The absence of prosecutions of individuals for the crime of aggression was not due to a lack of wars (civil or international) in the decades following the Second World War. Indeed, even the period of the Cold War was characterised by conflicts and the use of armed force by states, often in *prima facie* contravention of the prohibition of the use of force provided for in the UN Charter.[13] The lack of prosecutions should not be seen as a reflection on the normative legacy of Nuremberg. This legacy, discussed in Chapter IV, provided the legal and normative context of many attempts to build on the jurisprudence of Nuremberg (and Tokyo). These attempts were primarily aimed at keeping alive the ideal of an international criminal court with jurisdiction over the most serious crimes under international law, notably aggression, war crimes, crimes against humanity, and genocide. The United Nations and the International Law Commission, as well as numerous specialist organisations, scholars and human rights organisations worked on various proposals to create a *permanent international criminal court,* and to define or codify the most serious crimes. Some early successes, like the adoption of the Genocide Convention of 1948,[14] provided hope that the 'legacy of Nuremberg' (in the sense that individuals responsible for the worst international crimes should not go unpunished) would not be meaningless. The General Assembly of the UN – arguably the entity which is most representative of the 'international community' – adopted the Nuremberg Principles in 1950.[15] These Principles confirmed the notion of individual criminal liability for the most serious crimes under international law, and in particular the crimes tried at Nuremberg (crimes against peace, war crimes and crimes against humanity). The Genocide Convention, the Nuremberg Principles, and the four Geneva Conventions adopted in 1949,[16] indicated that the international community wanted to keep the legacy of Nuremberg alive, and to *expand* the scope of individual criminal liability for international crimes.

The irony is that the 'supreme international crime' (aggression) proved to be the most contentious of the four 'core crimes', referred to above. While the UN Charter reflected (especially in Article 2(4)) the commitment of the international

---

13 For instance the Iran/Iraq war during the 1980s; the Soviet invasion of Afghanistan in 1979.

14 Convention on the Prevention and Suppression of the Crime of Genocide (1948) *UN Treaty Series*, vol 78, 227, reproduced in Christine van den Wyngaert (ed) *International Criminal Law* 4th (2011) 405.

15 Nuremberg Principles, 29 Jul 1950, UNGAOR, 5th Session, Supp No 12, UN Doc A/1316 (1950), reproduced in Christine van den Wyngaert (International Criminal Law) (*supra*) 375.

16 Convention for the Amelioration of the Condition of the Wounded and Sick in Armed Forces in the Field; Convention for the Amelioration of the Condition of Wounded, Sick and Shipwrecked Members of Armed Forces at Sea; Convention relative to the Treatment of Prisoners of War; Convention relative to the Protection of Civilian Persons in Time of War, 12 Aug 1949.

community to end the use of force by states as a means to settle disputes or to further the national interest, neither the Charter nor any other international legal instrument provided for a definition of aggression. It was only in 1974 that the UN General Assembly adopted a so-called 'consensus' definition of aggression,[17] but this text was drafted with *state-responsibility* (and not individual criminal liability) in mind.

From the early 1950s to 1996 the International Law Commission (ILC) attempted to define aggression for purposes of individual criminal liability, but these attempts proved to be unsuccessful.[18]

The end of the Cold War did not result in global peace. But it provided the international community with an opportunity to react more decisively (and beyond the political restrictions of the Cold War) to threats to international peace and security. The establishment of two *ad hoc* international criminal tribunals by the Security Council in the last decade of the twentieth century, to deal with massive human rights violations in the Former Yugoslavia and in Rwanda, provided the essential political and legal impetus for the formation of a permanent international criminal court. The fusion of *political* and *criminal justice* responses to mass atrocities that shocked the conscience of the world and threatened international peace and security, provided a paradigm conducive to a more effective approach to the core crimes. In this spirit the Rome Statute of the International Criminal Court was adopted in July 1998, signalling a hopeful end to a bloody century.

The Rome Statute establishes a permanent International Criminal Court (ICC) to try individuals responsible for the most serious crimes under international law, namely war crimes, crimes against humanity and genocide. This Statute also includes aggression as a crime within the ICC's jurisdiction, but the ICC can only *exercise* jurisdiction over the crime after the adoption of a definition and conditions for the exercise of jurisdiction. The 'supreme international crime' proved too contentious for direct and immediate inclusion in the Rome Statute of the ICC.

The Assembly of States Parties delivered at the Kampala Review Conference of 2010, via a Special Working Group, a package of proposals that completed the task eschewed by the drafters of the original Article 5(2) of the Rome Statute of the ICC.

Regional criminal law takes the process further, as exemplified by the adapted definition of aggression provided for in the Protocol on Amendments to the Protocol on the Statute of the African Court of Justice and Human Rights – in short – the Malabo Protocol of 2014.

---

17 Definition of Aggression, GA Res 3314 (xxix), 29 UN GAOR Supp No 31, 142 UN Doc A/9631 (1974). See Ch IV section 2.3.1 *infra* for the text of the definition.

18 See discussion in Ch IV *infra*.

The criminalisation of aggression occurred in the aftermath of the Second World War and in the context of the international community's efforts to outlaw the use of force by states. In Chapter II it is shown that the development of the *jus ad bellum* – today best described as the *jus contra bellum* – represents one of the outstanding features of the international political and legal system. The prohibition of the use of force by states is one of the highest norms of the international legal system. This system, of which collective security forms a key characteristic, provides the institutional context for the discussion and analysis of the developments surrounding the various efforts to build on the post-Second World War prosecutions of individuals for the crime of aggression. It is shown in this book that the various efforts to define and codify the crime of aggression for purposes of individual criminal liability are fundamentally informed by the historical, institutional and normative factors referred to above.

The historical attempts to define and codify the crime of aggression are also analysed in the context of the evolving system of international criminal law. This system is characterised by national, regional and international efforts to end impunity for the worst crimes affecting the international community as a whole, notably the core crimes of aggression, war crimes, crimes against humanity and genocide. This evolving system comprises efforts to establish *national criminal jurisdiction* over the core crimes. In order to complement this, states party to the permanent *International Criminal Court* are obliged to provide for the necessary domestic legal mechanisms that would make it possible for such states to effectively co-operate with the ICC. To this end, the complementary jurisdiction of the ICC ensures that where a state party to the Rome Statute of the ICC is either unwilling or unable to prosecute an individual or individuals responsible for one or more of the crimes within the ICC's jurisdiction, the ICC can try the case. *Regional efforts* like the 'African Criminal Court' may yet complement or complicate the international criminal justice project.

2. KEY CONCEPTS AND DEBATES

2.1 THE MAIN FEATURES AND FOUNDATIONS OF THE EVOLVING SYSTEM OF INTERNATIONAL CRIMINAL LAW

2.1.1. The international community's reaction to atrocities

One way of looking at the system of international criminal law is to view it as a *reaction* of the *international community* to atrocities.[19] This must be seen in

[19] Antonio Cassese *International Criminal Law* (2003) Oxford University Press, Oxford, 3–14.

context: states are (still) the primary actors in the international system, but the *constitutionalist* notion of an international community (or, *civitas maxima*) entails that this international community is governed by norms, not power.[20] It means that the international system (traditionally anarchist, where sovereign states – in the absence of an overarching sovereign – acted in their own interest and where the exercise of state power was central)[21] is moving towards the *supra*-national *limitation of state power*. The UN Charter has been described as a 'constitutional' limitation on the raw power of sovereign states, regulating the exercise of state power, notably the use of force by states. The ICC has also been described as such a 'constitutional' development,[22] albeit not limiting, but rather *complementing*,[23] the exercise of state jurisdiction over the most serious crimes under international law. The ICC is arguably in a position to *limit the sovereignty* of states party to the Rome Statute of the ICC in the sense that it can influence state behaviour and policy, for instance with respect to human rights practices. The international community is thus more than a *political* community; it is also a *legal* community. It is a community characterised by norms such as the desire to act in the common good, and by actions to advance the collective interest. This constitutionalist view of the international community also emphasises the importance of certain fundamental values, especially 'super-norms' like *jus cogens* obligations – for instance the prohibition of the use of force by states.[24]

The criminal justice reaction to international atrocities is prompted in part by the failure of other measures (for instance diplomatic and economic sanctions) to stop or prevent atrocities like genocide, crimes against humanity, war crimes, and indeed, aggression. In terms of the criminal justice response, various modalities exist to address the atrocities that affect the whole of humankind. Antonio Cassese listed the following modalities: the exercise by national courts of jurisdiction over offences on grounds of territoriality or nationality; the exercise by national courts of extraterritorial jurisdiction (the latter can also be

20 See in general Wouter Werner 'Consitutionalisation, fragmentation, politicization, the constitutionalisation of international law as a janus-faced phenomenon' 8 *Griffin's View on International and Comparative Law* (2007) 17–30, in particular 18–23; and in particular Gerhard Kemp 'Constitutionalization and the International Criminal Court: Whither individual criminal liability for aggression?' 4 *South African Law Journal* (2008) 694–714.

21 David Caron pointed out that the condition of anarchy is a basic feature of international relations. David Caron 'Framing political theory of international courts and tribunals: Reflections at the Centennial' *ASIL Proceedings* (2006) 56.

22 Wouter Werner (Constitutionalisation, fragmentation, politicisation) (*supra*) 27; Kemp (*supra*) 695–696.

23 Under the principle of complementarity, the ICC will only exercise jurisdiction over a matter if a state party is either unwilling or unable to prosecute.

24 See in general Anne Peters 'There is nothing more practical than a good theory: An overview of contemporary approaches to international law' 44 *German Yearbook of International Law* (2001) 25–37, 35.

the result of obligations in terms of the *aut dedere, aut judicare*[25] enforcement model in international criminal law); the establishment of truth commissions to complement traditional criminal justice responses to atrocities; the establishment of international criminal tribunals.[26]

2.1.2. *Individual criminal liability*

This book concerns *individual criminal liability* for the crime of aggression. Individual criminal liability is one of the fundamental features of the evolving system of international criminal law.

The main purpose of traditional international law is the regulation of the relations between states. The prosecution of *individuals* for crimes under international law in the post-Second World War international criminal tribunals at Nuremberg and Tokyo represents a paradigm shift and can be seen as the confirmation of the *separateness* of international criminal law from classic (public) international law:[27] individuals are the subjects of international criminal law, and individuals can be held liable for crimes under international law. Individual (*personal*) criminal responsibility[28] is necessary to establish liability. In *Prosecutor v Tadic* the ICTY Appeals Chamber put it as follows:

> 'The basic assumption must be that in international law as much as in national systems, the foundation of criminal responsibility is the principle of personal culpability: nobody may be held criminally responsible for acts or transactions in which he has not personally engaged or in some other way participated (*nulla poena sine culpa*).'[29]

---

25 Many international instruments contain this model of enforcement of international criminal law. It imposes on states parties the duty to either 'extradite or prosecute' individuals responsible for crimes under international law. Hugo Grotius used the term *aut dedere aut punire*, but this was in 1973 reformulated by Cherif Bassiouni to '*aut dedere aut judicare*', in order to emphasise the judicial process in the form of a trial that is necessary to determine criminal culpability. See Cherif Bassiouni *International Criminal Law* 2nd Vol I (1999) Transnational Publishers, New York, 5.

26 Cassese (International Criminal Law) (*supra*) 6–14.

27 Kriangsak Kittichaisaree *International Criminal Law* (2001) Oxford University Press, Oxford, 9. Lyal Sunga wrote that the term international criminal law 'is accurate only if used in any one of three senses: 1) to refer to the accumulation of international legal norms on individual criminal responsibility (without implying that they form a coherent system); 2) to refer to international criminal law as an incipient field of international law currently in a stage of emergence (without implying that it already exists as a relatively self-sufficient or autonomous system); or 3) to refer to the decisions, law and procedure of a permanent international criminal court'. See Lyal Sunga *The emerging system of International Criminal Law – Developments in Codification and Implementation* (1997) Kluwer Law International, The Hague, 7. It is submitted that international criminal law has (especially after the adoption of the Rome Statute of the ICC in 1998) indeed emerged as a separate system in all three respects as identified by Sunga.

28 See in general Cassese (International Criminal Law) (*supra*) 136–139.

29 ICTY *Prosecutor v Dusko Tadic* (Appeals Chamber) Case No IT-94-1-A, 15 Jul 1999, par 186.

Article 25 of the Rome Statute of the ICC provides for individual criminal responsibility:

> '1. The Court shall have jurisdiction over natural persons pursuant to this Statute.
> 2. A person who commits a crime within the jurisdiction of the Court shall be individually responsible and liable for punishment in accordance with this Statute.
> 3. In accordance with this Statute, a person shall be criminally responsible and liable for punishment for a crime within the jurisdiction of the Court if that person:
>   (a) Commits such a crime, whether as an individual, jointly with another or through another person, regardless of whether that other person is criminally responsible;
>   (b) Orders, solicits or induces the commission of such a crime which in fact occurs or is attempted;
>   (c) For the purpose of facilitating the commission of such a crime, aids, abets or otherwise assists in its commission or its attempted commission, including providing the means for its commission;
>   (d) In any other way contributes to the commission or attempted commission of such a crime by a group of persons acting with a common purpose. Such contribution shall be intentional and shall either:
>   (i) Be made with the aim of furthering the criminal activity or criminal purpose of the group, where such activity or purpose involves the commission of a crime within the jurisdiction of the Court; or
>   (ii) Be made in the knowledge of the intention of the group to commit the crime;
>   (e) In respect of the crime of genocide, directly and publicly incites others to commit genocide;
>   (f) Attempts to commit such a crime by taking action that commences its execution by means of a substantial step, but the crime does not occur because of circumstances independent of the person's intentions. However, a person who abandons the effort to commit the crime or otherwise prevents the completion of the crime shall not be liable for punishment under this Statute for the attempt to commit that crime if that person completely and voluntarily gave up the criminal purpose.
> 4. No provision in this Statute relating to individual criminal responsibility shall affect the responsibility of States under international law.'

This detailed description of the elements of individual criminal responsibility is a reflection of the maturation of international criminal law as the international community's criminal justice response to atrocities that affect the whole of humankind.

2.1.3. *The importance of the principle of legality*

The question of individual criminal liability for the international crime of aggression also involves the principle of legality – one of the core principles of criminal law (often expressed in terms of the maxim *nullum crimen, nulla poena sine lege*). Indeed, the history of the various efforts to define aggression (described and analysed in Chapters III and further) is testimony to the impact that this principle had (and is still having) on the aggression-debate. The historically important international trials at Nuremberg and Tokyo (discussed in Chapter III) established individual criminal liability for crimes against peace, including the crime of waging a war of aggression. It is shown that these trials were controversial because of the way in which the tribunals dealt with the principle of legality. The historic first criminalisation of the crime of aggression was marred by the controversy surrounding the application of the principle of legality. It is shown how the 'legacy of Nuremberg' had an impact on various aspects of the aggression debate. It is pointed out in that the principle of legality plays a particular role in the debate about the possible application of international criminal law in national legal systems. The principle of legality is one of the foundational principles informing the scope and understanding of the substantive law elements of the crime of aggression.

The principle of legality entails that no crime (or punishment) exists without a norm or rule in law criminalising the conduct in question and providing for punishment.[30] Jonathan Burchell summarised the theory of the German scholar JP Anselm von Feuerbach (who formulated the *nullum crimen* principle in 1801) as follows: criminal laws should be made 'by a competent legislature that announced in advance and with clarity and certainty the definition of crimes and the details of their punishments.'[31]

The principle of legality is also well-established in international criminal law.[32] Gerhard Werle and Florian Jessberger point out that the principle of legality is part of customary international law.[33] The Rome Statute of the ICC provides for both *nullum crimen sine lege* (Article 22)[34] and *nulla poena sine*

30 CR Snyman Criminal Law 6th (2014) LexisNexis Butterworths, Durban, 36.

31 Jonathan Burchell *Principles of Criminal Law* 3rd (2005) Juta, Cape Town, 95.

32 Cassese (International Criminal Law) (*supra*) 139–158; Gerhard Werle and Florian Jessberger *Principles of International Criminal Law* 3rd (2014) Oxford University Press, Oxford, 39; Geert-Jan Knoops *Defenses in Contemporary International Criminal Law* (2001) Transnational Publishers, New York, 168. For a discussion of the principle of legality in international criminal tribunals, see Mia Swart 'Legality as inhibitor: The special place of *nullum crimen sine lege* in the jurisprudence of international criminal tribunals' 30 *SAYIL* (2005) 33–49.

33 Gerhard Werle and Florian Jessberger (Principles of International Criminal Law) (*supra*) 39.

34 Art 22: '1. A person shall not be criminally responsible under this Statute unless the conduct in question constitutes, at the time it takes place, a crime within the jurisdiction of the Court. 2. The definition of a crime shall be strictly construed and shall not be extended by analogy. In case of ambiguity, the definition shall be interpreted in favour of the person being

lege (Article 23).[35] Article 24 furthermore provides for the principle of non-retroactive application of criminal responsibility under the Rome Statute.[36]

2.2. STATE SOVEREIGNTY

State sovereignty (states exercising exclusive power over their territories) has been the organising principle of the modern international political and legal system since at least the Peace of Westphalia of 1648 (in terms of the Treaties of Osnabrück and Münster).[37] These Treaties, which ended the Thirty Years' War between Sweden, France and Germany, not only confirmed the concept of sovereign states as the organising principle of the international system, but also provided for the *enforcement* of the peace treaties. Leo Gross pointed out that Europe therefore received 'an international constitution, which gave to all its adherents the right of intervention to enforce its engagements'.[38] Thus, the treaties were more than just confirmations of state sovereignty, or of peace between two or more sovereign states: the treaties came to represent the first attempt to create a 'constitutional' order in an international system dominated by sovereign states. In this sense the Peace of Westphalia can be considered as an important precursor[39] to the international system of sovereign states, governed by the principles of collective security contained in the Charter of the United Nations.[40]

The Charter of the UN provides that the Organisation 'is based on the principle of the sovereign equality of all its Members'.[41] This principle forms the basis of modern public international law and is also 'the fundamental premise on which all international relations rest.'[42] The UN Charter confirms the Westphalian notion of sovereignty as a foundation of the international system, and protects the *legal equality* between states.[43] The principle of non-intervention and the prohibition of the threat or use of force are two features of the international system that are closely associated with the concept of sovereignty.[44] These

---

investigated, prosecuted or convicted. 3. This article shall not affect the characterization of any conduct as criminal under international law independent of this Statute.'

35 Art 23: 'A person convicted by the Court may be punished only in accordance with this Statute.'

36 Art 24: '1. No person shall be criminally responsible under this Statute for conduct prior to the entry into force of the Statute. 2. In the event of a change in the law applicable to a given case prior to a final judgment, the law more favourable to the person being investigated, prosecuted or convicted shall apply.'

37 For an historical overview, see Leo Gross 'The Peace of Westphalia, 1648–1948' 42 *AJIL* (1948) 20–41.

38 Leo Gross (Peace of Westphalia) (*supra*) 24.

39 Leo Gross (Peace of Westphalia) (*supra*) 20.

40 See further Ch I *infra*.

41 Art 2(1) UN Charter.

42 Antonio Cassese *International Law* 2nd (2005) Oxford University Press, Oxford, 48.

43 Antonio Cassese (International Law) (*supra*) 48.

44 See in general Ch II *infra*.

notions, however, are not static. The dynamics of collective security, the constitutionalisation of the international system, and the normative impact of human rights are some of the factors that shape the content and scope of 'state sovereignty', 'non-intervention', and 'the prohibition of the threat or use of force'. Since 'sovereignty', 'territorial integrity', and 'political independence' of states are also protected interests in the context of the criminalisation of international aggression,[45] these concepts are of great relevance for purposes of this book.

The notion of sovereignty – the organising principle of the international system and a protected interest underlying the prohibition of the use of force – has to be understood in the light of the normative impact of international human rights and the evolving system of international criminal law. 'Sovereignty' is thus a very complex notion. Although the 'sovereign equality of states' can be regarded as the *raison d'être* of the present international system, the normative impact of human rights and the evolving system of international criminal law are changing the meaning and scope of 'sovereignty'. The recognition of the notion of individual criminal liability for crimes under international law, and the creation of international criminal tribunals to try individuals responsible for these crimes, marked a fundamental departure from the traditional (Westphalian) notion of sovereignty. Bruce Broomhall has put it as follows:

> 'The idea that sovereignty does not arise in a vacuum, but is constituted by the recognition of the international community, which makes its recognition conditional on certain standards, has become increasingly accepted in the fields of international law and international relations. Such limits are held always to have been imposed by the community on the recognition of its members, but to be subject to development over time. From this perspective, crimes under international law can be understood as a formal limit to a State's legitimate exercise of its sovereignty, and so in principle justify a range of international responses (subject to the rest of international law, including that relating to the use of force).'[46]

It is submitted that the constitutionalisation of the international system and the system of collective security as well as the evolving legal and political processes within this paradigm, are important for the development of an effective dispensation regarding the question of individual criminal liability for aggression. It is shown that the interrelationship between the principal organs of the collective security system and the institutions and processes of the evolving system of international criminal law is of fundamental importance to the issue at hand: *Individual criminal liability for the crime of aggression in its proper context.*

---

45 See for instance Art 15(2) of Draft Code of Crimes against the Peace and Security of Mankind (1991) (discussed in Ch IV), and Art 1 of UN Gen Assembly Def of Aggression (1974) (discussed in Ch IV).

46 Bruce Broomhall *International Justice & The International Criminal Court – Between Sovereignty and the Rule of Law* (2003) Oxford University Press, Oxford 43.

PART II

COLLECTIVE SECURITY AND THE *JUS CONTRA BELLUM*

CHAPTER I

AGGRESSION IN THE CONTEXT OF COLLECTIVE SECURITY

'World history is largely a history of wars. All have been fought in a world without governance – where national "defence", regional military alliances, balance of power and hegemonic imperialism have been the prevailing regimes. There is a manifest need for a system under universal auspices for maintaining global peace and security.'[1]

1. COLLECTIVE SECURITY AS A MEANS TO PROMOTE AND SUSTAIN INTERNATIONAL PEACE AND SECURITY

The prohibition of aggression under international (criminal) law must be considered against the background of the collective security system. This system is primarily concerned with the maintenance of international peace and security. The criminalisation of aggression is analysed in terms of the international peace and security regime which developed during the twentieth century in the wake of two devastating world wars. While the focus of this book is the question of individual criminal liability as a *response* to (and *possible deterrent* for) international aggression, this must be seen contextually. Indeed, it will be shown that the criminal justice response to international aggression is ultimately not only intertwined with, but also to a considerable degree dependent upon, the key institutions of the system of collective security.

At present, the primary embodiment of the international collective security regime is the United Nations (UN).[2] The UN Charter (1945) provides for three pillars[3] of the system of collective security:

---

1 Ruben P Mendez 'Peace as a global public good' in Inge Kaul, Isabelle Grunberg and Marc Stern (eds) *Global Public Goods – International Cooperation in the 21st Century* (1999) Oxford University Press, Oxford, 382.

2 For an overview, see James Crawford *Brownlie's Principles of Public International Law* 8th (2012) Oxford University Press, Oxford, 746–768.

3 See Ruben Mendez (Peace as a global public good) (*supra*) 392–393.

(a) pacific behaviour by states: Article 2(3) of the Charter provides that member states 'shall settle their international disputes by peaceful means'. Furthermore, Article 2(4) provides that states 'shall refrain in their international relations from the threat or use of force against the territorial integrity or political independence of any state';[4]
(b) collective responses and mechanisms aimed at the settling of disputes (notably in terms of Chapter VI of the Charter), and Chapter VII powers and mechanisms to deal with threats to or breaches of the peace and with aggression;
(c) international co-operation to deal with socio-economic development, decolonisation, and the advancement of human rights, as means to prevent international conflict.

For present purposes, the focus is on the second pillar of the UN collective security system, namely the various powers (especially under Chapter VII of the Charter) to deal with threats to or breaches of the peace, and with aggression. It is important to understand the principles and practical implications of this second pillar. The institutional dynamics and relationship between the various organs of the UN that form the system of collective security have important implications for the criminal justice response to aggression, as is clear from the analysis in later chapters. Thus, the question of individual criminal liability for the crime of aggression must be analysed with due regard to the collective security system.

The Security Council of the UN has the primary[5] obligation to address threats to international peace and security. Where the Security Council cannot fulfil this obligation, the Uniting for Peace Resolution of 1950 provides the General Assembly of the UN with a complementary role to address threats to peace and security.[6] For present purposes, but also in the light of discussions in later Chapters on the relationship between the UN organs and the International Criminal Court (ICC), it is important to understand the roles of the Security Council and the General Assembly in the Charter system of collective security.

---

4 For the full text, see the Charter of the UN, 26 June 1945, UNCIO XV, 335, as reprinted in Bruno Simma (ed) *The Charter of the United Nations – A Commentary* 2nd (2002) Vol I CH Beck Verlag/Oxford University Press, Oxford.

5 Art 24 UN Charter; Stefan Talmon 'The Security Council as World Legislature' 99 *AJIL* (2005) 175–193, 179; Danesh Sarooshi *The United Nations and the Development of Collective Security – The delegation by the UN Security Council of its Chapter VII powers* (1999) Oxford University Press, Oxford, 1.

6 Uniting for Peace Resolution adopted by the UN General Assembly 3 Nov 1950 GA Res 337A, in Do A/1775 (1951). For the collective security role of the UN, see Hans Kelsen 'Collective security and collective self-defense under the Charter of the United Nations' 42 *AJIL* (1948) 783–796. For a more recent understanding of the collective security role of the UN, see the *Report of the Independent International Commission on Kosovo* (2000) Oxford University Press, Oxford, 166–176.

1.1. THE UNITING FOR PEACE RESOLUTION

In June 1950 North Korea invaded South Korea. This invasion caught the collective security system envisaged by the UN Charter, in a state of paralysis. At the time, the Soviet Union was boycotting the Security Council (as well as other UN institutions) in protest against the UN's refusal to replace Taiwan with the People's Republic of China in the structures of the UN. Thus, when the United States asked the Security Council to act on the Korean crisis, the Soviet Union did not participate in the process that led to the Security Council resolutions calling on North Korea to withdraw from the South[7] and recommending assistance of the international community to South Korea.[8] According to Henry Kissinger, this Soviet boycott of the Security Council provided the United States with the opportunity to invoke military force in collaboration with its allies and to 'justify the American role in Korea in the familiar Wilsonian terms of freedom versus dictatorship, good versus evil.'[9] The United States could thus argue that the use of military force was justified in order to uphold the resolutions of the Security Council.[10] Five decades later, the US would use the same argument to justify the use of force against Iraq, challenging yet again the way in which the collective security system is suppose to deter the use of force by states other than in cases of self-defence or with Security Council permission.[11]

It was noted above that the Security Council is the organ of the UN primarily responsible for issues concerning international peace and security. During the Korean crisis the Security Council was in a position to act, only because the Soviet Union was not using its veto (the latter was boycotting the Security Council at the time). Kissinger pointed out that the Soviet ambassador to the UN would 'surely have vetoed the Security Council resolution proposed by the United States' if the ambassador was 'less terrified of Stalin or [had] been able to obtain instructions more rapidly'.[12] There was, however, a need to provide for the inevitable return of the Soviet Union to the Security Council and the real possibility that the Soviet Union, or one or more of the other permanent members of the Security Council, would (in the context of the Cold War politics of that time) use their veto and thus cause paralysis in the UN's primary organ for international peace and security. To provide for this scenario, the General Assembly adopted the Uniting for Peace Resolution[13] in 1950. Paragraph 1 of the Resolution provides as follows:

---

7 UN SC Res 82 (1950).

8 UN SC Res 83 (1950).

9 Henry Kissinger *Diplomacy* (1994) Touchstone, New York, 477.

10 Kissinger (Diplomacy) (*supra*) 477.

11 See discussion in Ch II *infra*.

12 Kissinger (Diplomacy) (*supra*) 477.

13 UN GA Res 377 (V) 3 Nov 1950.

'[If] the Security Council, because of lack of unanimity of the permanent members, fails to exercise its primary responsibility for the maintenance of international peace and security in any case where there appears to be a threat to the peace, breach of the peace, or act of aggression, the General Assembly shall consider the matter immediately with a view to making appropriate recommendations to Members for collective measures, including in the case of a breach of the peace or act of aggression the use of armed force when necessary, to maintain or restore international peace and security. If not in session at the time, the General Assembly may meet in emergency special session within twenty-four hours of the request therefor. Such emergency special session shall be called if requested by the Security Council on the vote of any seven members, or by a majority of the Members of the United Nations'.[14]

Early commentators on the UN Charter, like Hans Kelsen, observed that the Charter envisages a *primary* role for the Security Council in collective security matters, and a *secondary* role for other organs, like the General Assembly. However, Kelsen submitted that 'no other central organ of the United Nations but the Security Council' has the power of using force.[15] The Uniting for Peace Resolution was thus a pragmatic development and perhaps not in line with the rather rigid division of labour between the organs of the UN, as described by Hans Kelsen in 1948. This Resolution seems to confer upon the General Assembly the kind of duties and responsibilities associated with the Security Council, and is perhaps evidence of the need for a more flexible (and arguably more democratic, or representative) collective security system. At the very least, it is submitted that the pragmatism reflected by the Uniting for Peace Resolution serves to illustrate the difficulties in trying to reconcile the ideals of international peace and security with political realities and the complexities of international relations. These complexities also impact on the process (or processes) to operationalise the criminal justice response to aggression via the ICC; possibly also via regional criminal courts, and in national legal systems.[16]

It is submitted that the Uniting for Peace Resolution, although not providing for a parallel collective security regime, does at least establish a potentially complementary role for the General Assembly in matters of peace and security, including cases of aggression. Michael Cowling pointed out that the General Assembly has acted under the Uniting for Peace Resolution on a number of occasions during the Cold War, and the practice in this regard is of growing importance.[17] Farhad Malekian argued that, because of the perception that the Uniting for Peace Resolution was essentially adopted to by-pass potential

14 Uniting for Peace Resolution, par 1.

15 Hans Kelsen (Collective security) (*supra*) 786.

16 See Chapters VII and VIII *infra*.

17 Michael Cowling 'The relationship between the Security Council and the General Assembly with particular reference to the ICJ Advisory Opinion in the "Israeli Wall" case' 30 *SAYIL* (2005) 50–81, 62.

Security Council vetoes by Russia, it was widely perceived to be anti-Soviet. Therefore, according to Malekian, the Resolution 'lost its potential to create a democratic approach to the machinery of the collective security system of the United Nations'.[18] It is submitted, though, that the Uniting for Peace Resolution holds out some potential for purposes of finding a mechanism to make the collective security system more democratic, especially in light of demands for Security Council reforms. The latter process will probably take some time and assumes considerable political will.

1.1.1. The Uniting for Peace Resolution and the Wall in the Occupied Palestinian Territory case

One of the world's enduring conflicts (that outlived the Cold War, apartheid and various civil wars that plagued the post-Second World War international system) is the Israeli-Palestinian conflict. This conflict not only generates much international political and diplomatic attention, but it also raises important legal questions. In December 2003 the International Court of Justice (ICJ)[19] was asked[20] to deliver an advisory opinion on the legal consequences of the construction of a very controversial wall in Israeli-occupied Palestinian territory. Israel contended that the construction of the wall was necessary for the security of Israel, while a number of states as well as human rights groups argued that the construction of the wall was contrary to international law (notably humanitarian and human rights law).

For present purposes, the importance of the ICJ's advisory opinion in the *Construction of a Wall* case lies in the way the Court dealt with the intricate question of the role of the General Assembly vis-à-vis the Security Council in matters that affect international peace and security. The meaning and impact of the Uniting for Peace Resolution of 1950 was considered by the ICJ. It is submitted that the opinion of the ICJ in the *Construction of the Wall* case has implications for one of the pertinent aspects addressed later in this book, namely the conditions for the exercise of jurisdiction by the International Criminal Court (ICC) over the crime of aggression. This is fully explored in Chapters VI

---

18 Farhad Malekian *The Monopolization of International Criminal Law in the United Nations* (1993) Almqvist & Wiksell International, Uppsala, 158.

19 *Legal Consequences of the Construction of a Wall in the Occupied Palestinian Territory (Advisory Opinion)* 9 Jul 2004 ICJ Reports 2004, 136.

20 GA Res ES-10/14 8 Dec 2003. The GA requested the ICJ for an advisory opinion on the following question: 'What are the legal consequences arising from the construction of the wall being built by Israel, the occupying Power, in the Occupied Palestinian Territory, including in and around East Jerusalem, as described in the report of the Secretary-General, considering the rules and principles of international law, including the Fourth Geneva Convention of 1949, and relevant Security Council and General Assembly resolutions?' See *Construction of a Wall* case (*supra*) par 1.

and further. The relationship between the General Assembly and the Security Council is thus important, not only for a discussion of collective security, but also for pertinent debates in international criminal law.

The present features of the collective security system (and the ongoing debate about the different roles of the UN organs in this system) need to be put in historical, theoretical and normative perspective.

2. COLLECTIVE SECURITY AND THE CONSTITUTIONALISATION OF THE INTERNATIONAL SYSTEM

Hugo Grotius, in his *Prolegomena to the Law of War and Peace*, noted the following about the legal dimension of international security:

> '[There] is no state so powerful that it may not at some time need the help of others outside itself, either for purposes of trade, or even to ward off the forces of many foreign nations united against it. In consequence we see that even the most powerful peoples and sovereigns seek alliances, which are quite devoid of significance according to the point of view of those who confine law within the boundaries of states. Most true is the saying that all things are uncertain the moment men depart from law.'[21]

In *Swords into Plowshares*, by Inis Claude, the basic assumption on which collective security rests is described as follows:

> 'The necessary assumption of collective security is simply that wars are likely to occur and that they ought to be prevented. The conflicts may be the fruit of unreflective passion or of deliberate planning; they may represent efforts to settle disputes, effects of undefinably broad situations of hostility, or calculated means to realize ambitious designs of conquest. They may be launched by the irresponsible dictate of cynical autocrats or the democratic will of a chauvinistic people – although the champions of collective security have frequently evinced the conviction that most wars are likely to stem from the former type of initiative. The point is that the theory of collective security is not invalidated by the discovery that the causes, functional purposes, and initiatory mechanisms of war are varied.'[22]

---

21 Hugo Grotius *Prolegomena to the Law of War and Peace* translated by Francis W Kelsey (1957) The Bobbs-Merrill Company, New York, par 22. This statement of Grotius must be seen in context: Grotius acknowledged (especially with reference to the Just War theory) the role of politics in international law. In that sense Grotius was more of a *realist* than his fellow Dutchman Erasmus, who was described by Grotius as an idealist who would forbid *all* use of arms. See Hugo Grotius (Prolegomena) (*supra*) par 29. For further analysis see BVA Röling '*Jus ad bellum* and the Grotian heritage' in *International Law and the Grotian Heritage* (1985) TMC Asser Institute, The Hague.

22 Inis L Claude *Swords into Plowshares* 4th (1971) Random House, New York, 249.

The rationale and assumed working of collective security have been described by Margaret Karns and Karen Mingst as follows:

> 'Collective security is based on the conviction that peace is indivisible and that all states have a collective interest in countering aggression whenever and wherever it may appear. It assumes that potential aggressors will be deterred by the united threat of counterforce mobilized through an international organization like the league [the League of Nations] or the UN. If enforcement is required, however, then a wide range of economic and diplomatic sanctions as well as armed force may be utilized.'[23]

Karns and Mingst observed that while Chapter VII of the UN Charter provides for the legal foundations of collective security, the veto power of the five permanent members of the Security Council 'assures that no collective security measures can ever be instituted against any of them'.[24] Because of this, the authors concluded that the UN is in fact a *limited* collective security organisation.

Danesh Sarooshi (like Inis Claude) linked the notion of collective security with the concept of legitimacy in international political and legal theory. In this regard, Sarooshi argued that while an important aspect of collective security consists of the maintenance of the *status quo* of the system, the perception of states 'that their individual interest is best served by ensuring that the interests of the community' of states is preserved, is actually a condition for the acceptance of the preservation of the *status quo*.[25] This seems to be a more nuanced mixture of idealism and realism as motivating factors informing states' participation in the collective security system.

In the light of the above, a brief outline of the theoretical underpinnings of the collective security system is given. Following on from that, the practice of collective security will be discussed with reference to the main features of the UN organs that form the focus of the present collective security system.

3. THE THEORY OF COLLECTIVE SECURITY

Inis Claude viewed the place of collective security in international law and policy as follows:

> 'Collective security is a specialized instrument of international policy in the sense that it is intended only to forestall the arbitrary and aggressive use of force, not to provide enforcement mechanisms for the whole body of international law; it

23 Margaret P Karns and Karen A Mingst *International Organizations – The politics and processes of global governance* (2004) Lynne Rienner Publishers, London, 297.

24 Karns and Mingst (International Organizations) (*supra*) 297.

25 Danesh Sarooshi (Collective Security) (*supra*) 5–6.

assumes that, so far as the problem of world order is concerned, the heart of the matter is the restraint of military action rather than the guarantee of respect for all legal obligations. Moreover, it assumes that this ideal may be realized, or at least approximated, by a reformation of international policy, without the institution of a revolution in the structure of the international system.'[26]

Claude has identified a number of subjective and objective requirements of collective security. One of the subjective requirements (referring to the acceptability of the responsibilities of collective security) rests on the Kantian notion of a constantly integrating world community: a community of peoples and nations that are becoming more and more interdependent and integrated into a true world community.

3.1. LIBERAL THEORY OF INTERNATIONAL RELATIONS AND GOVERNANCE

Immanuel Kant articulated the relationship between democracy and peace and put forward the idea that free communities and states would co-operate to promote peace.[27] These Enlightenment ideas were later reflected in what became known as the *liberal theory* of global governance and international co-operation.[28] Apart from the notion of a common humanity, one of the major threads running through the liberal theory of international relations is the respect for international law. Liberals, who are often also being regarded as *idealists*, have expectations of an international system not based on power alone, but power being exercised within the framework of rules (international law,)[29] and the institutions of collective security.[30]

---

26 Claude (Swords into Plowshares) (*supra*) 249.

27 For a critique of Kant's *For a Perpetual Peace: A Philosophical Sketch* (1795), and the way the modern political philosophers Jürgen Habermas, John Rawls and Norberto Bobbio treat the ideas of Kant (via Hegel) and the liberal/cosmopolitan view of international law, see commentary by Perry Anderson, 'Arms and Rights – Rawls, Habermas and Bobbio in an Age of War' 31 *NLR* (2005) 5–40. For a discussion of the impact of the so-called neo-conservative view of international relations on the UN-dominated collective security system, and how neo-conservative thinking differs from the realist school of international law and relations, see Jürgen Habermas, 'Interpreting the Fall of a Monument' 4(7) *German Law Journal* (2003) 701–708. The commentary appeared in reaction to the American-led invasion of Iraq in March 2003. The invasion was carried out without UN Security Council authorisation.

28 See Karns and Mingst (International Organizations) (*supra*) 35–36.

29 The creation of *ad hoc* international criminal tribunals and the permanent ICC can be regarded as flowing from the Kantian notion of a liberal/cosmopolitan international order based on the rule of law. On another level, the interaction between international criminal law and national criminal law, and the harmonisation that may occur as a result, can also be seen as consistent with a liberal/cosmopolitan view of international law and relations. For an international criminal law perspective, see Mireille Delmas-Marty, 'The contribution of comparative law to a pluralistic conception of International Criminal Law' 1 *JICJ* (2003), 13–25.

30 Karns and Mingst (International Organizations) (*supra*) 37.

In terms of collective security, this notion of a common humanity implies that the large majority of states must positively commit to 'the value of world peace'.[31] Authors like Hans Kelsen described collective security in terms of a continuum with 'a highest possible degree' of collective security. This 'highest degree' would have one central organ for the maintenance of peace and security, which would exercise an *exclusive* right to take enforcement actions against member states. Kelsen further described the 'highest form of collective security' in terms of the disarmament of individual states, and the commitment to *community*.[32]

The commitment to a more abstract value-oriented view of world order is perhaps the one feature that distinguishes collective security from the balance of power international system that existed before.[33] Both systems rely on the deterrent effect of overwhelming military power (be it in the form of alliances, or the international community collectively), but collective security is premised on the commitment to a higher international order – hence the irrelevance of the geographical remoteness of aggression.[34] Inis Claude linked the normative element of the community of nations to the essential characteristic of the international system as a rules-based system – not for the sake of rules, but for the deeper commitment to peace and harmony:

> 'The responsibilities of participation in a collective security system are too onerous to be borne by any but a people actuated by genuine sympathy for any and all victims of aggression, and loyalty to the values of a global system of law and order.'[35]

The ideal of peace is thus served by the certainty that the international rule of law is suppose to bring about: the certainty that acts of aggression will be met by the collective opposition of the nations of the world.[36]

3.2. LIBERALISM AND REALIST CRITIQUE

Whereas the liberal view of international relations and collective security is to a certain extent idealistic (there is an expectation that states will adhere to certain norms or would want to act for the *global good* of peace and security); *realists* view the international system as basically anarchic. Karns and Mingst summarise the realist theory of international relations as follows:

---

31 Inis Claude (Swords into Plowshares) (*supra*) 250.

32 See Hans Kelsen (Collective Security) (*supra*) 784.

33 On the rise and fall of the Balance of Power system, see Henry Kissinger *World Order – Reflections on the character of nations and the course of history* (2014) Allen Lane, New York, 49–95.

34 Inis Claude (Swords into Plowshares) (*supra*) 251.

35 *Ibid.*

36 Inis Claude (Swords into Plowshares) (*supra*) 252–253.

> 'Within the international system, realists see states as the primary actors, entities that act in a unitary way in pursuit of their national interest, generally defined in terms of maximizing power and security. States co-exist in an anarchic international system characterized by the absence of an authoritative hierarchy. As a result, states must rely primarily on themselves to manage their own insecurity through balance of power and deterrence.'[37]

The realist view of international relations often regards the application of international law as problematic. The functioning of the collective security system is thus viewed from a national/sovereign policy perspective. While realists are not absolutely opposed to the idea of international law,[38] they would scrutinise the application of international law very critically.[39] In extreme cases, there could be severe tension between the policy decisions of a sovereign state (acting in national self-interest) and the constraints imposed by international law. Consider the following statement by Stephen Krasner: 'For realists, the defining characteristic of the international system is anarchy, and the most important empirical reality is that national power, including but not limited to the ability to wage war, matters more than anything else.'[40]

4. THE FEATURES OF THE PRESENT COLLECTIVE SECURITY SYSTEM

4.1. THE LEGACY OF THE LEAGUE OF NATIONS

The United Nations, particularly the Security Council, is the institutional embodiment of the present collective security system. The UN was created in the wake of the Second World War. This war shook the international system to the core and exposed the failures of its institutional predecessor, the League of Nations.

The League of Nations was created as a result of the liberal ideal that the horrors of the First World War should never be repeated. Apart from the peace treaty that was signed at Versailles to end hostilities, the League of Nations was created to serve the ideal of collective security and to prevent war. The Covenant of the League of Nations took effect on 10 January 1920, the date on which Germany

---

37 Karns and Mingst (International Organizations) (*supra*) 45.

38 See comments by Richard Steinberg 'Overview: Realism in International law' *ASIL Proceedings* (2002) 260–262.

39 For a realist critique on the role of international law, specifically in terms of American responses to acts of terrorism and humanitarian intervention, see Edwin D Williamson 'Realism versus legalism in international relations' *ASIL Proceedings* (2002) 262–265.

40 Stephen D Krasner 'Realist views of international law' *ASIL Proceedings* (2002) 265.

deposited its instrument of ratification of the Treaty of Versailles.[41] Despite the fact that the League in many respects represented the ideals of liberal internationalists like President Woodrow Wilson of the US, it is ironic that the US declined to become a member of the League.[42] The reasoning of the US at the time seemed to be that some provisions in the Covenant of the League would diminish or bring an end to an important aspect of US foreign policy which had at that time been in place for almost a century: the Monroe Doctrine. This political doctrine was essentially a policy statement that the US would not tolerate interference or colonial projects in its 'sphere of influence', namely the continents of North and South America. The US considered some of the provisions of the Covenant of the League of Nations to form a basis for possible European influence and interference in the American continents. Higgins pointed out that part of the reason of American refusal to become a member of the League was the provisions of Article 10 of the Covenant.[43] This article contained the general principle that aggression was unlawful.[44] It imposed a legal obligation on states to respect the territorial integrity and political independence of all members of the League. The crucial political problem for the US seemed to lie in the fact that the Council of the League could decide on measures to be taken in cases where the political independence or territorial integrity of states was violated as a result of aggression. This dispensation created tension with the Monroe Doctrine which provided that the US (and by implication not other countries or international bodies or alliances) would be the guarantor of political independence and territorial integrity in the American continents. Although the wording of Article 10 of the Covenant were criticised as being too vague, authors like Ian Brownlie regarded the principle contained in the article as a clear and important declaration on the illegality of aggression.[45] Indeed, the League of Nations adopted resolutions which expressed the norm in strong terms; a resolution of 25 September 1925 and another of 24 September 1927 stated that wars of aggression were crimes under international law and prohibited under international law.[46] However, geopolitical considerations of the US trumped the normative impact of Article 10, and the emerging superpower was not willing to partake in the collective security regime of the League of Nations.

---

41 Pearce Higgins (ed) *Hall's A Treatise on International Law* 8th (1924) Clarendon Press, Oxford, 71.

42 Pearce Higgins (International Law) (*supra*) 72.

43 Pearce Higgins (International Law) (*supra*) 79.

44 See Ian Brownlie *International Law and the Use of Force by States* (1963) Clarendon Press, Oxford, 62–65.

45 Ian Brownlie (Use of Force) (*supra*) 65; James Crawford (Public International Law) (*supra*) 744. Other commentators, like Hans Kelsen, pointed out that the prohibition of the use of force was much weaker under the Covenant of the League of Nations than it is under the UN Charter. See Hans Kelsen (Collective Security) (*supra*) 787–788.

46 Spanish and Polish proposals adopted by the Sixth Assembly (1925) and the Eighth Assembly (1927) of the League, respectively. See further James Crawford (Public International Law) (*supra*) 745.

Ultimately, neither the legal provision in Article 10, nor the working of the League of Nations, could prevent the disastrous war of aggression that became the Second World War. Inis Claude, who viewed the League of Nations as the embodiment of the liberal ideal of collective security, concluded as follows on the nature of the Covenant of the League:

> '[All] the basic concepts of nineteenth-century liberalism – democracy, nationalism, natural harmony, law, limited government, rationalism, discussion, consent – made their imprint upon the Covenant of the League of Nations.'[47]

The fact that these ideals were shattered by the Second World War obviously called into question not only the practical impact of the League, but also the ideal of a collective security regime based on international law. Authors like Inis Claude, however, seemed to have had a more optimistic prognosis for collective security after the Second World War. Claude viewed the United Nations as 'a revised version of the League', and not a radically new concept. Of course, for tactical and political reasons, the resemblances between the League and the UN were understated. Essentially, Inis Claude regarded the UN as a continuation of the 'progressive trends' of the period between the two world wars.[48] In other words, the *idea* of collective security was not dead, but the organisational aspects were certainly in need of adjustment and reform. Hans Kelsen pointed out that decentralisation and self-help were key features (and weaknesses!) of the Covenant of the League of Nations. Thus, it 'was for the members, and not for a central organ of the League to decide whether a violation of the Covenant by illegal resort to war had occurred, and to decide what enforcement action had to be taken.'[49] Members were also not legally bound by the recommendations of the Council of the League. According to commentators like Kelsen, these features of the Covenant of the League led to the League's ultimate ineffectiveness.[50]

4.2. THE UNITED NATIONS AS PRINCIPAL EMBODIMENT OF COLLECTIVE SECURITY

The establishment of the United Nations was an attempt by the international community to create a more effective collective security system. The ideal of collective security, together with other areas of concern for the international community, is set out in Article 1 of the UN Charter:

47 Inis Claude (Swords into Plowshares) (*supra*) 54.
48 Inis Claude (Swords into Plowshares) (*supra*) 60–61.
49 Hans Kelsen (Collective Security) (*supra*) 787.
50 Hans Kelsen (Collective Security) (*supra*) 788.

'The Purposes of the United Nations are:

1. To maintain international peace and security, and to that end: to take effective collective measures for the prevention and removal of threats to the peace, and for the suppression of acts of aggression or other breaches of the peace, and to bring about by peaceful means, and in conformity with the principles of justice and international law, adjustment or settlement of international disputes or situations which might lead to a breach of the peace;
2. To develop friendly relations among nations based on respect for the principle of equal rights and self-determination of peoples, and to take other appropriate measures to strengthen universal peace;
3. To achieve international co-operation in solving international problems of an economic, social, cultural, or humanitarian character, and in promoting and encouraging respect for human rights and for fundamental freedoms for all without distinction as to race, sex, language, or religion; and
4. To be a center for harmonizing the actions of nations in the attainment of these common ends.'[51]

It is clear from Article 1 of the UN Charter that, although international peace and security is the primary objective of the organisation, the UN was also created, as Inis Claude put it, 'as a general organization in the additional sense that it was to deal with a comprehensive range of subject matter.'[52] While the UN Charter, like its predecessor the Covenant of the League of Nations, represented the old liberal ideal of international co-operation and collective security, the Charter also signalled the development of a new understanding of the liberal ideal: a far more *active* role for international organisations like the UN to enhance the ideals set out in the UN Charter.[53]

Apart from peace and security, the UN is also active in the fields of human rights,[54] refugees and migration,[55] the emancipation of women,[56] labour

51 Art 1 UN Charter.

52 Inis Claude (Swords into Plowshares) (*supra*) 67.

53 Inis Claude (Swords into Plowshares) (*supra*) 79.

54 For a concise discussion of the 'three stages' of international protection of human rights by the UN, see Antonio Cassese *International Law in a divided world* (1986) Oxford University Press, Oxford, 293–316. See further the work and publications of the UN Centre for Human Rights (www.un.org). The most important instruments in this regard are the Universal Declaration of Human Rights, GA Res 217A (III) UN Doc A/810 (1948); International Covenant on Civil and Political Rights (ICCPR) of 16 Dec 1966, 999 UNTS 171 (1966); and the International Covenant on Economic, Social and Cultural Rights of 16 Dec 1966, 999 UNTS 3 (1966).

55 The most important instrument in this regard is the Statute of the Office of the UN High Commissioner for Refugees, GA 428 (V) (Annex) (Dec 14, 1950). The UNHCR is based in Geneva, Switzerland. For a discussion of the work of the UNHCR see David Martin 'Refugees and Migration' in Christopher Joyner (ed) *The United Nations and International Law* (1997) Cambridge University Press, Cambridge, 155–180.

56 Notably the Convention on the Elimination of All Forms of Discrimination against Women, Dec 18, 1979, UN GAOR, 34th Sess, Supp No 21, at 193, UN Doc A/Res/34/180; 19 *ILM* 33

issues,[57] economic relations and development,[58] the environment and sustainable development,[59] the law of the sea,[60] outer space,[61] and international and transnational substantive and procedural criminal justice issues (notably terrorism, drug trafficking and organised crime).[62] It is submitted that the role of the UN is by no means limited to issues of peace and security. Indeed, the role of the UN as an agent for the advancement of human development and human rights prompts the suggestion that the UN Charter should not be seen as a static document, set in the time-frame of 1945. Issues of security and social development; the environment and security; and socio-economic issues, trade and human rights are all interrelated. It would therefore be wrong to regard the role of the UN's primary organ for collective security, the Security Council, as a very limited role – only concerned with questions of interstate aggression. International practice, especially since the early 1990s, has shown that the Security Council is willing to view for instance human rights violations to be a threat to international peace and security, thus triggering the collective security machinery of the UN Charter. The latter is also relevant for purposes of the debate on so-called humanitarian intervention,[63] which is dealt with below.[64]

From the above it is clear that the present collective security system, which is dominated by the UN, has its roots in liberal ideals and efforts to foster international peace and security; first attempted through the failed League of Nations. Authors like Inis Claude regarded the Charter of the UN as a more

---

(1980). See further discussion of efforts to combat trafficking in persons (especially women and children) in Gerhard Kemp 'The United Nations Convention Against Transnational Organized Crime: A milestone in international criminal law' 2 *SACJ* (2001) 152.

57 Especially through the work of the International Labour Organisation (ILO), which is a specialised agency of the UN. For ILO documents visit www.ilo.org.

58 See Art 55 UN Charter on the UN's role in socio-economic sphere. International trade is a specialised area of international law, with the work of the World Trade Organisation (WTO) at the centre. See in general www.wto.org.

59 Especially through the UN Environment Programme (UNEP), UN Doc A/8730 (1972). See further Draft Principles on Human Rights and the Environment (Final Report of the Special Rapporteur, Sub-Commission on Prevention of Discrimination and Protection of Minorities) UN Doc E/CN.4/Sub.2/1994/9, Annex I (1994) and Commission on Human Rights (Res 2003/71) on human rights and the environment as part of sustainable development.

60 Notably in terms of the Law of the Sea Convention of 1982, 21 *ILM* 1261 (1982).

61 It is generally assumed that international law also applies in space. There are a number of specific treaties dealing with specific outer space related issues, eg the Treaty on Principles Governing the Activities of States in the Exploration and Use of Outer Space, Including the Moon and Other Celestial Bodies, GA Res 2222 (XXI) Dec 19, 1966, 610 UNTS 205. Some international treaties have implications for activities in outer space, eg the Multilateral Treaty Banning Nuclear Weapons Tests in the Atmosphere, in Outer Space, and Under Water, 5 Aug 1963, 480 UNTS 43.

62 For this vast area of international law, see in general Cherif Bassiouni *International Criminal Law Conventions and their penal provisions* (1997) Transnational Publishers, New York.

63 See G Barrie 'Forcible intervention and international law: legal theory and realities' 116(4) *SALJ* (1999) 791–809, 804.

64 See Ch II *infra*.

satisfactory basis for collective security than the Covenant of the League. With reference to the core provisions of the Charter that constitute the essence of the limits put on the use of force by states, namely Article 2(4) (prohibition on the threat or use of force by states), Article 51 (individual or collective self-defence by states) and Article 53 (regional enforcement action with Security Council authorisation), Claude concluded as follows:

> '[The Charter] leaves no such convenient gaps in the legal fence for aggressors to crawl through as did the [Covenant of the League]; it substitutes for a limited prohibition of war the more comprehensive proscription of the threat or use of force, and it even undertakes to close the gap of fictitious defensive and law-enforcement measures by subjecting all coercive activity to the control and supervision of the Security Council.'[65]

The most important legal framework for the maintenance of international peace and security by the UN can be found in Chapter VII of the UN Charter. The key provision is Article 39, which provides as follows:

> 'The Security Council shall determine the existence of any threat to the peace, breach of the peace, or act of aggression and shall make recommendations, or decide what measures shall be taken in accordance with Articles 41 and 42, to maintain or restore international peace and security.'

Once the Security Council has determined under Article 39 that there exists a violation of or threat to international peace and security or an act of aggression, Articles 40 to 42 can potentially take effect. According to Erika de Wet, it is clear that the Security Council has a discretion both in terms of the determination of a threat or breach of peace or an act of aggression, and a further discretion as to what measures should be taken in response to these situations. She has also identified three schools of thought on the full extent of the Security Council's discretion:

> 'Some authors claim that both types of action fall within the absolute discretion of the Security Council. Others argue that the decision as to when the Security Council should intervene in terms of Article 39 lies purely within its discretion, but that general international law, in particular *ius cogens*, as well as the purposes and principles of the United Nations would pose limits to the type of action that may be taken by the Security Council. Yet others argue the exact opposite and state that once the Security Council is acting in terms of Article 39, there are no limits as to what it can do. However, whether it has passed the threshold constituted by Article 39 is something that can be measured by means of judicial criteria.'[66]

---

65 Inis Claude (Swords into Plowshares) (*supra*) 264.

66 Erika de Wet *The Chapter VII Powers of the United Nations Security Council* (2004) Hart Publishing, Portland, 133–134.

There seems to be an underlying divide between those who view the discretionary powers of the Security Council as primarily of a *political* nature and those who regard the exercise of the powers as closely resembling a *judicial* function involving legal interpretation. De Wet points out that supporters of the view that the Security Council is basically acting in terms of *political* considerations when interpreting Article 39, would point to the fact that the phrases 'threat to the peace', 'breach of the peace' and 'an act of aggression', as used in Article 39, are not defined – not in Article 39 or anywhere else in the Charter. Thus, the *modus operandi* of the Security Council would be to look at the factual situation and political realities when exercising its discretion. This, coupled with the veto power of the five permanent members of the Security Council (France, Russia, China, United Kingdom and United States) underpins the 'clear indication that decisions in the interest of peace and security will be based exclusively on (national) political considerations'.[67] Another indication of the political nature of the Article 39 discretionary powers of the Security Council is the fact that there is no obligation on the Security Council to act, despite the apparent seriousness of a given situation. The Security Council can in other words act 'selectively and with discretion'.[68]

However, there are those who argue that Article 39 does not provide the Security Council with unlimited discretion.[69] The fact that the Security Council can muster the political will (and overcome the veto threshold) to act on a specific situation that might constitute an act of aggression or a breach of peace, does not imply that it also has unlimited discretion to act. De Wet points to the fact that the 'imprecision and vagueness' of the terms used in Article 39 does not necessarily support the argument that the exercise of the Article 39 discretion by the Security Council is essentially a political act: 'The concretisation of vague terms is, in the first instance, a matter of legal interpretation.'[70] And further:

> 'There is nothing inherently special about the terms used in Article 39 that would *ab initio* remove them from the ambit of legal interpretation. On the contrary, the mere fact that Article 39 distinguishes between three criteria that trigger binding resolutions of the Security Council, implies that it does not have an unbound discretion. If an unbound discretion had been intended, such a distinction would have been obsolete. The Charter would only have contributed to the Security Council the general power to adopt binding measures in the interest of international peace and security and nothing more.'[71]

67 Erika De Wet (Chapter VII Powers) (*supra*) 135.
68 Erika De Wet (Chapter VII Powers) (*supra*) 136.
69 *Ibid.*
70 Erika De Wet (Chapter VII Powers) (*supra*) 136.
71 Erika De Wet (Chapter VII Powers) (*supra*) 136–137.

Erika de Wet pointed out that the International Court of Justice has not yet taken a position on the meaning of Article 39.[72] However, in *Prosecutor v Tadic*,[73] the Appeals Chamber of the International Criminal Tribunal for the Former Yugoslavia did have the opportunity to address not only the meaning of Article 39 but also the broader question of Security Council powers under Chapter VII. The ICTY was established by the Security Council in 1993[74] to try persons 'responsible for serious violations of international humanitarian law committed in the territory of the former Yugoslavia since 1991'.[75] At the Trial Chamber, one of the three grounds on which the appellant attacked the jurisdiction of the ICTY was the 'illegal foundation' of the Tribunal. The other two grounds were the 'wrongful primacy' of the ICTY over national courts and the 'lack of jurisdiction *ratione materiae*'. The motion challenging the jurisdiction of the Tribunal was denied in the Trial Chamber. The matter came before the Appeals Chamber, and for present purposes the focus will be on the first aspect of the motion on jurisdiction, namely the foundation of the ICTY in terms of the Chapter VII powers of the Security Council of the UN. The Appeals Chamber accepted that the Security Council has a 'very wide discretion' under Article 39 of the UN Charter. But the Appeals Chamber also stated that these discretionary powers are not unlimited.[76] The UN Charter cannot be interpreted in such a way as to depict the Security Council as '*legibus solutus* (unbound by law)'.[77] The structure of the UN Charter is such that the Security Council is indeed given wide powers to maintain international peace and security, but these powers are specifically laid down in Chapters VI, VII, VIII and XII of the Charter. Regarding the Chapter VII powers, the Appeals Chamber acknowledged the complex political and legal dimensions to an Article 39 determination, as also pointed out above. But importantly, the Appeals Chamber emphasised that the exercise of the discretion by the Security Council is ultimately still bound by the letter and spirit of the UN Charter:

> 'While the "act of aggression" is more amenable to a legal determination, the "threat to the peace" is more of a political concept. But the determination that there exists

---

72 Erika De Wet (Chapter VII Powers) (*supra*) 135.

73 Decision on the Defence Motion for interlocutory appeal on jurisdiction, *Prosecutor v Dusko Tadic*, Case No IT-94-1-AR72, Decision of 2 Oct 1995, reproduced in Andre Klip and Göran Sluiter (eds) *Annotated Leading Cases of International Criminal Tribunals – Student Ed* (2005) Intersentia, Antwerp, 9. Decision also available on www.un.org/icty.

74 SC Res 827 (1993) on Establishing an International Tribunal for the Prosecution of Persons Responsible for Serious Violations of International Humanitarian Law committed in the Territory of the Former Yugoslavia, *ILM* (1993) 1192 (Statute) and 1203 (Resolution); Amended by SC Res 1166 of 13 May 1998, Res 1329 of 30 Nov 2000, Res 1411 of 17 May 2002, Res 1431 of 14 Aug 2002 and Res 1481 of 19 May 2003 – see www.un.org/icty.

75 Art 1 ICTY Statute.

76 *Prosecutor v Tadic* (Appeal on Jurisdiction) (*supra*) par 28.

77 *Prosecutor v Tadic* (Appeal on Jurisdiction) (*supra*) par 28.

> such a threat is not a totally unfettered discretion, as it has to remain, at the very least, within the limits of the Purposes and Principles of the Charter.'[78]

The Appeals Chamber in *Tadic* had to consider whether the establishment of an international criminal tribunal (such as the ICTY) was within the Chapter VII powers of the Security Council – powers aimed at the maintenance or restoration of peace after a determination under Article 39 that there was a threat to peace or an act of aggression occurred. The Chamber noted that '[t]he establishment of an international criminal tribunal is not expressly mentioned among the enforcement measures provided for in Chapter VII, and more particularly in Articles 41 and 42.'[79] The Appeals Chamber held that Article 41 provides the necessary legal grounds for the Security Council to establish an international criminal tribunal in response to a threat to peace or an act of aggression. Article 41 of the UN Charter provides as follows:

> 'The Security Council may decide what measures not involving the use of armed force are to be employed to give effect to its decisions, and it may call upon the Members of the United Nations to apply such measures. These may include complete or partial interruption of economic relations and of rail, sea, air, postal, telegraphic, radio, and other means of communication, and the severance of diplomatic relations.'

The Appeals Chamber held that the measures listed in Article 41 are merely illustrative examples of appropriate measures; the use of armed force clearly excluded. Thus, the establishment of an international tribunal can also be an appropriate way of responding to an act of aggression or a threat to peace and security.[80]

The primary role of the Security Council as guardian of international peace and security is not only to determine whether the acts listed in Article 39 have occurred, but also to decide on appropriate responses to maintain peace and security. From the *Tadic* decision of the ICTY Appeals Chamber discussed above, it is clear that the creation of international criminal tribunals can also be an appropriate measure to restore peace and security. It is however prudent to guard against the view that international criminal tribunals can by themselves bring about peace. Michael Reisman has pointed out that the ICTY, for instance, was created as a Chapter VII measure, to 'stop the war' in Yugoslavia and not in the first instance to 'prosecute persons responsible for serious violations of international humanitarian law'.[81] Reisman's criticism is that the Security

78 *Prosecutor v Tadic* (Appeal on Jurisdiction) (*supra*) par 29.

79 *Prosecutor v Tadic* (Appeal on Jurisdiction) (*supra*) par 33.

80 *Prosecutor v Tadic* (Appeal on Jurisdiction) (*supra*) par 35–36.

81 Michael Reisman 'Stopping wars and making peace: Reflections on the ideology and practice of conflict termination in contemporary world politics' (1998) 6 *Tulane Journal of International and Comparative Law* 48.

Council, with the creation of the ICTY in the midst of a conflict, has abdicated its primary function of maintaining international peace and security. Reisman stated the following about the apparent paradoxical role of the ICTY as a Chapter VII measure:

> 'In the ordinary course of events, it is precisely at the end of a conflict that the operation of an international criminal tribunal kicks into operation. However, the purpose and essential design of the former Yugoslav Tribunal was to use it to accomplish other goals; it was to be terminated as soon as those goals were secured. Meanwhile, efforts at securing a political settlement had to continue, for no outsider was then willing to invest what was militarily necessary to force one of the parties to relent. However, the same people who should have been agreeing to a political solution were also the individuals who were assumed to be the prime candidates for indictment and trial. With two contradictory political strategies being pursued, the possibility of contribution by the Tribunal was not auspicious.'[82]

It falls beyond the scope of this book to evaluate the historical role of the ICTY in contributing to the end of the conflict in the former Yugoslavia. However, it is common cause that the conflict continued for years after the creation of the ICTY and a major conflict erupted in 1998/1999 in the (then) province of Kosovo. As discussed in section 4.3.1 below, the conflict eventually led to military intervention by NATO forces. In February 2008 Kosovo unilaterally declared independence from Serbia.[83] In a decision that can be regarded as significant for both post-conflict politics and international criminal justice, in August 2015 the Kosovo parliament agreed to the establishment of a special tribunal or special criminal chambers to try ex-Kosovo Liberation Army members accused of war crimes during the 1998/1999 conflict with Serbia.[84] This development can be seen as a continuation of the complex political, military and criminal justice reactions to the conflict in the Balkans.

The Security Council can decide on military action if the Article 41 measures 'would be inadequate or have proved to be inadequate'.[85] Article 43 of the

---

82 Michael Reisman (Stopping Wars) (*supra*) 48–49.

83 Kosovo Declaration of Independence, 17 February 2008 (www.assembly-kosova.org/?cid=2,128,1635). For perspectives on the unilateral declaration of independence, see Marc Weller *Contested Statehood: Kosovo's struggle for independence* (2009) Oxford University Press, Oxford; Milena Sterio 'Creating and building a "state": international law and Kosovo' *ASIL Proceedings* (2010) 361–365.

84 See statement by the European Union External Action Service, 3 Aug 2015 (www.europa.eu/statements-eeas/2015/150803_01_en.htm).

85 Art 42 Un Charter provides as follows: 'Should the Security Council consider that measures provided for in Article 41 would be inadequate or have proved to be inadequate, it may take such action by air, sea, or land forces as may be necessary to maintain or restore international peace and security. Such action may include demonstrations, blockade, and other operations by air, sea, or land forces of Members of the United Nations.'

Charter provides for the contribution of military forces to be made available to the Security Council in order to maintain peace and security.[86] This provision has proved to be unsuccessful, since states were very reluctant to enter into agreements with the Security Council. Of course, this state of affairs does not mean that the Security Council cannot make use of military forces assigned for *ad hoc* peace keeping or for peace enforcement under Article 42 of the Charter.[87]

The framework of collective security as set out in the UN Charter also provides in Article 51 for individual and collective self-defence. States which are under military attack are entitled to use force in self-defence, but only until the Security Council has taken the necessary measures to restore peace and security.

4.3. COLLECTIVE SECURITY AND REGIONAL SECURITY ARRANGEMENTS

4.3.1. The notion of regional self-defence and the evolving role of NATO

During the Cold War, the bipolar international political system, which was dominated by two superpowers (the United States and the Soviet Union), caused the collective security system of the UN to be complemented by *selective* security regimes like the North Atlantic Treaty Organisation (NATO).[88] Inis Claude viewed NATO as an elaboration of the alliance concept, 'in contrast to the collective security ideal of obtaining the abandonment and replacement of the alliance concept'.[89] Indeed, NATO's constituting treaty makes it clear that it is first and foremost an alliance or pact formed to collectively defend any *member* or *members* against external attacks. Article 5 of the NATO Treaty confirms that the pact is subject to the collective security regime provided for in the UN Charter:

---

86 Art 43 UN Charter provides as follows: '(1) All members of the United Nations, in order to contribute to the maintenance of international peace and security, undertake to make available to the Security Council, on its call and in accordance with a special agreement or agreements, armed forces, assistance, and facilities, including rights of passage, necessary for the purpose of maintaining international peace and security. (2) Such agreement or agreements shall govern the numbers and types of forces, their degree of readiness and general location, and the nature of the facilities and assistance to be provided. (3) The agreement or agreements shall be negotiated as soon as possible on the initiative of the Security Council. They shall be concluded between the Security Council and Members or between the Security Council and groups of Members and shall be subject to ratification by the signatory states in accordance with their respective constitutional processes.'

87 See in general commentary by Jochen Frowein in Bruno Simma (*supra*) Vol I 749–759.

88 For an overview and analysis of the key features of NATO, see Julian Lindley-French *The North Atlantic Treaty Organization – The enduring alliance* (2007) Routledge, Oxford.

89 Inis Claude (Swords into Plowshares) (*supra*) 267.

> 'The Parties agree that an armed attack against one or more of them in Europe or North America shall be considered an attack against them all and consequently they agree that, if such an armed attack occurs, each of them, in exercise of the right of individual or collective self-defence recognised by Article 51 of the Charter of the United Nations, will assist the Party or Parties so attacked by taking forthwith, individually and in concert with the other Parties, such action as it deems necessary, including the use of armed force, to restore and maintain the security of the North Atlantic area.
>
> Any such armed attack and all measures taken as a result thereof shall immediately be reported to the Security Council. Such measures shall be terminated when the Security Council has taken the measures necessary to restore and maintain international peace and security.'[90]

It can be argued that after the end of the Cold War the role of NATO as a regional defence alliance changed from a purely defence alliance to a more active (and assertive) regional collective security organisation. One event that certainly changed the way NATO views its mission and role as a 'selective security organisation' (as Inis Claude labelled it), was the military intervention in Kosovo in the Balkans in 1999. Indeed, during the Kosovo conflict, NATO acted far more actively as a collective security apparatus and not so much in self-defence of any of its members.

The conflict in Kosovo during 1998–1999 must be viewed within the context of the bigger regional conflict of the 1990s in the Balkans. After the disintegration of the old Yugoslav Federation with its six republics (Serbia, Croatia, Slovenia, Montenegro, Macedonia and Bosnia-Herzegovina) and two autonomous provinces in Serbia (Vojvodina and Kosovo), President Slobodan Milosevic of the new, smaller Federal Republic of Yugoslavia (Serbia and Montenegro) wanted to change the identity of Kosovo from being mainly Albanian to being more Serbian. By 1998 Milosevic's policies involved acts of violence and gross human rights violations against ethnic Albanians in Kosovo. There was a real concern that another genocide was about to begin in the Balkan region – the other being the Bosnian genocide of the early 1990s. There were diplomatic efforts to end the conflict and human rights abuses in Kosovo. These efforts were accompanied by a series of UN Security Council Resolutions aimed at ending the conflict. The situation in Kosovo was also grave enough for the Prosecutor of the ICTY to declare the violations of international humanitarian law in Kosovo to fall within the Tribunal's jurisdiction.[91] By September 1998 the conflict in Kosovo deteriorated to such an extent that the UN Security Council acted under Chapter VII of the UN Charter and passed Resolution 1199, demanding a ceasefire

---

90 Art 5 of The North Atlantic Treaty of 4 April 1949, available on www.nato.int/docu/basictxt/treaty.htm.

91 *Kosovo Report of the Independent International Commission on Kosovo* (2000) 69–70.

and the withdrawal of Yugoslav armed forces from Kosovo.[92] On 23 March 1999 NATO informed the Secretary-General of the UN about the worsening humanitarian situation and escalation of conflict in Kosovo. The next day the NATO air campaign against Yugoslav targets started.[93]

The military intervention by NATO armed forces in response to the ongoing conflict in Kosovo during the first half of 1999 was the first time that NATO acted beyond its narrow mandate of self-defence. The official basis for the military intervention was not so much out of concern for direct security threats against NATO members, but out of *humanitarian* concerns primarily, and *security* concerns secondary. Broadly speaking, NATO justified the military intervention in Kosovo on two grounds, namely humanitarian concerns for the people of Kosovo and, further, the enforcement of UN Security Council resolutions and other relevant international agreements.[94] However, it needs to be stressed that NATO's armed intervention was carried out without prior UN Security Council approval.[95]

It is true that the political statements by NATO leaders at the time seem to provide a more nuanced rationale for the military action – from pure humanitarian concerns to concerns for the peace, security and stability of the Balkan region and the rest of Europe.[96] Questions as to the legality (and political wisdom) of the intervention were raised. There was no UN Security Council approval of the intervention. In fact, two permanent members – China and Russia – were strongly opposed to the NATO action.[97] In light of the legal and political ramifications of the conflict in Kosovo, and in particular the controversial NATO military action, the Independent International Commission

92 *Kosovo Report* (*supra*) 75.

93 *Kosovo Report* (*supra*) 85.

94 See Press Statement by Dr Javier Solana, Secretary General of NATO, 23 March 1999, reproduced in Marc Weller *The Crisis in Kosovo 1989–1999* Vol I (1999) Documents & Analysis Publishing Ltd, Cambridge, 495.

95 See Statement made by the UN Secretary-General on NATO military action against Yugoslavia, 24 March 1999; and SC Provisional Record, 3988th Meeting, 24 March 1999 (reprinted in Marc Weller (Crisis in Kosovo) (*supra*) 498–501.

96 See for instance statements by UK Prime Minister Tony Blair (23 March 1999) and US President Bill Clinton (24 March 1999). Both leaders from the prominent NATO members cited not only humanitarian concerns, but also peace, stability and security in Europe as reasons for NATO to intervene militarily to end the conflict in Kosovo. Marc Weller (Crisis in Kosovo) (*supra*) 495–496 and 498–499.

97 See SC Provisional Record, 3988th Meeting, 24 March 1999 reproduced in Marc Weller (Crisis in Kosovo) (*supra*) 499–501. The Russian ambassador stated that Russia was 'profoundly outraged' by the NATO use of force in Yugoslavia. Mr Lavrov, the Russian ambassador, stated that the NATO action was illegal and in violation of the UN Charter. Russia even linked the NATO action to the 1974 definition of aggression (further discussed in Ch IV *infra*) and referred to the fact that under that definition, 'no consideration of whatever nature, whether political, economic, military or otherwise, may serve as a justification for aggression.'

on Kosovo (the Kosovo Commission) was convened by the Prime Minister of Sweden, Göran Persson. The Commission was endorsed by Kofi Annan, the UN Secretary-General. Justice Richard Goldstone from South Africa and Mr Carl Tham from Sweden served as co-chairmen. The findings of the Kosovo Commission were published in a comprehensive report.[98]

One of the important themes that were addressed in the Kosovo Report is of particular interest for the collective security debate in the post Cold War world: The impact of claims of legitimate use of force (often referred to as humanitarian intervention) outside the framework of the UN Charter. In this Chapter the aim is not to analyse possible new justifications for the use of armed force, for instance the contested notion of humanitarian intervention,[99] but rather to investigate to what extent the collective security system that was created in the wake of the Second World War, is still in place.

4.3.2. Regional security arrangements under Article 52 of the UN Charter

Article 52 of the UN Charter provides as follows:

> '(1) Nothing in the present Charter precludes the existence of regional arrangements or agencies for dealing with such matters relating to the maintenance of international peace and security as are appropriate for regional action, provided that such arrangements or agencies and their activities are consistent with the Purposes and Principles of the United Nations.
> (2) The Members of the United Nations entering into such arrangements or constituting such agencies shall make every effort to achieve pacific settlement of local disputes through such regional arrangements or by such regional agencies before referring them to the Security Council.
> (3) The Security Council shall encourage the development of pacific settlement of local disputes through such regional arrangements or by such regional agencies either on the initiative of the states concerned or by reference from the Security Council.
> (4) This Article in no way impairs the application of Articles 34 [Security Council may investigates disputes] and 35 [referral of disputes by states to the Security Council].'

Waldemar Hummer and Michael Schweitzer analysed the different aspects of Article 52 and proposed the following definition of a regional arrangement or agency within the meaning of Article 52:

98 *Kosovo Report* (*supra*).
99 On this debate, see in general Gerhard Kemp 'Mission Impossible? "Humanitarian intervention" and the new paradigm of international criminal law' 3 *Stell LR* (2002) 460–472; James Crawford (Public International Law) (*supra*) 752–754.

'[It] refers to a union of States or an international organization based upon a collective treaty or a constitution and consistent with the Purposes and Principles of the UN, whose primary task is the maintenance of peace and security under the control and within the framework of the UN. Its members, whose numbers must be smaller than that of the UN, must be so closely linked in territorial terms that effective local dispute settlement by means of a specially provided procedure is possible. Accordingly, regional agencies are internally focussed, thereby distinguishing themselves from, *inter alia*, externally focussed systems of collective self-defence under Art. 51.'[100]

In terms of the above definition, three organisations were identified by Hummer and Schweitzer as regional arrangements or agencies within the ambit of Article 52. These are: the Organisation of American States, the League of Arab States and the Organization of African Unity.[101] The latter has since been replaced by a potentially more assertive (interventionist) regional organisation, the African Union, which is briefly discussed below as an example of an organisation within the meaning of Article 52 of the UN Charter. The fact that the AU also has a growing *criminal justice* agenda (in addition to the more traditional agenda of a regional political body) is relevant to the topic of this book.[102] The criminal justice agenda adds significance to the role of the AU as active in both the political and criminal justice responses to aggression; a theme that is further developed in Chapter VIII below.

4.3.3. The African Union as regional security organisation

The African Union is the institutional successor of the Organisation of African Unity (OAU), which had a broad political and social agenda. The OAU evolved into the AU on 9 July 2002 with an aspiration to not only build upon the Pan-African ideals of the OAU, but also to eradicate the sources of conflict on the African continent.[103] To this end the AU, unlike its predecessor, is able to actively intervene on the African continent in order to prevent human rights violations on the scale of crimes against humanity and genocide.[104]

---

100 Waldemar Hummer and Michael Schweitzer 'Chapter VIII Regional Arrangements' in Bruno Simma (The Charter of the United Nations Vol I) (*supra*) 828.

101 Waldemar Hummer and Michael Schweitzer in Bruno Simma (The Charter of the United Nations Vol I) (*supra*) 828–831.

102 See further the discussion of the criminal jurisdiction of the 'African Court under the Malabo Protocol' in Ch VIII *infra*.

103 For a critical comparison between the objectives of the OAU and the AU, see Michael Cowling, 'The African Union – an evaluation' 27 *SAYIL* (2002) 193–205.

104 See Stephan Klingebiel, 'Africa's new peace and security architecture' 14(2) *African Security Review* (2005) 35–44. The author argues that the AU will be able to actively intervene to prevent conflicts and mass human rights violations on the African continent. However, the author also points out that external actors like the UN and regional groupings like NATO, the

Article 5(2) of the Constitutive Act of the AU provides for the creation of peace and security structures. In December 2003 the Peace and Security Council was established.[105] The crucial provisions on collective security can be found in the Protocol on the Peace and Security Council (PSC).[106] On the importance of this regional security body, Hennie Strydom noted that the UN regards the African continent as particularly prone to conflict and that this poses a major challenge to the UN.[107] In terms of the Protocol on Peace and Security, the Council can recommend to the Assembly of Heads of State intervention in a member state in respect of certain situations constituting serious crimes under international law, namely war crimes, genocide and crimes against humanity. The use of force may also be authorised to safeguard democracy and for broader humanitarian purposes, for instance in the context of natural disasters. It is clear that 'intervention' could include military intervention and the use of force.[108] An African Standby Force can be deployed on instructions from the PSC. Although the AU's peace and security structures might seem to constitute a complete collective security regime for Africa, the Protocol on the Peace and Security Council provides for close co-operation with the UN.[109] Having said that, it is also prudent to consider the following observations by Timothy Murithi on the role of the AU vis-à-vis that of the UN which, according to Murithi, has failed Africa on several occasions, including the Rwandan genocide in 1994:

> 'The Constitutive Act of the African Union has introduced a principle that if individual states are unable to live up to their responsibilities to protect people affected in internal conflicts then in theory the African Union is empowered to intervene. In effect African governments by signing up to the Union have accepted external intervention in the internal affairs in serious crisis situations which basically dilutes the provision found in the UN Charter on the non-intervention in the affairs of a member state.'[110]

The Peace and Security Council of the AU will have a function unlike that of the Security Council of the UN. Strydom has pointed out that the PSC has the typical collective security aim of '*promoting* peace, security and stability',[111]

EU and even individual states like former colonial powers Britain and France will still play a significant interventionist role in Africa.

105 See, in general, Jeremy Levitt *Africa: Mapping new boundaries in international law* (2008) Bloomsbury, London, 143 *et seq.*

106 See Art 1 of the Protocol Relating to the Establishment of the Peace and Security Council of the African Union, 9 Jul 2002.

107 Hennie Strydom 'Peace and Security under the African Union' 28 *SAYIL* (2003) 60.

108 Jeremy Levitt (Africa) (*supra*) 144.

109 Art 17(1) and (3) Protocol Relating to the Establishment of the Peace and Security Council of the African Union.

110 Timothy Murithi, *The African Union – Pan-Africanism, Peacebuilding and Development* (2005) Ashgate Publishing, Aldershot, 97.

111 Hennie Strydom (Peace and Security) (*supra*) 62.

but this is linked to broader economic, social and environmental objectives. Time will tell whether this broader approach to peace and security will be more successful in securing peace and stability than the narrower approach to security as provided for by the UN Charter and as practised by the UN Security Council.

The humanitarian crisis in the Darfur region of Sudan – where thousands of people have died in a conflict that some have labelled 'genocide' – provided an acid test for the effectiveness of the AU's peace and security structures.[112] This crisis, which has already prompted a criminal justice response in the form of a Security Council referral of the situation to the International Criminal Court,[113] turned out to be the first real test of whether the AU has the necessary political will and resources to bring the crisis to an end. On 31 July 2007 the Security Council adopted a resolution[114] providing for the deployment of one of the biggest peacekeeping forces ever. This force is a so-called 'hybrid' force – consisting of both AU and UN personnel.[115] The joint operation became a test case for the relationship between the UN, regional organisations like the AU, and the ICC in complex humanitarian situations affecting international peace and security. As far as the joint UN/AU operation is concerned, the assessment is not very positive. Indeed, a critical and evidence-based report in *Foreign Policy* is indicative of the perceived failure of the peace and security operation by the UN and the AU.[116] The deteriorating relationship between the AU and the ICC, which is further explored in Chapter VIII, adds to a sense of institutional impotence – in terms of both the political and criminal justice responses to the situation in Darfur.

---

112 See CDR Seth Appiah-Mensah 'AU's critical assignment in Darfur' 14(2) *African Security Review* (2005) 7–21; Stephan Klingebiel 'Africa's new peace and security architecture' 14(2) *African Security Review* (2005) 35–44.

113 UN SC Res 1593 (2005). Par 1 of the Resolution provides for the referral of the situation in Darfur to the ICC. This was the first time that the SC referred a situation to the ICC. The SC has on a number of occasions determined that the situation in Darfur continues to constitute a threat to international peace and security. For further analysis see Luigi Condorelli and Annalisa Ciampi 'Comments on the Security Council referral of the situation in Darfur to the ICC' 3 *JICJ* (2005) 590–599; Cécile Aptel Williamson 15(1) *African Security Review* (2006) 20–31.

114 UN SC Res 1769 (2007).

115 UN SC Res 1769 (*supra*) par 1. For an assessment, see Robert Barnidge 'The United Nations and the African Union: Assessing a partnership for peace in Darfur' 14(1) *Journal of Conflict & Security Law* (2009) 93–113.

116 Colum Lynch 'They just stood watching' *Foreign Policy* 7 April 2014 (www.foreignpolicy.com/2014/04/07/they-just-stood-watching-2/). The author observes: 'U.N. officials concede that the Darfur operation is deeply flawed. The mission, which is administered jointly by the U.N. and the African Union (A.U.), has been hobbled since its birth by a range of disabilities: conflicting visions of its role between U.N. headquarters and African leaders; a lack of cooperation by the Sudanese government; poor leadership; and badly-equipped troops that lacked the helicopters, trucks, and other military hardware needed to patrol a region as vast as France.'

While the operation in Darfur can be described as a failure; an assessment of the AU's peace and security work on the continent as a whole is more nuanced. For instance, the AU response to the conflict in Libya in 2011 can be described as another failure of the peace and security mechanism, while the intervention in Mali (2012/2013) received better reviews,[117] albeit still critical[118] of the institutional problems and apparent lack of co-operation between the AU, the UN and sub-regional groups like ECOWAS.[119] At the risk of oversimplification, the best way to summarise the situation is perhaps to say that 'the AU and the sub-regional peace and security organisations are faced with the challenge of responding to crises on the continent at the same time as they are developing the capacity to do so.'[120] Whether the addition of a regional criminal justice framework will be meaningful in terms of the peace and security needs of the continent is an open question. All indications are there that a regional criminal justice mechanism will become part of the AU response to regional peace, security and justice challenges.[121]

5. CONCLUDING REMARKS

The collective security system, dominated by the UN and in particular the powers of the UN Security Council under Chapter VII of the UN Charter, has been described as a 'perfect representative' of a collective security system.[122] However, it should be clear from the discussion above that this system is in practice not working as well as in theory. There are a number of problematic areas of a systemic nature that were pointed out by commentators to be the crucial weaknesses of the UN dominated collective security system. First, the political (and legal) implications of the veto power of the five permanent members of the UN Security Council: Craig Barker observed as follows:

> 'This problem [the veto power] is particularly acute in relation to the operation of the collective security system of the Charter because it places the permanent members of

117 Julian Brett 'The interrelationship between the African peace and security architecture, the global peace and security architecture and regional initiatives' 24 October 2013 (www.um.dk/en/~/media/UM/English-site/Documents/Danida/About-Danida/Danidatransparency/Documents/Grantcommittee/2013/Extdoc/02aAnnexAAPSAstudy.pdf).

118 Simone Haysom 'Security and humanitarian crisis in Mali – the role of regional organisations' (March 2014) Humanitarian Policy Group (www.odi.org/sites/odi.org.uk/files/odi-assets/publications-opinion-files/8829.pdf).

119 Economic Community of West African States.

120 Julian Brett (African peace and security architecture) (*supra*) 32.

121 See further the discussion of the criminal jurisdiction of the African Court for Justice and Human Rights in Ch VIII.

122 Craig Barker *International law and international relations* (2000) Continuum, London/New York, 99.

the Council above the system, ensuring that they can never properly be regarded as aggressor states under that system.'[123]

A second problem derives from the unfulfilled ideal expressed in the UN Charter that the system of collective security should be supported by a standing UN military force that would help with the maintenance of peace and security.[124] Barker submitted that this aspect of the collective security regime is in fact a crucial prerequisite of military action under Chapter VII of the Charter. The unwillingness of especially the big powers to enter into agreements with the UN to establish such a permanent UN force undermined the structure and credibility of the collective security system.[125] It was also pointed out by Dinstein that the Security Council in the past was quite reluctant to actively pursue agreements with potential contributing states to a UN standby force.[126]

Third, the political realities of the Cold War (1945 to 1990) resulted in the Security Council being unable to fully utilise the powers under Chapter VII of the Charter. During the Cold War a number of conflicts or possible threats to international peace occurred, but the Security Council proved to be reluctant to actively intervene, or to make determinations in terms of Article 39. Three conflicts in this period were labelled 'breaches of the peace', namely the Korean War (1950), the Falklands Island War (1982) and the Iran–Iraq War (1987).[127] The Security Council also determined that certain situations were 'threats to peace', for example during Israel's 1948 War of Independence.[128] The fact is that during the period of the Cold War the collective security system was virtually paralysed by political manoeuvring, and the reluctance of states to heed calls for military action, even with Security Council authorisation.[129] It was only after the Cold War ended effectively in 1989/1990,[130] that a dramatic increase in Security Council action under Chapter VII could be seen.[131] In this regard the role of the Uniting for Peace Resolution (referred to above) must also be noted.

---

123 Craig Barker (International law) (*supra*) 100.

124 See Art 43 of the UN Charter.

125 Craig Barker (International law) (*supra*) 100–101.

126 Yoram Dinstein (War Aggression Self-Defence) (*supra*) 304.

127 For a list of the relevant SC resolutions see Yoram Dinstein (War Aggression Self-Defence) (*supra*) 292.

128 Yoram Dinstein (War Aggression Self-Defence) (*supra*) 293.

129 For an analysis of various SC Resolutions in this period, see Yoram Dinstein (War Aggression Self-Defence) (*supra*) 293.

130 The Cold War ended symbolically when the Berlin Wall came down in 1989. Of course, the end of this 'war' was a much more gradual affair that really ended in the demise of the Soviet Union and the crumbling of Russian (Soviet) influence in Eastern Europe.

131 See examples listed by Yoram Dinstein (War Aggression Self-Defence) (*supra*) 300.

Ultimately, the response of international bodies like the UN Security Council to threats to international peace and security can take many different forms. Security Council responses (under Chapter VII) to threats to international peace and security can be regarded as the 'legalization of international politics'.[132] An example of the power of the Security Council to act as *lawmaker* as part of its Chapter VII powers,[133] is the adoption of Resolution 1373 in reaction to the terrorist attacks on New York and Washington on 11 September 2001. In terms of this Resolution the UN Convention for the Suppression of the Financing of Terrorism, 1999, effectively became binding on all states, because of the fact that it was adopted as a Chapter VII measure.[134]

In the collective security context an important fusion of politics and law can be seen. It is simply not possible to draw clear lines between 'political' and 'legal' responses to threats to international peace and security. One can ascribe *primary* roles or responsibilities to international organisations like the UN (and its organs the Security Council, the General Assembly and the ICJ); or collective self-defence or regional security organisations like NATO or the AU. Their responses to threats to peace and security have political and legal consequences relevant for purposes of this book.

132 See Stefan Oeter 'International Law and General Systems Theory' 44 *German Yearbook of International Law* (2001) 77.

133 See in general Stefan Talmon 'The Security Council as World Legislature' 99 *AJIL* (2005) 175–193.

134 Stefan Oeter (International law) (*supra*) 77.

CHAPTER II

FROM *JUS AD BELLUM* TO *JUS CONTRA BELLUM*: THE PROHIBITION OF THE USE OF FORCE IN NORMATIVE AND INSTITUTIONAL PERSPECTIVE

1. INTRODUCTION: THE SHIFT FROM *JUS AD BELLUM* TO *JUS CONTRA BELLUM*

In Chapter I it was shown how the collective security system as it stands today developed primarily in response to the two devastating world wars. The anarchic international system where war was part of international politics (and regarded as an extension of a sovereign state's right to pursue the national interest), gave way to the liberal ideal of a collective security system based on respect for international law and institutions of collective security. Part of this shift away from power politics at international level involved a move away from what was known as the *jus ad bellum*, or the right that states would assert in order to use war in the national interest. The *jus ad bellum* was not limited by legal constraints to the extent that we have today in the Charter of the United Nations, and under customary international law. Ian Brownlie pointed out that in the period before 1914 (outbreak of the First World War) the right to resort to war was often asserted as a sovereign right. But even then statesmen and writers on the topic often linked the *jus ad bellum* to some or other justification, such as self-defence.[1] By 1928, with the conclusion of the so-called Kellogg-Briand Pact (General Treaty for Renunciation of War as an Instrument of National Policy),[2] the contracting parties declared that war would no longer be used as an instrument of national policy or to solve international disputes.[3] This, according to Yoram Dinstein, was the historical moment when 'international law progressed from *jus ad bellum* to *jus contra bellum*.'[4]

1 See Ian Brownlie *International Law and the use of force by states* (1963) Oxford University Press, Oxford, 40–41.

2 International Treaty for Renunciation of War as an Instrument of National Policy, 27 Aug 1928, reproduced in McNair *The Law of Treaties* (1961) Clarendon Press, Oxford, 234–236.

3 Art 1 Kellogg-Briand Pact.

4 Yoram Dinstein *War Aggression and Self-Defence* 4th (2005) Cambridge University Press, Cambridge, 83.

In Chapter I the prohibition on the use of force was explained with reference to the theory and practice of the liberal ideal of collective security. The Security Council of the UN is the primary institutional guarantor of this ideal. The institutional framework designed to maintain international peace and security as discussed in Chapter I will serve as background to a discussion in Chapter II of the *content* of the prohibition of the use of force and the criminalisation of crimes against peace, which will be discussed in Chapter III.

2. THE PROHIBITION OF THE USE OF FORCE AS A PEREMPTORY NORM IN INTERNATIONAL LAW

Alexander Orakhelashvili defines the notion of a peremptory norm in international law as follows:

> 'In order to qualify as peremptory, a norm, while protecting a given actor, legal person or value, must safeguard interests transcending those of individual States, have a moral or humanitarian connotation, because its breach would involve a result so morally deplorable as to be considered absolutely unacceptable by the international community as a whole, and consequently not permitting division of these interests into bilateral legal relations.'[5]

One of the peremptory norms in international law that does satisfy the above definition is the prohibition of the use of force. The International Law Commission (ILC) is of the opinion that the prohibition of the use of force protects not only the survival and security of individual states, but more than the sum of this, also the interests of the international community as a whole.[6] The collective security system (including regional manifestations) as discussed in Chapter I provides the theoretical and institutional framework for a discussion of the content of the prohibition of the use of force.

Orakhelashvili states that the prohibition of the use of force forms part of *jus cogens*.[7] The prohibition of the use of force and the inherent right of states to self-defence form the modern *jus ad bellum* (primarily Article 2(4) of the UN Charter and the customary international law prohibition of the use of force).[8]

For the purposes of this book the position as set out by Dinstein is preferred, namely that there was a shift from the *jus ad bellum* to the modern *jus contra*

---

5 Alexander Orakhelashvili *Peremptory Norms in International Law* (2006) Oxford University Press, Oxford, 50.

6 *ILC Report* 2001 322.

7 Orakhelashvili (*supra*) 50.

8 Orakhelashvili (*supra*) 51.

bellum.[9] Thus, states are generally prohibited from using force in their international relations and in the pursuit of their national interest. There is no longer a 'right to go to war'. This right is now governed by the collective security regime under the UN Charter. The legal position was summarised by the ICJ in the *Legality of the Threat or Use of Nuclear Weapons* case:[10]

> 'This [Art 2(4)] prohibition of the use of force is to be considered in the light of other relevant provisions of the Charter. In Article 51, the Charter recognizes the inherent right of individual or collective self-defence if an armed attack occurs. A further lawful use of force is envisaged in Article 42, whereby the Security Council may take military enforcement measures in conformity with Chapter VII of the Charter.'[11]

And further, regarding the method of armed force, or the kind of weapons employed, the ICJ stated:

> 'They [Articles 2(4), 42 and 51] apply to any use of force, regardless of the weapons employed. The Charter neither expressly prohibits, nor permits, the use of any specific weapon, including nuclear weapons. A weapon that is already unlawful per se, whether by treaty or custom, does not become lawful by reason of its being used for a legitimate purpose under the Charter.'[12]

Regarding self-defence, the ICJ held *in casu* that the well-established conditions of necessity and proportionality (as rules of customary international law on the use of force in self-defence) are also limitations on the use of force in terms of Article 51 of the UN Charter.[13]

3. THE PROHIBITION OF THE USE OF FORCE IN INSTITUTIONAL PERSPECTIVE

When it comes to the prohibition of the use of force in international law, many complexities can arise. It is important to take into account not only the texts and provisions of the relevant international instruments, but also the competencies of the different role players like the Security Council, the ICJ, the General Assembly of the UN, and, as will be seen in later chapters, the ICC.

---

9 See discussion of the implications of the Kellogg-Briand Pact of 1928 and Dinstein's opinion *supra*.

10 *Legality of the Threat or Use of Nuclear Weapons* Advisory Opinion (8 Jul 1996) ICJ Reports 1996, 226.

11 *Legality of the Threat or Use of Nuclear Weapons* case (*supra*) par 38.

12 *Legality of the Threat or Use of Nuclear Weapons* case (*supra*) par 39.

13 *Legality of the Threat or Use of Nuclear Weapons* case (*supra*) par 40–41.

Christine Gray points out that one should not *assume* that the Security Council has (or should have) the final say as to the legality or illegality of the use of force, or on the content of the norms in question.[14] She asks:

> 'How far is the law developed by institutions? That is, do states acting collectively through the UN have a more important role than they do outside the UN in the interpretation and application of the UN Charter? Does the Security Council have the final say as to not only what is an act of aggression, threat to the peace or breach of the peace under Chapter VII of the Charter, but also as to what is a threat or use of force under Article 2(4) or an armed attack and as to whether a state is acting in self-defence under Article 51?'[15]

The primarily *political* role of the Security Council in determining whether conduct amounts to prohibited conduct under Article 39 of the UN Charter seems to be still an outstanding characteristic of not only the collective security system, but also the international use of force regime. The role of the ICJ as a forum for judicial review of Security Council decisions (notably under Chapter VII of the Charter) is debatable and the ICJ itself has not pronounced in clear terms on its relationship with the Security Council in this regard.[16]

Apart from the ICJ's seeming unwillingness to play a significant role in terms of Article 39 determinations (regarding acts of aggression, breaches of peace or threats to peace), the Court does seem to play an increasingly active role in terms of Article 2(4) questions on the prohibition of the use of force.[17] The important case of *Nicaragua v United States*[18] not only provided a judicial interpretation of the prohibition of the use of force under the UN Charter, but also delineated the respective roles of the ICJ and the Security Council in determining various aspects of the UN Charter on the use of force. Nicaragua alleged that the US violated Nicaragua's sovereignty, territorial integrity and political independence with an 'army' of mercenaries. Nicaragua alleged that these mercenaries were trained and supplied by the US and 'directed their attacks against human and economic targets inside Nicaragua'.[19]

---

14 Christine Gray *International law and the use of force* (2000) Oxford University Press, Oxford, 9.

15 Gray (*supra*) 9.

16 See Gray (*supra*) 9–10.

17 Gray (*supra*) 11–12. Gray refers to a number of ICJ cases post *Nicaragua* where the Court were approached by states to rule on the legality of the use of armed force.

18 *Case concerning military and paramilitary activities in and against Nicaragua (Nicaragua v United States of America)* Merits, Judgment, *ICJ Reports* 1986, p 14; 25 *ILM* 1023 (1986).

19 See *Nicaragua v United States* (Judgment on Jurisdiction) (*supra*) par 85. For more historical and political background on this, see Max Hilaire *International law and the United States military intervention in the Western Hemisphere* (1997) Kluwer Law International, The Hague, 97–108.

Gray pointed out that it was the United States that tried to portray the situation in Nicaragua as one relating to Chapter VII of the Charter (threats or breaches of peace or acts of aggression). However, the ICJ held that it was in fact an Article 2(4) matter (prohibition of the use of force). On the basis of this jurisdictional finding the matter could be brought before the ICJ, 'the principal judicial organ of the UN'.[20]

Gray concludes that '[the] implication seems to be that matters under Chapter VII could not properly be entertained by the Court.'[21] Gray observed that the ICJ can at present play an important role in the development of the law on the use of force – not an exclusive role, but alongside the Security Council. Put differently, issues involving the use of force fall not only within the *political* domain of the Security Council, but the ICJ is quite willing to assert its right to hear matters arising from the use of force by states and resolve the legal implications of such conduct.[22] This view is in line with the ICJ's interpretation of its role vis-à-vis the Security Council:

> 'The Charter … does not confer *exclusive* responsibility upon the Security Council for the purpose [maintenance of international peace and security]. While in Article 12 there is a provision for a clear demarcation of functions between the General Assembly and the Security Council, in respect of any dispute or situation, that the former should not make any recommendation with regard to that dispute or situation unless the Security Council so requires, there is no similar provision anywhere in the Charter with respect to the Security Council and the Court. The Council has functions of a political nature assigned to it, whereas the Court exercises purely judicial functions. Both organs can therefore perform their separate but complementary functions with respect to the same events.'[23]

Two decades after the judgment in the *Nicaragua* case, in *Democratic Republic of Congo v Uganda* (hereinafter '*DRC v Uganda*'),[24] the ICJ had to consider, *inter alia*, the legality of military interventions by Uganda in the DRC and whether that constituted a violation of Article 2(4) of the UN Charter. Perhaps it is an indication of the ICJ's sensitivity to not taking on the conflict resolution or collective security responsibilities of the Security Council that the Court declared in *DRC v Uganda*:

---

20 Gray (*supra*) 11.

21 Gray (*supra*) 11.

22 Gray (*supra*) 11–12.

23 *Nicaragua v United States* (Judgment on Jurisdiction of the Court) (*supra*) par 95 (emphasis in the original).

24 *Case concerning armed activities on the territory of the Congo (Democratic Republic of Congo v Uganda)* 45 *ILM* 271 (2006).

'The Court is aware of the complex and tragic situation which has long prevailed in the Great Lakes region. There has been much suffering by the local population and destabilization of much of the region. In particular, the instability in the DRC has had negative security implications for Uganda and some other neighbouring States ... The Court is aware, too, that the factional conflicts within the DRC require a comprehensive settlement to the problems of the region ... However, the task of the Court must be to respond, on the basis of international law, to the particular legal dispute brought before it. As it interprets and applies the law, it will be mindful of context, but its task cannot go beyond that.'[25]

Two decades after the *Nicaragua* case the different but complimentary roles of the Security Council and the ICJ in matters of the use of force by states are still in place. The Security Council still has the *primary political function* to determine under Article 39 of the UN Charter whether there is a threat or breach of peace, or an act of aggression. The Security Council can then act in terms of Chapter VII to maintain peace and security. This is not to say that the Security Council action under Chapter VII cannot involve criminal liability for perpetrators of international crimes through criminal tribunals like the Rwanda Tribunal and the Yugoslav Tribunal.[26] The ICJ on the other hand is the *primary judicial organ* under the UN Charter. It is the duty of the ICJ to settle disputes between States in terms of its powers under the Charter. Thus, a dispute regarding the use of force by a state in contravention of Article 2(4) of the Charter falls within the jurisdiction of the ICJ.[27]

4. THE ROLE OF THE GENERAL ASSEMBLY IN RELATION TO UN CHARTER PROVISIONS ON THE USE OF FORCE

It was pointed out in Chapter I that the General Assembly has since the adoption of the Uniting for Peace Resolution of 1950, in theory if not always in practice, an increasingly important role to play in matters of peace and security. Indeed,

25 *DRC v Uganda* (*supra*) par 26.

26 Leslie Green *The Contemporary law of armed conflict* 2nd (2000) Manchester University Press, Manchester, 9–10. With reference to the SC's powers under Ch VII UN Charter to maintain peace and security, the author stated: '[As] with the Covenant and all other agreements seeking to control aggression, there is no suggestion that any individual responsible for resorting to aggression shall be subject to criminal proceedings. However, in view of the atrocities committed during the conflicts consequent upon the break-up of the former Yugoslavia and during the civil war in Rwanda, the Security Council decided that action was necessary under Chapter VII and authorised the despatch of military forces as well as the establishment of *ad hoc* war crimes tribunals.' Thus, a combination of military and legal responses to threats to international peace and security.

27 See *Nicaragua v United States* (Judgment on Jurisdiction) (*supra*) par 94.

it was argued in Chapter I that the General Assembly's role in peace and security matters could help to bring about a more democratic or representative collective security regime, especially in light of growing demands for Security Council reform, which is perhaps still a long way off.

It is tempting to think of the General Assembly as a 'world parliament' or the natural place to search for the voice or voices representing 'the international community'. However, the structure of the UN Charter and the powerful political role that the big powers, especially the permanent members of the Security Council (United States, the United Kingdom, Russia, China and France), play limit the impact and role of the General Assembly in the peace and security context, and also with regard to use of force matters. Siegfried Magiera commented that 'the [General Assembly] is a conference of states, not a world parliament of independent representatives of the peoples.'[28] But whether one regards the General Assembly as the (perhaps idealistic) 'Parliament of Man', or as an ineffective political talk shop,[29] this UN body has a role to play in questions surrounding the use of force by states. Christine Gray points out that since the end of the Cold War, the debates and resolutions of the General Assembly are often the results of consensus, rather than confrontation. During the Cold War it was much more common for blocs of states to object to the General Assembly adopting resolutions on perceived acts of 'aggression'. The argument was that only the Security Council could make determinations of aggression under its Chapter VII powers.[30] Even so, Gray further points out that resolutions of the General Assembly 'tend not to use the language in the Charter in Articles 2(4) [use of force] and 51 [self-defence], nor to refer to them expressly'.[31] Gray makes the argument (albeit tentatively) that condemnation of a particular use of force by an organ such as the General Assembly (or, for that matter, the Security

28 Siegfried Magiera 'Chapter IV. The General Assembly' in Bruno Simma (*supra*) Vol I 247–256.

29 Paul Kennedy, in his book *The Parliament of Man: The Past, Present, and Future of the United Nations* (2006) Random House, New York, argues that despite all the criticism against the UN, including the notorious ineffectiveness of General Assembly measures, the world needs the UN, and organs like the General Assembly needs *more* power, not less. Rosemary Righter, who reviewed Kennedy's book in the London *Times*, was very critical of Kennedy's assumptions and his idealistic view of the UN dominated international system. She wrote: 'The General Assembly's obsession with process, rather than results, is reflected in the inconsequentiality of most of its decisions. UN files are filled with mould-pocked resolutions which never stood a chance of being implemented, reports and requests for further reports. Few of these documents are read by delegates, let alone by their governments. In New York alone, a recent inventory – the first attempted since 1956 – identified no fewer than 9,000 "active mandates" which the secretariat is supposed to be implementing. A body that cannot even organize its own agenda is unlikely to contribute to the better ordering of the world. There and elsewhere in the UN, the grinding of the mill has come to matter more than the quality of the flour produced.' See review by Rosemary Righter 'What use the UN?' *Timesonline*, http://tls.timesonline.co.uk (5 Dec 2006).

30 Gray (*supra*) 13.

31 Gray (*supra*) 14.

Council) 'is conclusive or at least persuasive as to illegality.'[32] The author uses the curious argument that the closer the political ties between the states involved (for example condemnation by the United Kingdom of the use of force by the United States), the stronger the evidence of illegality. Must one deduce from this argument that other resolutions on the use of force might be so clouded by partisan political or other considerations that findings on the illegality of the use of force in such cases need to be treated with scepticism? This is not a simple matter. Gray points to the following:

> 'It is ... common for the Security Council and the General Assembly's initial response to a conflict to be to avoid any finding of responsibility and simply to call for an end to all [armed] intervention.'[33]

And further:

> 'Express findings of aggression (or of aggressive acts) are extremely unusual. It has been only states which were in some sense seen as outlaws which have been condemned for aggression by both the Security Council and the General Assembly; Portugal when it refused to relinquish its colonial possessions, Southern Rhodesia after its unilateral declaration of independence, Israel after its occupation of the West Bank, Gaza and other territory, South Africa during apartheid and its occupation of Namibia, and Indonesia after its invasion of East Timor.'[34]

The reluctance of the General Assembly (and also the Security Council) to name specific states and to apportion blame and responsibility for the illegal use of armed force can perhaps be explained with reference to a number of factors, including the powers given to these organs under the UN Charter, and also political factors.[35] The General Assembly's reluctance to apportion blame to parties to a conflict, or where a state has used armed force, should not necessarily be seen as a particular weakness of the General Assembly. The scope of the General Assembly's powers and duties was intended by the drafters of the UN Charter to create a real discussion forum for the world. This feature certainly has its own potential advantages from a peace and security perspective. In brief, the General Assembly's duties and powers should be seen as complementary to that of the Security Council and International Court of Justice. With reference to Article 10 of the UN Charter, Hailbronner and Klein summarised the role of the General Assembly as follows:

---

32 Gray (*supra*) 15.
33 Gray (*supra*) 16.
34 Gray (*supra*) 17.
35 See references to a number of General Assembly and Security Council decisions in Gray (*supra*) 17.

> 'Art. 10 vests the [General Assembly] with a general power of discussion and recommendation regarding any questions which come within the scope of the Charter (the "comprehensive jurisdiction" of the [General Assembly]). The [General Assembly] represents the most prominent forum for the discussion of world politics and is therefore also described as the "town meeting of the world' and the 'open conscience of humanity". Taking into account the wide-ranging goals and principles which are stipulated in the UN Charter, there are hardly any political questions of international importance not covered by the [General Assembly's] power of discussion contained in Art. 10. On the other hand, the breadth and vagueness of the formulation of the scope of its responsibility mirrors the lack of power to make binding decisions. *So long as the [General Assembly] may only make recommendations that are usually of a non-binding nature ... there is no real need in practice to lay down and define more precisely its area of responsibility.*'[36]

This last mentioned aspect of the General Assembly seems to be both a strength and a weakness, depending on one's perspective. If the General Assembly condemns the use of force in a particular instance, but the condemnation is not followed with action; such condemnation would amount to acquiescence.[37] Christine Gray rightly depicts this line of argument as rather extreme, for a number of reasons, but not the least because this argument does not take into account the reaction of states (other than formal, binding resolutions) to the use of force.[38] And reaction to the use of force in the General Assembly is always relevant, if not formally, at least as evidence of how the international community view a particular instance of the use of force.

5. A BRIEF OVERVIEW OF THE CONTENT OF THE PROHIBITION OF THE USE OF FORCE, AND SOME DEVELOPMENTS THAT MIGHT AFFECT THE INTERPRETATION OF THIS PROHIBITION

With the UN Charter's prohibition of the use of force (which also forms part of *jus cogens*) in mind, and against the background of the broader collective security and international legal context described in Chapter I, it is now necessary to turn to some of the specific problems regarding the content of the rule prohibiting the use of force, and the implications of that for the aggression debate, which will be the focus of Chapter III and further.

---

36 Kay Hailbronner and Eckart Klein 'Functions and Powers – Article 10' in Bruno Simma (*supra*) Vol I 258 (emphasis added).

37 Gray (*supra*) 18.

38 Gray (*supra*) 18.

There are obvious normative connections between the prohibition of the use of force (the *jus contra bellum*) and aggression as a crime under international law (discussed in the following chapters). These are, most notably, the respect for the sovereignty and political integrity of states and the very limited instances where the use of force would be allowed under international law. It is useful to examine a number of new developments that might alter the content of the *jus contra bellum*, and to determine how these developments would affect the aggression debate.

The UN Charter was drafted in the context of a world recovering from the Second World War, and with a view to prevent such wars from ever happening again. That explains the strict regime regarding the lawful use of force. The Charter regime provides for only two instances where armed force would be justified, namely armed intervention under the auspices of the Security Council,[39] and individual or collective self-defence in terms of Article 51.[40]

The political context in which the UN Charter regime operates is not static. Henry Kissinger, one of the most prominent exponents (and practitioners) of *realpolitik* in international relations, described the dynamics of international relations as follows:

> 'International systems live precariously. Every "world order" expresses an aspiration to permanence; the very term has a ring of eternity about it. Yet the elements which comprise it are in constant flux; indeed, with each century, the duration of international systems has been shrinking. The order that grew out of the Peace of Westphalia lasted 150 years; the international system created by the Congress of Vienna maintained itself for a hundred years; the international order characterized by the Cold War ended after forty years. (The Versailles settlement never operated as a system adhered to by the major powers, and amounted to little more than an armistice between the two world wars.) Never before have the components of world order, their capacity to interact, and their goals all changed quite so rapidly, so deeply, or so globally … Whenever the entities constituting the international system change their character, a period of turmoil inevitably follows.'[41]

There are a number of developments that have the potential to challenge the *jus contra bellum* as provided for in the UN Charter. Johan van der Vyver identified three instances that might pose challenges for the use of force regime of the Charter: anticipatory self-defence; humanitarian intervention; and wars of national liberation.[42] Especially *anticipatory self-defence* (for instance, as claimed

---

39 See in general Ch I *supra*.

40 See also limitations on the use of force in self-defence, as identified by the ICJ in the *Legality of the Threat or Use of Nuclear Weapons* case (*supra*). See further James Crawford (Public International Law) (*supra*) 747–752.

41 Kissinger (Diplomacy) (*supra*) 806.

42 Johan van der Vyver '*Ius contra bellum* and American foreign policy' 28 *SAYIL* (2003) 1–28.

by the US as a *casus bellum* for the invasion of Iraq in 2003), and *humanitarian intervention* (for instance, claimed by NATO member states as a justification for the 1999 use of force against Serbia to protect Kosovo) proved to cause the kind of turmoil that Kissinger referred to: Fundamental challenges to the underpinnings of the UN Charter regime on the use of force. Perhaps less controversial than, say, humanitarian intervention (but equally challenging in terms of the traditional construction of the Charter regime) is the developing notion of '*responsibility to protect*' (or 'R2P'), which will also be considered below.

5.1. AN EVOLVING CONCEPT OF SELF-DEFENCE?

Article 51 of the UN Charter protects the right of states to use force in self-defence:

> 'Nothing in the present Charter shall impair the inherent right of individual or collective self-defence if an armed attack occurs against a Member of the United Nations, until the Security Council has taken the measures necessary to maintain international peace and security. Measures taken by Members in the exercise of this right of self-defence shall be immediately reported to the Security Council and shall not in any way affect the authority and responsibility of the Security Council under the present Charter to take at any time such action as it deems necessary in order to maintain or restore international peace and security.'

Under the modern *jus contra bellum*, the only permissible exceptions to the prohibition of the use of force by states are cases of self-defence, and in terms of Security Council action under Chapter VII of the UN Charter.[43] Both individual state conduct and collective security measures[44] can be viewed as permissible exceptions to the prohibition of the use of force. In the *Legality of the Threat or Use of Nuclear Weapons* case (referred to above), the ICJ seemed to link the 'right to self-defence' of every state to a rather high threshold, namely when the 'survival' of the state is at stake. The Court stated:

> '[The] Court cannot lose sight of the fundamental right of every State to survival, and thus its right to resort to self-defence, in accordance with Article 51 of the [UN] Charter, when its survival is at stake.'[45]

The generally accepted position, however, seems to be that self-defence is available to states, not only in the most drastic instances when the very survival of the

---

43 For a detailed discussion, see Yoram Dinstein (War Aggression and Self-Defence*)* (*supra*) 175–325.

44 See also Ch I *supra*.

45 *Legality of the Threat or Use of Nuclear Weapons* case (*supra*) par 96.

state is at stake, but indeed more broadly speaking when the *rights* of the state are violated.[46] The analogy with inter-personal self-defence (which is a well-established notion under domestic criminal law of virtually all legal systems)[47] as well as notions such as the 'Just War theory', clearly underpin the modern international law concept of self-defence. One can even recognise elements of the modern (international law) notion of self-defence in older (*political*) doctrines like those of *raison d'état* and state-interest, in terms of which the self-preservation of the state was paramount.[48] But it is important to note the shift from doctrines like *raison d'état* and Just War (in terms of which states sought to use force as a means to advance *interests*), to self-defence under the modern *jus contra bellum*, where the use of force is an exception (employed to defend the *rights* of the state under international law).[49] But even this more limited scope of the modern right of states to use force in self-defence, need to be carefully considered.

Article 51 of the UN Charter does not define 'armed attack'. It is generally accepted that the customary notion of self-defence is broader than that implied by Article 51. States should be allowed to use force in self-defence when the attack is *imminent*, but publicists like Alexandrov pointed out that the use of force as part of preventive or pre-emptive actions are not justified.[50] Albrecht Randelzhofer noted that Articles 51 and 2(4) of the UN Charter do not correspond exactly in terms of scope. Thus, 'not every use of force contrary to [Article] 2(4) may be responded to with armed self-defence.' The rather startling conclusion is that 'any State affected by another State's unlawful use of force not reaching the threshold of an "armed attack", is bound, if not exactly to endure the violation, then at least to respond only by means falling short of the use or threat of force, which are thus often totally ineffective.'[51]

The limitations to the resort to force in self-defence are also described in terms of the twin qualifications of *necessity* and *proportionality*. The defending state

46 Yoram Dinstein (War Aggression and Self-Defence) (*supra*) 175–176.

47 On the doctrinal and jurisprudential underpinnings and contours of the right to self-defence under domestic criminal law and international law, see Onder Bakircioglu *Self-defence in international and criminal law* (2011) Routledge, Oxford.

48 See in general Richard Tuck *The Rights of War and Peace – Political thought and the International order from Grotius to Kant* (1999) Oxford University Press, Oxford, 3–6.

49 Yoram Dinstein (War Aggression and Self-Defence) (*supra*) 176.

50 SA Alexandrov *Self-Defense Against the Use of Force in International Law* (1996) Kluwer Law International, The Hague, 165. The author refers to a number of instances where force were used not in self-defence, but as preventive or pre-emptive actions: Israel on the Sinai Peninsula (1956), Israel in Beirut (1968), Israel against other targets in Lebanon (1966–1974, 1975, 1981, 1982), South Africa's actions against Angola, Botswana and other states in the region (1976–1984) (many of these were condemned by the UN SC), Turkey's use of force in Northern Iraq (1995).

51 Albrecht Randelzhofer 'Article 51' in Bruno Simma (Charter of the United Nations Vol I) (*supra*) 790.

will use force out of necessity when there is no other option, while the element of proportionality refers to the size, duration, and target of the response, which needs to correspond with the attack. The combined effect of these qualifications is that self-defence cannot be punitive or retaliatory in nature.[52]

The boundaries of necessity are contested in terms of a further qualification: *imminence.* In an age where technology makes possible devastating attacks without much or no warning at all, the notion of *imminent threat* is all but clear. The aggressive deployment of weapons of mass destruction (notably nuclear, chemical and biological weapons) should, as a matter of logic and of principle, be treated differently from the aggressive deployment or posturing of conventional weapons. The imminent invasion by ground troops and tanks is simply not the same as is the deployment of weapons of mass destruction. Even more problematic is imminent threats in the context of kinetic and cyber warfare. A key feature of cyber-attacks is the fact that an attack is often only detected when it has already been implemented. The notion of an 'imminent threat', then, is meaningless, since any cyber-attack capability would as a matter of fact qualify as an 'imminent threat'.[53] Even so, some argue that the impact of cyber-attacks would generally not qualify as attacks that can affect the survival of the victim state, thus precluding the use of force in self-defence. Of course, a cyber-attack can affect economic interests, government functions and so on, but would probably not qualify as an armed attack for purposes of self-defence as explained above. And where the very survival of the state is not in question, it is unlikely that the threat posed by the possibility of a cyber-attack will qualify as an 'imminent threat' for purposes of self-defence under international law[54] – not yet. The actualisation of virtual aggression and kinetic force will shape the debate about the precise boundaries of self-defence under international law in future. Indeed, the very notion of 'an act of aggression' will have to be (re)considered in light of 21st century technological capabilities. For present purposes it suffices to note that this issue is relevant for the discussion on the definition of aggression as well as the jurisdictional regime adopted at the Kampala Review Conference of the Rome Statute of the International Criminal Court, 2010. As noted by Carrie McDougall, there is a question of whether the Kampala definition of acts of aggression,[55] which 'focus on bullets and bombs leaves room for attack by bits and bytes'.[56]

---

52 James Crawford (Public International Law) (*supra*) 749.

53 Henry Kissinger (World Order) (*supra*) 346.

54 Heather Harrison Dinniss *Cyber Warfare and the Laws of War* (2012) Cambridge University Press, Cambridge, 91.

55 Article 8*bis*(2)(a)–(g), Amendments to the Rome Statute of the International Criminal Court on the crime of aggression (reproduced in Annex I).

56 Carrie McDougall *The crime of aggression under the Rome Statute of the International Criminal Court* (2013) Cambridge University Press, Cambridge, 110.

It falls beyond the scope of this Chapter, and is furthermore not the aim of this book, to fully explore the meaning and scope of the right to self-defence under modern international law. The aim here is rather to highlight the contentious nature of this right, and to use a particularly controversial phenomenon (the 'war on terror') to illustrate that the right to self-defence is indeed a notion in flux. This has certain implications for the debate on the contours of the crime of aggression post-Kampala, as well as for individual criminal liability for the crime of aggression more generally, that is, also in regional and domestic perspective.

5.1.1. The use of force and the 'war on terror(ism)'

One of the most profound challenges to the dual requirements of 'necessity' and 'proportionality',[57] as well as the condition of 'imminent threat', underlying the right to self-defence in terms of Article 51 of the UN Charter, came about as a result of the spectacular attacks on New York and Washington DC on 11 September 2001 that killed approximately 3,000 people. The immediate response of the US was in the form of 'Operation Enduring Freedom', by which the US invaded Afghanistan on the basis that the Taliban regime – at the time in power in that state – harboured the Al Qaeda terrorists responsible for the planning of the attacks. The US removed the Taliban regime and started a military campaign to destroy Al Qaeda bases in Afghanistan. The legal basis for the US invasion of Afghanistan was thus presented as a classical case of self-defence, in accordance with the relevant provisions of the UN Charter, notably Article 51.[58] UN Security Council Resolution 1368 (2001) of 12 September 2001, together with Resolution 1373, stated that the terrorist attacks constituted a threat to international peace and security. Both Resolutions confirmed the 'inherent right of individual or collective self-defence'.[59] But this initial use of force in self-defence was only the first chapter in the bigger 'War on Terrorism'.[60]

---

57 See *Legality of the Threat or Use of Nuclear Weapons* case (*supra*) par 41.

58 For views on the justification for the US invasion of Afghanistan in the wake of the 11 Sept 2001 attacks, see Christopher Bertram 'Afghanistan: A just intervention' 6(2) *Imprints* (2002) (http://info.bris.ac.uk/~plcdib/imprints/bertram.html); Darrel Moellendorf 'Is the War in Afghanistan just?' 6(2) *Imprints* (2002) (http://info.bris.ac.uk/~plcdib/imprints/moellendorf.html); Garth Abraham and Kevin Hopkins 'Bombing for humanity: The American response to the 11 September attacks and the plea of self-defence' 119(4) *SALJ* (2002) 783–801; Michael Reisman 'Aftershocks: Reflections on the implications of September 11' 6 *Yale Human Rights & Development Law Journal* (2003) 81–102; Onder Bakircioglu (Self-defence in international and criminal law) (*supra*) 161–164.

59 UN SC Res 1368 (2001); UN SC Res 1373 (2001).

60 The rhetoric and public discourse on these attacks reveal the political context of the later justifications for the notion of pre-emptive strikes against supposed terrorist targets and states that harbour terrorists, and also on states that allegedly possess weapons of mass destruction. For analyses of the rhetoric, see Parag Khanna 'Terrorism as War' 121 *Policy Review* (2003) (www.policyreview.org/oct03/khanna_print.html); Grenville Byford 'The wrong war' *Foreign Affairs* Jul/Aug 2002 (www.foreignaffairs.org/Sea.../printable_fulltext.asp?i=20020701FAEssay8518.xm). Although the Security Council did not call the terrorist

The National Security Strategy of the United States of 2002 – published in the wake of the 11 September 2001 attacks – linked the phenomenon of international terrorism with the risk of these terrorists acquiring 'weapons of mass destruction'. Furthermore, the National Security Strategy also identified the risk posed by so-called 'rogue states': states that not only harbour terrorists, but that are themselves interested in acquiring weapons of mass destruction, thus posing a threat to the security interests of the US. In response to these threats, the National Security Strategy of 2002 states:

> 'The United States has long maintained the option of preemptive actions to counter a sufficient threat to our national security. The greater the threat, the greater is the risk of inaction – and the more compelling the case for taking anticipatory action to defend ourselves, even if uncertainty remains as to the time and place of the enemy's attack. To forestall or prevent such hostile acts by our adversaries, the United States will, if necessary, act pre-emptively.'[61]

Since the drafters of the National Security Strategy was no doubt aware that more states would want to assert the right to use force pre-emptively, the document also made reference to aggression. Pre-emptive strikes should, according to the document, not serve as pretexts for aggression.[62] In 2006 the US restated its assertion of the right to use force pre-emptively:

> 'Taking action [against enemy state and non-state actors which possess weapons of mass destruction] need not involve military force. Our strong preference and common practice is to address proliferation concerns through international diplomacy, in concert with key allies and regional partners. If necessary, however, under long-standing principles of self-defence, we do not rule out the use of force before attacks occur, even if uncertainty remains as to the time and place of the enemy's attack. When the consequences of an attack with [weapons of mass destruction] are potentially so devastating, we cannot afford to stand idly by as grave dangers materialize. This is the principle and logic of preemption. The place of preemption in our national security strategy remains the same. We will always proceed deliberately, weighing the consequences of our actions. The reasons for our actions will be clear, the force measured, and the cause just.'[63]

In terms of its stated policy to strike pre-emptively against (rogue) states that harbour terrorists and/or possess weapons of mass destruction (thus posing

attacks of 11 September 2001 'acts of aggression', the Council declared that 'acts of international terrorism constitute one of the most serious threats to international peace and security in the twenty-first century'. See UN SC Res 1377 (2001) Annex.

61 The National Security Strategy of the United States of America, 17 Sept 2002, 15.

62 National Security Strategy 2002 (*supra*) 15.

63 The National Security Strategy of the United States of America, 16 March 2006, 23.

a threat), US and allied forces attacked Iraq in 2003.[64] The reason for this was that US President Bush believed (and his Vice-President, Dick Cheney, seemed to be convinced) that Iraq was somehow also involved in the 11 September 2001 attacks on US cities. This, together with Iraq's alleged possession of weapons of mass destruction (including biological and chemical weapons, and an alleged programme to acquire nuclear weapons) formed the rationale for the US's decision to go to war with Iraq, even without Security Council authorisation.[65] Britain supported the US in this, and put forward the same reasons as *casus belli*.[66] By mid-2003 the government of President Saddam Hussein was removed from power and US and allied forces occupied the whole of Iraq.[67]

The assertion by the US of the right to use force pre-emptively (that is, not in cases of self-defence or as a collective security measure) came in for strong criticism.[68] In the case of pre-emptive self-defence, the problem is articulated by Van der Vyver as follows: 'Article 51 of the UN Charter authorises individual and collective self-defence "if an armed attack occurs". Would, therefore, pre-emptive strikes by a country under the threat of attack be lawful?'[69] Van der Vyver uses the concepts 'anticipatory self-defence' and 'pre-emptive strikes/action' interchangeably. The way the author formulates his observations in this regard seems as if he regards 'pre-emptive strikes/action' as manifestations of or at least part of 'anticipatory self-defence'. The author has a restrictive view of anticipatory self-defence:

> 'Anticipatory self-defence must ... remain confined to "situations in which the imminence of an attack is so clear and the danger so great that defensive action is essential for self-preservation".'[70]

---

64 Somewhat lost in the sound and fury of the invasion of Iraq, and the rhetoric that preceded the invasion, is the fact that the Allied governments did rely on Security Council resolutions as the primary empowering legal basis for the invasion of Iraq (see also comments by James Crawford (Public International Law) (*supra*) 752). However, the broader point here is that the US (if not the other allies) would have invaded Iraq, with or without Security Council authorisation. The fundamental claim of pre-emptive military action was the focus; the rather technical issue of Security Council authorisation was really a side-issue in the end.

65 See in general Bob Woodward *Plan of Attack* (2004) Simon & Schuster, New York, for an account of the Bush Administration's planning for the invasion of Iraq, and of the reasoning behind the invasion in 2003. See also transcript of Pres Bush's State of the Union Address of 2003, published in *The New York Times* 29 Jan 2003 (www.nytimes.com/2003/01/29/).

66 For the UK, see Iraq's Weapons of Mass Destruction – The Assessment of the British Government ID 114567 9/2002 776073, The Stationary Office (www.official-documents.co.uk). This document not only mentions the alleged weapons of mass destruction, it also refers (albeit as an afterthought) to reports of human rights abuses by the regime of Saddam Hussein.

67 For an historical and international law account of the Iraq War of 2003, see in general Lori Fisler Damrosch and Bernard H Oxman (eds) *Future Implications of the Iraq Conflict* (2003) The American Society of International Law, Washington DC.

68 For a critique of the 2002 National Security Strategy, see Stanley Hoffmann 'America goes backward' 50(10) *The New York Review of Books* 12 Jun 2003 (www.nybooks.com/articles/16350).

69 Johan Van der Vyver (*Ius contra bellum*) (*supra*) 4.

70 Johan Van der Vyver (*Ius contra bellum*) (*supra*) 5.

The use of armed force against Iraq in 2003 went beyond anticipatory self-defence. The invasion was furthermore not authorised by the UN Security Council (US arguments to this effect notwithstanding)[71] as a Chapter VII collective security measure. This distinguishes the Iraq invasion from the use of armed force against and the eventual removal of the Taliban regime of Afghanistan in the wake of the 11 September 2001 attacks on US cities.[72] Rhetorically, the phrases 'war on terror' and 'war on terrorism' became powerful instruments in the international media and in domestic and international political discourse. From a legal perspective, the question is whether the 'war on terror/terrorism' presents a paradigmatic shift from the traditional *jus contra bellum* as embodied in the UN Charter, notably Articles 2(4), 51 and the powers of the Security Council under Chapter VII. The High-level Panel (convened by the Security Council) drew a distinction between 'the right to intervene in the event of an imminent or proximate threat' (anticipatory self-defence) and 'the right to intervene based on pure threat' (preventive self-defence). The Panel concluded that international law recognises anticipatory self-defence, but on condition that the act of self-defence must be proportional to the imminent or proximate threat. The Panel indicated that 'preventive self-defence' would normally be regarded as contrary to international law. However, in certain circumstances (the Panel used the example of terrorists armed with a nuclear weapon) a state that would want to use preventive force, can put arguments before the Security Council which can authorise the necessary action.[73]

In light of the above, it is submitted that, although the National Security Strategy (and, indeed, *practice*) of the most powerful state on earth might present a new paradigm of justification for the use of force, 'terrorism' should in principle be treated as a criminal phenomenon[74] and not necessarily as an attack by a

71 Ruth Wedgwood argued that the US had the necessary legal basis (as presented by UN SC resolutions on weapons inspections in Iraq) to invade Iraq, after the latter did not adhere to relevant resolutions on its weapons programme. See Ruth Wedgwood 'The fall of Saddam Hussein: Security Council mandates and Preemptive Self-Defense' 97 *AJIL* (2003) 577.

72 For this argument, see Stephen P Marks 'Branding the "War on Terrorism": Is there a "New Paradigm" of International Law?' 14(1) *Michigan State Journal of International Law* (2006) 71–119.

73 'A more secure world: Our shared responsibility. Report of the Secretary-General's High-level Panel on Threats, Challenges and Change' UN Doc A/59/565, 1 Dec 2004. See further discussion of the report by Mireille Delmas-Marty 'The Paradigm of the War on Crime – Legitimating inhuman treatment?' 5 *JICJ* (2007) 584–598, in particular 593–594.

74 It is difficult to define international terrorism. A proposed definition is: '"Terrrorism" [is] "an ideologically strategy of internationally proscribed violence designed to inspire terror within a particular segment of a given society in order to achieve a power-outcome or to propagandize a claim or grievance, irrespective of whether its perpetrators are acting for and on behalf of themselves, or on behalf of a state."' See Cherif Bassiouni (International Criminal Law Vol I) (*supra*) 777–778. For comments on the proper doctrinal basis for reactions to mass violence (including acts of terror), see M Delmas-Marty 'Violence and massacres – Toward a criminal law of inhumanity?' 7(1) *Journal of International Criminal Justice* (2009) 5–16.

state (although the acts of terrorism can be committed on behalf of or with the backing of a state). The use of armed force (even when it is primarily aimed at terrorists) as against Afghanistan and Iraq, should remain firmly within the paradigm of the UN Charter prohibition of the use of armed force. The UN Charter does not (as yet) provide for individual or collective self-defence and collective security measures beyond Article 51, and measures sanctioned by the Security Council under Chapter VII.[75]

By 2004 it became clear that the two main reasons for the US and its allies' invasion of Iraq – weapons of mass destruction and Iraq's alleged links with Al Qaeda terrorists – were without factual basis. President Bush himself admitted that there was no evidence to support the initial theory that Saddam Hussein had links to the 11 September 2001 attacks. It also became clear that Iraq did not possess weapons of mass destruction, and even the alternative rationale of going to war on the basis that Iraq had 'programmes' to develop weapons of mass destruction, turned out to be rather weak.[76]

In the absence of the two main reasons for going to war, the US and the UK started to present a somewhat *ex post facto* (or at the least understated) rationale for the invasion, namely that the invasion was *justified*, because it rid Iraq of the oppressive regime of Saddam Hussein. This justification seemed more akin to 'humanitarian intervention' than to self-defence.[77]

5.2. THE NOTION OF HUMANITARIAN INTERVENTION

Perhaps even more controversial than anticipatory self-defence, is the claim of humanitarian intervention.[78] With reference to the NATO intervention in Kosovo in 1999, Michael Ignatieff observed that a motive of *humanitarian concern* to justify the use of armed force renders it more controversial than the use of armed force for *interests*;[79] the latter motive being unacceptable in

75 See also Stephen Marks (Branding the "War on Terrorism") (*supra*).

76 Christopher Scheer, Robert Scheer and Lakshmi Chaudhry 'Bush's lies about Iraq' *The Nation* 29 March 2004 (www.thenation.com/doc.mhtml?i=20040329&s=scheer).

77 Jutta Brunnée and Stephen J Toope 'Slouching towards new "Just" Wars: International law and the use of force after September 11th' *NILR* (2004) 363–392, 382.

78 See in general Francis Kofi Abiew *The Evolution of the Doctrine and Practice of Humanitarian Intervention* (1999) Kluwer Law International, The Hague. The author uses the following 'general' definition of humanitarian intervention: '[The] reliance upon force for the justifiable purpose of protecting the inhabitants of another state from treatment which is so arbitrary and persistently abusive as to exceed the limits of that authority within which the sovereign is presumed to act with reason and justice.' See Francis Kofi Abiew (Humanitarian Intervention) (*supra*) 31.

79 Michael Ignatieff *Virtual War – Kosovo and beyond* (2000) Chatto & Windus, London, 72.

terms of the modern *jus ad bellum*. It is interesting to note how Van der Vyver deals with humanitarian intervention from an essentially international law and politics perspective. He explains his understanding of humanitarian intervention by way of the following scenario: '[State] A takes military action against state B to protect the citizens of state B against severe atrocities committed by the powers-that-be of state B.'[80] This scenario closely resembles definitions and descriptions of the notion of humanitarian intervention from the early twentieth century.[81] Where a state would *invite* another state to intervene militarily or to use force against possible insurgents within its borders, it would not be regarded as humanitarian intervention.[82] This scenario (armed intervention by a state with the consent of the requesting or receiving state) is indeed provided for in the 1974 UN General Assembly Definition of Aggression. The armed intervention will only be regarded as an act of aggression if the intervening state contravened the conditions provided for in the agreement to intervene.[83]

There are many arguments for and against humanitarian intervention, especially in those instances where there is no clear UN mandate or UN Charter legal cover for the perceived intervention. Van der Vyver classifies the arguments in support of the legality (or moral legitimacy) of humanitarian intervention into three categories or approaches:

(a) the literalist approach;
(b) the flexible and teleological approach;
(c) the emergency mechanism argument.[84]

The first two schools of thought concern themselves with the interpretation of the UN Charter in such a way as to bring humanitarian intervention within the ambit of the Charter regime. For instance, Julius Stone (classified as a literalist by Van der Vyver)[85] argued that Article 2(4) of the UN Charter forbids the threat or use of force in a very specific way. The prohibition is directed at the use of force (or the threat of force) aimed at the territorial integrity or political independence of a state, or in any other manner inconsistent with the aims of the

80 Johan Van der Vyver (*Ius contra bellum*) (*supra*) 5.
81 See references to older sources by Lyal Sunga *The Emerging System of International Criminal Law – Developments in Codification and Implementation* (1997) Kluwer Law International, London, 81.
82 Francis Kofi Abiew (Humanitarian intervention) (*supra*) (1999) 31.
83 UN GA Def of Aggression art 3(e). For the text of the Def, see Ch VII *infra*. For a discussion of various ('legitimate') military interventions in Africa on the basis of *inter alia* requests by incumbent governments, see Francois van As 'African Peacekeeping: Past practices, future prospects and its contribution to international law' 45 *Revue de Droit Militaire et de Droit de la Guerre* (2006) 329–354.
84 Johan Van der Vyver (*Ius contra bellum*) (*supra*) 6.
85 Johan Van der Vyver (*Ius contra bellum*) (*supra*) 6.

United Nations. Stone thus maintained that the authors of proper humanitarian intervention should normally not have the above-mentioned ill intentions. Stone also referred to Article 2(3)[86] of the UN Charter and the value of 'justice' as one of the elements to be considered when deciding on the legality of the threat or use of force.[87]

Perhaps the most progressive (but also potentially most controversial) argument in support of humanitarian intervention is the flexible and teleological approach. Van der Vyver regards the scholar Michael Reisman as the principal exponent of this school. The argument is basically that the Charter's prohibition of the threat or use of force 'must be read in conjunction with the overarching human rights concerns of the United Nations as recorded in several provisions of the UN Charter and of which humanitarian intervention is a logical extension.'[88]

The third school of thought referred to by Van der Vyver is perhaps less of a school of interpretation of the UN Charter, but rather sceptical commentators on international affairs, or as some would put it, *realists*. Van der Vyver quotes the following from Richard Baxter (an exponent of the 'emergency mechanism argument'): '[It] is almost as if we were thrown back on customary international law by a breakdown of the Charter System'.[89] The context of this statement by Baxter is the often ineffective way in which the Security Council operates in the face of massive human rights violations. This was especially true during the Cold War, but even post-Cold War inaction by the Security Council (for example in the face of the Rwanda genocide of 1994 and the initial stages of the conflict in the Former Yugoslavia during the early 1990s) lends considerable credibility to the arguments of commentators like Baxter and Richard Lillich.[90] The 'emergency mechanism' argument is summarised as follows:

> '[T]here is a need for humanitarian intervention exactly because the Security Council has been immobilised by the veto power of the permanent members. This presupposes that humanitarian intervention is to be "deactivated" should the Security Council ever begin to function smoothly.'[91]

---

86 Art 2(3) of the UN Charter provides as follows: 'The Organization and its Members, in pursuit of the Purposes stated in Article 1, shall act in accordance with the following Principles: ... 3. All Members shall settle their international disputes by peaceful means in such a manner that international peace and security, and justice, are not endangered.'

87 See Johan Van der Vyver's description (*supra* at 6) of Stone's main argument on the proper construction of Art 2(4) of the UN Charter.

88 Johan Van der Vyver (*Ius contra bellum*) (*supra*) 6.

89 *Ibid.*

90 Johan Van der Vyver (*Ius contra bellum*) (*supra*) 6 refers to Lillich's contribution 'A United States policy of humanitarian intervention' in Donald P Kommers and Gilburt D Loescher (eds) *Human Rights and American Foreign Policy* (1979).

91 Johan Van der Vyver (*Ius contra bellum*) (*supra*) 6.

The third instance of the use of force that might pose a challenge to the prohibition of the use or threat of force-regime in Article 2(4) of the UN Charter is, according to Van der Vyver, wars of national liberation. Van der Vyver is not convinced that international armed conflict should always imply armed conflict between *states*:

> 'If an organised armed group engaged in protracted armed violence against a governmental authority, or against another organised group, were to include insurgents from another state, the hostilities would constitute an international armed conflict.'

And further:

> 'Wars of liberation, which may in some instances actually be armed conflicts not of an international character, are regulated by Protocol I of the Geneva Conventions of 12 August 1949 and have thus been made subject to the rules pertaining to international armed conflict.'[92]

The latter refers more to *jus in bello*, or international humanitarian law protection for certain categories of persons involved in armed conflict. It is certainly the case that a number of states from the so-called developing world regarded wars of national liberation as not only protected in terms of international humanitarian law but also as a further exception to the prohibition of the use of force.[93] In 1970 the General Assembly of the UN adopted the Declaration on Friendly Relations and Co-operation among States.[94] One of the principles that gained affirmation in the 1970s – and in no small measure as a result of the position taken by the General Assembly – was that the use of force as part of national liberation struggles were recognised as international matters and protected by international humanitarian law.[95] While it is quite clear that wars of national liberation are not regarded as 'purely domestic issues' and are also protected by the relevant instruments of international humanitarian law, it is a different matter whether wars of national liberation can be treated as exceptions to the general prohibition of the use of force contained in Article 2(4) of the UN Charter. The former is a matter for *jus in bello*; the latter for *jus contra bellum*.

Wars of national liberation in the context of *jus contra bellum* must be considered with due regard to the ideological divide that was very much apparent during the 1970s – the era of the big surge in anti-colonial struggles, as well as the deepening of the Cold War rift between the former Soviet Union and the Western powers.

92 Johan Van der Vyver (*Ius contra bellum*) (*supra*) 13.
93 See comments by Albrecht Randelzhofer 'Article 2(4)' in Bruno Simma (Charter of the UN Vol I) (*supra*) 128–129.
94 GA Res 2625 (XXV) 24 Oct 1970.
95 See Lyal Sunga (Emerging system) (*supra*) 102.

Against this background, Randelzhofer pointed out that the former Soviet Union and much of the 'third world' (where the anti-colonial struggles typically took place) propagated the notion that wars of liberation were indeed exceptions to the Article 2(4) prohibition of the use of force. Thus, liberation movements could be supported by third states to help them in their anti-colonial struggles. This argument was principally based on the idea that colonialism was regarded to be 'a permanent armed attack, against which individual and collective self-defence is allowed.'[96] This revolutionary idea was for obvious reasons not accepted by Western States – especially not by states with colonial histories. However, it is interesting to note that the non-binding 1974 Definition of Aggression[97] (adopted by the General Assembly) incorporates the idea that people can 'struggle'[98] for self-determination. As Randelzhofer pointed out, the Definition of Aggression does not relate to either Article 2(4) (the use of force) or Article 51 (individual and collective self-defence) of the UN Charter. Wars of liberation as exceptions to the prohibition of the use force seems doubtful, not only because of the notion's contentious doctrinal basis, but also because of the deep divide among states regarding the interpretation and application and proper place of wars of national liberation in the modern *jus contra bellum*.

'Humanitarian intervention' and 'wars of national liberation' (as well as the more recent notion of 'responsibility to protect' – dealt with below) share, of course, certain moral claims. In the context of the criminalisation of aggression, some commentators argue, for instance, that, while they support ICC jurisdiction over the crime of aggression, an *exception* for those engaged in 'bona fide unilateral humanitarian intervention' should be included in the conditions of ICC jurisdiction over the crime of aggression.[99] This is now a moot point in light of the definition of the crime of aggression and conditions for the exercise of ICC jurisdiction over the crime adopted at the Kampala Review Conference; a package that turned out to be rather less progressive than what these commentators were perhaps hoping for.

State practice on humanitarian intervention is still very limited, and the contentious nature of the notion is reflected in the divided opinion on this topic in the Security Council.[100]

96 Randelzhofer in Bruno Simma (Charter of the UN Vol I) (*supra*) 128.

97 For a discussion see Ch IV *infra*.

98 The draft of the relevant article referred to a right 'to use force', but this language was successfully opposed by Western States. See Randelzhofer in Bruno Simma (Charter of the UN Vol I) (*supra*) 128.

99 Elise Leclerc-Gagne and Michael Byers 'A question of intent: The crime of aggression and unilateral humanitarian intervention' 41 *Case Western Reserve Journal of International Law* (2009) 379–390.

100 James Crawford (Public International Law) (*supra*) 754.

5.3. THE RESPONSIBILITY TO PROTECT

The Outcome Document of the September 2005 high-level plenary meeting of the UN General Assembly (one of the biggest gatherings of heads of state and government in history), included two paragraphs that form the basis of the developing notion of responsibility to protect (R2P). Paragraphs 139 and 139 of the Outcome Document read as follows:

> '138. Each individual State has the responsibility to protect its populations from genocide, war crimes, ethnic cleansing and crimes against humanity. This responsibility entails the prevention of such crimes, including their incitement, through appropriate and necessary means. We accept that responsibility and will act in accordance with it. The international community should, as appropriate, encourage and help States to exercise this responsibility and support the United Nations in establishing an early warning capability.
>
> 139. The international community, through the United Nations, also has the responsibility to use appropriate diplomatic, humanitarian and other peaceful means, in accordance with Chapters VI and VIII of the Charter, to help protect populations from genocide, war crimes, ethnic cleansing and crimes against humanity. In this context, we are prepared to take collective action, in a timely and decisive manner, through the security Council, in accordance with the Charter, including Chapter VII, on a case-by-case basis and in cooperation with relevant regional organizations as appropriate, should peaceful means be inadequate and national authorities manifestly fail to protect their populations from genocide, war crimes, ethnic cleansing and crimes against humanity. We stress the need for the General Assembly to continue consideration of the responsibility to protect populations from genocide, war crimes, ethnic cleansing and crimes against humanity and its implications, bearing in mind the principles of the Charter and international law. We also intend to commit ourselves, as necessary and appropriate, to helping States build capacity to protect their populations from genocide, war crimes, ethnic cleansing and crimes against humanity and to assisting those which are under stress before crises and conflicts break out.'[101]

In certain quarters, the notions of 'humanitarian intervention' and 'responsibility to protect' are viewed as two sides of the same coin. Some label R2P as the 'legalisation of humanitarian intervention'.[102] However, the more sensible view is that R2P (although still in its early development) is simply not the same as (unilateral or unauthorised) humanitarian intervention. The notion of R2P is based on collective action, and very much in terms of the UN Charter

---

101 For the full text of this (and other related documents), see documentation centre of International Coalition for the Responsibility to Protect (available at www.responsibilitytoprotect.org).

102 For more on the different (national) perspectives of R2P, see Report on the General Assembly Debate on the Responsibility to Protect, 15 Sept 2009 (available at www.responsibilitytoprotect.org).

regime. It is *aspirational*, of course, since in practice it does not articulate (as yet) any new exception to the UN Charter prohibitions on the use of force.[103]

During July 2009 a plenary debate on R2P took place in the General Assembly. The result was that the 2005 commitment to further the goals of R2P (referred to above) was reiterated by the General Assembly. Consequently, the General Assembly decided (per Resolution)[104] to 'continue its consideration of the responsibility to protect'.

The future will tell whether R2P is going to become part of (an expanded) collective security (and humanitarian) regime under the UN Charter. It is submitted that any grey areas or uncertainties (or possibilities for abuse) also affect the debate about aggression, even in the aftermath of the adoption of the Kampala Review Conference package of provisions on the crime of aggression. This is so because the definition of aggression does not provide for an explicit subjective element, thus excluding references to 'purpose', or 'motive' in the context of the use of armed force. Individual criminal liability for the state act of aggression is rather based on the general mental element provided for in the Rome Statute of the ICC.

6. CONCLUDING REMARKS

In Chapter III the focus shifts from the *jus contra bellum* to the international criminal law paradigm of individual liability for the crime of aggression. This development has its roots in the Nuremberg trials after the Second World War, where individuals were held responsible for crimes against peace, including aggression. The content of the crime of aggression, as it was defined and applied at Nuremberg, will be analysed to serve as a starting point for the further discussion on the question of individual criminal liability for the crime of aggression, not only in terms of customary international law, but particularly in terms of the definition and conditions for the exercise of jurisdiction with respect to the crime of aggression under the Rome Statute of the International Criminal Court (ICC). It is shown that the criminalisation of aggression has its normative roots in the *jus contra bellum*. To the extent that this is a body of rules and norms in flux, due to developments such as expanded claims of self-defence under international law, and claims of justified humanitarian intervention, it is expected that the unsettled *jus contra bellum* will have an impact on the future development of criminal liability for the crime of aggression under international, regional and national law.

---

103 James Crawford (Public International Law) (*supra*) 757.

104 GA Res 63/308, *Official records of the General Assembly, Sixty-third Session, Plenary Meetings*, 96th to 101th meetings, and corrigendum (A/63/PV.96–101).

PART III

THE CRIMINALISATION OF AGGRESSION

CHAPTER III

FROM *JUS CONTRA BELLUM* TO THE CRIMINALISATION OF AGGRESSION

1. INTRODUCTION

This chapter charts the historical development of the criminalisation of aggression as a crime under international law. It also traces the development in international criminal law towards the acceptance of individual (as opposed to state) criminal liability for aggression.

In the previous chapters it was explained how the use of force by states became outlawed. The use of force is no longer acceptable as an instrument of foreign policy. The *jus ad bellum* became the *jus contra bellum*.

The liberal ideal of collective security manifested in the twin reactions to the use of force by states: The essentially *political* response, where the Security Council of the UN determines when a situation is regarded as a threat to or breach of peace, or an act of aggression; and the *legal* response where the International Court of Justice (ICJ) has a prominent role to play to determine whether the use of force violates the relevant provisions of the UN Charter, notably the prohibition of the use of force provided for in Article 2(4). The Security Council, which is the most important body to maintain international peace and security under the UN-dominated collective security system, may also create international criminal tribunals as a response to threats to peace and security, as it did in reaction to the conflict in the Former Yugoslavia in the early 1990s and with the genocide in Rwanda in 1994. Thus it can be said that the Security Council has set precedents in terms of Chapter VII of the UN Charter whereby international peace and security can be maintained by various methods like the use of armed force (for example during the Korea conflict in the 1950s), economic sanctions (for instance against *apartheid* South Africa), and also the creation of international criminal tribunals to try individuals responsible for serious crimes under international law (the aforementioned creation of the *ad hoc* tribunals for Rwanda and the former Yugoslavia).

The shift from *jus ad bellum* to *jus contra bellum* has been an important historical development in international law. Another important development in international law has been the acceptance of individual criminal liability for certain serious crimes under international law.[1] The emerging system of international criminal law, with its modern roots in the Nuremberg and Tokyo trials of the major Nazi and Japanese war criminals of the Second World War, confirmed the fact that states are no longer the only actors in international law and politics. Individuals (and not only states) are subjects of international law – not only in terms of responsibility for crimes under international law,[2] but to an ever-growing extent in other areas of international law as well.[3] States are subject to the prohibition of the use of force and those who would act contrary to the *jus contra bellum* can expect political and legal responses from the principal organs of the United Nations as described in Chapters I and II. The discussion will now turn to the other important dimension of the response to the illegal use of force and specifically acts of aggression, namely individual criminal liability for such acts. First, attention will be given to the historic precedents of the Nuremberg and Tokyo trials – including a discussion of attempts predating these two *ad hoc* tribunals to hold individuals liable for crimes of aggression.

2. PRECURSORS TO NUREMBERG AND TOKYO: HISTORICAL ATTEMPTS TO ESTABLISH INDIVIDUAL CRIMINAL LIABILITY FOR THE UNLAWFUL USE OF FORCE

Military conflict between two or more states not only involves the military apparatus of the states involved, but also the political leadership. It is after all usually the political leadership which has the constitutional ability to command the military. For a state to 'make war'[4] in the conventional sense involves a concerted political and military effort. The question about the individuals

1 See also discussion in Introduction *supra*.

2 See comments by Ian Brownlie (Use of Force) (*supra*) 165 on the implications of the principles of the Charter of the IMT (Nuremberg Charter). The author states: '[Those] who state their acceptance of the principles of the Nuremberg Charter but deny the proposition that the individual is a subject of international law invite charges of illogicality.'

3 In the context of international co-operation in criminal matters, it can be argued that individuals are also subjects, and not objects of international law. See Christine van den Wyngaert 'The criminal justice systems facing the challenge of organised crime' (1999) 70 *Revue Internationale de Droit Penal* 204. For a South African perspective on the position of individuals in international co-operation matters, see Gerhard Kemp 'Foreign relations, international co-operation in criminal matters and the position of the individual' 16(3) *SACJ* (2003) 370–392.

4 For a definition of 'war' see Yoram Dinstein (War Aggression and Self-Defence) (*supra*) 15: 'War is a hostile interaction between two or more States, either in a technical or in a material sense. War in the technical sense is a formal status produced by a declaration of war. War in the material sense is generated by actual use of armed force, which must be comprehensive on the part of at least one party to the conflict.'

involved in the decision to use armed force will come into play when determining possible liability for aggression. It was pointed out in the Introduction to this book that historically the notion that individuals can be held liable for what amounts to essentially an act of state (the use of force by the military of a state) was an ideal of non-governmental pressure groups and academics, but the road to the *actualisation* of international criminal tribunals was a long and tortuous one.

2.1. THE DEBATE: SHOULD STATES OR INDIVIDUALS BE HELD CRIMINALLY LIABLE FOR CRIMES UNDER INTERNATIONAL LAW?

After the First World War a number of non-governmental organisations and writers[5] suggested that states or a combination of states and individuals should be held liable for the initiation of the war of aggression. However, Brownlie pointed out that in terms of criminal liability for aggression, the debate initially leaned in favour of *state* liability. The early advocates of state liability or cumulative state and individual liability '[regarded] the state as a unit susceptible to certain penalties in the form of indemnities and various measures of security such as military occupation, demilitarization, and destruction of existing war potential, and international control of certain aspects of governmental activity.'[6] The notion that collective criminal liability in the form of state (criminal) liability was appropriate in post-conflict situations was particularly relevant in the context of liability for aggressive wars as serious violations of international law and order.[7] International instruments that came in the wake of the First World War, like the Kellogg-Briand Pact of 1928, referred to aggression as *international wrongful acts*.[8] This, together with (unsuccessful)[9] attempts to try individuals like Kaiser Wilhelm of Germany

5 These included prominent organisations in the fields of international law and international criminal law like the International Law Association (ILA) and the Association Internationale de Droit Penal (AIDP), the latter which was instrumental in the diplomatic conference in 1998 in Rome, which lead to the creation of the permanent ICC. The AIDP was working for the creation of some or other form of international criminal court since 1924. See Cherif Bassiouni 'Preface' in *International Criminal Law Quo Vadis?* (2004) Association Internationale de Droit Penal, Ramonville Saint-Agne, 11–15. For references to writers and organisations which advocated for state and/or individual liability for the outbreak of the First World War, see Ian Brownlie (Use of Force) (*supra*) 150.

6 Ian Brownlie (Use of Force) (*supra*) 150.

7 Ian Brownlie (Use of Force) (*supra*) 151.

8 Antonio Cassese *International Criminal Law* (2003) Oxford University Press, Oxford, 111 opined that a state that engaged in aggression committed 'an *international wrongful act* entailing State responsibility' (emphasis in the original).

9 Art 227 of the Treaty of Versailles provided that 'William II of Hohenzollern, formerly German Emperor' was to be publicly arraigned 'for a supreme offence against international morality and the sanctity of treaties'. The government of the Netherlands refused to surrender

for the initiation of hostilities that lead to war,[10] in fact implied state liability (the Kaiser represented the state) and not so much individual liability. Brownlie pointed out that instruments like the Kellogg-Briand Pact could 'at that time only refer, to state responsibility'.[11] The emphasis, in other words, still fell on *collective responsibility* and not the liability of individuals *per se*. However, looking back, the idea that a whole state should be 'punished' collectively for the policies and decisions of individuals (and without also punishing the responsible individuals who have made crucial policy decisions) seemed to be misdirected.

Georg Schwarzenberger, one of the prominent early writers on international criminal law, argued that states cannot be held criminally liable for crimes under international law. He analysed a number of cases before international tribunals and concluded that these cases all concerned breaches of treaties or international torts and not *crimes* under international customary law. Indeed, Schwarzenberger (writing in 1950) pointed out that no international tribunal has ever (at that stage, on the basis of customary international law) classified an act of state as an international crime.[12]

In terms of state responsibility for acts in violation of international law, Brownlie suggested that the emphasis should rather fall on *reparation* and *compensation*.[13] Brownlie explained the doctrinal basis for the aforementioned argument as follows:

> 'War guilt is simply an explanation, a moral justification for demanding reparation and for trying those individuals responsible for launching aggressive war. The imposition of collective sanctions would in any case violate general principles of justice and there is a strong presumption against vicarious responsibility in criminal law.'[14]

Indeed, the International Military Tribunal (IMT) sitting at Nuremberg after the Second World War, which will be discussed in the next section, took a practical approach (and essentially followed the arguments put forward by American prosecutor Jackson). The IMT stated as follows:

Kaiser Wilhelm to stand trial. See Pearce Higgins (ed) *Hall's A Treatise on International Law* 8th (1924) Clarendon Press, Oxford, 498–499.

10 See Cherif Bassiouni *International Criminal Law* 2nd Vol I (1999) Transnational Publishers, New York, 63 and Cherif Bassiouni *The legislative history of the International Criminal Court: Vol I Introduction, Analysis, and Integrated Text* (2005) Transnational Publishers, New York, 47.

11 Ian Brownlie (Use of Force) (*supra*) 151.

12 Georg Schwarzenberger 'The problem of an international criminal law' (1950) 3 *Current Legal Problems* 276–280.

13 Ian Brownlie (Use of Force) (*supra*) 153.

14 Ian Brownlie (Use of Force) (*supra*) 154.

> 'Crimes against international law are committed by men, not by abstract entities, and only by punishing individuals who commit such crimes can the provisions of international law be enforced.'[15]

Significantly, one finds an echo of the IMT's statement decades later in a statement by the Appeals Chamber of the International Criminal Tribunal for the Former Yugoslavia (ICTY):

> 'Under present international law it is clear that States, by definition, cannot be the subject of criminal sanctions akin to those provided for in national criminal systems.'[16]

John Dugard – a proponent of state criminal liability for crimes under international law[17] – pointed out that the International Law Commission (ILC), which was initially of the opinion that certain international wrongful acts should give rise to state criminal liability, is not advancing this notion any longer.[18] It is furthermore interesting to note that the 2001 Principles of State Responsibility rejected the concept of criminal liability for states.[19] Whatever the reason or reasons, it is clear that criminal liability for states seems to be not only *impractical*, but also problematic from a *doctrinal* point of view.[20]

The position taken by the driving forces for the acceptance of individual criminal liability for crimes under international law during the twentieth century were vindicated with the creation of a number of *ad hoc* international tribunals with jurisdiction to try individuals for international crimes, as well as a number of investigatory commissions which investigated international crimes.[21] The

---

15 From the *Nuremberg Judgment*, quoted by Ian Brownlie (Use of Force) (*supra*) 154.

16 *Prosecutor v Blaskic*, Judgment on the Request of the Republic of Croatia for a review of the Decision of Trial Chamber II of 18 July 1997, Case No IT-95-14-AR 108*bis* (1997) 110 *ILR* 688 at 698 par 25, reproduced in André Klip and Göran Sluiter *Annotated Leading Cases of International Criminal Tribunals – Student Ed* (2005) Intersentia, Antwerp/Oxford, 179–215. For commentary on the decision, see Göran Sluiter in Klip and Sluiter (*supra*) 216–219.

17 For arguments in support of criminal responsibility of states, see John Dugard 'Criminal Responsibility of States' in Bassiouni (International Criminal Law) (*supra*) 239–253.

18 For a discussion of the ILC's position regarding state criminal liability, see John Dugard *International Law – A South African Perspective* 4th (2011) Juta, Cape Town, 269–271.

19 See Cherif Bassiouni (Legislative History Vol I) (*supra*) 48. See further ILC 2001 Report at 279 (available at www.un.org/law/ilc/texts/State_responsibility/responsibilityfra.htm).

20 See arguments of Ian Brownlie and Georg Schwarzenberger (*supra*).

21 Bassiouni (Legislative History Vol I) (*supra*) 45–46 lists the following tribunals and commissions: Tribunals: The International Military Tribunal (IMT) at Nuremberg to try the major war criminals of the European Axis; the International Military Tribunal for the Far East (IMTFE) at Tokyo to try the Japanese war criminals; the International Criminal Tribunal for the Former Yugoslavia (ICTY) at The Hague to try individuals accused of genocide, war crimes and crimes against humanity which occurred in the Former Yugoslavia since 1991; and the International Criminal Tribunal for Rwanda (ICTR) at Arusha for the prosecution of individuals responsible for war crimes, genocide and crimes against humanity between 1 Jan

pre-Nuremberg and -Tokyo attempts were not very successful, mainly because of the lack of political will on the side of the international community[22] (basically the victors of the First World War). The Treaty of Versailles,[23] which ended the war, made provision for *ad hoc* tribunals, but, the political will to actually establish tribunals were lacking.[24] In 1920 the Commission on the Responsibility of the Authors of War came out in support of criminal liability for the violations of international law at the outbreak of and during what became the First World War. To make this more concrete, an Advisory Committee of Jurists proposed a 'High Court of International Justice' to try violations of international law. However, the realities of international politics at the time, as well as the relative weak position of the League of Nations, were not factors favourable to individual

1994 and 31 Dec 1994. The five investigatory commissions are: the 1919 Commission on the Responsibilities of the Authors of War and on Enforcement of Penalties, investigating crimes occurring during First World War; the 1943 UN War Crime Commission for the investigation of German war crimes during Second World War; the 1946 Far Eastern Commission for the investigation of Japanese war crimes during World War II; the Commission of Experts Established Pursuant to SC Res 780 for the investigation of violations of international humanitarian law in the Former Yugoslavia; and the Independent Commission of Experts established in terms of UN Security Council Resolution 935 (Rwanda Commission) for the investigation of violations committed during the 1994 Rwanda genocide. More recent developments in international criminal law include the creation of so-called 'mixed tribunals' and a report by an international commission of inquiry that lead to a referral to the ICC. The category of so-called 'mixed tribunals' concern national courts with some degree of international involvement or support. Two recent examples of mixed tribunals are: The Extraordinary Chambers of Cambodia (ECC) for the prosecution of individuals responsible for crimes committed during the reign of the *Khmer Rouge* and the Sierra Leone Special Court (SLSC) for the prosecution of individuals responsible for mass human rights violations in the 1990s (A Truth and Reconciliation Commission was also created to help with the reconstruction and normalisation of society in Sierra Leone). For the ECC see Agreement between the UN and the Royal Government of Cambodia concerning the prosecution under Cambodian Law of Crimes Committed during the period of Democratic Kampuchea, 6 Jun 2003, UN Doc A/RES 57/228B (Annex) (13 May 2003) (available at www.cambodia.gov.kh/krt/pdfs/Agreement%20between%20UN%20and%20RGC.pdf). For the SLSC see SC Res UN Doc S/RES/1315 (2000). See further comments by William Schabas 'Conjoined twins of transitional justice? – The Sierra Leone Truth and Reconciliation Commission and the Special Court' 2 *JICJ* (2004) 1082–1099. One of the big humanitarian disasters of the early 21st century – the mass human rights violations (many regard it to be a genocide) in the Sudanese area of Darfur, lead to an International Commission of Inquiry. See Report of the International Commission of Inquiry on Darfur to the Secretary General, Pursuant to SC Res 1564, 18 Sept 2004 (available at www.un.org/News/dh/sudan/com_inq_darfur.pdf). For commentary on the Report see George Fletcher and Jens David Ohlin 'Reclaiming fundamental principles of criminal law in the Darfur Case' 3 *JICJ* (2005) 539–561. Acting on the recommendations of the Commission of Inquiry, the Security Council referred the situation in Darfur to the permanent ICC. The SC acted in terms of its Ch VII powers. For a comment on this historic referral of a situation that poses a threat to international peace ands security to the ICC, see Luigi Condorelli and Annalisa Ciampi 'Comments on the Security Council Referral of the situation in Darfur to the ICC' 3 *JICJ* (2005) 590–599.

22 Cherif Bassiouni (Legislative History) (*supra*) 47.

23 Treaty of Peace Between the Allied and Associated Powers and Germany (Treaty of Versailles), 28 Jun 1919.

24 Cherif Bassiouni (Legislative History) (*supra*) 47.

(or state) criminal liability for crimes under international law. Brownlie summed up the political atmosphere of the time:

> 'The idea that states themselves, or state officials, should be subject to criminal jurisdiction in respect of acts of state, acts within their legal capacity according to classical international law, was naturally regarded as utopian and exotic. The subject of international criminal jurisdiction and penal law was for the next decade [the 1920s] principally the domain of writers and specialist institutions.'[25]

After the First World War there was a tentative commitment of the international community to pursue justice while establishing peace. But, as pointed out above, no actual criminal trials occurred at international level to punish individuals for international crimes. Nevertheless, the period following the Treaty of Versailles (1919) and later the Kellogg-Briand Pact (1928) were important milestones on the way to the criminalisation of aggression and the eventual prosecution at Nuremberg and Tokyo of individuals for crimes against peace.

2.2. PRE NUREMBERG EFFORTS TO ESTABLISH INDIVIDUAL CRIMINAL LIABILITY FOR THE INTERNATIONAL CRIME OF AGGRESSION

In the aftermath of the First World War, and in the context of international processes that were aimed at bringing about peace in Europe (notably in terms of the Treaty of Versailles and later the Kellogg-Briand Pact), the drive for individual criminal liability for the crime of aggression also became stronger. Brownlie pointed out that this effort was basically the result of the work of organisations like the International Association of Penal Law, as well as a number of academic writers.[26]

The problem with post First World War instruments on the use of force was that these instruments (notably the Kellogg-Briand Pact of 1928) were quite clear in their intent to outlaw the use of force, but less clear on the question of criminal liability for aggression.[27] However, Brownlie pointed out that the Kellogg-Briand Pact did have some impact on the criminalisation of aggression, but that was at national level (a number of states incorporated the provisions of the Pact into their domestic legislation). It became clear that even this development was not unequivocally aimed at individual liability for aggression – neither at international nor national level.[28] It was left to academics and

25 Ian Brownlie (Use of Force) (*supra*) 155.

26 See Ian Brownlie (Use of Force) (*supra*) 155 fn 6.

27 See Antonio Cassese (International Criminal Law) (*supra*) 111.

28 See Ian Brownlie (Use of Force) (*supra*) 156. The author also made reference to instruments like the draft Treaty of Mutual Assistance (1923), the Geneva Protocol (1924) and certain

non-governmental organisations to promote the notion of individual criminal liability for aggression. An important development in this regard was the adoption of 'Fundamental Principles of an International Legal Code for the Repression of International Crimes' of 1925 by the Inter-Parliamentary Union which met in Washington DC and Ottawa. Farhad Malekian summarised the most important principles set out in the document as follows:

> '(a) there must be an international criminal code applicable to all nations; (b) measures of repression should not only apply to the act of declaring a war of aggression, but to all acts on the part of individuals of bodies or persons with a view to preparation of the setting in motion of a war of aggression; (c) there must be a principle for the criminal responsibility of individuals alongside the international responsibility of states for violations of public international legal order and international law as a whole; (d) a list of crimes which can be committed by states and individuals should be formulated with relevant applicable penalties; moreover, international repression should be based on the principles of *nulla poena sine lege*.'[29]

From the above discussions two observations can be made. First, although there were proposals made in this regard, the international community in the aftermath of the First World War clearly lacked the political will to create the necessary tribunals with the jurisdiction to try individuals responsible for international crimes. Second, in the context of aggression, the combined effect of the above mentioned lack of political will to create *ad hoc* tribunals and the fact that international instruments (drafted in the wake of the war) did not clearly criminalise international aggression, was that individual criminal liability for aggression was still an academic notion rather than reality. The notion of individual responsibility for crimes under international law, and in particular, for the crime of aggression, would only become a reality after the Second World War, at Nuremberg and Tokyo.[30] The efforts of the League of Nations to avoid another world war with *inter alia* attempts to end impunity for international crimes, were poignantly described as follows by Geoffrey Robertson:

> '[It] seemed that the only way to stop war crimes was to stop war – a solution embraced in 1928 with the Kellogg-Briand Pact, by which state signatories falsely promised to renounce war as an instrument of national policy. The League of Nations, concerned by random assassinations of politicians and diplomats, managed

---

resolutions of the Assembly of the League of Nations (in 1925 and 1927) which referred to wars of aggression as *international crimes*.

29 Farhad Malekian 'International Criminal Responsibility' in Bassiouni (International Criminal Law) (*supra*) 178.

30 For an eloquent exposition of the international political and legal legacy of the First World War, and the period 1920–1945, see Antonio Cassese *International Law in a divided world* (1986) Clarendon Press, Oxford, 57–64. See further comments by Farhad Malekian in Bassiouni (International Criminal Law) (*supra*) 179.

by 1937 to draft a convention for the creation of an International Criminal Court with jurisdiction to try terrorist offences, but it failed to attract many signatories before most of its members slid into another world war.'[31]

3. THE IMPORTANCE AND MEANING OF THE NUREMBERG PRECEDENT

Aggression has been described as the most serious crime under international law. The International Military Tribunal (IMT) at Nuremberg (which tried the major Nazi war criminals after the Second World War) articulated the special status of aggression as follows:

> 'War is essentially an evil thing. Its consequences are not confined to the belligerent States alone, but affect the whole world.
>
> To initiate a war of aggression, therefore, is not only an international crime; it is the supreme international crime differing only from other war crimes in that it contains within itself the accumulated evil of the whole.'[32]

The trial at Nuremberg seems from a historical point of view as the zenith of individual criminal liability for aggression; the strongest possible legal response to international aggression. It will however be shown that historical precedent is not enough to rely on for purposes of creating an effective regime to regulate individual criminal liability for aggression.

3.1. THE CHARTER OF THE IMT NUREMBERG

The process to establish an international criminal tribunal for the trial of Nazi war criminals already began while the Second World War was still ongoing (and an Allied victory seemed probable). During 1943 and 1944 academic writers and Allied Governments began to look into the question of possible individual criminal liability for the crime of aggression. However, at that stage there was still some confusion regarding the question whether aggression was indeed *criminal* in terms of positive international law. Despite this confusion, some Allied leaders (notably Josef Stalin of the Soviet Union) came out strongly in support of the punishment of Nazi leaders who were responsible for the

---

31 Geoffrey Robertson *Crimes Against Humanity – The struggle for global justice* (1999) The New Press, New York, 211.

32 International Military Tribunal (Nuremberg trial) Judgment (1946), IMT 171, at 186. Yoram Dinstein pointed out that the passage from the judgment is based on an article by Lord Wright, 'War Crimes under International Law' 62 *LQR* (1946) 40, 47. See Yoram Dinstein (War Aggression Self-Defence) (*supra*) 120 fn 23.

war. While Stalin was adamant about 'punishment' (or 'show trials'),[33] other leaders like Churchill and Roosevelt were in favour of a formal trial in terms of international law.[34] On 8 August 1945 the four Allied nations[35] concluded the London Agreement, including the Charter of the IMT Nuremberg.[36]

The problem of the legal basis for the prosecution of individuals for aggression became a contentious issue at various junctures prior to the conclusion of the London Agreement on the Charter of the IMT. Robert H Jackson, at the time Chief Counsel of the US and later Chief Prosecutor at Nuremberg, explained the legal basis for the inclusion of the crime of aggression within the jurisdiction of the IMT as follows:

> 'International law ... is an outgrowth of treaties or agreements between nations and of accepted customs. But every custom has its origin in some single act ... Unless we are prepared to abandon every principle of growth for International Law, we cannot deny that our own day has its right to institute customs and to conclude agreements that will themselves become sources of a new and strengthened International Law.'[37]

Brownlie pointed out that Jackson referred to the post First World War instruments that outlawed war, namely the Kellogg-Briand Pact (1928), the Geneva Protocol (1924), the Assembly of the League of Nations Resolution (1925 and 1927), and the Resolution of the American States (1928).[38]

The IMT Charter provisions on the crime of aggression were the result of much debate and disagreement between Britain, the US, France and the Soviet Union. These states had to agree on a compromise text in the end. The differences were more than just political, or strategic, they were also dogmatic. While the US regarded aggressive war to be criminal *per se*,[39] France wanted the Charter provisions on aggression to be linked to violations of treaties and other international instruments (to avoid problems of retroactive application of criminal law).[40] Incidentally, references to 'violations of treaties' would also relieve the drafters of having to *define* aggression.[41] Because of the compromises

---

33 Geoffrey Robertson (Crimes against Humanity) (*supra*) 213.
34 Ian Brownlie (Use of Force) (*supra*) 160–161. See further Geoffrey Robertson (Crimes against Humanity) (*supra*) 211–213.
35 The UK, the Soviet Union, the US and France.
36 For comments on the legal nature of the Nuremberg Charter, see Hans-Heinrich Jescheck 'The General Principles of International Criminal Law set out in Nuremberg, as mirrored in the ICC Statute' 2 *JICJ* (2004) 38–55.
37 As quoted in Ian Brownlie (Use of Force) (*supra*) 162.
38 Ian Brownlie (Use of Force) (*supra*) 162, fn 5.
39 See also discussion of the legislative history of the Nuremberg Charter section 3.1.1 *infra*.
40 Ian Brownlie (Use of Force) (*supra*) 163.
41 See reference in Ian Brownlie (Use of Force) (*supra*) 164 to the opinion of Sir David Maxwell Fyfe, who pointed to this result.

necessitated by the different dogmatic positions taken by the four Allied states, the final provisions on the crime of aggression in the IMT Charter were – in the words of Ian Brownlie – a 'clumsy formula'.[42] Indeed, this formula was the result of different, but valid, concerns about the content of a *crime* that was at that stage all but established under international law. The French concerns about retroactivity proved to be relevant, because the application of the law on aggression by the IMT was one of the main criticisms against the judgment at Nuremberg.[43] With respect to *aggression*, Article 6 of the Charter of the IMT[44] provided as follows:

> 'The Tribunal established … for the trial and punishment of the major war criminals of the European Axis countries shall have the power to try and punish persons who, acting in the interests of the European Axis countries, whether as individuals or as members of organizations, committed any of the following crimes. The following acts, or any of them are crimes coming within the jurisdiction of the Tribunal for which there shall be individual responsibility:
>
> (a) Crimes against peace: namely, planning, preparation, initiation or waging of a war of aggression, or a war in violation of international treaties, agreements or assurances, or participating in a common plan or conspiracy for the accomplishment of any of the foregoing …'

It has to be pointed out that, although the definition of aggression as set out in the Nuremberg Charter was accepted, not only by the Nuremberg Tribunal, but also by the international community's confirmation of it subsequent to the Nuremberg trial, the controversy regarding the *ex post facto* criminalisation of aggression remained. Even authors clearly in favour of individual responsibility for international crimes (including aggression) saw the definition of aggression *as contained in the Nuremberg Charter* as not only a (dogmatic) compromise of the drafters,[45] but also more of a 'political-legal' rather than a 'purely juridical' definition.[46] In other words, the Nuremberg Charter definition was criticised because it potentially violated the principles *nulla poena sine lege/nullum crimen*

42 Ian Brownlie (Use of Force) (*supra*) 164.

43 FB Schick 'The Nuremberg Trial and the International Law of the Future' 41 *AJIL* (1947) 770, 783–784. For comments on the defence objections against *ex post facto* application of procedural and substantive law at Nuremberg, see Leo Gross 'The criminality of aggressive war' 41(2) *The American Political Science Review* (1947) 205–225.

44 Charter of the International Military Tribunal (1945) UN Treaty Series, vol 82, 279, reproduced in Christine van den Wyngaert (ed) *International Criminal Law – A collection of International and European Instruments* 4th (2011) Martinus Nijhoff Publishers, Leiden, 53–59. Apart from the four Allied powers (the US, the UK, France and the Soviet Union) the London Agreement (to which the IMT Charter was attached) was also adhered to by 19 other Allied nations. See Yoram Dinstein (War Aggression Self-Defence) (*supra*) 118.

45 Compare comments by Ian Brownlie (*supra*) on the different dogmatic positions of the French and US drafters of the IMT Charter.

46 See Farhad Malekian in Bassiouni (International Criminal Law) (*supra*) 179.

sine lege (the legality principles) in terms of the retroactivity implicit in the fact that aggression was never defined or regarded as an international crime with individual responsibility attached to it (despite provisions in the Kellogg-Briand Pact that could form a basis for such liability).[47]

The above description of the genesis of the Nuremberg Charter (later followed by the Tokyo Charter) is quite well-known. However, it is necessary to look at the particular circumstances and factors that made these developments possible. It is important to note the *pre*history of the Nuremberg Charter and the subsequent criminal processes at Nuremberg and elsewhere in order to understand *why* and *how* the international law prohibition on the use of force was transformed or interpreted to form the basis of individual criminal liability for the crime of aggression (or crimes against peace).

3.1.1. A legislative history of the crime of aggression under the Nuremberg Charter

The customary law *status* of aggression as a crime under international law (and the implications of this for individual criminal liability) is today quite well established.[48] The principle that individuals can be held liable for the crime of aggression (at least for *wars of aggression*) is at present regarded as customary international law.[49] International lawyers and legal historians might speculate on the factors that made it possible for the drafters of the Nuremberg Charter and consequently the judges at the IMT Nuremberg to have held individuals responsible for 'crimes against peace'. From an international criminal law point of view, it is important to look at some of the compelling arguments that ultimately made the transition from the prohibition of the use of force to the criminalisation and individual liability for aggression possible.

Many legal and political factors made the trials at Nuremberg and later Tokyo possible. However, the inclusion of the crime of aggression first at Nuremberg and later at Tokyo was one of the most remarkable developments in international criminal law.[50] The extraordinary advocacy and intellectual input that made this possible were well documented, but one of the most comprehensive narratives

---

47 On the legality-debate, see Leo Gross (Criminality of aggressive war) (*supra*); Telford Taylor 'The Nuremberg Trials' 55(4) *Columbia Law Review* (1955) 488–525 (Taylor, Jackson's successor as prosecutor at Nuremberg, eloquently addressed the legal-cultural differences between the Allied lawyers that often informed fundamental notions of legal doctrine, including the *nullum crimen, nulla poena sine lege* principle).

48 See Ch VIII *infra*.

49 Gerhard Werle and Florian Jessberger (Principles of International Criminal Law) (*supra*) 534; Antonio Cassese (International Criminal Law) (*supra*) 112–113.

50 For an early prognostic view on the impact of the Nuremberg judgment on international law, see Philip C Jessup 'The Crime of Aggression and the Future of International Law' 62(1) *Political Science Quarterly* (1947) 1–10.

on the legislative history of the crime of aggressive war was written by Jonathan Bush, who had access to some of the behind-the-scenes correspondence between lawyers and academics that ultimately had a great impact on the drafting of the Nuremberg Charter and the subsequent prosecutions and judgments.[51]

It is quite well known that during the negotiations in London to draft a legal framework for what would later become the Nuremberg Charter, objections regarding the inclusion of aggression/waging a war of aggression were raised. These objections were based on concerns that to try German war criminals for the crime of aggression would violate the legality principle (*nullum crimen/ nulla poena sine lege*), as was already pointed out above. It is also well known that proponents of the inclusion of aggression in the legal framework for the trial of the major war criminals of the European Axis mostly relied on the Kellogg-Briand Pact (1928) as the principal instrument that outlawed aggressive war. But, with reference to the Kellogg-Briand Pact, Jonathan Bush stated: 'Neither friend nor foe mentioned the possibility of criminal trials for individual aggressors.'[52] But during the course of the Second World War the intellectual, political and ultimately practical conditions that led to the inclusion of individual criminal liability for aggression aligned. This important moment in the history of international criminal law was seized by a number of lawyers who for some time had advocated the criminalisation of aggression.

Throughout the Second World War, an influential community of exiled intellectuals, writers and lawyers lived and worked in London. Their publications were aimed at bringing to attention the atrocities of the Nazi regime and to create awareness of the allegations of massive war crimes and other atrocities committed on the European Continent by the Nazis. For present purposes it is interesting to note what Jonathan Bush pointed out in his narrative:

> '[It] was common in both popular and scholarly literature to denounce the Nazi leaders for starting the war, as well as for their brutal means of waging it, and occasionally to speak of the need for Nazis to face a reckoning for starting the war. Typically aggression, war-making, expansionism, militarism, or the like was used as a description and a political charge, to which responses – political or military, but possibly legal – would be required. ... In short, there were many articles that approached the notion of criminal liability for initiating war.'[53]

Bush also pointed out that few of these writers (lawyers or non-lawyers) called for trials for 'an identifiable legal crime of planning, initiating, or waging aggressive

51 See in general Jonathan A Bush '"The Supreme... Crime" and its origins: The lost legislative history of the crime of aggressive war' 102(8) *Columbia Law Review* (2002) 2324–2424.

52 Jonathan Bush (Legislative history) (*supra*) 2335.

53 Jonathan Bush (Legislative History) (*supra*) 2338–2339.

war.'[54] Bush's narrative identified a number of American criminal lawyers and criminologists as the key group of individuals who eventually conceptualised and introduced individual criminal liability for aggression as a workable part of the legal framework for what would later become the Nuremberg Trials. In essence, this notion took shape in the correspondence in 1944 between William Chanler, an American criminal lawyer who also served in the American military, and the Harvard criminologist Sheldon Glueck.[55] Professor Glueck also served as the American delegate on the United Nations War Crimes Commission[56] that started work in 1944. It is important to note that by 1944, both Glueck and Marcel de Baer, the influential Belgian delegate on the War Crimes Commission, concluded that the Nazi leadership could *not* be tried for aggression – both found that the pre-war legal framework (consisting primarily of the Kellogg-Briand Pact and the Treaty of Versailles) did not sufficiently establish individual criminal liability. Thus, for them the legality concerns trumped any notions of possible criminal liability for aggression.[57]

In 1944 the War Crimes Commission invited its member nations to express their views on the crime of aggression. This presented William Chanler with the opportunity to submit to various American role-players his views and theories on the criminality of aggression. Jonathan Bush summarised Chanler's theory as follows:

> '[The] solution [for the legality concern] was to recognize that Kellogg-Briand and related instruments had determined that aggressive wars – wars not fought in self-defense – were illegal. If they were, then it followed, for example, that persons carrying guns and committing killings in Poland or Czechoslovakia were not privileged combatants, as they would be if they were lawful fighters in a lawful war under the traditional laws and customs of war. They were, instead, legally unprivileged fighters – men using violence without legal justification or excuse, men whom the law terms ordinary criminals – committing violations of Polish or Czech domestic criminal law.'[58]

---

54 Jonathan Bush (Legislative History) (*supra*) 2339.

55 The eventual influence of Prof Sheldon Glueck on the Prosecution at Nuremberg was recognised by early commentators on the Nuremberg trial. See for instance Franz B Schick 'Crimes against Peace' 38(5) *Journal of Criminal Law and Criminology* (1948) 445–465. Schick stated (458–459) as follows: 'Relying greatly, it appears, on the opinion of an American criminologist [Glueck] the Allied Prosecution declared that "the only innovation which this [Nuremberg] Charter has introduced is to provide machinery, long over-due, to carry out the existing law; and there is no substance in the complaint that the Charter is a piece of *post facto* legislation, either in declaring wars of aggression to be criminal, or in assuming that the State is not immune from criminal responsibility".'

56 This Commission of the Allied nations served as an advisory and fact-gathering body. Its first meeting was in Jan 1944. See further Jonathan Bush (Legislative History) (*supra*) 2347.

57 Jonathan Bush (Legislative History) (*supra*) 2346.

58 Jonathan Bush (Legislative History) (*supra*) 2355.

It would be obvious for any international (criminal) lawyer that the above theory represented a fusion of the *jus ad bellum* and the *jus in bello*.[59] The theory also did not advance any compelling argument or basis to regard aggression as an *international* crime with individual liability attached to it. Because of this apparent weakness in the theory, William Chanler at first advanced the argument that although Kellogg-Briand did not establish individual criminal liability for aggression, this Pact could at least serve as a legal basis to argue that the war was illegal under international law. With that as starting point, the argument can then proceed to say that aggression is not an international crime *yet*, but because the German conduct in the various occupied territories were illegal, that would permit domestic criminal jurisdiction over the soldiers. In turn, on the basis of *respondeat superior* (or command responsibility) the Nazi leadership could ultimately be held responsible. But responsible for what? Jonathan Bush explains the way Chanler crossed this bridge as follows:

> '[Chanler] reasoned ... that, at a minimum, Kellogg-Briand had declared the illegality of aggression on an international plane. Based on that, some individual or institution – perhaps even the victim nation itself – could determine that the invader had launched an act of aggression against it. That determination in turn would strip the protective layer from German soldiers, who now became in legal contemplation ordinary violent criminals under [for instance] Polish law, subject to domestic criminal law.'[60]

Creative though this argument was at the time, it obviously did not address the central problem of how to establish substantive jurisdiction over the crime of aggression for purposes of a possible *international* criminal tribunal. The alternative was to use the illegality of the war (in terms of the legal regime provided for under the Kellogg-Briand Pact) as not only a starting point, but as the legal focus point. Chanler pushed the idea that for the prosecution of Nazi war criminals to be effective, America had to insist on the inclusion of the charge of aggression in the legal framework of any future international war crimes tribunal. His arguments prevailed, and via his contacts in the American war administration (notably the Pentagon) his ideas won the favour of President Roosevelt. In January 1945 a memorandum from the President stated that charges against the Nazis 'should include an indictment for waging aggressive warfare, in violation of the Kellogg Pact.' And further, '[perhaps] these and other charges might be joined in a conspiracy indictment.'[61] The ideas of Chanler advanced from a rather novel idea to hold individuals criminally liable at domestic level,

---

59 For a brief discussion of the scope and application of international humanitarian law, see Christopher Greenwood 'Scope of Application of Humanitarian Law' in Dieter Fleck (ed) *The Handbook of Humanitarian Law in Armed Conflicts* (1995) Oxford University Press, Oxford, 39–63.

60 Jonathan Bush (Legislative History) (*supra*) 2355.

61 Statement by Pres Roosevelt as quoted in Jonathan Bush (Legislative History) (*supra*) 2363.

for violent conduct that was deemed illegal under international law, to the theory that became accepted as part of the legal framework of the Nuremberg Charter, namely that aggressive war was part of an overall 'Axis criminal conspiracy', and 'aggressive war as a free-standing substantive crime'.[62] Once the notion of individual criminal liability for aggression had been accepted as part of American policy, the inclusion of this notion as part of the legal framework for the Nuremberg Tribunal became a much more realistic prospect.[63]

The substantive definition of aggression that was ultimately included in the Nuremberg Charter was the result of much advocacy and negotiation. The fact that it was a 'neutral' definition (in other words not limited to acts of aggression by the Axis powers) meant that it could serve as the basis for future prosecutions of aggressive war. Jonathan Bush described the opening arguments of the American and British prosecutors at Nuremberg as follows:

> 'On November 21 [1945], Jackson gave one of the great arguments in forensic history as he opened the case, using the notions of conspiracy and Crimes against Peace to knit together acts that had occurred over two decades and around the world. Two weeks later, Sir Hartley Shawcross opened the British case with a speech almost as eloquent, focused on Crimes against Peace by means of forcibly violating treaties.'[64]

Indeed, it is no exaggeration to state that the Nuremberg trial and judgment constituted not just an unprecedented legal and forensic feat, but also a history of the Third Reich.[65] This, in itself, is valuable. For present purposes, the focus is on a more controversial aspect of the judgment, namely the criminalisation of aggression, or, crimes against peace.

3.2. JUDGMENT AT NUREMBERG

The trial of the major Nazi war criminals (in all twenty-four Nazi leaders were indicted) started on 20 November 1945 and lasted till 1 October 1946 in the Palace of Justice at Nuremberg. Only twenty-one of the twenty-four defendants were present during the trial.[66]

---

62 Jonathan Bush (Legislative History) (*supra*) 2364.

63 The notion of individual criminal liability for the crime of aggression was also strongly supported by Robert Jackson, who later became the American chief prosecutor at Nuremberg. During the negotiations in London in 1945 on the legal framework for the war crimes tribunal (that resulted in the Nuremberg Charter) Jackson was one of the few who advocated a 'neutral' definition of aggression, i.e. a definition not limited to aggressive acts of the Axis powers only. Jackson's overall view prevailed and can be found in the language of art 6(a) of the Nuremberg Charter. See comments by Jonathan Bush (Legislative History) (*supra*) 2369.

64 Jonathan Bush (Legislative History) (*supra*) 2370.

65 Gerhard Werle and Florian Jessberger (Principles of International Criminal Law) (*supra*) 8.

66 Gustav Krupp von Bohlen was too sick, Martin Bormann was tried in absentia, and Robert Ley committed suicide. See Quincy Wright 'The law of the Nuremberg Trial' 41(1) *AJIL* (1947)

The indictment at the IMT contained two counts related to the war of aggression conducted by the European Axis powers:

> 'Count One: [The] common plan or conspiracy embraced the commission of crimes against peace, in that the defendants planned, prepared, initiated and waged wars of aggression, which were also wars in violation of international treaties, agreements or assurances.
>
> Count Two: All the defendants with divers other persons, during a period of years preceding 8th May, 1945, participated in the planning, preparation, initiation and waging of wars of aggression, which were also wars in violation of international treaties, agreements or assurances.'[67]

The strategy of the prosecution was to first set out the aggressive Nazi foreign policy objectives and the way in which the German people were prepared for war in the period 1933 to 1939.[68] In this way the prosecution introduced the Common Plan that led to the wars of aggression. Germany's seizure of Austria and Czechoslovakia (the latter first had to cede part of her territory – Sudetenland – to Germany in terms of the infamous Munich Agreement)[69] were used by the Prosecution at Nuremberg to show Germany's aggressive foreign policy that eventually resulted in the Second World War.[70]

38–72, 40; Gerhard Werle and Florian Jessberger (Principles of International Criminal Law) (*supra*) 7–8.

67 Ian Brownlie (Use of Force) (*supra*) 167. 8 May 1945 is significant, because at 23h01, Central European Time, on that day, the German High Command surrendered to the Allied Expeditionary Force and the Supreme High Command of the Red Army. See Act of Military Surrender, signed at Berlin on 8 May 1945, reprinted in Walter Consuelo Langsam *Historic Documents of World War II* (1958) Greenwood Press Publishers, Westport, Connecticut, 145–146.

68 The Tribunal held: 'The first acts of aggression referred to in the Indictment are the seizure of Austria and Czechoslovakia and the first war of aggression charged in the Indictment is the war against Poland begun on the 1st September, 1939. ... The war against Poland did not come suddenly out of an otherwise clear sky; the evidence has made it plain that this war of aggression, as well as the seizure of Austria and Czechoslovakia, was pre-meditated and carefully prepared, and was not undertaken until the moment was thought opportune for it to be carried through as a definite part of the pre-ordained scheme and plan. For the aggressive designs of the Nazi Government were not accidents arising out of the immediate political situation in Europe and the world; they were a deliberate and essential part of Nazi foreign policy.' See *Judgment of the IMT (Nuremberg)* reprinted in Wise and Podgor (Cases and Materials) (*supra*) 518. See further Franz Schick (Crimes against Peace) (*supra*) 447 *et seq.*

69 The Munich Agreement of 29 Sept 1938 was signed by Germany, the UK, France and Italy. In terms of this agreement (which became known as the primary example of the policy of 'appeasement' of Hitler by Prime Minister Neville Chamberlain of Britain), Czechoslovakia had to cede to Germany the territory of Sudetenland, inhabited by many German speaking people. It became clear that Germany obtained the territory because of the threat of force and the policy of appeasement of Britain and France to avert war. For the text of the Munich Agreement, see Walter Langsam (Historic Documents) (*supra*) 10–13.

70 See further Franz Schick (Crimes against Peace) (*supra*) 447–449.

The rather tricky issue of retroactivity (as referred to in the previous paragraphs) was next addressed. As shown above, the prosecution argued that aggressive war was illegal in terms of international law since 1920 (the Treaty of Versailles, followed by various other instruments and treaties outlawing the use of force, notably the Kellogg-Briand Pact of 1928).[71]

3.2.1. *Political and legal problems at Nuremberg: Legality, foreign policy and Allied 'complicity'*

The defence in the Nuremberg trials of the German major war criminals developed an interesting argument to counter the prosecution's apparent insistence that international law not only outlawed war, but also that the criminalisation of aggression could be applied retroactively.[72] The defence argument focused on the status of international instruments and treaties like the Covenant of the League of Nations and the Kellogg-Briand Pact and concluded that by 1939 the collective security system were all but in ruins.[73] Indeed, it was ironic that the Soviet Union – one of the states most outraged by German aggression – was herself expelled from the League of Nations because of the Soviet invasion of Finland in 1939.[74] Thus, the defence argued that the distinction between 'legal' and 'illegal' wars became unworkable because of the failure of the League of Nations' dominated collective security system.[75] The annexation of Austria and Czechoslovakia by Germany (events, the prosecution alleged, were the precursors to what would become the Second World War) occurred, as also shown above, with a great degree of Allied complicity. Franz Schick has pointed out that 'the prosecuting governments [at Nuremberg] recognized the annexation of Austria without delay.'[76] Furthermore, in the case of Germany's attack on Poland (an attack which the IMT labelled 'plainly an aggressive war')[77] the murky political reality of foreign relations before and during the Second World War was illustrated by the fact that the Soviet Union, one of the Allied prosecuting nations at Nuremberg, had in fact reached an agreement on the partition of Poland with Nazi Germany in September 1939. This act of cold political manoeuvring by the Soviet Union did not stop them from accusing

---

71 Ian Brownlie (Use of Force) (*supra*) 167–168. See also discussion of the legislative history of the crime of aggression in terms of the Nuremberg Charter section 3.1.1 *supra*.

72 Quincy Wright (Nuremberg Trial) (*supra*) 62–66.

73 Ian Brownlie (Use of Force) (*supra*) 169.

74 The Soviet Union invaded Finland on 30 Nov 1939. The League of Nations expelled the Soviet Union on 14 Dec 1939. See Resolution Adopted by the Council of the League of Nations, Dec 14, 1939, League of Nations *Official Journal* 1939, 506; Resolution of the Assembly on 540. Reprinted in Walter Langsam (Historic Documents) (*supra*) 31–32.

75 Ian Brownlie (Use of Force) (*supra*) 169–170.

76 Franz Schick (Crimes against Peace) (*supra*) 447.

77 Nuremberg judgment 34.

Nazi leaders of aggression at Nuremberg.[78] The defence arguments at Nuremberg illustrate the peculiar political and legal dilemmas that the IMT faced. This was also compounded by the obvious weak collective security environment of the post-war international system.

The gist of the defence's argument was that this collapse of the collective security system that came into existence after the First World War signalled a return to the *jus ad bellum;* the anarchical international system where the use of force as part of foreign policy was quite acceptable. But, however interesting (or even compelling) some of these *tu quoque* ('you do it so I can do it too')[79] defence arguments might have been, the IMT rejected them as irrelevant. Geoffrey Robertson opined that the IMT was wrong to treat these *tu quoque* arguments as inadmissible: 'So far as the counts alleging the conspiracy to wage aggressive war and the commission of crimes against the peace were concerned, the *tu quoque* argument was most pertinent: the Germans were charged *inter alia* with violating the rearmament provisions of the Versailles Treaty which the French had ignored and the British had joined the Germans in circumventing.'[80] According to Robertson, the relevance of *tu quoque* evidence and arguments lie in the assessment of *justification* for war or modes of warfare.[81] Others, like Albin Eser, suggests that the IMT Nuremberg was right in its general disregard of the *tu quoque* defence arguments, for, 'by opening this door, even if just a crack, the way is paved for an ever-increasing escalation of competing crimes.'[82]

Apart from the *tu quoque* arguments, the Tribunal also dealt with the issue of legality with reference to the *jus contra bellum* of the time (and the defence arguments about the retroactive application of criminal provisions on aggression) by referring to the fact that the defendants (senior leaders of the Nazi regime) must have known that Germany's aggressive foreign policy was *in violation of treaties* like the Kellogg-Briand Pact, *which outlawed the use of force.* The Tribunal furthermore used the analogy of criminal liability for war crimes (which were also not always expressly criminalised under international law) to

78 Walter Langsam described the German-Soviet Boundary Agreement of 28 Sept 1939 as follows: 'While the outmanned and outmaneuvered Poles were trying to make a stand against the Nazis in southern and eastern Poland, the Soviet Union on September 17, 1939, invaded the unhappy country. The official explanation was the protection of the Ukrainian and White Russian minorities living in eastern Poland. Berlin and Moscow promptly divided the spoils.' Walter Langsam (Historic Documents) (*supra*) 28. For the text of the partition agreement and confidential correspondence between the Russian and German foreign ministers, see Walter Langsam (Historic Documents) (*supra*) 28–31.

79 For an explanation of the *tu quoque* argument as a possible defence in international criminal trials, see Albin Eser '"Defences" in War Crime Trials' in Yoram Dinstein and Mala Tabory (ed) *War Crimes in International Law* (1996) Kluwer Law International, The Hague, 269.

80 Geoffrey Robertson (Crimes Against Humanity) (*supra*) 215.

81 *Ibid.*

82 Albin Eser (Defences in War Crime Trials) (*supra*) 269.

support its opinion that, read together with the particular history of the Kellogg-Briand Pact and other international instruments and draft instruments actually providing for the criminalisation of aggression,[83] there could be no doubt that retroactive criminal liability for aggression in terms of the IMT Charter was justified.[84]

The issue of retroactivity (and criticism that the IMT disregarded the principles of *nullum crimen sine lege, nulla poena sine lege*) can *today* be regarded as an important, but largely academic debate.[85] The fact is that since the Judgment at Nuremberg, aggression has been established as a crime under international law by not only national legal systems,[86] but also by the International Military Tribunal for the Far East (IMTFE) in Tokyo, and other trials subsequent to the Nuremberg proceedings. This crime of aggression must, however, be seen in the context of the liability that the IMT Nuremberg had ultimately attached to the individual accused.

Regarding the scope of aggression as an individual crime and the extent of individual liability for this crime, it is important to note the difference between the 'individual crime of aggressive war' and 'aggressive war as an international

83 The IMT referred to Art 227 of the Versailles Treaty as well as instruments like the Geneva Protocol (1925) which intended aggressive war to be a crime under international law. See *Judgment* of the IMT at 40–41; see also Ian Brownlie (Use of Force) (*supra*) 171.

84 Ian Brownlie (Use of Force) (*supra*) 170–171.

85 One should however, not take lightly the criticisms against the IMT's treatment of the principle *nullum crimen, nulla poena sine lege*. Some commentators argued that the 'improvising' spirit at Nuremberg should not serve as a general example for the future development of International criminal law and procedure. See the critical observations by Hans Leonhardt 'The Nuremberg Trial: A legal analysis' 11(4) *The Review of Politics* (1949) 449–476. For an argument in favour of the dynamic nature of international law and the development of customary law (and for the basis of the crime of aggression in customary law *before* the Nuremberg trial), see Leo Gross 'The criminality of aggressive war' 41(2) *The American Political Science Review* (1947) 205–225. Compare also the following passage from the Nuremberg judgment, as quoted by Telford Taylor: 'International law is not capable of development by the normal processes of legislation, for there is no continuing international legislative authority … It grows, as did the common law, through decisions reached from time to time in adapting settled principles to new situations.' Telford Taylor 'The Nuremberg Trials' 55(4) *Columbia Law Review* (1955) 516. For a succinct assessment of the Nuremberg Judgment, see Gerhard Werle and Florian Jessberger (Principles of International Criminal Law) (*supra*) 8–10.

86 See Ian Brownlie (Use of Force) (*supra*) 175–182 for a discussion of the provision for the crime of aggression in national legal systems. For a discussion of the trials that were conducted under the so-called Control Council Laws, see Ian Brownlie (Use of Force) (*supra*) 174–175. The latter provided for military tribunals in the various areas of Germany under the control of the Allied forces. These tribunals also had jurisdiction to try individuals for aggression (crimes against peace). Many of the judgments in these tribunals relied on the precedent of the IMT Judgment at Nuremberg. The application of international criminal law (in particular the crime of aggression) before national courts (either on the basis of national laws or international law (customary or treaty) will be discussed in Chapter VIII *infra*.

delinquency'. The latter concept refers to the often broadly stated international obligations of states. Violations of treaty obligations, the use of armed force in the absence of the necessary conditions for collective or individual self-defence, or the use of armed force without the authorisation of international organs would fall in this category. As Quincy Wright observed, '[the] international delinquency arises from an act or omission of the state, and the element of individual intention is not involved.'[87] Wright distinguished this concept from the individual crime of aggression, as developed at Nuremberg: '[In] the individual crime of aggression, the element of individual intention is of major importance. This crime as stated in the [Nuremberg] Charter consists in "planning, preparation, initiation or waging of a war of aggression, or a war in violation of international treaties, agreements or assurances, or participation in a common plan or conspiracy for the accomplishment of any of the foregoing."' Wright emphasised the extent of individual liability for aggression with reference to the particular defendant's subjective intention, linked to that individual's position of authority: 'To determine whether an individual is guilty of [aggression] it is necessary to examine the extent of his authority over the armed forces involved or his importance as an advisor of, or collaborator with, the person exercising such authority, and his intention in authorizing, or in advising or collaborating in authorizing, the use of such forces.'[88]

4. THE JUDGMENT OF THE TOKYO TRIBUNAL

The trial of the Japanese war criminals at the International Military Tribunal for the Far East (IMTFE) in Tokyo started in 1947. It involved 28 senior Japanese military and political leaders, who were accused, *inter alia*, of the crime of aggression. Article 5(a) of the Charter of the IMTFE (Tokyo Charter) provided for individual criminal responsibility for Crimes against peace:

> '[The] planning, preparation, initiation or waging of a declared or undeclared war of aggression, or a war in violation of international law, treaties, agreements or assurances, or participation in a common plan or conspiracy for the accomplishment of any of the foregoing ...'[89]

There are similarities, but also striking differences, between the Nuremberg and Tokyo Tribunals and the judgments delivered by these *ad hoc* international

87 Quincy Wright (Nuremberg Trial) (*supra*) 66.
88 Quincy Wright (Nuremberg Trial) (*supra*) 67.
89 Charter of the International Military Tribunal for the Far East (1946), Special Proclamation by the Supreme Commander for the Allied Powers, as amended 26 April 1946, TIAS No 1589, reprinted in Christine Van den Wyngaert (International Criminal Law) (*supra*) 61–65.

criminal tribunals.[90] Although it can be said that both tribunals were ultimately examples of 'victors' justice',[91] the criticism against the establishment and judgment of the Tokyo Tribunal seems to strike at the very heart of the legitimacy of the Tribunal and the value of its jurisprudence.[92] The critique goes further than the legitimacy problem, and includes criticism against procedural and material aspects of the process and judgment.[93] As far as legitimacy is concerned, the most obvious difference between the IMT at Nuremberg and the Tokyo Tribunal is the fact that the Tokyo Tribunal was established *unilaterally* by the American Supreme Commander of the Allied Powers in the Pacific. The Charter of the Tribunal was furthermore not the result of international conferences, but was drafted largely by American officials.[94]

Apart from the perceived legitimacy problem and problems from a procedural perspective referred to above, one of the more fundamental problems with the judgment at Tokyo concerns for present purposes the Tribunal's adjudication on the crime of aggression and specifically the way the Tribunal employed the doctrine of conspiracy liability to hold individuals responsible for crimes committed in the Far East. All the defendants (the 28 senior political and military leaders) were charged with the offences of 'conspiring to wage an aggressive war' or 'waging a war of aggression'.[95] The critical point however is that these defendants were not necessarily in the same position as their Nazi counterparts at Nuremberg with regards to their perceived responsibility for formulating and executing aggressive Japanese foreign policy prior to the war. The *mens rea* of the specific individual accused were in other words of less concern for the prosecution. The defendants were thus chosen as *representatives*

90 See AS Comyns Carr 'The judgment of the International Military Tribunal for the Far East' *Transactions of the Grotius Society* Vol 34 *Problems of Public and Private International Law, Transactions of the Year 1948* (1948) Oxford University Press, Oxford, 141–151.

91 See comments by Christine van den Wyngaert 'De bijdrage van de internationale straftribunalen tot de ontwikkeling van het straf(process)recht vanuit internationaal en Belgisch perspektief', paper delivered at Delva cyclus, Ghent, Belgium, 17 March 2006 (copy on file). Prof Van den Wyngaert observed: '[Het] was een justitie van overwinnaars tegen overwonnenen (enkel Duitse en Japanse oorlogsmisdadigers stonden er terecht, en feiten zoals Hiroshima/Nagasaki en het bombardement van Dresden werden er niet beoordeeld), het was ten dele ex post facto rechtspraak (de Genocideconventie en de Rode Kruisconventies die genocide en oorlogsmisdaden omschreven kwamen pas tot stand achteraf), en op de procedure zelf was ook een en ander aan te merken.'

92 For a contextual analysis of the trial, see P Lowe 'An embarassing necessity: the Tokyo trial of Japanese leaders, 1946–48' in RA Melikan (ed) *Domestic and International Trials, 1700–2000, The Trial in History Vol II* (2003) Manchester University Press, Manchester, 137–156. For a brief assessment, see Gerhard Werle and Florian Jessberger (Principles of International Criminal Law) (*supra*) 10–11.

93 See in general Allison Marston Danner 'Beyond the Geneva Conventions: Lessons from the Tokyo Tribunal in prosecuting war and terrorism' 46 *Virginia Journal of International Law* (2005) 83–130.

94 See Allison Marston Danner (Lessons from Tokyo Tribunal) (*supra*).

95 Allison Marston Danner (Lessons from Tokyo Tribunal) (*supra*) 90.

of a certain influential political and military class, the members of which were regarded as being responsible for the formulation and direction of the militaristic and aggressive Japanese foreign policy – and anyone in this group could, according to the prosecution's theory, be held responsible on the basis of the perceived conspiracy to commit aggression.[96] AS Comyns Carr described the grand political plan to pursue an aggressive foreign policy as follows:

> 'The story as unfolded in the judgment is one of a grandiose plot which originated in the late 1920's in the minds of a few officers and civilians, and grew until it became the dominating purpose, in varying degrees and with occasional variations of emphasis, of every successive government of Japan.'[97]

As noted, neither the Nuremberg Charter nor the Tokyo Charter defined 'aggression'. The judges of the Tokyo Tribunal had the opportunity to study the proceedings at Nuremberg, but did not define aggression. With reference to the legal basis for the criminalisation of aggression and the impact of the Kellogg-Briand Pact in this regard, Brownlie quoted the following passage from the opinion of the President of the IMTFE:

> 'This Pact [Kellogg-Briand Pact] does not contain the word "crime" or the word "criminal"; but having regard to the language of the Pact – the solemn condemnation of war, the renunciation of war as an instrument of national policy, and the agreement not to resort to it to settle or solve disputes or conflicts, and to the natural and probable, if not inevitable consequences of recourse to war – the conclusion is irresistible that the illegality of aggressive war and its criminality were perceived and acknowledged ... Every State that became a party to the Pact of Paris perceived and acknowledged the illegality and criminality of recourse to war for the solution of international controversies ... If, nevertheless, any State resorts to aggressive war, those individuals through whom it acts, knowing as they do that their State is a party to the Pact, are criminally responsible for this delict of State'.[98]

The *Tokyo* judgment ultimately linked the aggressive foreign policy of Japan[99] to a *single conspiracy* of the defendants before the war to use the Japanese military

96 Allison Marston Danner (Lessons from Tokyo Tribunal) (*supra*) 90.

97 AS Comyns Carr (Military Tribunal for the Far East) (*supra*) 146.

98 Ian Brownlie (Use of Force) (*supra*) 173.

99 The aggressive Japanese foreign policy was first and foremost aimed at establishing Japan as the dominant power in Asia, and specifically Pacific-Asia. When the war in Europe started in 1939 Japan was already at war with China (Japan occupied Manchuria and wanted to occupy the whole of China). On 27 Sept 1940 Japan, Germany and Italy entered into an alliance. For the text of the German-Italian-Japanese Pact, see Walter Langsam (Historic Documents) (*supra*) 76–77. The first 3 articles set out the geo-political vision of the Pact: '[Art 1] Japan recognizes and respects the leadership of Germany and Italy in the establishment of a new order in Europe. [Art 2] Germany and Italy recognize and respect the leadership of Japan in the establishment of a new order in Greater East Asia. [Art 3] Germany, Italy and Japan agree to co-operate in their efforts on the aforesaid basis. They further undertake to assist

and political apparatus to dominate the Far East. Allison Marston Danner explained this *conspiracy* as follows:

> 'The Tokyo indictment first alleged that "a conspiracy between the defendants, joined in by the rulers of other aggressive countries, namely Nazi Germany and Fascist Italy, was entered into. The main object of this conspiracy was to secure the domination and exploitation by the aggressive States of the rest of the world." Count One of the indictment then charged the defendants with the more specific (although still breathtakingly broad) conspiracy.'[100]

On the matter of conspiracy to plan and commit aggression, dissenting judge Pal from India made the critical observation[101] that to characterise national foreign policy as a criminal conspiracy was rather simplistic, especially where such a characterisation would lead to a finding of individual criminal responsibility.[102] With this warning in mind, Allison Marston Danner warned against the dangers of relying on the doctrine of conspiracy to hold individuals responsible for a crime like aggression – a crime so closely associated with state conduct and the political processes of that state:

> 'Alleging a conspiracy against a broader historical and political canvas has several potential failings. It allows prosecutors to overreach on the scope of the overall wrongdoing by rolling up what turns out to be disparate activity into one legal package. It also bears the significant risk of sweeping up too many defendants into its ambit. ... A clear link between wrongdoing and conviction helps overcome the negative perception that may attach to criminal cases with strong political overtones.'[103]

There was an attempt by Judge Röling in his dissenting opinion to limit the convictions for conspiracy only to those defendants who were in actual fact formulators of Japanese government policy. Broadly speaking, the Tribunal – although less cautious than Judge Röling – also emphasised that one of the conditions for individual liability for conspiracy to commit aggression was that such defendants had to have the capacity or official position to influence Japanese

one another with all political, economic, and military means, if one of the three Contracting Parties is attacked by a Power at present not involved in the European war or in the Chinese-Japanese conflict.' See further Stephen E Ambrose *Rise to Globalism – American foreign policy since 1938* 7th (1993) Penguin Books, New York, 9–14 for a brief but eloquent description of the aggressive Japanese foreign policy, and the eventual US involvement in the war in East Asia.

100 Allison Marston Danner (Lessons from Tokyo Tribunal) (*supra*) 114.

101 For commentary on the extent and impact of Judge Pal's dissenting opinion, see E Kopelman 'Ideology and International Law: the dissent of the Indian Justice at the Tokyo War Crimes Tribunal' 23 *New York University Journal of International Law and Politics* (1991) 373.

102 Allison Marston Danner (Lessons from Tokyo Tribunal) (*supra*) 118.

103 Allison Marston Danner (Lessons from Tokyo Tribunal) (*supra*) 119.

government policy.[104] The approach in the Tokyo judgment nevertheless represented a wider understanding of conspiracy liability than at Nuremberg. In the more restrictive interpretation of 'conspiracy' in the Nuremberg judgment only those defendants who actively participated in the planning of the aggressive war were held responsible on the basis of conspiracy.[105]

The Tokyo Tribunal confirmed the individual criminal responsibility for aggression under international law. However, it is clear that the Tokyo judgment, although in some respects more nuanced than the Nuremberg judgment as a result of some dissenting opinions, was always far less celebrated and influential than the Nuremberg judgment.[106] The reasons for this may vary, but one factor is certainly the perceived problem of legitimacy of the Tokyo Charter and Tribunal. Apart from that, aspects of the judgment like the broader interpretation of conspiracy (discussed above) might add to the present debate about the suitability of the definition of aggression under the Statute of the ICC. But one must also be realistic: the narrower approach regarding the elements of aggression for purposes of individual criminal liability (as formulated by the Nuremberg Tribunal) seem to set the parameters of aggression under customary international law. In this respect, the legacy of Nuremberg is indeed the fact that the debate about the definition of aggression was influenced to a far greater degree by the judgment at Nuremberg (and also the judgments under the Control Council Laws)[107] than by the judgment of the Tokyo Tribunal – the latter's legacy tainted (perhaps more than Nuremberg's) by the problems of legitimacy. Nevertheless, the judgment of the Tokyo Tribunal certainly adds value to the ongoing debate about individual criminal liability for aggression, apart from the fact that it brought to justice at least some of the individuals closely associated with the aggressive Japanese regime that caused much suffering in East Asia.[108]

5. THE PROCEEDINGS IN OCCUPIED GERMANY UNDER THE CONTROL COUNCIL LAWS

On 29 April 1945 Hitler realised that his Reich had ended. In his bunker in Berlin he prepared his 'Private and Political Testament'. In terms of this document the Presidency of the Reich was handed to Grand Admiral Karl Doenitz, who became Hitler's successor as German Head of State. Hitler committed suicide

104 Allison Marston Danner (Lessons from Tokyo Tribunal) (*supra*) 123–124.
105 Gerhard Werle and Florian Jessberger (Principles of International Criminal Law) (*supra*) 262.
106 See in general the critical assessment by BVA Röling and A Cassese *The Tokyo trial and beyond: Reflections of a peacemaker* (1993) Polity Press, Cambridge.
107 See discussion under section 5 *infra*.
108 See concluding remarks by AS Comyns Carr (Military Tribunal for the Far East) (*supra*) 150–151.

shortly after the testament was signed. On 1 May 1945 Admiral Doenitz assumed the position of German Head of State and Commander-in-Chief of the armed forces. Less than a week later Doenitz agreed to Germany's unconditional surrender to the Allied forces.[109] After the German surrender and the conference of the Allied forces at Potsdam, the sovereign state of Germany seized to exist. Doenitz was no longer Head of State. In the place of the Nazi government, the Allied Forces created a *Condominium* over the German territory, which was exercised by the Allied Control Council at Berlin. This Control Council consisted of the Commanders in Chief of the four Allies.[110]

While the major war criminals were tried at the IMT Nuremberg, the Control Council issued Control Council Law No 10 on the Punishment of Persons Guilty of War crimes, Crimes against Peace and against Humanity (1945).[111] The aim of this legislation was to make sure that the trials of Nazi war criminals subsequent to the IMT Nuremberg trial would have a sound legal basis and to enhance legal uniformity throughout occupied Germany. A number of important judgments were delivered by tribunals that operated in terms of the Control Council Law, for example the prosecution of powerful industrialists who supported the Nazi war effort (*Krupp*), the case against high officials of the Nazi state not tried at Nuremberg (*Von Weizsakcker et al*), and the so-called High Command Trial of the senior military officers (*Von Leeb et al*).[112] While these cases confirmed the law on aggression[113] as applied by the IMT Nuremberg, a common feature of these judgments is that they put the emphasis on the more nuanced personal positions and personalities of the accused. More emphasis was for example put on the 'actual power of individuals to shape or influence the war policy' of Germany. These statements by the tribunals under the Control Council Law later had an impact on the International Law Commission's work on the definition of aggression, especially on the meaning of 'waging of a war of aggression'.[114]

---

109 For the text of 'The Private and Political Testaments of Hitler 29 April 1945'; 'Assumption of Power by Doenitz, 1 May 1945'; and 'The German Surrender, 7–8/9 May 1945', see Walter Langsam (Historic Documents) (*supra*) 137–146.

110 See Franz Schick (Crimes against Peace) (*supra*) 452.

111 Control Council Law No 10 (*Official Gazette Control Council for Germany* No 3, Berlin, 31 Jan 1946 50 *et seq*), reprinted in Christine van den Wyngaert (International Criminal Law) (*supra*) 67–70. See further comments by Gerhard Werle and Florian Jessberger (Principles of International Criminal Law) (*supra*) 11–12.

112 See Gerhard Werle and Florian Jessberger (Principles of International Criminal Law) (*supra*) 12.

113 Art II 1(a) provided for Crimes against peace: 'Crimes against Peace. Initiation of invasions of other countries and wars of aggression in violation of international laws and treaties, including but not limited to planning, preparation, initiation or waging a war of aggression, or a war of violation of international treaties, agreements or assurances, or participation in a common plan or conspiracy for the accomplishment of any of the foregoing.'

114 See discussion of various cases under the Control Council Law in Caroline Fournet (International Crimes) (*supra*) 159–160. See further discussion of the work of the ILC in Ch IV *infra*.

6. CONCLUDING REMARKS

The judgments of the *ad hoc* tribunals at Nuremberg and, perhaps more controversially, Tokyo represent the maturation of international criminal law. This was no longer the utopian ideal of writers and non-governmental organisations, but as a consequence of the work of the tribunals important areas of the desired international criminal law (*de lege ferenda*) became *de lege lata* – the law in force.[115] Part of this historical development was the acceptance of individual criminal liability for the crime of aggression. Two important principles were thus established: (1) aggression is a crime under international law; and (2) individuals can be held liable for the crime of aggression.

Looking at the Nuremberg and Tokyo judgments of the two post-war *ad hoc* tribunals, one can say that both the political and legal conditions were optimum for their relative success. Yes, one can criticise the processes as 'victors' justice', and some dogmatic and jurisprudential critique against the *ex post facto* criminalisation of aggression at IMT Nuremberg seems (even today) to have some merit. However, the historical fact is that at Nuremberg (and later Tokyo) the long desired criminalisation of aggression reached its maturity. However, it is also prudent to make some critical preliminary observations regarding the 'legacy of Nuremberg', which will be more fully analysed in the next chapter.

The processes at Nuremberg (and later Tokyo) were, all matters considered, successful in making sure that peace was established not through political convenience, but at least with the help of justice. The two *ad hoc* tribunals represented important milestones on the long road to end impunity for crimes of international concern. As pointed out above, the political conditions were favourable to establish the *ad hoc* tribunals. The Allies could make sure that the logistics and political support for the tribunals were in place. Another important factor was that the big powers all committed themselves to the creation of a collective security system, dominated by the UN as successor of the failed League of Nations. This commitment to collective security and international co-operation was also later manifested in the important Nuremberg Principles,[116] which can be regarded as another cornerstone of the developing system of international criminal law. Apart from the fact that the political conditions after the Second World War were favourable for the creation of two *ad hoc* tribunals, one should not forget one of the contentions of the defence counsel before the

---

115 For a discussion of the distinction between *de lege lata* (the law in force) and *de lege ferenda* (the law in its primary stages; not in force, or desired law) in international criminal law, see Farhad Malekian *The Monopolization of International Criminal Law in the United Nations* (1993) Almqvist & Wiksell International, Stockholm, 34–37.

116 See discussion in Ch IV *infra*.

IMT (Nuremberg), namely that aggression could never have been a crime under international law, because the very powers who were at that stage prosecuting the Nazis for aggression, were themselves responsible for the collapse of the post First World War collective security system. Indeed, the US never took part in the League of Nations, and the Soviet Union was expelled from the League because of its invasion of Finland in 1939. Although that argument of the defence was rejected by the IMT, it is an important theme that may yet recur when we look at the present debate about the prognostics of the inclusion of aggression as a crime within the jurisdiction of the International Criminal Court. Although the criminalisation of aggression and the eventual judgments at Nuremberg and Tokyo were important historical milestones, the reality of the Cold War had a significant impact on the development of international criminal law, including the doctrine and enforcement mechanisms for the crime of aggression.

CHAPTER IV

THE 'LEGACY OF NUREMBERG': ESTABLISHING INDIVIDUAL CRIMINAL LIABILITY FOR THE CRIME OF AGGRESSION

1. INTRODUCTION

In Chapter III above it was observed that to a certain extent the trials at Nuremberg and Tokyo were remarkable historical events (and, to an important extent, exercises in history writing).[1] It was also noted that these trials represent the concretisation of the *ideal* to end impunity for international crimes. However, as far as individual criminal liability for aggression is concerned, the sometimes awkward jurisprudential positions concerning questions of legality (*nullum crimen, nulla poena sine lege*), the scope and ambit of the concept of aggression, the issue of conspiracy, and other factors impacting on the aggression debate were not definitively solved at Nuremberg and Tokyo. As William Schabas observed:

> '[It] is certainly striking to observe that the uncertainty about the role of aggression within the overall system of international criminal law is not only characteristic of the debate that immediately preceded Nuremberg, but it is also manifested in the approach to the issue in the decades that were to follow the landmark trial. The failure of the United Nations War Crimes Commission to even take a position on whether or not aggressive war should be a crime seems remarkably like the hesitations at the Rome Conference [on the International Criminal Court], more than half a century later.'[2]

1 The trials at Nuremberg and Tokyo involved long narrative presentations by the prosecution that showed the genesis of policies and practices beyond the involvement of the individuals concerned. In that sense the *ad hoc* tribunals were not only fact finders, but also history writers. See for instance the assessment of the work of the Tokyo Tribunal in this regard by AS Comyns Carr (Military Tribunal for the Far East) (*supra*) 146: 'The story as unfolded in the judgment is one of a grandiose plot which originated in the late 1920's in the minds of a few officers and civilians, and grew until it became the dominating purpose, in varying degrees and with occasional variations of emphasis, of every successive government of Japan.'

2 William A Schabas 'Origins of the criminalization of aggression: How crimes against peace became the "supreme international crime"' in Mauro Politi and Giuseppe Nesi (eds) *The International Criminal Court and the Crime of Aggression* (2004) Ashgate, Aldershot, 31.

Indeed, after Nuremberg, Tokyo and the subsequent trials under Control Council Law No 10 in Germany, no serious attempts were made to prosecute individuals for the crime of aggression in the post-Second World War era.[3] The aim of this chapter is to analyse the reasons for this state of affairs. First, the efforts of the United Nations to consolidate and preserve the legal legacy of Nuremberg will be examined. Second, this 'Legacy of Nuremberg' will be analysed *contextually*, with reference to some of the key developments in international criminal law in the post-Second World War period. Finally, some preliminary conclusions regarding the impact of the legacy of Nuremberg on the establishment of the permanent International Criminal Court will be identified.

2. EFFORTS TO CONSOLIDATE THE JURISPRUDENTIAL LEGACY OF NUREMBERG AND TOKYO

2.1. CREATING A NEW INTERNATIONAL LEGAL ORDER: THE UN CHARTER AND THE NUREMBERG PRINCIPLES

The judgment at Nuremberg, and the subsequent judgments at Tokyo and other tribunals, affirmed the criminalisation of aggression and the individual liability attached to this international crime. In order to assess the legal developments post-Nuremberg, it is necessary to briefly contextualise the collective security regime that emerged in the wake of the Second World War, and as identified in Chapters I and II above.

The provisions of the UN Charter on the use of force do not in themselves criminalise aggression, but they do reflect the development of principles that already took shape in the last part of the Second World War and in the immediate post-Second World War era. This must be viewed in light of the general prohibition of the use of force – *jus contra bellum* – that developed after the First World War. But these provisions also reflect a deliberate attempt *away* from the constraints or anomalies of the League of Nations era. Thus, while the Charter of the League of Nations prohibited resort to 'war', the UN Charter prohibits the 'threat or use of force against the territorial integrity or political independence of any state'.[4] While the UN Charter in this respect provides for a more realistic legal regime in the context of the use of force by states,

3 Yoram Dinstein (War Aggression Self-Defence) (*supra*) 121. See further critical comments by Jonathan Bush (The Supreme… Crime) (*supra*); Caroline Fournet (International Crimes) (*supra*) 143.

4 Art 2(4) UN Charter.

the Charter provisions can be criticised when considering the strides made at Nuremberg to criminalise international aggression. The problem seems to lie in the fact that Article 2(4), read with Article 39 of the UN Charter, does not contain a definition or explanation of the elements of aggression. It is essentially left to the political processes at the Security Council where the existence of acts of aggression, threats to peace and breaches of peace are determined.[5] Cherif Bassiouni and Benjamin Ferencz described the problem as follows:

> 'The text of Article 39 left the term "aggression" undefined and gave equal weight to the "threat to the peace, breach of the peace, or act of aggression." It was hoped that Article 2(4) would satisfactorily prohibit a use of force unless it was "consistent with the purposes of the United Nations." Should a "threat to the peace, breach of the peace, or act of aggression" take place, it is left in the hands of the Security Council to determine its existence and what sanctions should be used to end it. When the Charter was drafted, it was felt that (1) no definition of aggression could be established that could cover every possible case and (2) it was best to let the Security Council decide what had happened and what actions to take. Both reasons fall short of their objective.'[6]

While it is true that the UN Charter contains this apparent weakness because of the lack of any *definition* of aggression, one should also be mindful of the historical processes that led to the drafting of the Charter. Regarding aggression, it is clear that the Charter could never be a codification of the law as it was interpreted and developed at Nuremberg and the subsequent trials. The drafting of the Charter was of course a process quite independent from the conferences that preceded the Nuremberg and Tokyo Charters. The judicial processes at Nuremberg and the other post-Second World War trials (all of which were completed after the adoption of the UN Charter in 1945) were furthermore linked to the particular political situation at the end of the war and the dynamics of the peace settlement in Europe and eventually the Far East. The trials can in a certain respect be regarded as 'victor's justice', set in a particular political context.[7]

Having said the above, it is also clear that the international community had the desire to preserve the legacy of Nuremberg, if not in terms of a *permanent* international criminal court than at least suggestive of the desire to create such an institution with jurisdiction to hold individuals accountable for crimes under international law. Thus, the General Assembly of the UN adopted a number of resolutions aimed at consolidating and preserving the principles of individual criminal liability for certain international crimes.[8]

---

5 See discussion of Ch VII UN Charter powers of the SC in Ch I section 4.2 *supra*.

6 M Cherif Bassiouni and Benjamin B Ferencz 'The crime against peace' in Cherif Bassiouni *International Criminal Law* 2nd Vol 1 (1999) Transnational Publishers, New York, 322.

7 See comments on 'victors' justice' by Christine Van den Wyngaert Ch III section 4 *supra*.

8 See Herman von Hebel 'An International Criminal Court – A historical perspective' in Herman von Hebel, Johan Lammers and Jolien Schukking (eds) *Reflections on the*

the International Law Commission (ILC),[9] established in terms of Article 13 of the UN Charter, acted on a request by the General Assembly to 'formulate the principles of international law recognized in the Charter of the Nürnberg Tribunal and in the Judgment of the Tribunal'.[10] The Nuremberg Principles[11] were adopted in 1950, and were, generally speaking, more than just an attempt to preserve the jurisprudential legacy of Nuremberg.[12] In many ways the work of the ILC in this regard served as an impetus to keep many of the ideals of international criminal law alive; most important of which was the ideal of a permanent International Criminal Court with jurisdiction over the core international crimes.[13] Principle VI provides as follows:

> 'The crimes hereinafter set out are punishable as crimes under international law:
> (a) Crimes Against Peace:
> (i) Planning, preparation, initiation or waging of a war of aggression or a war in violation of international treaties, agreements or assurances;
> (ii) Participation in a common plan or conspiracy for the accomplishment of any of the acts mentioned under (i).
> (b) War Crimes: Violations of the laws or customs of war which include, but are not limited to, murder, ill-treatment or deportation to slave labour of for any other purpose of civilian population of or in occupied territory, murder or ill-treatment or prisoners of war, of persons on the seas, killing of hostages, plunder of public or private property, wanton destruction of cities, towns, or villages, or devastation not justified by military necessity.
> (c) Crimes Against Humanity: Murder, extermination, enslavement, deportation and other inhuman acts done against any civilian population, or persecutions on political, racial or religious grounds, when such acts are done or such persecutions are carried on in execution of or in connection with any crime against peace or any war crime.'

The ILC neither analysed nor commented in much detail on the Principles crystallised from the Charter and judgment of the Nuremberg Tribunal. The

---

International Criminal Court – Essays in Honour of Adriaan Bos (1999) TMC Asser Press, The Hague, 22–23.

9 The ILC was established in 1947 in terms of Art 13 of the UN Charter. The first session of the ILC opened on 12 April 1949. For an historical overview of the ILC, see Sir Arthur Watts *The International Law Commission 1949–1998* Vol I (1999) Oxford University Press, Oxford, 1–20.

10 GA Res 177 (II), of 21 Nov 1947. See also Arthur Watts (International Law Commission Vol III) (*supra*) 1657.

11 Nuremberg Principles, Geneva, 19 Jul 1950, UNGAOR, 5th Session, Supp No 12, UN Doc A/1316 (1950), reproduced in Christine van den Wyngaert (International Criminal Law) (*supra*) 375–376.

12 For a discussion of the impact of the Nuremberg Principles in various domestic legal contexts (mainly in American jurisprudence), see Gary Komarow 'Individual responsibility under International law: The Nuremberg Principles in domestic legal systems' 29(1) *ICLQ* (1980) 21–37.

13 Arthur Watts (International Law Commission Vol III) (*supra*) 1658.

ILC confirmed that, as far as the crime of aggression was concerned, the IMT at Nuremberg could not rely on any definition in the Nuremberg Charter, and the IMT also did not provide its own definition of 'aggression' or 'war of aggression'. The ILC noted the following:

> 'It was by reviewing the historical events before and during the war that it [the Nuremberg Tribunal] found that certain of the defendants planned and waged aggressive wars against twelve nations and were therefore guilty of a series of crimes.'[14]

One important clarification that the ILC included in their commentary on the Nuremberg Principles was on the meaning of the words 'waging of a war of aggression'. It was noted that some members of the ILC regarded this to extend criminal liability for 'waging' a war of aggression to all persons (in uniform) who fought in the war in question. However, the ILC interpreted the judgment at Nuremberg to limit responsibility for 'waging' a war of aggression to senior military officers and personnel and senior State officials.[15]

The language of Principle VI(a) affirms (with some measure of clarification) the criminality of international aggression, but does not provide for a definition of aggression. The desirability of an international criminal code and/or court with jurisdiction over aggression was thus clear. To affirm the jurisprudential legacy of Nuremberg was not enough; a clear definition of aggression (which could be applied beyond the political settlement of the Second World War) was needed, together with a tribunal to enforce this aspect of international criminal law. With the formulation of the Nuremberg Principles the ILC completed the first important part of the comprehensive project to preserve the legacy of Nuremberg. The second leg of this important project was to make the principles more concrete and relevant for future generations. A first draft Code of Offences against the Peace and Security of Mankind was finalised in 1954. Following on that, a number of further draft Codes were authored between 1954 and 1996. Sir Arthur Watts noted that one can in this regard distinguish between two phases, namely the draft Codes of the period 1947 to 1954; and the period 1982 to 1996.[16] It is clear, however, that the Nuremberg Principles were the foundational work from which the ILC draft codes cannot be separated.[17]

---

14 Arthur Watts (International Law Commission Vol III) (*supra*) 1665.

15 Arthur Watts (International Law Commission Vol III) (*supra*) 1665.

16 Arthur Watts (International Law Commission Vol III) (*supra*) 1669.

17 See references by Arthur Watts (International Law Commission Vol III) (*supra*) 1669 to the foundational GA Res 177 (II) of 21 Nov 1947, which requested the ILC to identify and formulate the Nuremberg Principles and to write a draft Code of Offences against the Peace and Security of Mankind.

2.2. BUILDING ON THE NUREMBERG PRINCIPLES: THE FURTHER WORK OF THE INTERNATIONAL LAW COMMISSION: SEARCHING FOR A DEFINITION OF AGGRESSION

Bassiouni and Ferencz pointed out that the drafters of the UN Charter did not view it necessary to provide for any definition of aggression, apart from the wording of Article 39.[18] *Aggression* was thus put firmly in the domain of international political processes via the Security Council, and not primarily in the judicial domain as it was done at Nuremberg and the other post-war trials. There were however attempts to define aggression for purposes of criminal responsibility. The most important work in this regard was done by the ILC in the context of its twin tasks of compiling the Nuremberg Principles and writing draft Codes on criminal liability for the most important crimes under international law, including aggression.

It is important to study the development of the various ILC draft Codes. These drafts shed some light on the trends in international legal thinking and are indeed important legal sources. Werle and Jessberger noted that the report of the ILC on the Nuremberg Principles reflect their recognition as customary international law. The important attempts to codify crimes under international law were driving forces to clarify the scope of substantive international criminal law. Various elements of customary international criminal law were also adopted in treaties, for instance the Genocide Convention of 1948.[19]

2.2.1. The Draft Code of Offences against Peace and Security of Mankind (1954)[20]

In 1951 the ILC adopted a draft of the Code of Offences against Peace and Security of Mankind for circulation among governments. They adopted the final text of the draft Code in 1954. One of the problematic aspects of the draft Code related to the *definition* of aggression. In the light of this, the General Assembly decided to task a Special Committee to deal with this particular problem. However, despite the fact that the definition of aggression (or lack of such a definition) remained a problematic aspect, the ILC nevertheless adopted the draft Code which included the crimes covered under 'offences against peace

18 Bassiouni and Ferencz in Bassiouni (International Criminal Law) (*supra*) 322.

19 Gerhard Werle and Florian Jessberger (Principles of International Criminal Law) (*supra*) 13.

20 Draft Code of Offences against the Peace and Security of Mankind (1954), *Yearbook of the ILC*, 1954, 151; UN Doc A/2693 (1954), reproduced in Christine Van den Wyngaert (International Criminal Law) (*supra*) 377–378.

and security', namely 'an act of aggression' and 'any threat of aggression'.[21] The relevant parts[22] of Article 2 of the draft Code provides as follows:

> 'The following acts are offences against the peace and security of mankind:
> 1. Any act of aggression, including the employment by the authorities of a State of armed force against another State for any purpose other than national or collective self-defence or in pursuance of a decision or recommendation of a competent organ of the United Nations.
> 2. Any threat by the authorities of a State to resort to an act of aggression against another State.
> 3. The preparation by the authorities of a State of the employment of armed force against another State for any purpose other than national or collective self-defence or in pursuance of a decision or recommendations of a competent organ of the United Nations.'

The ILC's 1951 comment on the draft Code referred to the fact that the inclusion of crimes against peace in the Code was confirmation of the General Assembly's resolution of 1950,[23] a resolution that reaffirmed that aggression is the gravest of all crimes against peace and security. In addition, the relevant paragraph of the draft Code also took the Charter of the Nuremberg Tribunal into consideration.[24] The 1951 comment further made reference to all the important instruments on the illegality of the use of force (Covenant of the League of Nations, Kellogg-Briand Pact etc) as well as the *jus contra bellum* dispensation in terms of the UN Charter, notably Article 2(4). The comment also referred to the ILC draft Declaration on Rights and Duties of States, which also provided for the prohibition of war as an instrument of national policy.[25] On criminal responsibility for aggression, the comment read as follows: 'The offence defined in this paragraph [Article 2, paragraph 1] can be committed only by the authorities of a State. A criminal responsibility of private individuals under international law may, however, arise under the provisions of paragraph [13] of [this] article.'[26]

From a criminal law perspective the provisions of Article 2 did not in fact address the problem of a suitable definition of aggression. Both the ILC and the Sixth Committee of the UN General Assembly (which deals with legal matters) could not agree on a definition. The disagreement was not confined to the

21 See Arthur Watts (International Law Commission Vol III) (*supra*) 1670.
22 The remaining provisions of Article 2 deal with other forms of intervention, violation of sovereignty, encouragement of civil strife, terrorism, annexation of territory contrary to international law etc. Art 2 also makes provision for the crimes of genocide, crimes against humanity and war crimes.
23 GA Res 380 (V), 17 Nov 1950.
24 Arthur Watts (International Law Commission Vol III) (*supra*) 1677.
25 Arthur Watts (International Law Commission Vol III) (*supra*) 1677.
26 Arthur Watts (International Law Commission Vol III) (*supra*) 1677.

substantive content of aggression. Indeed, the Sixth Committee itself was not capable of agreeing on whether aggression could (or should) be defined at all.[27]

In terms of the collective security system structured by the UN Charter, the task of the maintenance of international peace and security is allocated to the Security Council.[28] One of the main features of this dispensation is the paramount role of the Security Council in determining whether international incidents would qualify as 'acts of aggression'.[29] Thus, during the early 1950s this dispensation caused some political unease in the General Assembly and led the Assembly to further investigate the possibility to define aggression.

The work of the ILC on the draft Code, as well as processes within the General Assembly to establish the content of the crime of aggression, must be viewed against the background of not only the frustration over the lack of a definition of aggression, but also because of the *place* of the crime of aggression within the Security Council-dominated collective security system.[30] Should aggression be treated as primarily a political problem; or a criminal justice problem? This underlying dynamic formed an important impetus for the further quest for a definition of aggression – with important implications for the overall development of international criminal law.

While the ILC's draft Code certainly represented a real effort to 'define' aggression (albeit unsatisfactorily from a criminal law point of view), it is nevertheless important to consider the value of the draft Code's treatment of the subject of aggression contextually. The drafting process exposed the many political and legal dimensions impacting on the quest to define aggression at international level.

2.2.2. The Draft Code of Crimes against the Peace and Security of Mankind (1991)[31]

While the early 1990s were in many respects very hopeful and optimistic times (the fall of the Berlin Wall; the end of the Cold War; democratisation in Eastern Europe; the official end of *apartheid* in South Africa), there were also events

27 Cherif Bassiouni and Benjamin Ferencz 'The Crime against Peace' in Cherif Bassiouni (International Criminal Law Vol I) (*supra*) 323. See further Ian Brownlie (Use of Force) (*supra*) 353–355.

28 See discussion in Ch I above.

29 See Art 39 UN Charter; discussion of Ch VII powers of the SC in Ch I above.

30 See Bassiouni and Ferencz in Cherif Bassiouni (International Criminal Law) (*supra*) 323–324.

31 Draft Code of Crimes against the Peace and Security of Mankind (1991), *Report of the ILC*, 43rd Session, UNGAOR, 46th Session, Supp No 10, A/46/10 (1991), reprinted in Christine Van den Wyngaert (International Criminal Law) (*supra*) 379–385.

that threatened international peace and security. These events challenged the 'New World Order' that was supposed to have emerged after the end of the Cold War. Most vividly, the invasion of Kuwait by Iraq and the subsequent US-led armed response to liberate Kuwait were widely broadcasted by CNN and other media to make this war the first major 'media war'. This conflict was also a major test for the post-Cold War collective security system and the working of the Security Council.[32] The Security Council was indeed able to respond to the invasion in a way unimaginable during the Cold War era. In terms of Resolution 660 of 2 August 1990, the Security Council determined that the invasion was a breach of international peace and security. This determination was followed by a number of Resolutions setting out Security Council action under Chapter VII of the UN Charter, including the important Resolution 678 which served as the basis for an international coalition, led by the USA, to act in collective self-defence and to liberate Kuwait.[33]

The international political response to the violation of peace and security by Iraq was accompanied by calls for the creation of an international criminal tribunal to try senior Iraqi officials – including the Iraqi leader Saddam Hussein – for crimes under international law. The international community, while willing to co-operate to end the conflict, was not enthusiastic about the creation of an international criminal tribunal. However, as a consequence, the work of the ILC on international crimes, including the crime of aggression, gained renewed attention. After the issue was dormant for many years, the question of the definition of aggression received new prominence with the adoption of the 1991 draft Code of Crimes against Peace and Security of Mankind.[34]

Article 15 (Aggression) provides as follows:

> '1. An individual who as leader or organizer plans, commits or orders the commission of an act of aggression shall, on conviction thereof, be sentenced (to...).
> 2. Aggression is the use of armed force by a State against the sovereignty, territorial integrity or political independence of another State, or in any other manner inconsistent with the Charter of the United Nations.
> 3. The first use of armed force by a State in contravention of the Charter shall constitute *prima facie* evidence of an act of aggression, although the Security

32 For a brief description of the events that led to the (First) Gulf War in 1990–1991 and the role of the UN SC, see Stephen Ambrose (Rise to Globalism) (*supra*). For a legal analysis of the SC action in the wake of the invasion of Kuwait in 1990, see Arthur Mark Weisburd in Enzo Cannizzaro and Paolo Palchetti *Customary International Law on the Use of Force – A Methodological Approach* (2005) Martinus Nijhoff Publishers, Leiden, 51–53.

33 See in general Yoram Dinstein (War Aggression and Self-defence) (*supra*) 294–296.

34 Lyal Sunga (Emerging system) (*supra*) 10–11.

Council may, in conformity with the Charter, conclude that a determination that an act of aggression has been committed would not be justified in the light of other relevant circumstances, including the fact that the acts concerned or their consequences are not of sufficient gravity.

4. Any of the following acts, regardless of a declaration of war, constitutes an act of aggression, due regard being paid to paragraphs 2 and 3:
   (a) the invasion or attack by the armed forces of a State of the territory of another State, or any military occupation, however temporary, resulting from such invasion or attack, or any annexation by the use of force of the territory of another State or part thereof;
   (b) bombardment by the armed forces of a State against the territory of another State or the use of any weapons by a State against the territory of another State;
   (c) the blockade of the ports or coasts of a State by the armed forces of another State;
   (d) an attack by the armed forces of a State on the land, sea or air forces, or marine and air fleets of another State;
   (e) the use of armed forces of one State which are within the territory of another State with the agreement of the receiving State, in contravention of the conditions provided for in the agreement, or any extension of their presence in such territory beyond the termination of the agreement;
   (f) the action of a State in allowing its territory, which it has placed at the disposal of another State, to be used by that other State for perpetrating an act of aggression against a third State;
   (g) the sending by or on behalf of a State or armed bands, groups, irregulars or mercenaries, which carry out acts or armed force against another State of such gravity as to amount to the acts listed above, or its substantial involvement therein;
   (h) any other acts determined by the Security Council as constituting acts of aggression under the provisions of the Charter;
5. Any determination by the Security Council as to the existence of an act of aggression is binding on national courts.
6. Nothing in this article shall be interpreted as in any way enlarging or diminishing the scope of the Charter of the United Nations including its provisions concerning cases in which the use of force is lawful.
7. Nothing in this article could in any way prejudice the right to self-determination, freedom and independence, as derived from the Charter, of peoples forcibly deprived of that right and referred to in the Declaration on Principles of International Law concerning Friendly Relations and Co-operation among States in accordance with the Charter of the United Nations, particularly peoples under colonial and racist regimes or other forms of alien domination; nor the right of these peoples to struggle to that end and to seek and receive support, in accordance with the principles of the Charter and in conformity with the above-mentioned Declaration.'

Article 16 (Threat of aggression) provides as follows:

> '1. An individual who as leader or organizer commits or orders the commission of a threat of aggression shall, on conviction thereof, be sentenced (to…).
> 2. Threat of aggression consists of declarations, communications, demonstrations of force or any other measures which would give good reason to the Government of a State to believe that aggression is being seriously contemplated against that State.'

It is clear from the text of the 1991 draft Code that the ILC intended the proposed substantive provisions to be much broader in scope than the 1954 draft Code. The crimes provided for in the 1991 draft Code was intended by the ILC to form the competence *ratione materiae* of a future international criminal court.[35] At the time, the creation of what would become the first permanent international criminal court – the ICC in terms of the Rome Statute, 1998 – was still politically and legally unlikely. Nevertheless, some commentators viewed the draft Code as a possible set of guidelines for the prosecution of international crimes at national level. The formulation of some of the crimes or categories of crimes in the draft Code came in for strong criticism, especially from criminal and constitutional lawyers. John Murphy, one such commentator, identified a number of problematic aspects relating to the structure and formulation of the offences contained in the draft Code.[36] It has to be said that he analysed and criticised the various provisions, including the provisions on aggression, from a US constitutional and criminal law perspective. However, it is submitted that these criticisms were noteworthy at the time and are still relevant from an international criminal law point of view, since the system of international criminal law still relies (even after the coming into operation of the ICC) to a large extent on national courts to apply the norms of international criminal law, and, obviously, to co-operate with international criminal tribunals and mutually between states.[37]

Murphy raised the general objection that the provisions on aggression (Articles 15 and 16) were 'simply unacceptable', because they were too vague and were essentially designed to serve 'various political agendas'.[38] The Draft Code could serve a useful purpose in guiding the Security Council with its determination of 'acts of aggression', but not as a definition of a crime in a court of law. Murphy pointed to US case law that held that 'a criminal statute is void (as a constitutional

---

35 Lyal Sunga (*supra*) 11.

36 John F Murphy, 'Commentaries on the Draft Code of Crimes, 11 *Nouvelles Études Pénales* 209 (1993) (excerpts reprinted in Bassiouni (International Criminal Law Vol I) (*supra*) 338–340).

37 See Gerhard Erasmus and Gerhard Kemp 'The application of international criminal law before domestic courts in the light of recent developments in international and constitutional law' 27 *SAYIL* (2002) 64.

38 Murphy in Cherif Bassiouni (International Criminal Law Vol I) (*supra*) 338.

law matter) when it is so vague and imprecise that "men of common intelligence must guess its meaning and differ as to its application".'[39] Murphy referred to the fact that words like 'use of armed force by a State against the sovereignty, territorial integrity or political independence of another State, or in any manner inconsistent with the Charter of the United Nations' (Article 15(2)), are 'imprecise' and 'subject to too many varying interpretations'.[40]

These concerns from a national constitutional and criminal law perspective could equally have been made from an international criminal law perspective, where the legality principle (*nullum crimen, nulla poena sine lege*) is also protected. The principle of legality at international level is today protected in terms of treaty and customary international law.[41] It is submitted that from a national criminal law perspective, many of the criticisms against the formulation of Articles 15 and 16 of the draft Code could equally be informed by the principle of legality as protected in international criminal law.[42] Furthermore, the way in which the draft Code extended the notions of aggression and threat of aggression, seems to be unrealistic. It is clear that the notion of aggression in the draft Code was almost identical to that of the UN General Assembly Consensus Definition of Aggression (1974),[43] which was drafted with state liability (not individual criminal liability) in mind.[44]

2.2.3. *The Draft Code of Crimes against the Peace and Security of Mankind (1996)*[45]

The provision on aggression contained in the 1996 draft Code is much shorter than the 1991 draft and is basically a restatement of the interpretation and application of aggression by the Nuremberg Tribunal. Article 16 (Crime of aggression) provides as follows:

> 'An individual who, as leader or organizer, actively participates in or orders the planning, preparation, initiation or waging of aggression committed by a State shall be responsible for a crime of aggression.'

---

39 Reference to *Coronally v General Construction Company*, 296 US 385, 391 (1926); Murphy in Cherif Bassiouni (International Criminal Law Vol I) (*supra*) 339.

40 Murphy in Cherif Bassiouni (International Criminal Law Vol I) (*supra*) 339.

41 Hans-Heinrich Jescheck 'The general principles of International Criminal Law set out in Nuremberg, as mirrored in the ICC Statute' 2 *JICJ* (2004) 38–55.

42 See also Introduction section 1.3 *supra*.

43 See discussion in section 2.3 *et seq infra*.

44 See comments by Timothy McCormack and Gerry Simpson 'The International Law Commission's Draft Code of Crimes against the Peace and Security of Mankind: An appraisal of the substantive provisions' 5(1) *Criminal Law Forum* (1994) 1–55.

45 Draft Code of Crimes against the Peace and Security of Mankind, 5 Jul 1996, *Yearbook of the ILC* 1996 vol II (2), www.un.org/law/ilc/texts/dcodefra.htm. Reprinted in Christine Van den Wyngaert (International Criminal Law) (*supra*) 387–392.

Although the formulation of Article 16 was clearly not intended to shed any new light on the definition of aggression, the ILC was intent on confirming and emphasising individual criminal liability for the crime of aggression. In their commentary on Article 16 the ILC stated as follows:

> 'The phrase "An individual ... shall be responsible for a crime of aggression" is used to indicate that the scope of the present article is limited to the crime of aggression for the purpose of individual criminal responsibility. Thus, the present article does not address the question of the definition of aggression by a State which is beyond the scope of the present Code.'[46]

Bassiouni and Ferencz observed that the work of the ILC on the definition of aggression involved a process of 'gradual deletion'. Article 16 in the 1996 draft Code was a total replacement of the deleted (and much longer) definition of aggression contained in the 1991 draft Code. Thus, the 1996 provision on aggression contained no list of the elements of aggression – only the confirmation that individuals can be held liable for the crime of aggression.[47] It seems that the role of the Security Council as a *sine qua non* for determining the existence of an act of aggression loomed so large that it was politically and legally not possible (or desirable) to define aggression in the draft Code. After all the attempts to define aggression (with elements clear enough for purposes of criminal liability and in accordance with the internationally recognised principle of *nullum crimen, nulla poena sine lege*), the 1996 draft Code was a giant step backwards. The commentary of the ILC on Article 16 of the 1996 draft Code confirmed that '[the] Charter [of the UN] and Judgement of the Nürnberg Tribunal are the main sources of authority with regard to individual criminal responsibility for acts of aggression.' According to this comment, any court that would want to determine criminal responsibility of an individual for the crime of aggression, would have to determine whether the State in question violated the prohibition of the use of force in Article 2(4) of the UN Charter, and further, 'whether such conduct [constituted] a sufficiently serious violation of an international obligation'.[48]

---

46 Arthur Watts (The International Law Commission Vol III) (*supra*) 1738.

47 Bassiouni and Ferencz in Cherif Bassiouni (International Criminal Law Vol I) (*supra*) 342.

48 Arthur Watts (The International Law Commission Vol III) (*supra*) 1739. See further comments by Lyal Sunga (Emerging system) (*supra*) 13–14. On the deletions and 'slimming down' of the 1996 draft Code (compared to the much broader and more detailed 1991 draft Code) Sunga concluded as follows: 'A more restrictive and precise international criminal code would promote greater objectivity, fairness and predictability in implementation, which in turn, could enhance prospects for the emergence of an effective system of international criminal law. On the other hand, an overly narrow or restrictive material coverage could put international criminal law into a normative straitjacket, thereby reducing its flexibility and responsiveness to new challenges arising from crime in the perennially turbulent international panorama.' Sunga (*supra*) 14–15. See also comments by Yoram Dinstein (War Aggression and Self-Defence) (*supra*) 124–125.

2.3. THE UN GENERAL ASSEMBLY 'CONSENSUS DEFINITION' OF AGGRESSION (1974)

2.3.1. *The Definition in perspective*

In the decades that followed the establishment of the United Nations, and while the various efforts of the International Law Commission to define aggression (and to draft the legal framework for an international criminal court) were ongoing, international claims of 'aggression' were manifold.[49] As Bassiouni and Ferencz put it, '[it] was easier to commit aggression than to define it.'[50]

Bassiouni and Ferencz submitted that the compromises that were reached in the UN Special Committee that dealt with the question of a definition for aggression, was in part made possible by the 'spirit of détente' that was prevalent in international politics at the end of the Vietnam war in the early 1970s.[51] The 'spirit of détente' did not, of course, replace the divisions that characterised Cold War international relations,[52] but merely made it possible to reach certain key agreements at the UN. A close scrutiny of the text of the 'Consensus Definition of Aggression' reveals the political divisions of the time. Nevertheless, after much debate the Sixth (Legal Affairs) Committee of the General Assembly was able to accept (in substance) the proposed text of the Special Committee. The slightly amended text was adopted by the General Assembly as Resolution 3314 (XXIX) on 14 December 1974. This Resolution is not legally binding, but is nevertheless quite a significant text in terms of the development of the crime of aggression under international law.[53] Indeed, this resolution found its way into the text of the Kampala Resolution on the Crime of Aggression (2010), which is discussed in Chapter VII. Aspects of the 1974 Resolution also informed the definition of aggression contained in the Malabo Protocol on the 'African Criminal Court', discussed in Chapter VIII.

---

49 For instance: The invasion of Hungary by the Red Army of the Soviet Union, various military interventions in Latin America, and perhaps the most notorious conflict of the post-Second World War era – the conflict in Vietnam. For an 'insider's perspective' on many of these conflicts (especially the Vietnam conflict), see Henry Kissinger (Diplomacy) (*supra*). See further Stephen Ambrose (Rise to Globalism) (*supra*) 224–253 for a discussion of the foreign policy of US Pres Nixon and the impact of détente.

50 Bassiouni and Ferencz in Cherif Bassiouni (International Criminal Law Vol I) (*supra*) 327.

51 Bassiouni and Ferencz in Cherif Bassiouni (International Criminal Law Vol I) (*supra*) 327.

52 For a critical assessment of the geopolitical realities of the era of détente after the Vietnam conflict, see Henry Kissinger (Diplomacy) (*supra*) 733–761.

53 See Cherif Bassiouni *International Criminal Law Conventions and their Penal Provisions* (1997) Transnational Publishers, New York, 227.

The substantive provisions of the UN General Assembly 'Consensus Definition of Aggression'[54] provides as follows:

'Article 1
Aggression is the use of armed force by a State against the sovereignty, territorial integrity or political independence of another State, or in any other manner inconsistent with the Charter of the United Nations, as set out in this Definition.
Explanatory note: In this Definition the term "State":
(a) Is used without prejudice to questions of recognition or to whether a State is a member of the United Nations;
(b) Includes the concept of a "group of States" where appropriate.

Article 2
The first use of armed force by a State in contravention of the Charter shall constitute prima facie evidence of an act of aggression although the Security Council may, in conformity with the Charter, conclude that a determination that an act of aggression has been committed would not be justified in the light of other relevant circumstances, including the fact that the acts concerned or their consequences are not of sufficient gravity.

Article 3
Any of the following acts, regardless of a declaration of war, shall, subject to and in accordance with the provisions of article 2, qualify as an act of aggression:
(a) The invasion or attack by the armed forces of a State of the territory of another State, or any military occupation, however temporary, resulting from such invasion or attack, or any annexation by the use of force of the territory of another State or part thereof;
(b) Bombardment by the armed forces of a State against the territory of another State or the use of any weapons by a State against the territory of another State;
(c) The blockade of the ports or coasts of a State by the armed forces of another State;
(d) An attack by the armed forces of a State on the land, sea or air forces, or marine and air fleets of another State;
(e) The use of armed forces of one State which are within the territory of another State with the agreement of the receiving State, in contravention of the conditions provided for in the agreement or any extension of their presence in such territory beyond the termination of the agreement;
(f) The action of a State in allowing its territory, which it has placed at the disposal of another State, to be used by that other State for perpetrating an act of aggression against a third State;
(g) The sending by or on behalf of a State of armed bands, groups, irregulars or mercenaries, which carry out acts or armed force against another State of such

---

54 UN Res No 3314 (XXIX). Definition of Aggression (1974) GA Res of 14 Dec 1974, www.un.org/documents/ga/res/29/ares29.htm, reprinted in Christine Van den Wyngaert (International Criminal Law) (*supra*) 397–398; (1974) 13 *ILM* 710.

gravity as to amount to the acts listed above, or its substantial involvement therein.

Article 4
The acts enumerated above are not exhaustive and the Security Council may determine that other acts constitute aggression under the provisions of the Charter.

Article 5
1. No consideration of whatever nature, whether political, economic, military or otherwise, may serve as a justification for aggression.
2. A war of aggression is a crime against international peace. Aggression gives rise to international responsibility.
3. No territorial acquisition or special advantage resulting from aggression is or shall be recognized as lawful.

Article 6
Nothing in this Definition shall be construed as in any way enlarging or diminishing the scope of the Charter, including its provisions concerning cases in which the use of force is lawful.

Article 7
Nothing in this Definition, and in particular article 3, could in any way prejudice the right to self-determination, freedom and independence, as derived from the Charter, of peoples forcibly deprived of that right and referred to in the Declaration on Principles of International Law concerning Friendly Relations and Cooperation among States in accordance with the Charter of the United Nations, particularly peoples under colonial and racist regimes or other forms of alien domination: nor the right of these peoples to struggle to that end and to seek and receive support, in accordance with the principles of the Charter and in conformity with the above-mentioned Declaration.

Article 8
In their interpretation and application the above provisions are interrelated and each provision should be construed in the context of the other provisions.'

While the political *context* in which the consensus Definition of Aggression of 1974 was agreed on was clearly one of hope in a time of reduced international tension (the period of détente), the Definition itself was the subject of some strong criticism from legal scholars and commentators. Rhetoric about the virtues of this new Definition sprung forth to underline an achievement that was perhaps more of a testament to the politics of détente than clear legal drafting. Julius Stone, one of the Definition's strongest critics, put the central critique as follows: '[That] remarkable text rather appears to have codified into itself (and in some respects extended) all the main "juridical loopholes and pre-texts to unleash aggression" available under preexisting international law, as modified by the UN Charter.'[55]

Generally speaking, the Definition is quite useful as an indication of the international community's understanding of the *notion* of aggression, but less so from a purely legal (and certainly international criminal law) perspective.[56] It is perhaps appropriate to describe the value of the Definition – on its own – as a guide for the Security Council more than a legal definition for judicial interpretation.[57] Its value as part of the definition of the crime of aggression that was adopted at the Kampala Review Conference is considered in Chapter VII. As was noted above, the different acts of aggression listed in the 1974 Definition also informed the second part of the definition of aggression provided for in the Malabo Protocol. For now, the focus is on the 1974 Definition in its proper context and with reference to its own terms.

There seems to be many compromises in the text of the 1974 Definition that were the result of attempts to cover the deep-seated political and doctrinal divisions within the international community. Even more than that, the Definition also reflects the structural aspects of the UN-dominated collective security system that informed the process of finding an acceptable (and workable) definition of aggression. To an important extent the 1974 Definition exposed the inherent weaknesses caused by the powerful role of the Security Council in matters that affect the aggression-debate.

Article 1 of the Definition lists the basic protected interests of the generic notion of aggression. Bassiouni and Ferencz have pointed out that Article 1 has Article 2(4) of the UN Charter as its foundation. However there are some important differences in content and structure between the two texts.[58] While both the UN Charter and some of the Nuremberg judgments include 'threat of force' as part of the notion of aggression, the Definition does not include it as such.[59] An interesting addition to the notion of aggression is the reference

55 Julius Stone 'Hopes and loopholes in the 1974 Definition of Aggression' 71 *AJIL* (1977) 224.

56 See Justin Hogan-Doran and Bibi T van Ginkel 'Aggression as a crime under international law and the prosecution of individuals by the proposed International Criminal Court' *NILR* (1996) 321–351, 336.

57 Caroline Fournet (International Crimes) (*supra*) 160.

58 Bassiouni and Ferencz in Cherif Bassiouni (International Criminal Law Vol I) (*supra*) 329.

59 See reference to *The Ministries Case*, Military Tribunal IV, Case 11, *The United States of America against Weizsaeker et al*, Vol XII, XIII, Trials of War Criminals, Nuremberg Military Tribunals, Bassiouni and Ferencz in Cherif Bassiouni (International Criminal Law Vol I) (*supra*) 329. Defendants Wilhelm Keppler and Hans Heinrich Lammers were convicted on charges of crimes against peace, but the convictions of the other defendants – Ernst von Weizsaeker and Ernst Wörmann – were overturned on appeal. See further Gerhard Werle and Florian Jessberger (Principles of International Criminal Law) (*supra*) 535.

to 'sovereignty' in Article 1 of the Definition. Bassiouni and Ferencz found this to undermine at least some aspects of the prohibition of the use of force-dispensation:

> 'The ... reference to "sovereignty" in the definition seems to strengthen a concept that runs counter to the notion of the interdependence of states and the need for nations to yield some of their prerogatives if there is to be any effective control over the use of armed force.'[60]

The Definition was, on balance, not a very successful attempt to define aggression form an international criminal law perspective. However, it did help the Security Council on a number of occasions to make findings that certain state conduct amounted to 'aggression'.[61] In this respect one can say that the Definition helped to concretise the notion of aggression that is not defined as such in the UN Charter. And, of course, it ultimately forms an important part of Article 8*bis* (Crime of aggression) that was adopted at the Kampala Review Conference of the Rome Statute of the International Criminal Court, as well as Article 28M of the Malabo Protocol.

2.3.2. *Some observations on the usefulness of the Definition from an international criminal law perspective: Elements of criminal liability*

The notion of individual criminal responsibility is one of the key principles of modern international criminal law. In essence this entails that individuals are criminally liable for unlawful conduct (*actus reus*), provided that a mental element (*mens rea*) can in some way be 'directed to or linked with the commission of the crime'.[62]

2.3.2.1. *Actus reus*

The language and structure of the 1974 Definition reflects the two basic approaches to aggression that were advanced during the debates preceding the adoption of the consensus Definition. While Article 1 contains a more general approach to aggression (based on the language of Article 2(4) of the UN Charter), Article 3 (read with Article 2) contains a non-exhaustive list of acts that would typically constitute aggression (such as military invasion and occupation of territory). The fact that the Definition contains elements of both the general definition and enumerative approaches is yet another indication of not only the

60 Bassiouni and Ferencz in Cherif Bassiouni (International Criminal Law Vol I) (*supra*) 329.

61 For instance, the SC employed the 1974 Def in its finding that South Africa has committed 'acts of aggression' against Angola in the 1970s war. See SC Res 387 (1976) 31 March 1976. See further Hogan-Doran and Van Ginkel (*supra*) 334.

62 Antonio Cassese (International Criminal Law) (*supra*) 159.

political but also doctrinal compromises that were made to reach a Consensus Definition.[63]

2.3.2.2. *Mens rea*

The 1974 Definition of Aggression, which focuses on *state*-liability and not individual criminal liability, naturally does not provide for the element of *mens rea*. However, this means that the Definition as such cannot serve as a basis for individual criminal liability for the crime of aggression. In this regard the Definition does not move beyond the UN Charter dispensation where it is left to the Security Council to determine whether acts of aggression occurred.[64] There is therefore no specific mention of what would constitute the subjective mental element(s) necessary to prove criminal liability for aggression.[65]

Yoram Dinstein pointed out that, given the seriousness of aggression as an international crime, a special kind of subjective element (sometimes referred to as *animus aggressionis*) developed around the concept of crimes against peace.[66] The need for *actus reus* to be accompanied by *mens rea* was also confirmed by the Nuremberg Tribunal and subsequent trials of senior Nazis by the various Control Council-proceedings.[67] Kriangsak Kittichaisaree stated that the *mens rea*-element of aggression involves *intent* plus *knowledge*. In this regard, he quoted the following passage from the *High Command* case,[68] where the US Military Tribunal held that individuals accused of the crime of aggression must have

> 'actual knowledge that an aggressive war is being intended and that if launched it will be an aggressive war. It requires in addition that the possessor of such knowledge, after he acquires it shall be in a position to shape or influence the policy that brings about its initiation or its continuance after its initiation, either by furthering, or by hindering or preventing it. If he then does the former, he becomes criminally responsible; if he does the latter to the extent of his ability, then his action shows the lack of criminal intent with respect to such policy…'[69]

Dinstein summarised the *mens rea* requirement as follows:

> 'The intent to undertake war of aggression may be formed by only one or few individuals at the helm of a State. Others at the policy-making level need not be

---

63 Hogan-Doran and Van Ginkel (*supra*) 335.
64 See Stone (Hopes and Loopholes) (*supra*) 228.
65 See Hogan-Doran and Van Ginkel (*supra*) 336–337.
66 Yoram Dinstein (War Aggression and Self-Defence) (*supra*) 136.
67 See references and discussion by Yoram Dinstein (War Aggression and Self-Defence) (*supra*) 137.
68 *Wilhelm von Leeb and Others*, US Military Tribunal at Nuremberg, 28 Oct 1948, as quoted in Kittichaisaree (International Criminal Law) (*supra*) 221.
69 *Ibid.*

> personally guided by the same intent. The acid test is whether, in assisting the preparations for war, they actually know of the aggressive schemes. If they know that aggression is planned, this may suffice to establish the requisite mens rea. The obverse side of the coin is that when a person (who actively participates in honing the military machinery) does not possess personal knowledge as to aggressive plans, he cannot be convicted of crimes against peace.'[70]

The 1974 Definition constituted an important development towards a legal framework that built on the legacy of Nuremberg, while also providing for evolving state acts (short of aggressive war) that would be regarded as acts of aggression.

3. CONCLUDING REMARKS: ATTEMPTS TO DEFINE AGGRESSION IN THE LIGHT OF THE NUREMBERG LEGACY

There are different schools of thought on the desirability to define aggression. Julius Stone, one of the prominent exponents of the 'sceptical school' supported the criticism that a definition would provide a 'trap for the innocent and a signpost for the guilty'.[71] This school of thought opposed attempts to define aggression, regardless of whether a 'general definition' approach or 'enumerative' approach was taken. These sceptical voices were also informed by a desire not to restrict the functions of international bodies (notably the Security Council) in determining or identifying the occurrence of aggression.[72]

---

70 Dinstein (War Aggression and Self-Defence) (*supra*) 137. For a discussion of the element of *mens rea* in international criminal law, see Antonio Cassese (International Criminal Law) (*supra*) 159–178.

71 Julius Stone (1958) as quoted in Ian Brownlie (Use of Force) (*supra*) 355. Echoes of this scepticism can also be found in the debate about US opposition to the ICC, particularly in the context of the process of drafting a definition for the crime of aggression for purposes of ICC jurisdiction. For some of these arguments, see William Nash 'The ICC and the Deployment of US Armed Forces' in Sarah Sewall and Carl Kaysen *The United States and the International Criminal Court* (2000) Rowman & Littlefield Publishers, Lanham, Maryland, 153–164. The controversial nature of the crime of aggression, and the debate about a suitable definition, resulted in the compromise provision of Art 5(d) of the Rome Statute of the ICC, which lists aggression as one of the crimes within the jurisdiction of the ICC, but further provides that the ICC can only exercise jurisdiction over the crime after adoption of an acceptable definition. This aspiration came to pass with the adoption of art 8*bis* (crime of aggression) of the Rome Statute. See also Theodor Meron 'Crimes under the jurisdiction of the International Criminal Court' in Herman von Hebel, Johan Lammers and Jolien Schukking (eds) *Reflections on the International Criminal Court – Essays in Honour of Adriaan Bos* (1999) TMC Asser Press, The Hague, 47–48.

72 See Brownlie (International Law and the Use of Force) (*supra*) 355.

Ian Brownlie, a proponent of attempts to define aggression, stated the following about the requirements for a definition of aggression:

> 'Definition must involve generalization and employ elements which require further definition. It may also be said that no definition is "automatic", since the organ concerned must necessarily apply any criteria to particular facts. Particularly dubious is the argument that a criminal may take advantage of a precise definition; one might assume instead that he would welcome the absence of a definition.'[73]

Apart from the general comments on the desirability (and indeed *possibility*) to define aggression, Brownlie further argued that the international legal conditions were in place to define aggression, since 'states generally have accepted obligations relating to the use of force expressed in various forms of words, 'aggression' or its variants being merely one of these forms.'[74]

The real problem, according to Brownlie, was that since the Nuremberg trials and the creation of the new UN-dominated collective security system, 'the quest for a definition of aggression' became a 'vast law-making project with many facets'.[75] From being originally a military concept, it became much more of a legal concept after the First World War.[76] While the IMT at Nuremberg (and certainly the subsequent proceedings) interpreted and applied aggression rather narrowly, the attempts to define aggression in the post-Second World War era drew a number of state policies that might have an impact on the interests of other states[77] – thus making the 'law-making project' much more comprehensive, but less focused and certainly, in the end, less successful.[78] The concept of aggression was no longer limited to the use of armed force, but concepts like 'economic aggression'[79] and 'indirect aggression' (states acting vicariously)[80] were also entertained and played a role in the different drafting processes and debates on a suitable definition for aggression.

---

73 Ian Brownlie (Use of Force) (*supra*) 356.
74 Ian Brownlie (Use of Force) (*supra*) 356.
75 Ian Brownlie (Use of Force) (*supra*) 356.
76 Ian Brownlie (Use of Force) (*supra*) 356. See also discussion of the various post-First World War instruments in Ch II *supra*.
77 Ian Brownlie (Use of Force) (*supra*) 356.
78 See critical assessment of the various ILC Draft Codes of Crimes against Peace and Security of Mankind in sections 2.2.1–2.2.3 *supra*.
79 See also discussion by Julius Stone (Hopes and Loopholes) (*supra*) 230–231.
80 See further Julius Stone (Hopes and Loopholes) (*supra*) 237–239, for a discussion of 'Aggression and attack by armed bands and volunteers'.

PART IV

THE INTERNATIONAL CRIMINAL COURT AND THE CRIME OF AGGRESSION

CHAPTER V
THE INCLUSION OF AGGRESSION IN THE ROME STATUTE OF THE INTERNATIONAL CRIMINAL COURT

1. INTRODUCTION: THE INTERNATIONAL CRIMINAL COURT

The aim of this chapter is twofold. First, the process that led to the adoption of the Rome Statute of the ICC is described. Particular attention is given to the (unsuccessful) process to define aggression and the difficult task to draft a suitable definition in conformity with Articles 5(2), 121[1] and 123[2] of the

1 Art 121 provides as follows: '1. After the expiry of seven years from the entry into force of this Statute, any State Party may propose amendments thereto. The text of any proposed amendment shall be submitted to the Secretary-General of the United Nations, who shall promptly circulate it to all States Parties. 2. No sooner than three months from the date of notification, the Assembly of States Parties, at its next meeting, shall, by a majority of those present and voting, decide whether to take up the proposal. The Assembly may deal with the proposal directly or convene a Review Conference if the issue involved so warrants. 3. The adoption of an amendment at a meeting of the Assembly of States Parties or at a Review Conference on which concensus cannot be reached shall require a two-thirds majority of States Parties. 4. Except as provided in paragraph 5, an amendment shall enter into force for all States Parties one year after instruments of ratification or acceptance have been deposited with the Secretary-General of the United Nations by seven-eighths of them. 5. Any amendment to articles 5, 6, 7 and 8 of this Statute shall enter into force for those States Parties which have accepted the amendment one year after the deposit of their instruments of ratification or acceptance. In respect of a State Party which has not accepted the amendment, the Court shall not exercise its jurisdiction regarding a crime covered by the amendment when committed by that State Party's nationals or on its territory. 6. If an amendment has been accepted by seven-eighths of States Parties in accordance with paragraph 4, any State Party which has not accepted the amendment may withdraw from this Statute with immediate effect, notwithstanding article 127, paragraph 1, but subject to article 127, paragraph 2, by giving notice no later than one year after the entry into force of such amendment. 7. The Secretary-General of the United Nations shall circulate to all States Parties any amendment adopted at a meeting of the Assembly of States Parties or at a Review Conference.'

2 Art 123 provides: '1. Seven years after the entry into force of this Statute the Secretary-General of the United Nations shall convene a Review Conference to consider any amendments to this Statute. Such review may include, but is not limited to, the list of crimes contained in article 5. The Conference shall be open to those participating in the Assembly of States Parties and on the same conditions. 2. At any time thereafter, at the request of a State Party and for the purposes set out in paragraph 1, the Secretary-General of the United Nations shall, upon approval by a majority of States Parties, convene a Review Conference. 3. The provisions

Rome Statute of the ICC. Second, the process to define aggression is discussed contextually with reference to the relationship between the Security Council of the UN and the ICC. This contextual background serves as an introduction to Chapter VI, where the various definitional options for the crime of aggression will be critically analysed.

In Chapter VIII a number of factors relevant to the application of international criminal law at the national and regional levels are identified. It is pointed out that these concerns pose particular problems for prosecuting individuals in national and regional courts for the crime of aggression. It is concluded that, although the notion of universal jurisdiction and the possibility of so-called 'direct application of international criminal law' are today important features of the developing system of international criminal law, the peculiar nature of the crime of aggression leaves little scope for the prosecution of individuals in national courts for this crime. Regional courts may be better options, but there are significant limitations as well, as is pointed out in Chapter VIII.

Aggression is arguably the international crime *par excellence*.[3] It is therefore ironic that the first permanent International Criminal Court (ICC) is, more than a decade after the entry into force of the Rome Statute, still not in a position to hear cases of aggression. This may change soon after 2017, as will be explained in subsequent chapters. Indeed, the adoption at the Kampala Review Conference in 2010 of a definition of aggression as well as conditions for the exercise of ICC jurisdiction over the crime is a significant development.

The historic *first permanent* ICC has jurisdiction over the most serious crimes under international law – genocide, crimes against humanity, war crimes and aggression.[4]

Article 5 of the Rome Statute provides that aggression is a crime within the jurisdiction of the Court, but the Court will only have *effective* jurisdiction once a definition of aggression and conditions for the exercise of jurisdiction are agreed on by the Assembly of States Parties. The article provides as follows:

> '1. The jurisdiction of the Court shall be limited to the most serious crimes of concern to the international community as a whole. The Court has jurisdiction in accordance with this Statute with respect to the following crimes:

---

of article 121, paragraphs 3 to 7, shall apply to the adoption and entry into force of any amendment to the Statute considered at a Review Conference.'

3 Compare statement by the IMT Nuremberg that aggression is the 'supreme international crime'. See Ch III section 3.3 *supra*.

4 For an overview of the Rome Statute of the ICC, see Adreas O'Shea 'The Statute of the International Criminal Court' 116 *SALJ* (1999) 243–261. The Rome Statute of the ICC came into force on 1 Jul 2002.

(a) The crime of genocide;
(b) Crimes against humanity;
(c) War crimes;
(d) The crime of aggression.

2. The Court shall exercise jurisdiction over the crime of aggression once a provision is adopted in accordance with articles 121 and 123 defining the crime and setting out the conditions under which the Court shall exercise jurisdiction with respect to this crime. Such a provision shall be consistent with the relevant provisions of the United Nations.'[5]

In terms of the Amendments to the Rome Statute of the ICC on the Crime of Aggression, adopted by the Assembly of States Parties Review Conference at Kampala in 2010, article 5(2) of the Rome Statute is deleted.[6]

Three important underlying themes that have recurred in the many debates and proposals on the crime of aggression are the principle of complementarity, the concern of many states that the ICC will be abused for political reasons, and the role of the ICC vis-à-vis the United Nations in terms of international peace and security. The sometimes very technical discussions on a suitable definition for aggression must be seen in the context of the following important issues concerning the functioning of the ICC.

1.1. THE IMPORTANCE OF THE PRINCIPLE OF COMPLEMENTARITY

One of the outstanding features of the Rome Statute of the ICC is the *principle of complementarity*.[7] This means that national courts, provided that they have jurisdiction, will have the first option to exercise jurisdiction over a matter that would also fall within the jurisdiction of the ICC. Only if a state is unwilling or unable genuinely to investigate or prosecute a matter will the ICC be able to

5 Rome Statute of the International Criminal Court (1998), UN Doc.A/CONF.183/9, *ILM*, 1998, 999; reprinted in Christine Van den Wyngaert (International Criminal Law) (*supra*) 187.

6 For the text of the Amendments, see Resolution RC/Res. 6, Adopted by the 13th plenary meeting of the Assembly of States Parties on 11 June 2010, Annex I (reproduced in Annex I *infra*).

7 See, in general, William Burke-White 'Proactive complementarity: The International Criminal Court and national courts in the Rome system of international justice' 49 *Harvard International Law Journal* (2008) 53; Christopher Keith Hall 'Developing and implementing an effective positive complementarity prosecution strategy' in Carsten Stahn and Göran Sluiter (eds) *The emerging practice of the International Criminal Court* (2009) Martinus Nijhoff, The Hague, 219; Sarah Nouwen *Complementarity in the line of fire: The catalysing effect of the International Criminal Court in Uganda and Sudan* (2013) Cambridge University Press, Cambridge; Cedric Ryngaert 'Applying the Rome Statute's complementarity principle: Drawing lessons from the prosecution of core crimes by states acting under the universality principle' 19 *Criminal Law Forum* (2008) 153.

step in.[8] Jann Kleffner describes the role of the ICC vis-à-vis national courts as follows:

> 'The ICC only assumes the role of a "permanent reserve court", which completes the "international criminal order", while national criminal jurisdictions are regarded as remaining indispensable for achieving the ultimate goal of ending impunity.'[9]

Regarding the respective roles of the ICC and national courts in the system of international criminal justice, it is important to note that there are other mechanisms that can also play a role. *Ad hoc* international criminal tribunals (for instance the ICTY and ICTR) and other forms of internationalised criminal courts (including so-called 'hybrid' courts)[10] complete the picture of the system of international criminal justice, which is aimed at ending impunity for the most serious international crimes.[11] There is also the possibility of regional criminal courts, for instance the proposed 'African Criminal Court'[12] which will be discussed in Chapter VIII.

There are certain situations where the Security Council can refer matters to the ICC. In these cases the ICC will have the necessary jurisdiction regardless of any national claims to exercise jurisdiction.[13] In general, however, the principle of complementarity will apply.

1.2. THE RISK OF POLITICISED TRIALS OR ABUSE OF PROCESS

The 'risk of abuse of process' was one of the bogeymen at the Rome Conference on the ICC. However, the risk of 'political trials' can even be bigger at national level. Jann Kleffner referred to an extreme example to illustrate this point:

> 'That risk [of abuse of process for political reasons] is amply demonstrated by the proceedings against senior NATO leaders, including [former] US President Bill

---

8 See par 10 of the Preamble, and Art 17 of the Rome Statute of the ICC. See further Sharon Williams 'Issues of admissibility' in Otto Triffterer (Commentary on the Rome Statute) (*supra*) 383–394.

9 Jann Kleffner *Complementarity in the Rome Statute and National Criminal Jurisdiction* (2007) Doctoral dissertation, University of Amsterdam, 115.

10 For instance the Special Court for Sierra Leone (SCSL). For an assessment, see Chandra Lekha Sriram 'Wrong-sizing international justice? The hybrid tribunal in Sierra Leone' 29 *Fordham Int'l LJ* 472–506. Courts like the SCSL combine international and domestic elements – in terms of both applicable law and staff.

11 Jann Kleffner (Complementarity) (*supra*) 379–380.

12 See Protocol on Amendments to the Protocol on the Statute of the African Court of Justice and Human Rights.

13 Art 13(b) Rome Statute of the ICC. See further Sharon Williams 'Exercise of jurisdiction' in Otto Triffterer (Commentary on the Rome Statute) (*supra*) 350.

Clinton, [former] UK Prime Minister Tony Blair and [former] French President Jacques Chirac, before a court in Belgrade which resulted in their sentencing in absentia, on 21 September 2000, to 20 years in prison for "inciting an aggressive war, war crimes against the civilian population, use of prohibited combat means, attempted murder of the Yugoslav president, as well as with the violation of the country's territorial integrity" committed during NATO's bombing campaign against Yugoslavia [during the Kosovo conflict]. Slavisa Mrdakovic, who was appointed to defend French President Chirac, was quoted by the news agency Beta as saying: "If I were the judge, and it's a good thing that I am not, I would … take a gun and shoot both Clinton and the other scum for all the evil they have done", to applause in the courtroom. In January 2001, the new Serbian justice minister Vladan Batic was reported as saying that the verdict would be revised, stating that "This was not a trial, but a farce, a comedy" … The judgment was subsequently annulled.'[14]

The risk of abuse of process and the possibility of so-called 'politicised trials' were addressed by the drafters of the Rome Statute. Some of the measures include the important role of the Pre-Trial Chamber[15] on the admissibility of cases,[16] and the role of states in the selection and removal from office of the Prosecutor. These measures constitute checks to prevent abuse of process or arbitrary use of power.[17]

1.3. THE ROLE OF THE ICC IN INTERNATIONAL PEACE AND SECURITY

It is important to note at the outset that the drafters of the Rome Statute were not only determined to create an international court with the jurisdiction to try individuals suspected of having committed serious international crimes, but also to *reaffirm* the 'Purposes and Principles of the Charter of the United Nations'.[18] Furthermore, the Statute reaffirms that 'all States shall refrain from the threat

14 Jann Kleffner 'The impact of complementarity on national implementation of substantive international criminal law' 1 *JICJ* (2003) 105.

15 See comments by Gideon Boas 'Comparing the ICTY and the ICC: Some procedural and substantive issues' *NILR* (2000) 267–292, in particular 289–290.

16 See for instance Art 15 and Art 18 Rome Statute of the ICC on, respectively, the rules regarding investigations by the Prosecutor, and preliminary rulings on admissibility.

17 For favourable assessments of the checks against abuse of process and power in the Rome Statute, see Steven Ratner and Jason Abrams *Accountability for Human Rights atrocities in International Law* 2nd (2001) Oxford University Press, Oxford, 216–219; Ruth Wedgwood in Sewall and Kaysen (United States and the International Criminal Court) (*supra*) 119–136. For a negative assessment of the ICC's 'lack of political accountability', see John Bolton 'Courting Danger: What's wrong with the International Criminal Court' *The National Interest* (1998/1999) 60, in particular 65–66. For a critical assessment of some of the objections to the powers and procedures of the ICC, see Douglas Edlin 'The anxiety of sovereignty: Britain, the United States and the International Criminal Court' 29 (1) *BC Int'l & Comp L Rev* (2006) 1–22.

18 For general comments on the relationship between the ICC and the UN, see Leila Nadya Sadat *The International Criminal Court and the Transformation of International Law: Justice for the New Millennium* (2002) Transnational Publishers, New York, 78–81.

or use of force against the territorial integrity or political independence of any State, or in any other manner inconsistent with the Purposes of the United Nations'. The drafters also emphasised that nothing in the Rome Statute 'shall be taken as authorizing any State Party to intervene in an armed conflict or in the internal affairs of any State'.[19]

It is thus clear that although the drafters of the Rome Statute could not agree on a definition of aggression or on conditions for the exercise of jurisdiction over the crime, they regarded the prohibition on the use of force in international law and the maintenance of peace and security as fundamental values informing the Rome Statute. Morten Bergsmo described the relationship between the UN Charter and the ICC Statute as follows:

> 'To the extent a reaffirmation of fundamental Charter principles may serve as a reminder to States to effectively prevent and stop armed conflicts pursuant to the settlement regimes of the Charter, it contributes to the international prevention of the crimes within the Court's jurisdiction. As international peace and criminal justice mandates gradually develop more mature modes of co-existence, it may be useful to remind ourselves of the commonality of the fundamental values of human life and person underlying both the Charter and the ICC Statute.'[20]

International peace and security was arguably one of the strongest interests informing the process that resulted in eventual agreement on a definition of aggression in the Rome Statute of the ICC. However, it is this very issue that also lies within the political domain of the Security Council of the UN. Throughout the negotiations and discussions that preceded the Rome Diplomatic Conference on the ICC, this tension between aggression as an international criminal justice issue and aggression as an international political issue proved to be a very difficult item to deal with.

2. AN OVERVIEW OF THE LEGISLATIVE HISTORY OF THE ROME STATUTE OF THE INTERNATIONAL CRIMINAL COURT, 1998

2.1. THE ROAD(S) TO ROME

Philippe Kirsch QC, who was elected as the first President of the ICC, has described the adoption of the Rome Statute of the ICC in 1998 as 'a major step in a longstanding effort to establish a permanent forum of international criminal

[19] See Preamble to the Rome Statute of the ICC (*supra*).

[20] Morten Bergsmo/Otto Triffterer 'Preamble' in Otto Triffterer (Commentary on the Rome Statute) (*supra*) 1–16.

justice'.[21] Indeed, for almost the entire duration of the twentieth century, there were many attempts to establish an international criminal court. Cherif Bassiouni traced the ideal back to early attempts to establish tribunals with jurisdiction to try individuals for international crimes such as war crimes and crimes against peace. These various efforts culminated in the adoption at Rome of the Statute of the ICC.[22]

The various attempts during the twentieth century to establish international criminal tribunals were not always successful. Adriaan Bos, who served as chairman of the preparatory committee that evaluated the draft Statute of the ICC prepared by the International Law Commission, described the genesis of the ICC from the Treaty of Versailles to the Rome Statute as follows:

> 'It is undeniable that something was achieved in 1998 that had proved elusive in 1919 at Versailles, throughout the existence of the League of Nations, and even after the Second World War – that is, agreement within the international community on the establishment of an international criminal court.'[23]

The realisation of the ICC with the adoption of the Rome Statute in 1998 can be explained with reference to two closely related historical processes. On the one hand there are the manifold norms and rules that developed through many centuries and in reaction to war and conflict. Various religious and philosophical thinkers had a great impact on what would during the nineteenth and twentieth centuries became the laws of war (the so-called 'law of The Hague' on the methods of warfare and the 'law of Geneva' on the protection of wounded combatants and civilians). The criminalisation of many of these rules and norms can be regarded as the necessary material precursors to the process that started in the early twentieth century to create international criminal tribunals to try individuals accused of crimes under international law.[24]

Bassiouni has identified the first quasi-international criminal trial as that of Conradin von Hohenstaufen and Frederic of Baden that took place in 1268 in Naples, Italy. The charges, which stemmed from acts that occurred after the battle

---

21 Philippe Kirsch 'Introduction' in Herman von Hebel, Johan Lammers and Jolien Schukking (eds) *Reflections on the International Criminal Court – Essays in Honour of Adriaan Bos* (1999) TMC Asser Press, The Hague.

22 Cherif Bassiouni 'Historical Chronology' and 'International Criminal Justice A historical perspective' in *The legislative history of the International Criminal Court* Vol I (2005) Transnational Publishers, New York, 3–121. See also a succinct description by Gerhard Werle and Florian Jessberger (Principles of International Criminal Law) (*supra*) 19–21.

23 Adriaan Bos 'The International Criminal Court: A perspective' in Roy Lee (ed) *The International Criminal Court – The making of the Rome Statute* (1999) Kluwer Law International, The Hague, 464.

24 See in general Cherif Bassiouni (Legislative History Vol I) (*supra*) 3–40.

of Tagliacozzo near Rome, included the 'plundering of civilian property', 'the killing of civilians' and 'destruction of private property, in violation of the laws of God and man'. Interestingly, there was also a charge identified by Bassiouni as the equivalent of aggression. The Hohenstaufens, who were supported by the ruling family of Baden from Germany, attacked Charles of Anjou of France, the king of Naples and Sicily. Bassiouni described the significance of this early example of a quasi-international criminal trial as follows:

> 'While this was one of the many inter-European wars that lasted until [the Second World War], it had an inter-regional character in that Germans fought French and Italians in Italy over territory in Italy and Sicily. Moreover, the trial was tantamount to a military field trial for crimes committed in the course of an armed conflict. While this may not exemplify an international criminal trial in the modern sense, it indicated the beginning of an effort to enforce certain laws in connection with the conduct of armed conflict.'[25]

After the First World War there were also attempts to prosecute individuals (and, notably, the German Kaiser) for war crimes and related crimes under international law. However, the trial at Leipzig for individuals accused of war crimes was not an international trial, but a national trial under German law. Attempts to try the German Kaiser were unsuccessful, since he was granted asylum in the Netherlands.[26]

The normative impetus for the creation of an international criminal court was, according to Bassiouni's chronology, the creation of rules and later also the criminalisation of behaviour that affected the whole of humankind. In the aftermath of the Second World War the Agreement for the Prosecution and Punishment of Major War Criminals of the European Axis (the London Charter) established the International Military Tribunal (IMT) at Nuremberg. This was an important milestone, and the IMT (and later the International Military Tribunal for the Far East sitting at Tokyo) signalled the resolve of the fledgling international community to punish individuals responsible for the most serious crimes affecting humankind. Criticism that the IMT at Nuremberg and the IMTFE at Tokyo represented 'victors' justice' notwithstanding, the two *ad hoc* tribunals achieved a measure of justice not seen before.[27]

The post-Second World War efforts to codify and further develop the legal legacy of Nuremberg was discussed in Chapter IV above. Projects like the draft Code of Crimes Against the Peace and Security of Mankind (in its various versions)

---

25 Cherif Bassiouni (Legislative History Vol I) (*supra*) 15–16.

26 Cherif Bassiouni (Legislative History Vol I) (*supra*) 22–26.

27 See discussion of the judgments at Nuremberg (section 3.2) and Tokyo (section 4) in Ch III *supra*.

were aimed at the development of substantive international criminal law. At the same time the UN General Assembly mandated a Committee to draft a statute for an international criminal court that could give effect to the norms and values of substantive international criminal law. By 1954 two draft statutes for an international criminal court were prepared. Ideally, the institutional process of drafting a statute for the court and the process to codify international crimes (the Draft Code of Crimes Against the Peace and Security of Mankind) should have been in tandem. Unfortunately for the development of both substantive and institutional international criminal law, the 1953 Revised Draft Statute for an International Criminal Court never got serious attention in the UN General Assembly, and no progress on this project was made. Bassiouni explained the apparent reason for this as follows:

> '[Splitting] up of subject matters and giving them to different committees was a cold-war tactic designed to forestall having to draft measures enhancing international criminal justice. Since the IMT and IMTFE precedents were still so close in time, the major powers on both sides of the Cold War used procedural maneuvers to postpone, delay and prevent progress. Aggression, being the political crime *par excellence*, was the object of delays and maneuvers to prevent its application.'[28]

In 1979 an important seed was planted that eventually developed into the draft Statute of the ICC adopted in Rome in 1998. During 1979 the Commission on Human Rights Working Group on Southern Africa mandated Cherif Bassiouni to draft a Statute for the Establishment of an International Criminal Jurisdiction to Enforce the Apartheid Convention of 1973.[29] Article V of the Apartheid Convention provides for the prosecution of individuals at national or international level for the crimes collectively known as the crime of apartheid:

> 'Persons charged with the acts enumerated in article II of the present Convention may be tried by a competent tribunal of any State Party to the Convention which may acquire jurisdiction over the person of the accused or by an international penal tribunal having jurisdiction with respect to those States Parties which shall have accepted its jurisdiction.'

Bassiouni prepared a Draft Statute[30] (based on Article V of the Apartheid Convention), but it was never adopted.[31] However, this Draft Statute for the prosecution of apartheid criminals was later used as a model for the International

28 Cherif Bassiouni (Legislative History Vol I) (*supra*) 32.

29 International Convention on the Suppression and Punishment of the Crime of Apartheid (1973), *ILM* 1974, 50; reprinted in Christine Van den Wyngaert (International Criminal Law) (*supra*) 413.

30 UN Doc E/CN4/AC/22CRP.19/Rev.1 (10 Dec 1980).

31 Cherif Bassiouni (Legislative History Vol I) (*supra*) 33.

Law Commission's 1994 Draft Statute for an International Criminal Court.[32] In 1995 this Draft Statute was submitted to the UN General Assembly's Ad Hoc Committee on the Establishment of an International Criminal Court. The work of the Ad Hoc Committee was followed by that of yet another General Assembly committee, the Preparatory Committee on the Establishment of an International Criminal Court. This Preparatory Committee eventually developed its own text for a draft Statute for an International Criminal Court. The work of the Preparatory Committee culminated in the Diplomatic Conference in Rome that lasted from 15 June to 17 July 1998. At the end of this conference, which was convened by the UN General Assembly, the Rome Statute of the ICC was adopted.[33] The legal framework for the first permanent International Criminal Court with jurisdiction to try individuals accused of the most serious international crimes thus became a reality.

It is important to note that even before the adoption of the Rome Statute of the ICC in 1998, the willingness of the post-Cold War international community to give effect to the ideals of international justice were signalled with the creation first of the International Criminal Tribunal for the Former Yugoslavia (ICTY) in 1993[34] and then the International Criminal Tribunal for Rwanda in 1994.[35] The creation of these *ad hoc* international criminal tribunals no doubt added to the momentum of the process that led to the adoption of the Rome Statute of the ICC in 1998.[36]

2.2. THE DRAFTING HISTORY OF THE ROME STATUTE WITH RESPECT TO THE CRIME OF AGGRESSION

The delegates at the Rome Diplomatic Conference on the establishment of an International Criminal Court were not all in favour of the inclusion of aggression as a crime within the jurisdiction of the ICC. Many delegations regarded the crime of aggression as essentially a crime committed by states, not individuals;

---

32 Report of the International Law Commission, 46th Sess., 2 May – 22 Jul 1994, UN GAOR, 49th Sess., Supp No 10, UN Doc A/49/10 (1994); Cherif Bassiouni (Legislative History Vol I) (*supra*) 36.

33 Cherif Bassiouni (Legislative History Vol I) (*supra*) 36.

34 Statute of the International Tribunal for the Former Yugoslavia (1993) SC Res 827 (1993) on Establishing an International Tribunal for the Prosecution of Persons Responsible for Serious Violations of International humanitarian law committed in the territory of the Former Yugoslavia, *ILM*, 1993, 1192; reprinted in Christine Van den Wyngaert (International Criminal Law) (*supra*) 73.

35 Statute of the International Tribunal for Rwanda (1994) SC Res 955 establishing the International Tribunal for Rwanda, *ILM*, 1994, 1598; reprinted in Christine Van den Wyngaert (International Criminal Law) (*supra*) 139.

36 Gerhard Werle and Florian Jessberger (Principles of International Criminal Law) (*supra*) 14–17.

other delegations regarded aggression as too 'political' a concept, not susceptible to legal definition. Some delegations were also concerned that the paramount role of the Security Council in matters of international peace and security would be eroded by the inclusion of aggression in the ICC Statute. Many delegations that were supportive of the inclusion of aggression shared some of the above mentioned concerns.[37]

The final text of the Statute of the ICC adopted at Rome reflected a compromise between the delegations opposed to and those in favour of the inclusion of aggression. It also reflects some of the concerns of many of the delegations regarding the conditions under which the ICC should exercise its jurisdiction, as well as the role of the Security Council in terms of its Chapter VII powers.

2.2.1. An overview of some of the main concerns at the Diplomatic Conference in Rome

Most delegations referred to the different approaches to define aggression (notably the Nuremberg definition and the much more detailed, but state-centred 1974 UN General Assembly Definition)[38] and the difficulties in formulating a definition that is precise enough to be able to serve as a basis for individual criminal liability. For these reasons, some delegations rejected the idea of including aggression in the Statute. But they also advanced international political concerns. The Records of the Diplomatic Conference show for instance the following position taken by the delegation from Pakistan, which reflects some of the common concerns of many delegations:

> '[Pakistan] agreed that the Statute should include the most heinous crimes of international concern but opposed the inclusion of aggression because of its controversial nature. The definition of aggression which had been adopted by the General Assembly in 1974 was considered by many States, including Pakistan, as being of a non-binding nature, and more political than legal. Regarding a role for the Security Council in the matter, any such role would introduce a political element which would undermine the trigger mechanism, and would also run counter to the basic philosophy of complementarity devised to preserve the jurisdiction of national legal systems ... Furthermore, aggression was traditionally considered a crime committed by States, whereas Pakistan favoured the principle that the Court's jurisdiction should be limited only to crimes committed by individuals. That raised the complex problem as to how an individual might be prosecuted and punished for aggression, unless the Security Council first determined the existence of aggression,

37 See in general 'Summary Records of the 1998 Diplomatic Conference' in Cherif Bassiouni (Legislative History Vol 3) (*supra*) 127–382.

38 See discussion of UN Res No 3314 (XXIX) Def of Aggression (1974) in Ch IV section 2.3 *et seq, supra*.

and that then those responsible were identified [sic]. In most cases those in authority would be the accused, something which threatened the concept of sovereignty of States.'[39]

In the sections that follow, some of the main concerns raised at the Diplomatic Conference will be highlighted. The intention is not to provide a summary of the positions taken by all the delegations[40] but rather to point to the main concerns insofar as these had an impact on the eventual adoption of Article 5 (crimes within the jurisdiction of the Court) of the Rome Statute. These concerns related to both the definition of aggression and the role of the Security Council.

The Preparatory Committee on the Establishment of an International Criminal Court (PrepCom) identified two sources as possible points of departure in its discussions on the crime of aggression, namely the provision on aggression in the Nuremberg Charter and the UN General Assembly Definition of Aggression, 1974. However, these two sources were not as such acceptable to the PrepCom as appropriate for inclusion in the Draft Statute.[41] PrepCom thus decided on three options for inclusion in the Draft Statute. The fact that PrepCom was able to present three options on the crime of aggression reflected the fact that a large number of delegations held the view that aggression should, as a matter of principle, be included as a crime in terms of the Statute.[42] On the definition of aggression, the following options were presented, but without prejudice to 'the discussion of the issue of the relationship of the Security Council with the [ICC]':[43]

'Option 1
[For the purpose of the present Statute, the crime [of aggression] [against peace] means any of the following acts committed by an individual [who is in a position of exercising control or capable of directing political/military action in a State]:
(a) planning,
(b) preparing,
(c) ordering,
(d) initiating, or
(e) carrying out
[an armed attack] [the use of armed force] [a war of aggression,] [a war of aggression, or a war in violation of international treaties, agreements or assurances, or participation in a common plan or conspiracy for the accomplishment of any of

39 Cherif Bassiouni (Legislative History Vol 3) (*supra*) 130.

40 For a comprehensive account, see Stefan Barriga and Claus Kreß (eds) *The travaux préparatoires of the crime of aggression* (2012) Cambridge University Press, Cambridge, 255–331.

41 Cherif Bassiouni (Legislative History Vol 3) (*supra*) 127.

42 Cherif Bassuiouni (Legislative History Vol 2) (*supra*) 24 fn 10. At Rome, a core group of states insisted on the inclusion of the crime of aggression as a crime within the jurisdiction of the ICC. See Daniel Nsereko 'Bringing aggressors to justice: From Nuremberg to Rome' 2 *UBLJ* (2005) 5–32.

43 Cherif Bassiouni (Legislative History Vol 2) (*supra*) 24–25.

the foregoing] by a State against the [sovereignty,] territorial integrity [or political independence] of another State [when this] [armed attack] [use of force] [is] [in contravention of the Charter of the United Nations] [in contravention of the Charter of the United Nations as determined by the Security Council].]

Option 2

1. [For the purposes of this Statute, the crime of aggression is committed by a person who is in a position of exercising control or capable of directing political/ military actions in his State, against another State, in contravention of the Charter of the United Nations, by resorting to armed force, to threaten or violate the sovereignty, territorial integrity or political independence of that State.]

[2. [Acts constituting [aggression] [armed attack] include the following:]

[Provided that the acts concerned or their consequences are of sufficient gravity, acts constituting aggression [are] [include] the following:]

(a) the invasion or attack by the armed forces of a State of the territory of another State, or any military occupation, however temporary, resulting from such invasion or attack, or any annexation by the use of force of the territory of another State or part thereof;
(b) bombardment by the armed forces of a State against the territory of another State [, or the use of any weapons by a State against the territory of another State];
(c) the blockade of the ports or coasts of a State by the armed forces of another State;
(d) an attack by the armed forces of a State on the land, sea or air forces, or marine and air fleets of another State;
(e) the use of armed forces of one State which are within the territory of another State with the agreement of the receiving State in contravention of the conditions provided for in the agreement, or any extension of their presence in such territory beyond their termination of the agreement;
(f) the action of a State in allowing its territory, which it has placed at the disposal of another State, to be used by that other State for perpetrating an act of aggression against a third State;
(g) the sending by or on behalf of a State of armed bands, groups, irregulars or mercenaries, which carry out acts of armed force against another State of such gravity as to amount to the acts listed above, or its substantial involvement therein.]]

Option 3

[1. For the purpose of the present Statute [and subject to a determination by the Security Council referred to in article 10, paragraph 2, regarding the act of a State], the crime of aggression means either of the following acts committed by an individual who is in a position of exercising control or capable of directing the political or military action of a State:
   (a) initiating, or
   (b) carrying out

an armed attack directed by a State against the territorial integrity or political independence of another State when this armed attack was undertaken in [manifest] contravention of the Charter of the United Nations [with the object or result of

> establishing a [military] occupation of, or annexing, the territory of such other State or part thereof by the armed forces of the attacking State.]
> 2. Where an attack under paragraph 1 has been committed, the
>   (a) planning,
>   (b) preparing, or
>   (c) ordering
>
> thereof by an individual who is in a position of exercising control or capable of directing the political or military action of a State shall also constitute a crime of aggression.]'

During PrepCom deliberations it became clear that a number of states used the 1974 General Assembly Definition as a working definition, thus supporting an approach where the definition would contain an enumeration of acts constituting aggression. However, as was shown in Chapter IV above, the 1974 Definition was drafted with state liability, and not individual criminal liability, in mind. Thus a number of delegations at the PrepCom delegations favoured a definition that would address many of the concerns relating to issues of gravity, clarity and legality from a *criminal law perspective*. The German delegation presented an informal discussion paper (which contained many of the pivotal points of criticism against the 1974 Definition, as well as some important suggestions for a compromise definition). The summary records of the PrepCom deliberations[44] on the definition for aggression for inclusion in the Draft Statute of the ICC, reflects the efforts of some delegates to find a suitable alternative to the 1974 Definition:

> 'The definition must not lend itself to frivolous accusations of a political nature against the leadership of a Member State. Also, the definition must not negatively affect the legitimate use of armed force in conformity with the Charter of the United Nations, the necessity of which could not be ruled out in the future. Furthermore, the definition contained in option 3 was in line with historic precedents such as the Charter of the Nuremberg Military Tribunal. It also met the strict standard of legal precision, clarity and certainty that was necessary for a norm providing for individual criminal responsibility. The broad and enumerative approach of General Assembly resolution 3314 (XXIX) would not command general agreement.'[45]

The concerns reflected above stemmed not only from a critique of the 1974 Definition. Concerns were also raised regarding the content of the ICC Statute vis-à-vis the UN Charter, and in particular the relationship between the ICC and

---

44 As presented at the 6th meeting on the Draft Statute under the Chairmanship of Phillip Kirsch (Canada) on 18 Jun 1998, A/CONF.183/C.1/SR.6, reprinted in Cherif Bassiouni (Legislative History Vol 3) (*supra*) 126–140. The question of a definition of aggression was discussed further at the 7th meeting, on 19 Jun 1998, A/CONF.183/C.1/SR.7, reprinted in Cherif Bassiouni (Legislative History Vol 3) (*supra*) 140–148.

45 Cherif Bassiouni (Legislative History Vol 3) (*supra*) 128.

the Security Council. Many delegates felt strongly about the primary role of the Security Council in the context of collective security. In terms of Chapter VII of the UN Charter, the Security Council has the power to determine whether an act of aggression was committed by a state. Many states (especially states who are regular contributors to international peacekeeping operations) were opposed to any circumvention of the role of the Security Council. At the same time many states (including states who were opposed to a circumvention of the role of the Security Council) pointed to the need for an independent International Criminal Court – that is, that 'acknowledgment of the role of the Security Council would not and must not endanger the independence of the Court in determining individual criminal responsibility.'[46] Thus, delegations that favoured the inclusion of the crime of aggression in the draft Statute not only had to come up with a suitable definition, but also with a definition that took into account the powers and responsibilities of the Security Council.

At first, the inclusion of the crime of aggression in the Statute of the ICC experienced some opposition. However, the bloc of states known as the Non-Aligned Movement, plus Germany, insisted on the inclusion of the crime of aggression.[47] There were mainly two reasons for the initial opposition. First, the opponents regarded acts of aggression as acts of states – committed by states against states – and these did 'not belong to the category of offences committed by individuals in violation of international humanitarian law, which was what the [ICC] Statute was intended to deal with.'[48] Second, as was pointed out by the delegate from Israel, even if the crime of aggression was to be included in the Draft Statute, 'the exercise of jurisdiction [of the ICC] should be subject to determination by the Security Council that an act of aggression had occurred.'[49] And just to add to the scepticism, the Israeli delegate also submitted the following: '[A determination of an act of aggression] by the Security Council would adversely affect the major defences available to the accused before the Court, and might also affect the standing of the Court as an independent judicial organ.'[50]

The positions taken by the various delegations (before and during the Rome diplomatic conference) should be seen in context: the General Assembly resolutions that paved the way for the Diplomatic Conference in Rome have not resulted in legal-technical processes; the Conference was still characterised by the dynamics of diplomatic processes. Phillippe Kirsch and John Holmes pointed out that the positions that states took were to a large extent informed

46 Cherif Bassiouni (Legislative History Vol 3) (*supra*) 128.
47 Daniel Nsereko (Bringing aggressors to justice) (*supra*) 5–32, in particular at 5.
48 Cherif Bassiouni (Legislative History Vol 3) (*supra*) 131.
49 Cherif Bassiouni (Legislative History Vol 3) (*supra*) 131.
50 *Ibid.*

by their respective histories and political situations.[51] For instance, a core group of states from the developing world, the so-called Non-Alignment Movement (NAM), resolved that the crime of aggression should be included in the Statute of the ICC 'at all costs'.[52] Observers and participants closely associated with the diplomatic conference (and the processes that preceded the Rome conference) explained the NAM position with reference to the historical fact that many of the states comprising NAM were in the past victims of 'acts of aggression'. These states were also concerned about the risk that history might repeat itself.[53]

Equally informative to the position taken by the NAM states referred to above were those of the major powers (like Germany and Italy) who are regular contributors to multinational peacekeeping forces (like in Lebanon in 2006) or involved in collective security operations, like the NATO operations in Afghanistan (since 2002). The positions of the five permanent members of the UN Security Council (United States, France, Russia, United Kingdom and China) warrant special attention, not only because of their special role in the collective security system,[54] but also because of their military, economic and political reach.

The *German* position – that the need for a definition of aggression that does not 'negatively affect the legitimate use of armed force in conformity with the [UN] Charter' – was explained above. This, together with the important role of the Security Council with respect to collective security and the Council's responsibility of having to determine acts of aggression, was to Germany a *sine qua non* for the inclusion of the crime of aggression in the ICC Statute.[55] Germany thus favoured the definition of aggression under Option 3 above, since that option provided for a central role for the Security Council. However, Germany also emphasised the need for an independent ICC, which must determine individual criminal responsibility without the fear of interference. *Italy* favoured Option 2 above, where the definition of aggression was linked to the importance of the UN Charter provisions on the use of force, but where the Security Council would not play such a central role in determining whether conduct would constitute an act of aggression, as a jurisdictional prerequisite for purposes of the ICC.[56] Italy thus favoured an approach where the ICC alone would determine, on the basis of the definition contained in the Statute, whether conduct constitutes aggression.

51 Phillippe Kirsch and John Holmes 'The birth of the International Criminal Court: The 1998 Rome Conference' 36 *Canadian Yearbook of International Law*, 3–39, in particular at 8.
52 Phillippe Kirsch and John Holmes (Birth of the ICC) (*supra*) 10.
53 Phillippe Kirsch and John Holmes (Birth of the ICC) (*supra*) 10.
54 See discussion in Ch I *supra*.
55 Cherif Bassiouni (Legislative History Vol 3) (*supra*) 128.
56 Cherif Bassiouni (Legislative History Vol 3) (*supra*) 138.

The *United States*, economically and militarily the most powerful state in the world, and a permanent member of the Security Council, was one of the few states that voted against the Rome Statute of the ICC. During the diplomatic conference, the US raised a number of issues it deemed fundamental flaws in the draft Statute.[57] The US delegation at the diplomatic conference at Rome was sceptical whether any of the three options for the inclusion of the crime of aggression in the draft Statute would be suitable. In particular, Theodor Meron (US State Department) explained to the PrepCom that the US could not support the UN General Assembly Definition of 1974 as a basis for a definition of aggression for inclusion in the Rome Statute. The US's position was that the 1974 Definition is much wider in scope than aggression under customary international law. The US also rejected the notion that the 1974 Definition had become part of customary international law through state practice and *opinio juris*.[58]

For the US, the problematic substantive aspect of defining aggression was difficult enough, but the critical issue was the role of the Security Council. The US would not agree to any reduced role for the Security Council in matters concerning possible acts of aggression.[59] David Scheffer, who served as ambassador-at-large for war crimes under the Clinton administration, wrote that the US had a number of fundamental difficulties with the draft Statute of the ICC. While the US (at the time) was not opposed to the ICC in principle, these concerns were too serious for the US to vote for the Rome Statute. One of the concerns was that the United States could not vote for the inclusion of the 'undefined' crime of aggression.[60] The other concerns included the complementary jurisdiction of the ICC; the way in which crimes within the jurisdiction of the ICC can be amended; the processes involving the addition of new crimes to the Rome Statute; constitutional concerns (from the perspective of the US); and, in general, political concerns relating to the US global military presence. However, despite Scheffer's explanations for the US's opposition to the Rome Statute, it was already clear at the diplomatic conference that the US had serious doubts about the PrepCom draft and the three options for the definition of aggression as presented to the diplomatic conference. Even if the conference was able to define aggression, it is doubtful that that would bring the US to vote for the Rome Statute. The other concerns of the US were too fundamental for it

57 For an overview of some of the US concerns, see Marten Zwanenburg 'The Statute for an International Criminal Court and the United States: Peacekeepers under fire?' 10 *EJIL* (1999) 124–143.

58 Theodor Meron as quoted in 'Contemporary practice of the United States' 95 *AJIL* (2001) 400–401.

59 Cherif Bassiouni (Legislative History Vol 3) (*supra*) 135.

60 David Scheffer 'The US perspective on the ICC' in Sarah Sewall and Carl Kaysen (United States and the International Criminal Court) (*supra*) 115–118.

to support the draft Statute. The US was eventually one of only seven states[61] that voted against the Rome Statute of the ICC.[62]

With the exception of China and the US, the other permanent members of the UN Security Council (Russia, France and the United Kingdom) were generally supportive of the ICC and of the idea to include the crime of aggression in the ICC Statute. However, their support was qualified: *Russia* supported Option 3 (as quoted above) and strongly emphasised the role of the Security Council in cases of aggression.[63] This emphasis on the role of the Security Council as a condition for the ICC to exercise jurisdiction over the crime of aggression was also reflected in the statement by Russia after the adoption of the Rome Statute of the ICC. The position of Russia regarding a future definition for aggression (to be included in the Rome Statute) was based on the assumption that any definition of aggression 'would be linked directly to the *exclusive prerogative of the Security Council* to characterize the actions of a State as an act of aggression as a prerequisite for the institution of proceedings against an individual.'[64]

France and the *United Kingdom,* like the other delegations from Western Europe, were both supportive of the ICC and of the inclusion of the crime of aggression in the ICC Statute, but on the conditions that (a) an adequate and precise definition of aggression be drafted (both supported definition Option 3 above), and (b) that there must be a link between the prior determination of an act of aggression by the Security Council and the ICC's exercise of jurisdiction over individuals accused of the crime of aggression.[65]

China ultimately voted against the Rome Statute, but was initially supportive of the inclusion of the crime of aggression in the Statute of the ICC. The Chinese delegation, like the other permanent members of the Security Council, was adamant that, apart from a clear definition of aggression, the central role of the Security Council in determining acts of aggression must be linked to the ICC's exercise of jurisdiction. China, with the United States and five other countries,

---

61 Only three states (China, Israel and the US) publicly explained why they have voted against the Rome Statute. The other four states decided not to make their positions known. Since the vote on the adoption of the Rome Statute was a non-recorded vote, it is not possible to identify the other four states. See Roy Lee (The International Criminal Court) (*supra*) 26.

62 Press Release, UN Diplomatic Conference of Plenipotentiaries on the Establishment of an International Criminal Court, L/ROM/22, 17 Jul 1998, Dept of Public Information, United Nations; Roy Lee (The International Criminal Court) (*supra*) 26. See further Sarah Sewall, Carl Kaysen and Michael Scharf 'The United States and the International Criminal Court: An overview' in Sarah Sewall and Carl Kaysen (United States and the ICC) (*supra*) 1–27.

63 Cherif Bassiouni (Legislative History Vol 3) (*supra*) 136.

64 Roy Lee (International Criminal Court) (*supra*) 617 (emphasis added).

65 Cherif Bassiouni (Legislative History Vol 3) (*supra*) 136–137.

ultimately voted against the Rome Statute, mainly because of the perceived jurisdictional overreach of the ICC.[66]

2.2.2. Inclusion of the crime of aggression, The compromise text of Article 5

Although there was no general support for any of the proposals regarding the inclusion of the crime of aggression in the Draft Statute of the ICC, Option 3 (as set out above) received wide support. However, because of the many debates and viewpoints on aggression, the three proposals were included in the draft text that served as a basis for discussion at the diplomatic conference in Rome.[67]

At the Rome Conference two opposing views emerged on the inclusion of the crime of aggression in the Statute of the ICC. These two blocs were much more intransigent in their respective points of view than the delegations at the meetings that preceded the Rome Conference. On the role of the Security Council, many states, but especially those from the Non-Alignment Movement (NAM), wanted an absolutely independent court with no role for the Security Council. This included no role for the Security Council regarding the crime of aggression. Directly in opposition to this were many Western states and Russia who wanted a central role for the Security Council. Indeed, the permanent members of the Security Council persisted in their view that the role of the Security Council is an absolute condition for the inclusion of the crime of aggression in the ICC Statute.[68]

At the Diplomatic Conference Option 3 (as set out above), that came about as a result of an informal discussion document distributed by Germany during meetings preceding the Rome Conference, was met with some resistance. A number of states (notably states from the developing world) wanted to expand the scope of the definition in Option 3 to include the 'right to self-determination, freedom and independence' as interests protected by the definition of aggression. The states that favoured the more minimalist definition contained in Option 3 feared that an expanded definition could be too politicised and open to abuse. The opposing views were such that no compromise seemed possible. However, the NAM states (who were committed to include the crime of aggression in the ICC Statute) proposed the basis for a legal framework on aggression that was eventually adopted as part of the ICC Statute. The proposal was to include the crime of aggression, but to leave the definition and conditions for exercise of jurisdiction for future deliberations.[69]

---

66 Cherif Bassiouni (Legislative History Vol 3) (*supra*) 141; Roy Lee (International Criminal Court) (*supra*) 582–586.

67 PrepCom Draft Statute 14–16; Roy Lee (International Criminal Court) (*supra*) 83.

68 Roy Lee (International Criminal Court) (*supra*) 84.

69 Roy Lee (International Criminal Court) (*supra*) 85.

Article 5(2) is thus a reflection of the NAM proposal, but there is also an important nod in the direction of those states who favour a role for the Security Council in cases of aggression. Article 5(2) (now deleted in terms of the Resolution on Aggression that was adopted at Kampala in 2010) provides that any future definition of aggression 'shall be consistent with the relevant provisions of the Charter of the United Nations.' Some commentators saw this as an indication that the language of Article 5(2) provided for some threshold of Security Council role to play in the ICC jurisdictional regime over the crime of aggression.[70]

3. THE QUEST TO DRAFT A DEFINITION OF AGGRESSION, AND CONDITIONS UNDER WHICH THE ICC CAN EXERCISE JURISDICTION OVER THE CRIME OF AGGRESSION

3.1. THE CONTEXT: POLITICAL AND CRIMINAL JUSTICE RESPONSES TO INTERNATIONAL AGGRESSION

The Assembly of States Parties to the Rome Statute established a Special Working Group (SWG) in order to take further the matter of the definition and related issues concerning the crime of aggression. The SWG has met on a number of occasions (including informal discussions and workshops).[71] Before the various discussions and proposals of the SWG are discussed, these debates have to be put in perspective.

In previous chapters it was shown that two basic responses to the phenomenon of aggressive war emerged in the wake of the Second World War. Michael Reisman described these as 'strategies' born from the desire by the Allied victors who could no longer tolerate the fact that there was 'no general prohibition in international law against the waging of war.'[72] He described the two responses as follows:

> 'The first was a *political* response to aggression: the United Nations Charter prohibited "the threat or use of force against the territorial integrity or political

---

70 D Sarooshi 'Aspects of the relationship between the International Criminal Court and the United Nations' Vol XXXII *NYIL* (2001) 27–53, especially 43–44; Daryl Mundis 'The Assembly of States Parties and the Institutional Framework of the International Criminal Court' 97 *AJIL* (2003) 132–147.

71 The Special Working Group on Aggression held a number of 'Inter-sessional meetings' at the Liechtenstein Institute on Self-Determination, Woodrow Wilson School, Princeton University.

72 Michael Reisman 'Introduction: The definition of aggression and the ICC' *ASIL Proceedings* (2002) American Society of International Law, Washington DC, 181.

> independence of any state" and authorized the Security Council to "take such action by air, sea, or land forces as may be necessary to maintain or restore international peace and security." The second was a *criminal justice* response to aggression: the victors established international tribunals for finding "individual responsibility" for "planning, preparation, initiation or waging of a war of aggression."'[73]

Reisman pointed to the 'latent tension' between these two responses or strategies. From the discussion above of the opinions of the various delegations at the conferences preceding the Rome Statute of the ICC, as well as at the Conference itself, this 'latent tension' clearly manifested itself in the way the delegations viewed the role of the Security Council vis-à-vis the ICC.

In Reisman's opinion the Security Council is assigned the task of restoring and maintaining peace and order and this necessarily imports a 'broad competence to engage in a contextual appreciation of whether to characterize certain uses of force as aggression.'[74] On the other hand, according to Reisman, a criminal law approach 'is not charged with world order concerns and does not admit a comparable contextual appreciation.'[75]

It is submitted that the political approach (that is basically the collective security approach, dominated by the Security Council) differs in substance, methodology and outcome from the criminal justice response to international aggression. Article 5(2) of the Rome Statute of the ICC reflects a compromise reached at the Diplomatic Conference in 1998. Underlying Article 5(2) is the tension between the political and criminal justice approaches to aggression referred to above. Phani Dascalopoulou-Divada noted the following in relation to the two conditions provided for in Article 5(2): 'Both issues are of course intimately interrelated; there can be no watertight separation between them.'[76] Most importantly, Dascalopoulou-Livada linked both issues to the broader question of the definition of aggression and the conditions for the exercise of ICC jurisdiction over the crime. The substantive definition of aggression and the issue of the relationship between the jurisdiction of the ICC over the crime of aggression and the powers of the Security Council stemming from Article 39 of the UN Charter are all interdependent.

---

73 Michael Reisman (Definition of aggression) (*supra*) 181 (emphasis in the original).

74 Michael Reisman (Definition of aggression) (*supra*) 181.

75 *Ibid.*

76 Phani Dascalopoulou-Livada 'The crime of aggression: making operative the jurisdiction of the ICC – Tendencies in the PrepCom' *ASIL Proceedings* (2002) American Society of International Law, Washington DC, 185.

3.2. THE SPECIAL WORKING GROUP ON THE CRIME OF AGGRESSION

A Review Conference on the Rome Statute was held in 2010.[77] This event presented the Assembly of States Parties with the opportunity to amend the Rome Statute, including any progress made on the definition of aggression and the conditions under which the ICC could exercise its jurisdiction with respect to aggression, as prompted by Article 5(2) of the Rome Statute.

In preparation of the Review Conference, the Special Working Group on the Crime of Aggression was set up in 2002. It was the task of the Special Working Group to discuss proposals for a provision on aggression. These discussions have produced many discussion documents with different options and models on both the definition of aggression and the conditions of exercising of jurisdiction by the ICC.[78] The main proposals that culminated in the adoption of Articles 8*bis*, 15*bis*, and 15*ter* are discussed in Chapter VI.

---

77 For a firsthand account, see Claus Kreß and Leonie von Holtzendorff 'The Kampala Compromise on the Crime of Aggression' 8 *Journal of International Criminal Justice* (2010) 1179–1217.

78 For background see 'Press conference by Chairman of Working Group on Crime of Aggression' 31 Jan 2007 (available at www.un.org/News/briefings/docs/2007/070131_Wenaweser.doc.htm).

CHAPTER VI

DRAFTING AND DIPLOMACY: THE SPECIAL WORKING GROUP ON THE CRIME OF AGGRESSION

1. THE PROCESS TO ADOPT A DEFINITION OF AGGRESSION AND CONDITIONS FOR THE EXERCISE OF JURISDICTION BY THE ICC

The aim of this chapter is to describe and analyse some of the important debates and processes that resulted in the adoption of the necessary amendments to the Rome Statute to provide for effective ICC jurisdiction over the crime of aggression. The different approaches that emerged in the aftermath of the Rome Conference are highlighted. The aim is not to reproduce or summarise the *travaux préparatoires* of the adoption of the amendments to the Rome Statute of the ICC at the 2010 Review Conference in Kampala. That has been done elsewhere.[1] Where appropriate, reference is made to the relevant drafts, non-papers, reports, country proposals and other relevant materials.

1.1. IN THE AFTERMATH OF THE ROME DIPLOMATIC CONFERENCE: THE PROPOSALS AT THE PREPARATORY COMMISSION

Since the adoption of the Rome Statute of the ICC in 1998,[2] the process prompted by Article 5(2) to find a suitable definition of aggression, involved many discussions at diplomatic and legal-technical level. A number of issues remained to be finalised, *inter alia* the Elements of Crimes and the Rules of Procedure and Evidence. At the first session of the Preparatory Commission (which had the task of carrying these processes forward) a group of states (mainly the states from the Non-Alignment Movement (NAM) as well as a number of Arab states) insisted

1 See Stefan Barriga and Claus Kreß *The travaux préparatoires of the crime of aggression* (2012) Cambridge University Press, Cambridge.

2 Rome Statute of the International Criminal Court (1998) UN DocA/CONF.183/9, *ILM*, 1998, 999, reproduced in Christine Van den Wyngaert (International Criminal Law) (*supra*) 187.

that the issue of the crime of aggression be put on the agenda as well. Although the aggression question was not a priority at that stage, the NAM and Arab states made sure that the issue was put on the agenda for the second meeting of the Preparatory Commission.[3]

During the first number of meetings of the Preparatory Commission, three distinct approaches to the question of a definition for aggression and conditions for the exercise of jurisdiction of the ICC emerged. The three approaches were reflected in proposals represented to a special coordinator on the issue of aggression. Proposal 1 (by the Arab and NAM states) was a compilation of proposals that were made before, during and after the Rome Diplomatic Conference of 1998. It reflected a very broad approach to the crime of aggression and included references to the UN General Assembly Definition of Aggression of 1974.[4] Proposal 2 was submitted by Russia. It contained a concise and generic definition of aggression:

> 'For the purposes of the present Statute [of the ICC] and subject to a prior determination by the UN Security Council of an act of aggression by the State concerned, the crime of aggression means any of the following acts: planning, preparing, initiating, carrying out a war of aggression.'[5]

Proposal 3 was presented by Germany and focused on a narrower concept of aggression, with the element of 'occupation' as a central element. The German proposal represented a move away from the illustrative list contained in the UN General Assembly Definition of Aggression of 1974.[6]

1.2. THE ASSEMBLY OF STATES PARTIES' SPECIAL WORKING GROUP ON THE CRIME OF AGGRESSION

Little progress was made at the various meetings of the Preparatory Commission. However, the discussion papers compiled by the Coordinators (first from Tanzania and then Argentina) served as valuable points of departure for the discussions of the Special Working Group on Aggression. The Special Working Group (which was created in 2002) had resolved to present the Assembly of States

---

3 See analysis of the work of the PrepCom by Muhammad Shukri 'Will aggressors ever be tried before the ICC?' in Mauro Politi and Giuseppe Nesi (eds) *The International Criminal Court and the Crime of Aggression* (2004) Ashgate Publishing, Aldershot, 37–42.

4 For the text of this Def, see Ch IV section 2.3 *supra*.

5 Discussion document PCNICC/1999/DP/12 presented at the Jul-Aug 1999 Session of Preparatory Commission. See further Muhammad Shukri (Will aggressors ever be tried before the ICC?) (*supra*) 38.

6 Muhammad Shukri (Will aggressors ever be tried before the ICC?) (*supra*) 38–39.

Parties with proposals on the crime of aggression before the Review Conference on the ICC Statute, which was held in 2010.[7]

2. THE MAIN PROPOSALS EMERGING FROM THE SPECIAL WORKING GROUP ON AGGRESSION

It is important to note that the debates and discussions in the Special Working Group were symptomatic of the difficulties of reaching consensus on the definition of aggression – as also experienced during previous attempts by international bodies to define aggression.[8] A fundamental difference, however, is the fact that the process post-1998 was conducted against the background of a functioning International Criminal Court.[9] This was not the case during the various earlier attempts by the International Law Commission (ILC) to define aggression or during the adoption of the UN General Assembly Definition of Aggression. The sense of urgency[10] to resolve the issue of aggression certainly prompted members of the Special Working Group to adopt realistic positions on the crime of aggression. Thus, the Chairman of the Special Working Group could note in January 2007 that the various proposals on aggression can be narrowed down to two different approaches: the 'differentiated' and 'monistic' approaches.[11] This is in contrast to the manifold opinions expressed and approaches taken by states before and during the Rome Diplomatic Conference.

2.1. THE CRIME OF AGGRESSION: TWO APPROACHES TAKEN AT THE SPECIAL WORKING GROUP

The discussion paper of January 2007 proposed by the Chairman of the Special Working Group reflected the two above mentioned approaches. It proposed an Article 8*bis* to be inserted into the Rome Statute of the ICC. The proposed Article

7 Press Conference by Chairman of Working Group on Crime of Aggression, 31 Jan 2007 (available at www.un.org/News/briefings/docs/2007/070131_Wenaweser.doc.htm); Report of the Special Working Group on the Crime of Aggression, ICC-ASP/5/35 Annex II, 9 (available at www.icc-cpi.int/asp). See further Res ICC-ASP/8/Res 6 on the Review Conference of 31 May–11 June 2010 (available at www.icc-cpi.int/asp).

8 See concluding remarks in Ch IV section 3 *supra*.

9 Information on cases before the ICC, as well as ongoing investigations into crimes within the jurisdiction of the Court, see www.icc-cpi.int.

10 The Report of the Informal inter-sessional meeting of the Special Working Group of the Crime of Aggression, held at the Liechtenstein Institute on Self-Determination, Woodrow Wilson School, Princeton University, US (8–11 Jun 2006) (available at www.icc-cpi.int/library/asp/ASP_Advancecopy_Aggression200629jun.pdf).

11 Explanatory note, Discussion Paper proposed by the Chairman, ICC-ASP/5/SWGCA/2 (16 Jan 2007) par 5 (available at www.icc-cpi.int).

provided for two variants. Variant (a) reflected the *differentiated* approach and Variant (b) the *monistic* approach.

'*Variant (a):*
1. For the purpose of the present Statute, a person commits a "crime of aggression" when, being in a position effectively to exercise control over or to direct the political or military action of a State, that person (leads) (directs) (organizes and/or directs) (engages in) the planning, preparation, initiation or execution of an act of aggression/armed attack

Variant (b):
1. For the purpose of the present Statute, a person commits a "crime of aggression" when, being in a position effectively to exercise control over or to direct the political or military action of a State, that person orders or participates actively in the planning, preparation, initiation or execution of an act of aggression/armed attack

continue under both variants:
[which, by its character, gravity and scale, constitutes a manifest violation of the Charter of the United Nations] [such as, in particular, a war of aggression or an act which has the object or result of establishing a military occupation of, or annexing, the territory of another State or part thereof].

2. For the purpose of paragraph 1, "act of aggression" means an act referred to in [articles 1 and 3 of] United Nations General Assembly resolution 3314 (XXIX) of 14 December 1974.

under variant (a) above:
3. The provisions of articles 25, paragraph 3(f), and [28] of the Statute do not apply to the crime of aggression.

under variant (b) above:
3. The provisions of articles 25, paragraph 3, and [28] of the Statute do not apply to the crime of aggression.

4. Where the Prosecutor intends to proceed with an investigation in respect of a crime of aggression, the Court shall first ascertain whether the Security Council has made a determination of an act of aggression committed by the State concerned. If no Security Council determination exists, the Court shall notify the Security Council of the situation before the Court.

5. Where the Security Council does not make such a determination within [six] months after the date of the notification,
Option 1: the Court may proceed with the case.
Option 2: the Court may not proceed with the case.

Option 3: the Court may, with due regard to the provisions of articles 12, 14 and 24 of the [UN] Charter, request the General Assembly of the United Nations to make such a determination within [12] months. In the absence of such a determination, the Court may proceed with the case.
Option 4: the Court may proceed if it ascertains that the International Court of Justice has made a finding in proceedings brought under Chapter II of its Statute that an act of aggression has been committed by the State concerned.'[12]

2.2. DEFINING THE CONDUCT OF THE INDIVIDUAL

The two approaches above entail the typologies of individual criminal responsibility provided for in the general principles provisions of the ICC Statute.[13] Article 25, which provides for the principle of individual criminal responsibility, is central to the function of the ICC, being an international court with jurisdiction over *individuals* (natural persons) accused of the crimes listed in the Statute.[14]

2.2.1. Variant (a): The differentiated approach

Variant (a) above (the differentiated approach) provided for direct (immediate) perpetration, co-perpetration and perpetration by means ('through another

12 Assembly of States Parties, Resumed fifth session, Discussion paper on the crime of aggression proposed by the Chairman (16 Jan 2007), Annex, ICC-ASP/5/SWGCA/2 (available at www.icc-cpi.int/asp).
13 See Part 3 of the Rome Statute of the ICC.
14 Art 25 of the Rome Statute of the ICC provides as follows: '1. The Court shall have jurisdiction over natural persons pursuant to this Statute. 2. A person who commits a crime within the jurisdiction of the Court shall be individually responsible and liable for punishment in accordance with this Statute. 3. In accordance with this Statute, a person shall be criminally responsible and liable for punishment for a crime within the jurisdiction of the Court if that person: (a) Commits such a crime, whether as an individual, jointly with another or through another person, regardless of whether that other person is criminally responsible; (b) Orders, solicits or induces the commission of such a crime which in fact occurs or is attempted; (c) For the purpose of facilitating the commission of such a crime, aids, abets or otherwise assists in its commission or its attempted commission, including providing the means for its commission; (d) In any other way contributes to the commission or attempted commission of such a crime by a group of persons acting with a common purpose. Such contribution shall be intentional and shall either: (i) Be made with the aim of furthering the criminal activity or criminal purpose of the group, where such activity or purpose involves the commission of a crime within the jurisdiction of the Court; or (ii) Be made in the knowledge of the intention of the group to commit the crime; (e) In respect of the crime of genocide, directly and publicly incites others to commit genocide; (f) Attempts to commit such a crime by taking action that commences its execution by means of a substantial step, but the crime does not occur because of circumstances independent of the person's intentions. However, a person who abandons the effort to commit the crime or otherwise prevents the completion of the crime shall not be liable for punishment under this Statute for the attempt to commit that crime if that person completely and voluntarily gave up the criminal purpose. 4. No provision in this Statute relating to individual criminal responsibility shall affect the responsibility of States under international law.'

person').[15] In addition, it provided for the criminal responsibility of individuals who order, solicit, or induce the crime of aggression (whether it occurs in fact or is attempted).[16] The forms of criminal responsibility that emanate from Article 25(3)(b) are actually quite distinct. The first form of responsibility in this context is for a *perpetrator by means*. As Kai Ambos noted, '[a] person who orders a crime is not a mere accomplice but rather a perpetrator by means, using a subordinate to commit the crime.'[17] In this sense Article 25(3)(b) actually complements Article 28, which provides for command-responsibility.[18] However, in the case of aggression, Variant (a) explicitly stated that Article 28 (Responsibility of commanders and other superiors) of the Rome Statute of the ICC does not apply to the crime of aggression. There was some logic to that proposal. The nature of the crime of aggression is such that it is really inconceivable that members of the military (who are not in a position to *direct* the political or military apparatus of the state) can commit the crime of aggression, for which their superiors will then (on the basis of Article 28) be held responsible.[19]

The second form of responsibility provided for in Article 25(3)(b) is 'soliciting'. Kai Ambos commented as follows on the meaning of 'solicits' and 'induces' in this context:

> 'Soliciting a crime means, inter alia, to command, encourage, request or incite another person to engage in specific conduct to commit it. To induce basically means to influence another person to commit a crime. Inducing is a kind of umbrella term covering soliciting which, in turn, has a stronger and more specific meaning than inducing ... In sum, both forms of complicity are applicable to cases in which a person is influenced by another to commit a crime. Such influence is normally of psychological nature but may also take the form of physical pressure within the

15 Art 25(3)(a) Rome Statute of the ICC.

16 Art 25(3)(b) Rome Statute of the ICC.

17 Kai Ambos 'Individual criminal responsibility' in Otto Triffterer (ed) (Commentary on the Rome Statute) (*supra*) 480. See further *Prosecutor v Jean Paul Akayesu*, Case No ICTR-96-4-T, 2 Sept 1998, par 483: 'By ordering the commission of one of the crimes ... a person also incurs individual criminal responsibility. Ordering implies a superior-subordinate relationship between the person giving the order and the one executing it. In other words, the person in a position of authority uses it to convince another to commit an offence. In certain legal systems, including that of Rwanda, ordering is a form of complicity through instructions given to the direct perpetrator of an offence. Regarding the position of authority, the Chamber considers that sometimes it can be just a question of fact.' For further comment on this case see William Schabas in André Klip and Göran Sluiter (eds) *Annotated Leading Cases of International Criminal Tribunals – Student Ed* (2005) Intersentia, Antwerp/Oxford, 427–442.

18 See comment by Kai Ambos in Otto Triffterer (Commentary on the Rome Statute) (*supra*) 480.

19 Despite significant agreement in the Special Working Group that Art 28 should not apply to the crime of aggression, there was disagreement on whether the non-applicability needs to be specified or not. See Discussion paper on the crime of aggression (ICC-ASP/5/SWGCA/2) (*supra*).

meaning of *vis compulsiva*. Unlike in the case of "ordering" a superior-subordinate relationship is not necessary.'[20]

Variant (a) of the definition of aggression further provided for responsibility on the basis of aiding, abetting and assistance.[21] In the context of aggression the meaning and application of the words 'providing the means for its commission' (as per Article 25(3)(c)) could have far-reaching consequences for individuals who are not necessarily political or military leaders. In this regard the historical examples of the so-called Nuremberg industrialists' prosecutions[22] could hold lessons for the criminal liability of individuals for the crime of aggression under the Rome Statute of the ICC. Although the prosecutions of a number of rich industrialists sympathetic to the Nazi regime's aggressive foreign policy were not successful as far as the charges relating to aggression were concerned, the implications for possible future prosecutions of individuals who made an aggressive war effort possible (through resources or other forms of assistance) should be considered. Allison Marston Danner noted the following:

> 'International prosecutors contemplating bringing charges of aggression against corporate officers will have to consider the Nuremberg precedents carefully. They must assess whether the political climate and legal understanding of aggression has changed sufficiently in the past sixty years to garner a different result than that recorded in the earlier cases.'[23]

With reference to the jurisprudence of the *ad hoc* ICTY and ICTR, Kai Ambos concluded that aiding and abetting (in terms of the Rome Statute) should mean the following:

> '[Aiding] and abetting encompasses any assistance, whether physical or psychological, which, however, had a substantial effect on the commission of the main crime. In other words, the limiting element is the "substantial effect" requirement. Thus, the question arises when an effect is "substantial". This cannot be decided by an abstract formula but only on a case by case basis taking into account modern theories of attribution. At any rate, a concrete inquiry may be a mere academic exercise since the subsidiary mode of complicity of "assist otherwise" introduces an even lower threshold for accomplice liability than aiding and abetting. Although this concept is already included in the aiding and abetting formula as interpreted by the case law it makes quite clear that there should be virtually no objective threshold for accomplice liability.'[24]

---

20 Kai Ambos in Otto Triffterer (Commentary on the Rome Statute) (*supra*) 480–481.

21 See Art 25(3)(c) of the Rome Statute of the ICC.

22 For a discussion of the implications of these post-Second World War prosecutions see Allison Marston Danner 'The Nuremberg Industrialist prosecutions and aggressive war' 46 *Virginia Journal of International Law* (2006) 651–676. See further Ch III section 5 (*supra*).

23 Allison Marsten Danner (Nuremberg industrialist prosecutions) (*supra*) 676.

24 Kai Ambos in Otto Triffterer (Commentary on the Rome Statute) (*supra*) 482–483.

The subjective element contained in Article 25(3)(c) – 'for the purpose of facilitating' – means that the accomplice (the individual aiding or abetting) must have special knowledge about the circumstances in which the assistance is taking place. Kai Ambos commented that this formulation goes further than the *mens rea* requirement in terms of Article 30[25] of the Rome Statute of the ICC. The accomplice will thus have to be more than just aloof or nonchalant about his or her assistance. This is a 'specific subjective requirement stricter than mere knowledge.'[26]

Variant (a) also included criminal responsibility on the basis of common purpose,[27] as provided for in Article 25(3)(d) of the Rome Statute of the ICC. That means an intentional contribution by each participant to a certain intended outcome, as well as alternative additional requirements complementing the individual contributions.[28]

The alternative additional requirements refer to 'the aim of furthering the criminal activity or criminal purpose of the group, where such activity or purpose involves the commission of a crime within the jurisdiction of the Court';[29] or a contribution 'made in the knowledge of the intention of the group to commit the crime'.[30] The first alternative typically involves a specific intent to 'promote the practical acts and ideological objectives of the group'.[31] The second alternative refers to the participant's knowledge or awareness of the crime that the group intends to commit.[32] It is submitted that the language of the Rome Statute in this regard favours 'active association' rather than 'conspiracy' or 'mandate' as a basis for the doctrine of common purpose. 'Active association' seems to be a wider notion than 'agreement'.[33]

---

25 Art 30 of the Rome Statute of the ICC provides for the mental element of criminal liability: '1. Unless otherwise provided, a person shall be criminally responsible and liable for punishment for a crime within the jurisdiction of the Court only if the material elements are committed with intent and knowledge. 2. For the purposes of this article, a person has intent where: (a) In relation to conduct, that person means to engage in the conduct; (b) In relation to a consequence, that person means to cause that consequence or is aware that it will occur in the ordinary course of events. 3. For the purposes of this article, "knowledge" means awareness that a circumstance exists or a consequence will occur in the ordinary course of events. "Know" and "knowingly" shall be construed accordingly.'

26 Kai Ambos in Otto Triffterer (Commentary on the Rome Statute) (*supra*) 483.

27 See in general (including references to comparative material) Gerhard Kemp et al *Criminal Law in South Africa* (2012) Oxford University Press, Cape Town, 234–245; Kai Ambos in Otto Triffterer (Commentary on the Rome Statute) (*supra*) 483–486, for commentary on the meaning of common purpose in the context of the Rome Statute of the ICC, including references to French, German and Spanish legal doctrine on common purpose.

28 Kai Ambos in Otto Triffterer (Commentary on the Rome Statute) (*supra*) 484.

29 Art 25(3)(d)(i).

30 Art 25(3)(d)(ii).

31 Kai Ambos in Otto Triffterer (Commentary on the Rome Statute) (*supra*) 486.

32 *Ibid.*

33 CR Snyman (Criminal Law) (*supra*) 259.

Variant (a) did not provide for attempt (as per Article 25(3)(f) of the Rome Statute). It is curious that Article 25(3)(f) was excluded from variant (a). At Nuremberg and Tokyo attempt liability was not explicitly provided for, but, as Kai Ambos has pointed out, the criminalisation of 'preparation' and 'planning' of a war of aggression was indeed made punishable 'as a complete offence' at the two *ad hoc* tribunals.[34] However, it seems doubtful that 'preparation' and 'planning' of aggression can be understood as having the same meaning as 'attempted aggression'. Werle and Jessberger comment that the ICC Statute does not criminalise the *preparatory* phase.[35] Preparatory here means that actions not involving an execution of the crime and the absence of any realisation of material elements of the definition of the crime.[36]

The present position seems to be that, under customary international law, the planning and preparation phases are regarded as criminal with regard to the crime of aggression.[37] This rule of customary international law follows from the prosecutions at Nuremberg and Tokyo,[38] as well as the Control Council Law No 10[39] in Germany after the Second World War. Planning, preparation, initiation or waging of a war of aggression was criminalised in terms of the Nuremberg Charter,[40] the Tokyo Charter[41] and Control Council Law No 10.[42] With regard to the criminality of 'planning and preparation' of a war of aggression, Werle and Jessberger submitted that there can only be criminal responsibility for planning and preparation if such activities 'actually result in the initiation of hostilities.'[43] From the Nuremberg judgments it is clear that much of the aggressive display of military force by Nazi Germany that led to the occupation of Austria and Czechoslovakia, was regarded as 'aggressive action' by the IMT Nuremberg.[44] These actions were referred to as evidence of Germany's aggressive foreign policy, but did not form the basis of criminal liability as such.[45] Thus, while variant (a) of the proposed definition of aggression provided for the planning, preparation, or initiation of an act of aggression/ armed attack, it is submitted that this would add a very specific dimension of individual criminal responsibility to the Rome Statute. While the Rome Statute

34 Kai Ambos in Otto Triffterer (Commentary on the Rome Statute) (*supra*) 488.
35 Gerhard Werle and Florian Jessberger (Principles of International Criminal Law) (*supra*) 265.
36 *Ibid.*
37 Gerhard Werle & Florian Jessberger (Principles of International Criminal Law) (*supra*) 263.
38 See Ch III section 3 *et seq*, *supra*.
39 See Ch III section 3.5 *supra*.
40 Nuremberg Charter Art 6(a).
41 Tokyo Charter Art 5(a).
42 Control Council Law No 10 Art II(1)(a).
43 Gerhard Werle and Florian Jessberger (Principles of International Criminal Law) (*supra*) 537.
44 See Ch III section 3.2 *supra*.
45 See Gerhard Werle and Florian Jessberger (Principles of International Criminal Law) (*supra*) 537 for a discussion of the judgment of the IMT Nuremberg with respect to the 'planning' of aggression. See further Ch III section 3.2 *et seq* (*supra*).

does provide for responsibility on the basis of 'attempt' (but not on the basis of preparatory conduct), the customary law position (namely that individuals can be held liable for the preparation of a war of aggression), should be reflected in any definition of aggression for purposes of the Rome Statute of the ICC. This aspect is more fully explored below (in the context of the discussion of the November 2009 Resolution adopted by the Assembly of States Parties).

2.2.2. Variant (b): The 'monistic' approach

Variant (b) (as quoted in section 2.1 above) did not provide for any of the grounds of individual responsibility as listed in Article 25(3) of the Rome Statute of the ICC. While some delegations who participated in the discussions in the Special Working Group on Aggression supported the 'simple and pragmatic' approach contained in variant (b), the more detailed approach reflected in variant (a) received more support. The delegations that supported variant (a) felt that this approach 'would preserve consistency among the crimes contained in the Statute and with the "General Principles of Criminal Law" contained in Part 3 of the Statute, *in particular [Article 25(3)*].'[46] Thus, while both variants (a) and (b) defined aggression as a leadership crime, variant (b) seemed to be too restrictive in its approach. It is submitted that variant (a) was much closer to the understanding of individual criminal liability for aggression as applied at Nuremberg and the subsequent trials. Aggression is a leadership crime *par excellence*; however, the criminalisation of forms of criminal liability such as incitement or common purpose (as per Article 25(3) of the Rome Statute) best reflects the complexities of leadership and the structures that often make leadership (and decision making) effective.

The classical proponents of the Just War Theory argued that '[monarchs] and those who command the sovereign power of the state are assigned exclusive responsibility for recourse to aggressive war, that is, for matters of *jus ad bellum*, whereas the responsibility of soldiers is limited to the use of proper methods of fighting and other issues of *jus in bello*.'[47] At present a distinction is still drawn between the crime of aggression (in essence, the criminalisation of the use of armed force) and war crimes (the criminalisation of conduct during the war, irrespective of the legality of the war).[48] However, it is submitted that the criminalisation of aggression as proposed in variant (a) was not only a better reflection of the scope and understanding of aggression as a leadership crime

---

46 Discussion paper proposed by the Chairman, Assembly of States Parties, Resumed 5th session (29 Jan–1 Feb 2007) Annex II, Report of the Special Working Group on the Crime of Aggression, ICC-ASP/5/35 (available at www.icc-cpi.org) (emphasis added).

47 David Rodin *War & Self-Defense* (2002) Clarendon Press, Oxford, 167.

48 See Introduction section 2 (*supra*) for a discussion on the distinction between *jus ad bellum* and *jus in bello* as issues of demarcation.

since the Nuremberg and Tokyo judgments, but was certainly more in line with the complexities of the very notion of 'leadership'. With reference to the distinction between 'leaders' and 'soldiers' in the context of aggression, David Rodin noted the following:

> 'It seems plausible to conclude that soldiers, and not just sovereigns, are responsible for the aggressive wars in which they engage. This is true in the sense that anyone who participates in, and contributes towards, a larger communal project is responsible for the legality or morality of that project: *they are responsible for their contribution*.'[49]

The notion that an individual should be held liable for his or her *contribution* to the criminal conduct certainly lies at the heart of the general principles of individual criminal responsibility as provided for in Article 25 of the Rome Statute.

2.3. THE ACT OF AGGRESSION AND THE CONDUCT OF THE STATE

The two above-mentioned variants of the draft provisions on aggression provided not only for the conduct and responsibility of the individual, but also for the required state conduct.[50] Both variants (a) and (b) referred to 'act of aggression' and 'armed attack' to describe the act of the state. Although both terms were retained in the two variants, the 2007 Report of the Special Working Group on the Crime of Aggression noted that 'broad support' was expressed for the term 'act of aggression'. The latter is a term that is used in Article 39 of the UN Charter and was furthermore defined in the General Assembly Definition of Aggression of 1974 (Resolution 3314 (XXIX)). The Special Working Group regarded the use of the term 'act of aggression' as a well-established term (with some Security Council resolutions on 'acts of aggression' to help guide interpretation in this regard). Future interpretation of the term could thus be guided by Article 39 and the General Assembly Definition.[51]

It was noted in the 2007 Report of the Special Working Group that, although the term 'armed attack' was linked to the concept of self-defence under Article 51[52]

49 David Rodin (War & Self-Defense) (*supra*) 173 (emphasis added).

50 See para 1 and 2 of the Special Working Group's draft Art 8*bis* as quoted in section 2.1 *supra*.

51 ICC, Assembly of States Parties, Resumed 5th Session, 29 Jan–1 Feb 2007, Discussion paper proposed by the Chairman, Annex II, Report of the Special Working Group on the Crime of Aggression, ICC-ASP/5/35 par 14 (available at www.icc-cpi.org).

52 Art 51 of the UN Charter provides as follows: 'Nothing in the present Charter shall impair the inherent right of individual or collective self-defence if an *armed attack* occurs against a Member of the United Nations, until the Security Council has taken the measures necessary to maintain international peace and security. Measures taken by Members in the exercise of

of the UN Charter, it lacked a specific definition. It was not defined in the Charter or in other international instruments.[53] There is also a difference in wording between Article 2(4) and Article 51 of the Charter. While the latter refers to 'armed attack', Article 2(4) refers to the broader notion of 'threat or use of force'. The difference between the narrower concept of 'armed attack' in Article 51 and the broader notion of 'threat or use of force' in Article 2(4) led Albrecht Randelzhofer to the following conclusion:

> '[Any] state affected by another state's unlawful use of force not reaching the threshold of an "armed attack", is bound, if not exactly to endure the violation, then at least to respond only by means falling short of the use or threat of force, which are thus often totally ineffective. This at first sight unacceptable result is undoubtedly intended by the Charter, since the unilateral use of force is meant to be excluded as far as possible. Until an armed attack occurs, states are expected to renounce forcible self-defence ... Only if and when the prohibited use of force rises to an armed attack can the state concerned resort to forcible measures for its defence.'[54]

The difference between the two notions does make sense in terms of the UN Charter's general intention to discourage the use of force by states. In terms of the criminalisation of aggression, the view was expressed in the Special Working Group that 'the notion of "armed attack" should be retained as it reflected the idea that only [the] gravest violations of the United Nations Charter are covered by the crime of aggression.'[55] This view is also consistent with the commentary of the International Law Commission on Article 16 of the 1996 Draft Code of Crimes against the Peace and Security of Mankind, as discussed in Chapter IV above.[56] The conduct of the State will thus have to be of a *serious nature*. This could be a violation of Article 2(4) of the UN Charter[57] or conduct that constituted 'a sufficiently serious violation of an international obligation'.[58]

The 2007 Report of the Special Working Group reflected the general view that the conduct of the state will in essence be 'the use of armed force'[59] and will in all probability be an act listed in Article 3 of the General Assembly Definition of

---

this right of self-defence shall be immediately reported to the Security Council and shall not in any way affect the authority and responsibility of the Security Council under the present Charter to take at any time such action as it deems necessary in order to maintain or restore international peace and security' (emphasis added). See further Ch II section 5.1 *supra*.

53 See Report of the Special Working Group (*supra*) par 14.

54 Albrecht Randelzhofer 'Article 51' in Bruno Simma (Charter of the United Nations Vol I) (*supra*) 790.

55 Report of the Special Working Group (*supra*) par 15.

56 See discussion in Ch IV section 2.2.3 (*supra*).

57 See discussion in Ch II, in particular section 3 *et seq*, *supra*.

58 Arthur Watts (The International Law Commission Vol III) (*supra*) 1739.

59 See Art 1 of the UN General Assembly Def of Aggression (1974) quoted in Ch IV section 2.3 *supra*.

Aggression of 1974.[60] Of course, the list contained in the 1974 Definition is not exhaustive and 'the Security Council may determine that other acts constitute aggression under the provisions of the Charter.'[61] The 1974 list does not explicitly provide for 'attacks' other than armed attacks. During the operational period of the Special Working Group there occurred events that could have had an impact on the debate about the type of attacks to be included in the eventual list of attacks to be covered by the acts of aggression for purposes of the definition of the crime of aggression. For instance, the impact of technology on the means by which states could 'attack' other states (and cause the kind of damage that could equal or surpass any armed attack), could have been considered. In May 2007 it was reported that Russia (or at least entities in Russia acting in a concerted fashion) unleashed a so-called 'cyberwar' to massively disable the Estonian government and financial institutions, which are all heavily dependent on functioning websites. Estonia, a member of NATO, regarded the attacks as very serious and raised the issue with other countries in Europe and with NATO. However, the Estonian defence minister conceded that Article V of the North Atlantic Treaty (concerning collective self-defence) could not be activated, since the Treaty does not define cyber-attacks as 'clear military action'.[62] The lack of definitive engagement during the drafting process with the phenomenon of cyber-attacks and the question of whether cyber-attacks could under certain circumstances be regarded as akin to armed attacks, clearly resulted in the eventual Article 8*bis* being silent on the matter; its focus on 'bullets and bombs'[63] essentially following the 1974 list.

The nature or object and the result of the act of the State were further contentious issues that the Special Working Group had to consider. These matters essentially concern the nature of the act of aggression or the armed attack. The text in the two sets of brackets under the proposed paragraph 1 (in terms of the 2007 Report) described the nature of the act of aggression/armed attack with reference to 'a manifest violation of the Charter of the United Nations' and links that with a 'war of aggression' (which was the term used by the Nuremberg Tribunal), or, alternatively, 'an act which has the object or result of establishing a military occupation of, or annexing, the territory of another State or part thereof'. The threshold provided for in the first sets of brackets ('manifest violation of the Charter of the United Nations') received broad support in the Special Working

60 For the full text of the UN General Assembly Def of Aggression (1974), see Ch IV section 2.3 *supra*.

61 Art 4 UN General Assembly Def of Aggression (*supra*).

62 See statements by Defence Minister Jaak Aaviksoo in 'Russia accused of unleashing cyberwar to disable Estonia' *The Guardian* 17 May 2007 (available at www.guardian.co.uk/print/0,,329864981-103610,00.html).

63 Carrie McDougall *The crime of aggression under the Rome Statute of the International Criminal Court* (2013) Cambridge University Press, Cambridge, 110.

Group – the supporters of this threshold wanted to exclude 'borderline' cases from the jurisdiction of the ICC.[64] It is true that the Preamble as well as Article 1 of the Rome Statute of the ICC also make reference to the inherent limitation of the jurisdiction of the ICC to 'the most serious crimes of international concern'. It is submitted that this threshold contained in the first set of brackets provided an important context. The jurisdictional threshold provided for in the Rome Statute of the ICC must be seen in the context of the collective security framework of the UN Charter. This would provide the proper threshold to determine whether state conduct is serious enough to be regarded as an act of aggression. Apart from this, one should also be mindful of the envisaged role of the Security Council, which is considered below.

The text in the second set of brackets under paragraph 1 of the above version of Article 8*bis* linked the threshold in the first set of brackets to a *non-exhaustive list* of instances of violations, but highlighted the two particular instances of 'manifest violations' of the UN Charter, namely 'a war of aggression' or 'an act which has the object or result of establishing a military occupation of, or annexing, the territory of another State or part thereof'. The 2007 Report of the Special Working Group on the Crime of Aggression noted the following:

> 'Different views were expressed concerning the usefulness of retaining the second set of brackets. While some support was voiced for the notion of "war of aggression", mainly so as to utilize the Nuremberg precedent, other delegations emphasized that such a reference was not desirable as it was closely linked to the modalities of warfare in World War II and would unduly limit the scope of the crime of aggression. It was also pointed out that the non-exhaustive list of examples in the second set of brackets was difficult to reconcile with the principle of legality. Some delegations therefore called for the deletion of the content of the second set of brackets.'[65]

It was pointed out in Chapter IV above that although the UN General Assembly Definition of Aggression (1974) was the result of political compromises (in an era of détente) and does not constitute a legally binding instrument,[66] it nevertheless has the potential to serve as a valuable text for purposes of determining possible acts of aggression.[67] It was however also pointed out that a number of international legal scholars criticised the text as being weak from a (criminal) law perspective. Thus it is concluded that the 1974 text could best serve as a guide to the Security Council to help determine acts of aggression, which is essentially a political and not a legal exercise.[68]

---

64 Report of the Special Working Group (*supra*) par 16.
65 Report of the Special Working Group (*supra*) par 18.
66 See Ch IV section 2.3.1 *supra*.
67 *Ibid.*
68 *Ibid.*

The 2007 Report of the Special Working Group on Aggression noted that 'broad support was expressed for the retention' of the reference to the UN General Assembly Definition of Aggression in paragraph 2 of the above version of Article 8*bis*.[69] According to one proposal an 'act of aggression' means the acts listed in Articles 1 and 3 of the General Assembly Definition. The supporters of this proposal at the Special Working Group argued that a reference to the General Assembly Definition as a whole would be a perpetuation of many of the criticisms raised against the Definition (as also pointed out in Chapter IV above). For instance, Article 4 of the General Assembly Definition contains references to *unspecified* acts, which is problematic from a legality point of view. However, a reference to Articles 1 and 3 was regarded by many delegates at the Special Working Group as 'pertinent and concrete' enough to satisfy the legality principle.[70] Some delegates argued that all the articles in the General Assembly Definition of Aggression are interlinked and should be interpreted as a whole. The supporters of the inclusion of the General Assembly Definition as a whole apparently gave a lot of weight to the fact that the 1974 Definition was a 'careful compromise' that should not lightly be tampered with.

2.4. CONDITIONS FOR THE EXERCISE OF JURISDICTION BY THE ICC

2.4.1. The role of the Security Council

Paragraphs 4 and 5 of the Special Working Group's 2007 proposal on aggression (as quoted in section 2.1 above) set out the proposed role of the Security Council as part of the conditions for the exercise of the ICC's jurisdiction over the crime of aggression. It was pointed out in Chapter V that most delegates at the Rome Conference on the ICC were adamant that the Security Council's primary responsibility for peace and security should be respected and accommodated in the context of ICC jurisdiction over the crime of aggression. The debate on the role of the Security Council continued as part of the process to find an acceptable definition for aggression as well as conditions for the exercise of jurisdiction of the ICC.

The 2007 Report of the Special Working Group on Aggression noted the following:

> 'Divergent views were expressed as to whether the exercise of jurisdiction over the crime of aggression should require a prior determination of the State act of

69 Report of the Special Working Group (*supra*) par 19.
70 Report of the Special Working Group (*supra*) par 20.

> aggression by the Security Council, and on the consequences of the absence of such determination. A view was expressed that in either case the [ICC] would benefit from the authority of the Security Council as there would be political backing for the Court's investigation of situations.'[71]

From the discussions in the Special Working Group four broad proposals emerged regarding the precise role of the Security Council vis-à-vis the ICC in cases of aggression.

The *first proposal* envisaged a dispensation where the Prosecutor of the ICC could proceed with an investigation into a possible case of aggression without prior determination by the Security Council as to the existence of an act of aggression. From the 2007 Report of the Special Working Group it seems that some delegates felt that the independence of the ICC (and thus also the Prosecutor's office) would be undermined if the Security Council (a political body) first had to determine the existence of a state act of aggression. The *second proposal* focused on Article 5(2) of the Rome Statute of the ICC which provides that any future provision on the crime of aggression 'shall be consistent with the relevant provisions of the Charter of the United Nations.' Thus, '[under] Article 39 of the Charter, the Security Council was the only organ competent to determine that a State act of aggression had occurred.'[72]

The *third proposal* also regarded the role of the Security Council as important, but slightly less important than the second proposal suggested. In terms of this point of view, the 'competence of the Security Council under Article 39 of the Charter [is] primary, but not exclusive'.[73] This third grouping also envisaged roles for the General Assembly and the International Court of Justice. It seems that this third proposal put the emphasis on the independence of the ICC (and the competence of the ICC to make an independent determination of a State act of aggression as a jurisdictional fact). However, unlike the first proposal above, this third proposal would want to allocate *complementary roles* to the main bodies of the United Nations (the Security Council, the General Assembly and the International Court of Justice) to help the ICC to determine the existence of a state act of aggression.

It is suggested in Chapter I above that the relationship between the main UN bodies – especially the Security Council and the General Assembly – should not be seen as a static relationship. The realities of international relations and political events can have an impact on the relationship between these bodies. It is furthermore submitted that the Uniting for Peace Resolution can play an

---

71 Report of the Special Working Group (*supra*) par 23.
72 Report of the Special Working Group (*supra*) par 26.
73 Report of the Special Working Group (*supra*) par 27.

important role in the relationship between the General Assembly and the Security Council. It needs to be pointed out here that paragraph 1 of the Uniting for Peace Resolution of 1950 provides that when the Security Council fails to exercise its primary responsibility for the maintenance of international peace and security, in particular in cases where there appears to be a threat to the peace, breach of the peace, or an act of aggression, then the General Assembly shall consider the matter immediately with a view to making appropriate recommendations to member states for collective measures (including the use of force) to be taken.[74]

The main purpose of the Uniting for Peace Resolution is to provide for a role for the General Assembly to take action when the Security Council is for some or other reason (most probably because of a veto by one of the permanent members) not in a position to take action when there are situations which could be acts of aggression or other threats to international peace. In the *Israeli Wall* case[75] the ICJ considered a request by the General Assembly (in terms of a resolution adopted at an emergency session of the General Assembly in terms of the Uniting for Peace Resolution) for an advisory opinion by the ICJ concerning the legal consequences arising from the wall constructed by the Israeli government. As pointed out in Chapter I above, this wall (which separates the territory of Israel from Palestinian territories) is very controversial and the effect of the wall is considered by many to violate the human rights of Palestinians, and to be a threat to the peace in the region. The reason why the General Assembly became involved in the matter was that the Security Council (the primary organ responsible for matters concerning peace and security) was not able to act because the US used its veto in the Security Council to block any discussions on the construction of the wall and the implications of that for peace and security. However, the matter remained on the Security Council's agenda. The ICJ held that the General Assembly can make recommendations (including a request for an advisory opinion form the ICJ) where the Security Council is incapable to act in situation affecting peace and security, or on acts of aggression. This power of the General Assembly is derived from the Uniting for Peace Resolution. The ICJ held that the General Assembly can even exercise this power while the particular situation is still on the Security Council's agenda.[76] The potential beneficial role of UN bodies other than the Security Council in the process to determine acts of aggression, did not find favour and is not part of the eventual articles 15*bis* and 15*ter*, to be analysed in the next chapter. The potentially progressive ideas

74 See discussion in Ch I section 1.1 *supra*.

75 See reference in Ch I section 1.1.1 *supra*.

76 See *Israeli Wall* case (*supra*) par 30 *et seq*. For a critical discussion of the case, see Michael Cowling 'The relationship between the Security Council and the General Assembly with particular reference to the ICJ Advisory Opinion in the "Israeli Wall" case' 30 *SAYIL* (2005) 50–81.

regarding a broader international involvement in the determination of acts of aggression (that is with the inclusion of the UN General Assembly) as contained in the third proposal, were not taken up in the final articles that were adopted at Kampala.

Emphasising the rights of the individual accused, the third proposal (wisely) suggested that the ICC should *not be bound* by any prior determinations of an act of aggression by UN bodies (including the General Assembly and the Security Council).[77]

A *fourth proposal* suggested that a system of checks and balances should be put in place in order to fulfil the requirements of Article 5(2) of the Rome Statute of the ICC. The challenge seemed to be to find a solution 'which duly takes into account the special responsibility of the Security Council under Chapter VII of the United Nations Charter, while allowing the [ICC] to act in the absence of a determination by the Security Council.'[78]

2.4.2. Procedural considerations

2.4.2.1. Security Council determination as a condition for the exercise of ICC jurisdiction

Paragraph 4 of the Special Working Group's 2007 proposals (quoted above) provided for Security Council involvement in cases of aggression before the ICC. The text of the proposed paragraph 4 reflected the fine balance between an independent ICC and the traditional role of the Security Council in matters concerning international peace and security. According to this proposal, before the Prosecutor can proceed with an investigation into a possible case of aggression, 'the Court shall first ascertain whether the Security Council has made a determination of an act of aggression committed by the State concerned.' If such a determination exists, the ICC 'shall notify the Security Council of the situation before the Court'.

On the face of it, Article 13(b) of the Rome Statute of the ICC might provide a procedural avenue for Security Council determinations of state acts of aggression, thus playing a role in the process of ICC jurisdiction over the crime of aggression. Article 13 provides as follows:

> 'The Court may exercise its jurisdiction with respect to a crime referred to in article 5 in accordance with the provisions of this Statute if:

---

77 Report of the Special Working Group (*supra*) par 27.
78 Report of the Special Working Group (*supra*) par 28.

(a) A situation in which one or more of such crimes appears to have been committed is referred to the Prosecutor by a State Party in accordance with article 14;[79]
(b) A situation in which one or more of such crimes appears to have been committed is referred to the Prosecutor by the Security Council acting under Chapter VII of the Charter of the United Nations; or
(c) The Prosecutor has initiated an investigation in respect of such a crime in accordance with article 15.'

The fact that a referral of a situation by the Security Council is one of the so-called 'trigger mechanisms' of the ICC, must be seen in context. Where cases are referred to the Prosecutor in terms of Article 13(a) or where the Prosecutor initiates an investigation *proprio motu* in terms of Article 13(c), state acceptance is a precondition for the exercise of jurisdiction by the ICC.[80] The trigger mechanism provided for in Article 13(b) was one of the controversial issues before and during the Rome Diplomatic Conference on the ICC in 1998. While the majority of delegations were in favour of a referral role for the Security Council, there was a small minority of delegations who argued that a referral role for the Security Council could lead to political abuse. In particular, these delegations were worried that the five permanent members of the Security Council could use their veto to stop referrals of situations where they, their allies or their interests were involved or affected.[81] These concerns were ultimately rejected in favour of the inclusion of the present Article 13(b) of the Rome Statute.

The majority of delegates accepted that the Security Council has a pivotal role to play in the collective security system. Furthermore, in the ICTY case *Prosecutor v Dusko Tadic*[82] the tribunal held (with reference to Article 41 of the UN Charter) that the Security Council has the necessary competency to refer situations that

---

79 Art 14 provides as follows: '1. A State Party may refer to the Prosecutor a situation in which one or more crimes within the jurisdiction of the Court appear to have been committed requesting the Prosecutor to investigate the situation for the purpose of determining whether one or more specific persons should be charged with the commission of such crimes. 2. As far as possible, a referral shall specify the relevant circumstances and be accompanied by such supporting documentation as is available to the State referring the situation.'

80 See Art 12(2) of the Rome Statute of the ICC: 'In the case of article 13, paragraph (a) or (c), the Court may exercise its jurisdiction if one or more of the following States are Parties to this Statute or have accepted the jurisdiction of the Court in accordance with paragraph 3: (a) The State on the territory of which the conduct in question occurred or, if the crime was committed on board a vessel or aircraft, the State of registration of that vessel or aircraft; (b) The State of which the person accused of the crime is a national.'

81 See in general Sharon Williams 'Article 13 – Exercise of jurisdiction' in Otto Triffterer (Commentary on the Rome Statute) (*supra*) 349.

82 See *Prosecutor v Tadic* (Appeal on Jurisdiction) (*supra*) par 33–36. See further discussion in Ch I section 4.2 *supra*. For critical comments on the role of international criminal tribunals as responses to threats to international peace or acts of aggression, see discussion in Ch I section 4.2 of Michael Reisman (Stopping wars and making peace) (*supra*).

affect international peace and security to international criminal tribunals. It was argued at the Rome Conference that the same competency should also apply with reference to the ICC.[83] In this regard, the delegates who supported the referral role of the Security Council pointed to the enforcement powers[84] of the Security Council which could add to the effectiveness of the ICC regime. Article 87(7) of the Rome Statute provides that where the Security Council has referred a matter to the ICC, the ICC can refer a state which fails to co-operate with the ICC to the Security Council. While states party to the Rome Statute are legally obliged to co-operate with the ICC, non-party states can, on the basis of Security Council referrals, be forced to co-operate with the ICC.[85]

It was also pointed out that once a 'situation' (which is a less specific term than the originally proposed term of 'matter')[86] has been referred to the ICC Prosecutor, the Prosecutor will be able to act independently and the Security Council will not be in a position to influence the proceedings or decisions of the Prosecutor with regard to the individual accused.[87]

2.4.2.2. Procedural options in the absence of a Security Council determination

Paragraph 4 of the Special Working Group's 2007 proposals provided that if no Security Council determination on aggression exists, the ICC must notify the Security Council of the situation (of possible aggression) before the ICC. *Paragraph 5* contained four options pertaining to those instances where the Security Council does *not* make a determination within six months after it was notified by the ICC of a situation of possible aggression.

The views expressed in the Special Working Group reflected the spectrum of ideas on the role of the Security Council vis-à-vis the organs of the ICC. The argument was made in the Special Working Group that, if the Security Council does not make a determination of a possible act of aggression within six months after it was notified by the ICC, the ICC should be in a position to proceed with the case. It was argued that this Option 1 under the proposed paragraph 5

---

83 Sharon Williams in Otto Triffterer (Commentary on the Rome Statute) (*supra*) 349.

84 See Security Council enforcement powers (under the UN Charter) in terms of Art 41 (eg severance of diplomatic relations, complete or partial interruption of economic relations, and interruption of rail, sea, air, postal, telegraphic, radio, and other means of communication); and Art 42 (the use of military force) of the UN Charter.

85 See comments by Claus Kreß and Kimberly Prost in Otto Triffterer (Commentary on the Rome Statute) (*supra*) 1064–1068.

86 It was argued that the term 'situation' is broad enough to only identify the possible criminal conduct, while the term 'matter' would be too specific and would give the Security Council the ability to pinpoint individual accused, thus playing a more substantive role in the conduct of criminal proceedings and undermining the independence of the Prosecutor. See Sharon Williams in Otto Triffterer (Commentary on the Rome Statute) (*supra*) 349.

87 Sharon Williams in Otto Triffterer (Commentary on the Rome Statute) (*supra*) 349.

was the only option consistent with the ICC's independence under the Rome Statute.[88]

The proposal that the ICC should be in a position to proceed with the case if the Security Council does not make a determination of an act of aggression within six months after referral by the ICC, must also be evaluated in the context of Article 16 of the Rome Statute, which provides as follows:

> 'No investigation or prosecution may be commenced or proceeded with under this Statute for a period of 12 months after the Security Council, in a resolution adopted under Chapter VII of the Charter of the United Nations, has requested the Court to that effect; that request may be renewed by the Council under the same conditions.'

The deferral of investigations or prosecutions under Article 16 represents a further aspect of the so-called 'three-pronged relationship' between the ICC and the Security Council.[89] The other two were already referred to above, namely the 'trigger mechanism' in Article 13(b) and the enforcement mechanism in Article 87(7) of the Rome Statute. This power of the Security Council to defer investigations or prosecutions is a clear manifestation of the *political* versus *criminal justice* approaches to aggression.[90] The linking of the deferral power of the Security Council with its Chapter VII powers under the UN Charter is a clear indication that, under certain conditions, the ICC will have to yield to requests by the Security Council where international peace and security issues are at stake. The fact that the Security Council is, in the context of Article 16 of the Rome Statute, obliged to issue its request for deferral via a Chapter VII (UN Charter) resolution, has, according to Bergsmo and Pejić, the following implications:

> '*First*, it ensures that the deferral of an investigation or prosecution is undertaken on the basis of a legally binding Security Council decision, thereby establishing a legal duty on the [ICC] to comply with the deferral request. *Secondly*, given that a Chapter VII resolution pertains to threats to the peace, breaches of the peace and acts of aggression, issuing such a resolution may make the Council acknowledge implicitly that ICC proceedings would be detrimental to the maintenance of international peace and security.'[91]

Those delegates participating in the Special Working Group most in favour of a central role for the Security Council, pointed to the 'primary responsibility of the [Council] for the maintenance of international peace and security and

---

88 Report of the Special Working Group (*supra*) par 36.

89 See Morten Bergsmo and Jelena Pejić 'Article 16 – Deferral of investigation or prosecution' in Otto Triffterer (Commentary on the Rome Statute) (*supra*) 373.

90 See also Introduction section 1.1 *supra*.

91 Morten Bergsmo and Jelena Pejić in Otto Triffterer (Commentary on the Rome Statute) (*supra*) 381–382 (emphasis in the original).

the powers of the Council under Article 39 of the Charter.'[92] Those delegates favoured Option 2 under paragraph 5 of the Special Working Group's proposed text of 2007, as quoted above. It is submitted that Option 2 would give too much power to the Security Council vis-à-vis the ICC and would fundamentally undermine the independence of the Court. Option 1 is arguably the better of the first two options – acknowledging the role of the Security Council without undermining the competency and independence of the ICC.

The two remaining options (3 and 4) under paragraph 5 of the Special Working Group's proposed text introduced two other international players in the context of those instances where the Security Council would not make a determination after having been notified by the ICC of a possible situation of aggression. Option 3 provided for the UN General Assembly to make (at the request of the ICC) a determination on aggression. Option 4 provided for the ICC to fall back on a determination of an act of aggression by the ICJ, and to then proceed with its own investigation and prosecution.

The 2007 Report of the Special Working Group noted that certain delegates were concerned that 'the involvement of the International Court of Justice ... would undermine the independence of the [ICC] and [would] create a hierarchy between these two institutions.'[93] A previous Report of the Special Working Group on Aggression noted that the concern was raised that to wait for an advisory opinion (on the existence of an act of aggression) from the International Court of Justice 'would seriously delay the case [before the ICC].'[94] Advisory opinions can be delivered by the International Court of Justice in terms of Chapter IV of its Statute. The January 2007 proposal of the Special Working Group thus reflected a move away from the proposal that the ICC would have to wait (under the circumstances referred to above) for an ICJ advisory opinion before proceeding with an investigation and prosecution of a case of aggression.

Option 4 above referred to the Chapter II competencies of the ICJ, which provide for the acceptance of compulsory jurisdiction of the ICJ in legal disputes between states.[95] For instance, in *Democratic Republic of Congo v Uganda*,[96] the Democratic Republic of Congo (DRC) instituted legal action in the ICJ against the Republic of Uganda in respect of a dispute concerning 'acts of armed aggression perpetrated by Uganda on the territory of the [DRC], in flagrant

---

92 Report of the Special Working Group (*supra*) par 37.

93 Report of the Special Working Group (*supra*) par 39.

94 Report of the Special Working on the Crime of Aggression (29 Jun 2006) par 80 (available at www.icc-cpi.int/library/asp/ASP_Advancecopy_Aggression200629jun.pdf).

95 See ICJ Statute (26 Jun 1945), Ch II, reprinted in Bruno Simma (*supra*) Vol I.

96 Case concerning Armed Activities on the territory of the Congo (*Democratic Republic of Congo v Uganda*). See also discussion of this case in Ch II section 3 *supra*.

violation of the United Nations Charter and of the Charter of the Organization of African Unity'.[97] Both parties in this matter accepted the ICJ's compulsory jurisdiction[98] under Chapter II of the ICJ Statute.[99] In its application before the ICJ, the DRC *inter alia* requested the Court to declare that:

> 'Uganda is guilty of an act of aggression within the meaning of Article 1 of resolution 3314 of the General Assembly of the United Nations of 14 December 1974 and of the jurisprudence of the International Court of Justice, contrary to Article 2, paragraph 4, of the United Nations Charter;'[100]

In casu the ICJ held that Uganda had 'violated the principle of non-use of force in international relations and the principle of non-intervention.'[101] There was no finding or declaration on possible 'acts of aggression'. This finding would arguably not have been suitable for purposes of Option 4 under paragraph 5 of the Special Working Group's 2007 proposal on aggression, as discussed above.

2.5. CONSOLIDATION AND REFINEMENT: THE PROPOSED AMENDMENTS TO THE ROME STATUTE, AND THE DRAFT ELEMENTS OF THE CRIME OF AGGRESSION (NOVEMBER 2009)

The Resolution of the Assembly of States Parties, adopted at the 8th plenary meeting on 26 November 2009, contained the consolidated and refined proposals for a provision on aggression, to be included in the Rome Statute of the ICC.[102] It was proposed that the following text be inserted after Article 8 of the Rome Statute:

> 'Article 8 *bis*
> Crime of aggression
> 1. For the purpose of this Statute, "crime of aggression" means the planning, preparation, initiation or execution, by a person in a position effectively to exercise control over or to direct the political or military action of a State, of an act of aggression which, by its character, gravity and scale, constitutes a manifest violation of the Charter of the United Nations.
> 2. For the purpose of paragraph 1, "act of aggression" means the use of armed force by a State against the sovereignty, territorial integrity or political independence of another State, or in any other manner inconsistent with the Charter of the United

---

97 *DRC v Uganda* (*supra*) par 1.
98 *DRC v Uganda* (*supra*) par 1–2.
99 Art 36(2) ICJ Statute.
100 *DRC v Uganda* (*supra*) par 23.
101 *DRC v Uganda* (*supra*) par 345.
102 ICC-ASP/8/20. Resolution ICC-ASP/8/Res.6 Adopted at the 8th plenary meeting, on 26 Nov 2009, by consensus (available at www.icc-cpi.int/asp).

Nations. Any of the following acts, regardless of a declaration of war, shall, in accordance with United Nations General Assembly resolution 3314 (XXIX) of 14 December 1974, qualify as an act of aggression:

(a) The invasion or attack by the armed forces of a State of the territory of another State, or any military occupation, however temporary, resulting from such invasion or attack, or any annexation by the use of force of the territory of another State or part thereof;
(b) Bombardment by the armed forces of a State against the territory of another State or the use of any weapons by a State against the territory of another State;
(c) The blockade of the ports or coasts of a State by the armed forces of another State;
(d) An attack by the armed forces of a State on the land, sea or air forces, or marine and air fleets of another State;
(e) The use of armed forces of one State which are within the territory of another State with the agreement of the receiving State, in contravention of the conditions provided for in the agreement or any extension of their presence in such territory beyond the termination of the agreement;
(f) The action of a State in allowing its territory, which it has placed at the disposal of another State, to be used by that other State for perpetrating an act of aggression against a third State;
(g) The sending by or on behalf of a State of armed bands, groups, irregulars or mercenaries, which carry out acts of armed force against another State of such gravity as to amount to the acts listed above, or its substantial involvement therein.'

It is further proposed that the following text be included after Article 15 of the Rome Statute:

'Article 15 *bis*
Exercise of jurisdiction over the crime of aggression
1. The Court may exercise jurisdiction over the crime of aggression in accordance with article 13, subject to the provisions of this article.
2. Where the Prosecutor concludes that there is a reasonable basis to proceed with an investigation in respect of a crime of aggression, he or she shall first ascertain whether the Security Council has made a determination of an act of aggression committed by the State concerned. The Prosecutor shall notify the Secretary-General of the United Nations of the situation before the Court, including any relevant information and documents.
3. Where the Security Council has made such a determination, the Prosecutor may proceed with the investigation in respect of a crime of aggression.
4. (*Alternative 1*) In the absence of such a determination, the Prosecutor may not proceed with the investigation in respect of a crime of aggression,
Option 1 – end the paragraph here.
Option 2 – add: unless the Security Council has, in a resolution adopted under Chapter VII of the Charter of the United Nations, requested the Prosecutor to proceed with the investigation in respect of a crime of aggression.

4. (*Alternative 2*) Where no such determination is made within [6] months after the date of notification, the Prosecutor may proceed with the investigation in respect of a crime of aggression,
Option 1 – end the paragraph here.
Option 2 – add: provided that the Pre-Trial Chamber has authorized the commencement of the investigation in respect of a crime of aggression in accordance with the procedure contained in article 15;
Option 3 – add: provided that the General Assembly has determined that an act of aggression has been committed by the State referred to in article 8 *bis*;
Option 4 – add: provided that the International Court of Justice has determined that an act of aggression has been committed by the State referred to in article 8 *bis*.
5. A determination of an act of aggression by an organ outside the Court shall be without prejudice to the Court's own findings under this Statute.
6. This article is without prejudice to the provisions relating to the exercise of jurisdiction with respect to other crimes referred to in article 5.'

The following text is to be inserted after article 25, paragraph 3 of the Rome Statute:

'3 *bis*. In respect of the crime of aggression, the provisions of this article shall apply only to persons in a position effectively to exercise control over or to direct the political or military action of a State.'

The last aspect of the package proposal on aggression makes reference to the elements of crimes. It is proposed that the first sentence of Article 9(1) of the Rome Statute is replaced by the following sentence:

'1. Elements of Crimes shall assist the Court in the interpretation and application of articles 6, 7, 8 and 8 *bis*.
6. *The chapeau of article 20, paragraph 3, of the Statute is replaced by the following paragraph; the rest of the paragraph remains unchanged:*
3. No person who has been tried by another court for conduct also proscribed under article 6, 7, 8 or 8 *bis* shall be tried by the Court with respect to the same conduct unless the proceedings in the other court: ...'

In an appendix to the November 2009 resolution, the following draft elements of crimes (aggression) were included:

'Article 8 *bis*
Crime of aggression
Introduction

1. It is understood that any of the acts referred to in article 8 *bis*, paragraph 2, qualify as an act of aggression.
2. There is no requirement to prove that the perpetrator has made a legal evaluation as to whether the use of armed force was inconsistent with the Charter of the United Nations.

3. The term "manifest" is an objective qualification.
4. There is no requirement to prove that the perpetrator has made a legal evaluation as to the "manifest" nature of the violation of the Charter of the United Nations.

Elements
1. The perpetrator planned, prepared, initiated or executed an act of aggression.
2. The perpetrator was a person[103] in a position effectively to exercise control over or to direct the political or military action of the State which committed the act of aggression.
3. The act of aggression – the use of armed force by a State against the sovereignty, territorial integrity or political independence of another State, or in any other manner inconsistent with the Charter of the United Nations – was committed.
4. The perpetrator was aware of the factual circumstances that established that such a use of armed force was inconsistent with the Charter of the United Nations.
5. The act of aggression, by its character, gravity and scale, constituted a manifest violation of the Charter of the United Nations.
6. The perpetrator was aware of the factual circumstances that established such a manifest violation of the Charter of the United Nations.'

Having regard to the discussions and submissions concerning earlier proposals on the crime of aggression (notably the proposals from 2007 discussed above), a number of issues from the 2009 (consolidated) proposals are highlighted below.

2.5.1. 'Crime'/'act'/'gravity'

In the context of earlier proposals on the criminalisation of aggression for purposes of ICC jurisdiction, it was submitted by this author[104] that a 'threshold of seriousness' must form part of any provision on the crime of aggression. The inclusion of the threshold language in the draft Article 8*bis* (on the character, gravity and scale of the act of aggression) that found its way to Kampala was therefore the sensible thing to do. This is not primarily a pragmatic view; it is also informed by this author's belief that any criminalisation of aggression for purposes of ICC jurisdiction should as closely as possible keep to the historical roots of the crime under international law – that is the criminalisation of the *jus contra bellum*,[105] and not mere (relatively) trivial international incidents or violations of international law. Of course, this evaluation is qualified with reference to the observation about lost opportunity regarding the impact of cyber-attacks (and other forms of kinetic warfare) that ultimately can also satisfy

103 The following appears as a footnote: 'With respect to an act of aggression, more than one person may be in a position that meets these criteria.'
104 See section 2.3 *supra*.
105 See in general Ch III and Ch IV *supra*.

the threshold of seriousness, but were not explicitly listed as possible acts of aggression – not in the draft texts or in the final article 8*bis*.

2.5.2. The mental element, and the element of unlawfulness

The so-called 'differentiated approach' to individual liability for aggression (discussed in section 2.2.1 above) implied certain forms of liability that would go further than the *mens rea* requirement in terms of Article 30 of the Rome Statute. The 2009 proposed Article 8*bis* paragraph 1, made no reference to 'intent'. It could be argued that this draft article should at any rate be read with Articles 25 and 30 of the Rome Statute (on individual criminal responsibility and the mental element, respectively). A specific reference to the mental element in Article 8*bis* would thus have been superfluous. The absence of an explicit mental element is not a fatal flaw, but for reasons explained in the next chapter, it would have been better to include it.

The absence of a reference to 'unlawfulness' in the draft Article 8*bis* paragraph 2 is understandable, given the clear references to violations of the UN Charter. It is thus understood that such violations would be unlawful *per se*, given the development of the *jus contra bellum* discussed in earlier chapters. Proponents of a qualified criminalisation of aggression (in other words, the possibility to exclude liability for *bona fide* humanitarian intervention,[106] or for military interventions based on the notion of the responsibility to protect (R2P))[107] might have found the draft (and adopted) Article 8*bis* paragraph 2, less than satisfactory.

2.5.3. The list of acts of aggression

The draft Article 8*bis* paragraph 2 represented a criminalisation of the *jus contra bellum*. Viewed in this way, it makes sense to have included a list of acts taken from the 1974 UN General Assembly Definition of Aggression (despite the fact that the latter was drafted with state liability, not individual criminal liability, in mind).[108] The combination of a general reference to the *jus contra bellum* (as contained in the UN Charter regime), and the more specific list of acts of the 1974 Definition, should be satisfactory from a legality point of view. Any argument that paragraph 2 should make reference to an open-ended list, should be rejected. The same concern about legality was also raised with respect to earlier proposals on the criminalisation of aggression for ICC purposes.[109] The emphasis on armed force (as opposed to serious threats in a material sense,

106 See Ch II section 5.2 *supra*.
107 See Ch II section 5.3 *supra*.
108 See Ch IV section 2.3 *supra*.
109 See discussion under section 2.3 *supra*.

including kinetic warfare) was arguably the biggest lost opportunity from a drafting perspective.

2.5.4. *Conditions for the exercise of jurisdiction*

Ever since the work on a definition and conditions for the exercise of jurisdiction over the crime of aggression started, the role of the Security Council remained a central and contentious issue. With reference to the earlier proposals on the role of the Security Council vis-à-vis the ICC Prosecutor, it was submitted that the only realistic option was to accept some form of Security Council involvement as a condition for the exercise of ICC jurisdiction.[110] The draft Article 15*bis*, paragraphs 1 to 4 (Alternative 2), Option 2, plus paragraphs 5 and 6, contained a *realistic* way forward (see also the discussion under section 2.4 above). The text balanced the different political and criminal justice approaches to aggression. Romantic or idealistic views of a totally independent role for the ICC Prosecutor (i.e. without any role for the Security Council, or other international bodies) proofed to be unhelpful. Alternative 1 (which granted an effective veto to the Security Council over the Prosecutor) represented the other extreme. That alternative indeed represented a worldview where international criminal justice would forever be at the mercy of international political concerns.

2.5.5. *Aggression as a leadership crime*

It is noted in section 2.2.2 above, that aggression is a leadership crime *par excellence*. It is also noted that leadership is a complex notion. The draft Article 25 paragraph 3*bis* which also eventually found its way to Kampala was a sensible proposal. The plural 'persons' was indicative of the acceptance that more than one individual (and individuals in different capacities) can 'exercise control' or 'direct' the political *or* military action of a state. The language was sufficiently broad to include powerful individuals who might not be members of the government, or the formal military structures, but who are nevertheless influential enough to move a country to war or aggression. As such the draft article seemed to be a nod in the direction of the criminalisation and liability of powerful industrial-military-political interests, as were recognised in the post Second World War trials of the German industrialists.[111]

2.5.6. *The elements of the crime of aggression, in particular the manifest nature of the violation of the Charter of the United Nations*

The draft Elements of Crimes with respect to aggression provided that, for liability, the perpetrator was aware of the factual circumstances that established

110 See discussion and submissions under section 2.4 *supra*.

111 See discussion in Ch III, section 5 *supra*.

that the use of armed force was inconsistent with the United Nations. However, there is no requirement 'to prove that the perpetrator has made a legal evaluation as to whether the use of armed force was inconsistent with the Charter'. The conduct elements and the mental element were curiously dealt with – at least from a domestic (ordinary) criminal law perspective. There was no mention that the crime of aggression is a crime of intent. Of course the references in Element 1 to planning, preparation, initiation or execution are understood to bring aggression within the scope of the mental element provided for in Article 30(2)(a) of the Rome Statute. The threshold of 'a manifest violation of the United Nations Charter' potentially complicated matters. The further reference (in the special Introduction to the Elements, paragraph 3) that the term 'manifest' is an *objective qualification*, introduced a possible test of *reasonableness*. The 'reasonable leader' assessing the (factual) nature of the act in question (but not the legal nature), might be compared to the situation of the 'reasonable soldier' assessing a situation in the context of 'manifestly unlawful orders (viz. Article 33 of the Rome Statute).

The 2007 proposals that culminated in the 2009 draft articles resulted in a package of proposals that were ultimately adopted at the Kampala Review Conference in 2010. This chapter explored a number of key features, strengths and weaknesses of the proposals and drafts. The next chapter takes the analyses further, but with reference to the final amendments to the Rome Statute that were adopted at the Kampala Review Conference. It will be shown that the drafting and diplomacy that preceded the Kampala Conference was obviously thorough in terms of the fact that the contours of the draft Article 8*bis* and the draft Articles 15*bis* and 15*ter* that emerged during the period 2007–2009, basically presaged what would ultimately turn out to be a successful Kampala Review Conference, at least from the perspective of those who advocated for the crime of aggression to come within the effective jurisdiction of the ICC.

CHAPTER VII
THE CRIME OF AGGRESSION UNDER THE ROME STATUTE OF THE ICC

1. THE KAMPALA REVIEW CONFERENCE

The first review Conference of the Rome Statute of the International Criminal Court took place in Kampala, Uganda, between 31 May and 11 June 2010. A number of proposals were discussed, ranging from proposals to include the crimes of terrorism and drug trafficking within the jurisdiction of the ICC, to the criminalisation of the use of nuclear weapons. The most prominent proposal – on the definition of the crime of aggression and the concomitant proposal on the conditions for the exercise of ICC jurisdiction over the crime of aggression – was eventually also one of the two successful substantive proposals. The other substantive proposal concerned the extension of the prohibition of certain types of weapons (including poisonous weapons) in the context of non-international armed conflicts as war crimes.[1]

Observers at the Kampala Conference noted the fact that the eventual decision on the crime of aggression was made by consensus. Big powers gave serious input. Even the United States, a non-party participant but not part of the final decision, also made a serious substantive contribution. The drafting and diplomacy of the preceding decade thus culminated in an historic agreement.[2]

---

1 Thomas Weigend 'Foreword' 8 *Journal of International Criminal Justice* (2010) 1177–1178. For a list of delegations at the Kampala Review Conference, see Delegations to the Review Conference of the Rome Statute of the International Criminal Court, 26 Aug 2010 (RC/INF.1) (available at www.icc-cpi.int/iccdocs/asp_docs/RC2010/RC-INF.1-reissued-ENG-FRA-SPA.pdf).

2 For first-hand accounts, see Claus Kreß and Leonie von Holtzendorff 'The Kampala compromise on the crime of aggression' 8 *Journal of International Criminal Justice* (2010) 1179–1217; Christian Wenaweser 'Reaching the Kampala compromise on aggression: The Chair's perspective' 23 *Leiden Journal of International Law* (2010) 883–887. See further Stefan Barriga and Claus Kreß (The travaux préparatoires of the crime of aggression) (*supra*) 727–817.

2. THE DEFINITION OF AGGRESSION

Article 8*bis*,[3] containing the definition of the crime of aggression under the Rome Statute, is the result of the work done by the Special Working Group. The main aspects of the proposals and draft texts were discussed in Chapter VI.

The unlawful behaviour is criminalised in the first part of Article 8*bis*. The second part of Article 8*bis* contains the acts of aggression that are unlawful use of force by a state in violation of international law (essentially, but with some modification, the *jus contra bellum* discussed in Chapter II).[4]

2.1. THE STATE ACT OF AGGRESSION

In order to understand the scope of criminal acts that are criminalised under Article 8*bis*, the starting point of the analysis is the list of acts provided for in the second part of Article 8*bis*. The criminal scope of these acts are determined by (a) the content of the state acts as unlawful use of armed force in violation of the UN Charter, and (b) the threshold provided for in the first part of Article 8*bis*.[5]

It was noted in Chapter IV that the 1974 UN General Assembly Definition of Aggression, containing a list of examples of acts of aggression, was not intended to serve as an instrument of criminalisation, at least not for purposes of individual criminal responsibility. The second part of Article 8*bis* contains essentially the same list, but now in a form that appears textually to be an exhaustive, as opposed to an illustrative list. Despite the textual difference in this regard between the 1974 Definition and the second part of Article 8*bis*, some commentators still note concerns that the list may serve as a basis for ICC judges to develop case law on other examples of the unlawful use of force, thus implicating the principle of legality.[6] This author argued in an earlier edition of this book that an open-ended list of acts of aggression would certainly violate the principle of legality.[7] Even in common law and mixed jurisdictions where 'judge-made law' is a central feature of the legal culture, criminalisation by analogy is regarded as unacceptable and in violation of the *jus acceptum* component of legality.[8] This does not mean, of course, that judges cannot interpret, or clarify,

---

3 For the full text of Art 8*bis*, see Annex I (*infra*).

4 Gerhard Werle and Florian Jessberger (Principles of International Criminal Law) (*supra*) 548.

5 Gerhard Werle and Florian Jessberger (Principles of International Criminal Law) (*supra*) 548–549.

6 Gerhard Werle and Florian Jessberger (Principles of International Criminal Law) (*supra*) 549.

7 Gerhard Kemp *Individual criminal liability for the international crime of aggression* (2010) Intersentia, Antwerp, 236, 249.

8 Gerhard Kemp et al (Criminal Law in South Africa) (*supra*) 17.

or refine existing forms of criminal conduct. The principle of legality is protected in the Rome Statute.[9] The definitions of crimes must be strictly construed. Those who argue that the list of acts of aggression in the second part of Article 8*bis* is a closed list, not even 'semi-open', are correct.[10] This does not mean that the list as it stands is satisfactory. It means that the judges of the ICC, tasked with evaluating, interpreting and judging the most serious crimes under international law in an increasingly complex and even delicate political environment, cannot and should not be expected to act as legislators for the international community. Certainly not with respect to the ambit of the crime of aggression, a crime that is political at the core.

2.2. THE CRIME OF AGGRESSION

It was pointed out in Chapter VI that the majority of states and ultimately the Special Working Group on the Crime of Aggression as well were generally inclined to expand the crime of aggression beyond wars of aggression. However, consensus on how best to demarcate the crime, without criminalising every instance of the unlawful use of force under international law, seemed elusive.[11]

The solution reached was to make use of a threshold of seriousness in the first part of Article 8*bis*. Criminal liability of the individual is triggered by acts of aggression that are manifest violations of the UN Charter. The focus is not on the subjective aim of the individual, but on the objective criteria determining the nature of the violation of the UN Charter. To assist in the objective analysis,[12] three further qualifications are mentioned in the first part of Article 8*bis*, namely that the character, gravity and scale of the violation of act of aggression must be such that it will be regarded as a manifest violation of the UN Charter.[13] Some commentators view the qualitative aspect of the first part of Article 8*bis* also as a filter designed to exclude 'minor incidents (e.g. border skirmishes) or legally controversial cases (e.g. humanitarian intervention) from criminalization'.[14] The 'character' criterion may turn out to be especially controversial in light of the ambiguities surrounding pre-emptive self-defence. Of course, none of the three

---

9 Articles 22–24 Rome Statute of the ICC.

10 See, for instance, analysis by Kai Ambos 'The crime of aggression after Kampala' 53 *German Yearbook of International Law* (2010) 463–509, 487.

11 See also comments by Gerhard Werle and Florian Jessberger (Principles of International Criminal Law) (*supra*) 549.

12 See Annex II (*infra*), Amendments to the Elements of Crimes, Rome Statute of the International Criminal Court, Introduction section 3: 'The term "manifest" is an objective qualification'.

13 Gerhard Werle and Florian Jessberger (Principles of International Criminal Law) (*supra*) 549.

14 Kai Ambos (The crime of aggression after Kampala) (*supra*) 482–483.

criteria will be analysed in isolation, since all three criteria must be fulfilled cumulatively.[15]

Apart from the objective threshold requirement contained in the first part of Article 8*bis*, the other outstanding feature of the crime of aggression is the fact that it is clearly limited to individuals in leadership positions as potential perpetrators. 'Leadership' in this context means political and military leadership. The material test is whether the person in such a leadership position was in a position 'effectively to exercise control over or to direct the political or military action of a State'. As far as the historical development of the crime of aggression is concerned, there is little doubt that the customary form of the crime of aggression (based on the Nuremberg and Tokyo judgments) is a leadership crime.[16] But it was pointed out in Chapter VI[17] that leadership is a rather complex notion with many possible persons falling within the ambit of 'leadership', depending on the relevant political and military context. The correct and realistic approach seems to be to follow a material test for leadership, thus looking at the element of *de facto* control or leadership. The test is not legalistic or formal.[18] Indeed, 'context is paramount'.[19] It is therefore correctly suggested by some commentators that persons beyond the political and military classes (notably private economic actors who may yield considerable influence and power) may also be potential perpetrators under Article 8*bis*.[20]

In addition to the interpretation of leadership in the context of Article 8*bis*, it is also necessary to note the inclusion of Article 25(3)*bis* in the package of provisions adopted at Kampala.[21] Article 25(3)*bis* limits criminal liability for the crime of aggression based on aiding and abetting or inducement to individuals who would also satisfy the leadership qualification discussed above. This does not make sense and has correctly been criticised.[22] Not only is it incompatible with general criminal law theory, but by echoing the qualification contained in Article 8*bis*, the limitation to leadership in the context of aiding and abetting may in reality boils down to a superfluous provision. The very nature of aiding and abetting typologies is the fact that individuals in those categories normally do not share the characteristics or circumstances of the main perpetrator. The

15 See critique of 'Understanding 7' (reproduced in Annex III *infra*) in Gerhard Werle and Florian Jessberger (Principles of International Criminal Law) (*supra*) 549–550.

16 Gerhard Werle and Florian Jessberger (Principles of International Criminal Law) (*supra*) 550.

17 See Chapter VI section 2.2.2.

18 Kai Ambos (The crime of aggression after Kampala) (*supra*) 490; Stefan Barriga and Claus Kreß (The travaux préparatoires of the crime of aggression) (*supra*) 22; Gerhard Werle and Florian Jessberger (Principles of International Criminal Law) (*supra*) 550.

19 Carrie McDougall (The crime of aggression under the Rome Statute) (*supra*) 180.

20 Gerhard Werle and Florian Jessberger (Principles of International Criminal Law) (*supra*) 550.

21 See Annex I *infra*.

22 Kai Ambos (The crime of aggression after Kampala) (*supra*) 491 et seq.

qualification contained in Article 25(3)*bis* has in fact the potential to cause effective impunity for the crime of aggression, even where individuals actively contributed to the commission of the crime in a material way. This is neither good law nor good policy.

3. CONDITIONS FOR THE EXERCISE OF ICC JURISDICTION OVER THE CRIME OF AGGRESSION

It was pointed out in previous chapters that the peace and security regime that emerged in the aftermath of the Second World War assigned a central role to the UN Security Council. That includes the specific authority of the Security Council to determine whether the use of military force by states amount to acts of aggression. This authority is governed by Article 39 of the UN Charter. The Security Council also plays a more general role in the collective security apparatus via Article 24 of the UN Charter, which assigns primary responsibility for the maintenance of peace and security to the Security Council.[23]

The dominant role of the Security Council in the collective security system translated into predictable reluctance on the side of the powerful permanent members on the Security Council to cede much, if any, of the powers of the Security Council in favour of the ICC. These states emphasised the legal framework under the UN Charter, in particular Articles 39 and 24.[24] At Kampala a compromise was reached. The view of those states who would want to see a less dominant role for the Security Council in the determination of whether conduct constitutes an act of aggression shifted the balance back to a system akin to the established system in terms of Article 13(b) of the Rome Statute, which provides for referrals of situations to the ICC in which one or more of the crimes under the jurisdiction of the Court appears to have been committed. In such a matter the Security Council, acting under Chapter VII of the UN Charter, can refer the situation to the Prosecutor of the ICC. This established role of the Security Council in the jurisdictional regime of the ICC is modified with the adoption at Kampala of Articles 15*bis* and 15*ter*.[25]

---

23 See in particular Chapter I *supra*.

24 See for instance the submissions by Russia and the United States at the Rome Diplomatic Conference on the centrality of the Security Council in matters of peace and security, described in Chapter V *supra*.

25 For the text of Art 15*bis* and 15*ter*, see Annex I *infra*.

3.1. SECURITY COUNCIL REFERRALS

As noted above, in terms of Article 13(b) of the Rome Statute the Security Council may refer a situation in which one or more of the crimes within the jurisdiction of the ICC appears to have been committed. This links the jurisdictional regime of the ICC with a power that the Security Council has in terms of Chapter VII of the UN Charter, namely to take decisions in order to deal with threats to peace and security. Since the creation of the ICTY[26] and later the ICTR,[27] it has become a prominent feature of Security Council practice to employ international criminal justice mechanisms in order to deal with peace and security matters. Article 15*ter*, which allows the ICC to act upon referral by the Security Council but without any further involvement by the Security Council, can thus be viewed as a part of a developing symbiotic relationship between the political role of the Security Council and the institutions of international criminal justice, including the ICC, in matters concerning peace and security.

3.2. STATE REFERRALS AND *PROPRIO MOTU* INVESTIGATIONS BY THE ICC PROSECUTOR

Whereas the referral and jurisdictional regime provided for in Article 15*ter* is to a large extent uncomplicated and essentially in line with the regime in terms of which the Security Council may refer situations potentially involving genocide, crimes against humanity and/or war crimes, the regime provided for in terms of Article 15*bis* is more complicated.

When a state party refers a situation potentially concerning the crime of aggression, or where the Prosecutor acts on his or her own initiative, the regime provided for in Article 15*bis* determines that (1) the Prosecutor is required to consult the Security Council, and (2) if the Security Council then determines that an act of aggression has indeed occurred, the Prosecutor may proceed with the further investigation of the matter. In the event that the Security Council fails to make a determination within a window of six months (not an unlikely scenario, given the historical track record of the Security Council on the question of determining the existence of acts of aggression) the Prosecutor may proceed with the investigation. There is a qualification though: the entire Pre-Trial Division of the ICC needs to give the Prosecutor the necessary permission to proceed. This is a deviation from the pre-trial decision-making regime for the other crimes, where the permission of only one Pre-Trial Chamber is required.[28]

26 Established by Security Council Resolution 827 (1993).

27 Established by Security Council Resolution 955 (1994).

28 See Art 15*bis*(8). For the usual pre-trial authorisation process, see Art 39(2)(b)(iii) of the Rome Statute of the ICC. Gerhard Werle and Florian Jessberger (Principles of International

The requirement that the entire Pre-Trial Division of the ICC needs to authorise the Prosecutor to proceed with an investigation into aggression also applies in the instance where the Security Council would make a determination that an act of aggression has not occurred. It is important to note that the ICC is not bound by the Security Council's characterisation of the act as an act of aggression or not. It is difficult to imagine what weight the Court would ultimately attach to the Security Council's negative or positive determination. Those who assume[29] that the ICC judges will attach considerable probative value to a Security Council determination are probably correct. However, it is equally probable (and indeed advisable) that judges sitting in the Pre-Trial Division would not be swayed by ostensible or perceived political manoeuvring by the Security Council, for instance to promote or to protect the interests of the most powerful members of the Council – a not inconceivable scenario.[30]

State referrals or *proprio motu* investigations by the Prosecutor into allegations of aggression under Article 15*bis*(4) are limited to alleged acts of aggression committed by states parties that have not previously declared that they do not accept ICC jurisdiction over the crime of aggression. Any acts of aggression committed by non-state parties are excluded from the jurisdiction of the ICC.[31] A further restriction is added in Article 15*bis*(5) which provides that in respect of a state that is not a party to the Rome Statute the ICC shall not exercise its jurisdiction over the crime of aggression when committed by that state's nationals or on its territory. It should further be noted that this restriction cannot be circumvented through an *ad hoc* acceptance of ICC jurisdiction via Article 12(3) by the non-state party that is the alleged victim of aggression. Kreß and Von Holtzendorff observed that Article 15*bis*(5) constitutes a *lex specialis*, thus preventing non-state parties from deriving 'asymmetrical benefits' from

Criminal Law) (*supra*) 553 correctly observed that the requirement in terms of Art 15*bis*(8) 'is likely to present the Court with a further organizational challenge'.

29 See Marina Mancini 'A brand new definition for the crime of aggression: The Kampala outcome' 81 *Nordic Journal of International Law* (2012) 227, 233 *et seq*; Gerhard Werle and Florian Jessberger (Principles of International Criminal Law) (*supra*) 553.

30 Compare for instance the critical remarks by Judges Fernández de Gurmendi, Trendafilova and Van den Wyngaert in the decision by Pre-Trial Chamber 1, Situation on Registered Vessels of the Union of the Comoros, the Hellenic Republic of Greece and the Kingdom of Cambodia, ICC-01/13, 29 Jan 2015, Public Redacted Version with Confidential Annexes 1, 2 and 3, Application for Review pursuant to Article 53(3)(a) of the Prosecutor's Decision of 6 November 2014 not to initiate an investigation in the Situation (available at www.icc-cpi.int/iccdocs/doc/doc1910341.pdf). The judges (at par 21) criticised the Prosecutor for her deference to the perceived interests of the world's most powerful states. If ICC judges are willing to articulate their frustration thus, it can be expected that any decision by the world's most powerful states (who also happens to be the permanent members of the Security Council) and which would amount to the promotion or protection of their perceived interests, will also not carry weight.

31 Claus Kreß and Leonie von Holtzendorff (The Kampala compromise on the crime of aggression) (*supra*) 1212.

the ICC jurisdictional regime concerning the crime of aggression.[32] The ICC will not be able to exercise jurisdiction over nationals of non-state parties who participated in acts of aggression committed by a state party – a thoroughly restrictive jurisdictional regime indeed.[33]

A distinction should be drawn between *state parties* that have ratified the Kampala Resolution and those who have not. If both the alleged aggressor state and the victim state have ratified the amendments contained in the Kampala Resolution, then there can be no doubt that the ICC has jurisdiction over the matter. If neither party has ratified, the ICC will not have jurisdiction.[34]

More problematic are those scenarios where only the alleged aggressor state or the victim state has ratified the amendments. It is important to note, once again, the restrictive jurisdictional regime of the ICC with respect to the crime of aggression. Article 15*bis*(4) provides that the ICC cannot exercise jurisdiction over the crime of aggression if the alleged aggressor state has previously lodged a so-called 'opt-out' declaration with the Registrar of the Court, in terms of which the relevant state party declares not to accept ICC jurisdiction over the crime of aggression.[35]

4. ENTRY INTO FORCE OF THE AGGRESSION AMENDMENTS

In order to determine the date of entry into force of the amendments to the Rome Statute regarding the crime of aggression, the relevant provisions contained in Articles 15*bis* and *ter* must be read with the Understandings adopted at Kampala (reproduced in Annex III *infra*). The amendments cannot enter into force before 1 January 2017, regardless of the number of ratifications.

For the initial entry into force of the package of amendments, both Article 15*bis*(2) and Article 15*ter*(2) provide that 30 states must ratify the amendments before the ICC can exercise jurisdiction over the crime of

32 Claus Kreß and Leonie von Holtzendorff (The Kampala compromise on the crime of aggression) (*supra*) 1213. See also Gerhard Werle and Florian Jessberger (Principles of International Criminal Law) (*supra*) 554.

33 Gerhard Werle and Florian Jessberger (Principles of International Criminal Law) (*supra*) 554.

34 Gerhard Werle and Florian Jessberger (Principles of International Criminal Law) (*supra*) 554.

35 For a critical assessment of this opt-out declaration, see Kai Ambos (Crime of aggression after Kampala) (*supra*) 505 *et seq*; Claus Kreß and Leonie von Holtzendorff (The Kampala compromise on the crime of aggression) (*supra*) 1215; Andreas Zimmermann 'Amending the Amendment Provisions of the Rome Statute: The Kampala compromise on the crime of aggression and the law of treaties' 10 *Journal of International Criminal Justice* (2012) 209, 223 *et seq*.

aggression.[36] However, the ICC will only be able to exercise jurisdiction over crimes of aggression committed at least one year after the above mentioned entry into force. Articles 15*bis*(3) and 15*ter*(3) provide for yet another jurisdictional activator in that ICC jurisdiction over the crime of aggression must be authorised in terms of a decision by a majority of at least two thirds of the states parties.[37] The latter requirement is in compliance with the general amendment procedure provided for in Article 121(3) of the Rome Statute.

With regard to Security Council referrals it is important to note that the ICC shall exercise jurisdiction over the crime of aggression irrespective of whether the state concerned has accepted ICC jurisdiction with respect to the crime of aggression. This can obviously only happen after the entry into force of the amendments on aggression, as described above.[38]

5. EVALUATING THE CRIME OF AGGRESSION UNDER THE ROME STATUTE

The bulk of this book is on the collective security and legal responses to aggression that culminated in the adoption of the definition of the crime of aggression for purposes of ICC jurisdiction, as well as the conditions for the exercise of ICC jurisdiction over the crime of aggression. In this sense it is clear that what was achieved at Kampala is nothing short of a monument to Nuremberg (warts and all, one may add) and a milestone on the road to the still evolving international criminal justice project's goal to end impunity for the most serious crimes under international law. Despite concerns about any formal role for a political body like the Security Council in this regard, the Kampala compromise seemed to have struck a realistic balance between the political role of the Security Council and the prosecutorial and judicial functions of the ICC.

The International Criminal Court is not the only player in international criminal justice. It is arguably today the single most important player, but, as will also be discussed in the next chapter, there are other players as well. Since the ICC

---

36 At the time of writing 23 states have ratified the Kampala amendments. The following website contains useful information regarding the ratification and implementation status: http://crimeofaggression.info/the-role-of-states/status-of-ratification-and-implementation/. The site of the UN Treaty Collection contains an official list of states that have ratified the Kampala amendments.

37 Thus, a collective decision by the Assembly of States Parties and individual acceptance decisions by at least 30 states parties. For this interpretation, see Kai Ambos (Crime of aggression after Kampala) (*supra*) 477–478.

38 See Understandings regarding the amendments to the Rome Statute of the ICC on the crime of aggression, reproduced in Annex III *infra*. See also Kai Ambos (Crime of aggression after Kampala) (*supra*) 478.

is the most important single player, the Kampala compromise on the crime of aggression is certainly a singular achievement in terms of the chequered history to hold individuals criminally liable for the crime of aggression. A few critical observations about this important achievement are offered below.

5.1. THE CRIME OF AGGRESSION, ITS DUAL NATURE, AND THE THRESHOLD CLAUSE: CONDUCT AND MENTAL ELEMENTS CONSIDERED

Kai Ambos neatly described the dual nature of the crime of aggression as encompassing the collective state act of aggression (macro level) and the individual crime (micro level). Thus, a collective state act of aggression, as listed in Article 8*bis*(2), does not imply individual responsibility for the crime of aggression. The macro and micro level aspects of determining whether the crime of aggression was committed in each instance, further involves the key threshold clause which unlocks the possibility of individual criminal liability. Without the threshold of seriousness ('an act of aggression which, by its character, gravity and scale, constitutes a manifest violation of the Charter of the United Nations') the state act of aggression in the second part of Article 8*bis* would simply be regarded as unlawful state conduct under international law, but not suitable for individual criminal liability. It is the qualitative nature of the state act that triggers the possibility of individual liability.[39] From a criminal law point of view, the question is whether the objective qualifier, the threshold clause, is enough to distinguish between the state act of aggression and the crime of aggression. Should there not have been an explicit subjective element, or is the subjective element implied?

The first part of Article 8*bis* does not provide for the requirement of *animus aggressionis* which one would find in the structure of the crime of aggression under customary international law.[40] Of course, by its nature, the crime under customary international law is not detailed with regard to the conduct element and criminal liability therefore demands a clear criminal intent. The drafters of the conduct element of the crime of aggression under Article 8*bis* deemed it to be sufficiently clear. No explicit mental element was therefore included and reliance on the default mental element in Article 30(2)(a) of the Rome Statute should be sufficient. The 2009 Princeton Report of the Special Working Group on the Crime of Aggression noted that a person has 'intent' where that person

39 Kai Ambos (Crime of aggression after Kampala) (*supra*) 482–483.

40 Carrie McDougal (Crime of aggression under the Rome Statute) (*supra*) 154. See also Ch VIII *infra*.

'means to engage in the conduct'.[41] This, I suppose, is good as far as it goes, but an explicit subjective qualifier – a modified *animus aggressionis* – would go a long way towards transforming the collective state act of aggression into a crime of aggression for purposes of individual criminal liability.[42] At any rate, a subjective qualifier would also be able to assist in distinguishing between the crime of aggression, as constructed by the combined effect of Article 8*bis* parts 1 and 2, and the *prima facie* unlawful but *bona fide* use of armed force, for instance in cases of humanitarian intervention.[43] Of course this is what the drafters wanted to avoid – difficult grey areas – but the objective qualifier is still there and judges of the ICC are expected to decide difficult cases. But this point is moot, since the qualifier in Article 8*bis*(1) is objective, and not combined with further subjective qualifiers, apart from the general application of Article 30(2)(a) of the Rome Statute.

5.2. THE CONDUCT ELEMENT: EXTREMELY BROAD, NOT BROAD ENOUGH, OR JUST RIGHT?

The legislative history of Article 8*bis* shows that the threshold qualification in the first part of the definition was the only viable method to distinguish between the state acts of aggression and the crime of aggression. The mental element of intent is implied, as pointed out above. Given the fact that an objective standard determines the existence of the crime of aggression, an additional concern from a legality point of view, then, is the potential scope of the conduct element provided for in the second part of Article 8*bis*.

Some describe the list as capturing 'an extremely broad range of conduct'.[44] I would say that the conduct in Article 8*bis*(2) is not extremely broad, but there is the risk that the drafters conveniently relied on the UN General Assembly Definition of 1974, without appreciating the fundamental difference between criminalisation for purposes of individual criminal liability on the one hand, and declaring certain conduct to be unlawful under international law, on the other hand. It is true that the result may have been essentially the same. However, if one consider, for instance, the normative ambiguities surrounding humanitarian intervention, or the 21st century realities of potential havoc caused by cyber attacks and 'kinetic warfare', the final list in Article 8*bis*(2) may represent a lost opportunity from a drafting and criminalisation perspective. At

---

41 See 2009 Princeton Report, reproduced in Stefan Barriga and Claus Kreß (Travaux préparatoires of the crime of aggression) (*supra*) 695.

42 For support for this view, see also Kai Ambos (Crime of aggression after Kampala) (*supra*) 485.

43 Kai Ambos (Crime of aggression after Kampala) (*supra*) 485–486.

44 Carrie McDougal (Crime of aggression under the Rome Statute) (*supra*) 154.

the same time it is prudent to note, once again, that the list – arguably defective as it may be – cannot be extended by analogy or creative interpretation.

5.3. ACTS OF PREPARATION

It is submitted that 'planning' and 'preparation' in the context of Article 8*bis*(1) must be interpreted as more than *mere* planning. It must involve some collective state action indicating *initiation*. The problem is to reconcile such a reading with the general criminalisation of individual attempt, under Article 25(3)(f) of the Rome Statute. Kai Ambos reads the interaction between Article 8*bis*(1) and Article 25(3)(f) to provide for the criminalisation of 'attempted preparatory acts' (planning and preparation) and 'attempted attempt' (initiation).[45] This seems to be the correct reading of the provisions. It is also correct to question the rather broad criminalisation of acts of preparation in this regard. One can think of many military and foreign policy preparations and initiatives that could be at risk of unnecessary and over-broad criminalisation as a result of the criminalisation of preparatory acts as indicated above.[46]

45 Kai Ambos (Crime of aggression after Kampala) (*supra*) 495.

46 See also Kai Ambos (Crime of aggression after Kampala) (*supra*) 495–496 who criticises the overcriminalisation of preparatory acts. For an opposing interpretation and view, see Carrie McDougal (Crime of aggression under the Rome Statute) (*supra*) 200–202.

PART V

NATIONAL AND REGIONAL CRIMINALISATION AND PROSECUTION OF THE CRIME OF AGGRESSION

CHAPTER VIII
NATIONAL AND REGIONAL PROSECUTION OF THE CRIME OF AGGRESSION

1. THE CRIME OF AGGRESSION AND THE COMPLEMENTARITY IMPERATIVE

The foundation of the international criminal justice system dominated by the International Criminal Court is the notion that states, and not the ICC, should take on the primary responsibility to investigate and prosecute cases of genocide, crimes against humanity and war crimes. The ICC should in principle only step in when states are unwilling or unable to deal with the matter at hand. This is known as the principle of complementarity. Needless to say, not all states are party to the ICC. However, other enforcement regimes beyond the Rome Statute of the ICC, for instance the UN Torture Convention, the Genocide Convention and the Geneva Conventions provide for an enforcement regime based on the domestication of crimes under international law and the concomitant possibility to enforce international criminal law at the national level.

The Kampala Resolution on the Crime of Aggression adopted by the Assembly of States Parties expresses the sentiment that the crime of aggression, unlike the other core crimes, should rather not be prosecuted at the national level. There is no prohibition of national prosecutions. But there is a strong hint that there should not be any progressive domestication of the crime of aggression. Understandings 4 and 5 regarding the amendments to the Rome Statute on the crime of aggression provide that the amendments to the Rome Statute are adopted for purposes of the Rome Statute only, and not to be interpreted as limiting or prejudicing in any way existing or developing rules of international law for purposes other than the Rome Statute.[1]

It is further understood that the amendments shall not be interpreted as creating the right or obligation to exercise domestic jurisdiction with respect to an act of

[1] Understanding 4, Annex III *infra*.

aggression committed by another state.[2] The latter Understanding is actually superfluous. The Rome Statute does not create a duty on the part of states parties to criminalise the core crimes under their domestic law. Of course, there is a duty on states parties to cooperate with the ICC, but there is no duty with respect to the implementation at national level of substantive international criminal law, safe for the modification of crimes against the administration of justice, thus including the ICC administration of justice as duly protected under domestic law as well.[3]

From the perspective of states parties to the Rome Statute, there is, in light of the Understandings regarding the amendments to the Rome Statute on the crime of aggression, the suggestive understanding that the crime of aggression should rather not be prosecuted at the national level. At the same time, there is an understanding that existing or developing rules of international law are in no way limited by the adoption of the amendments on the crime of aggression. Whether states are party to the Rome Statute or not, there exists the crime of aggression under customary international law and states not party to the Rome Statute can still criminalise the crime in that form as part of their domestic law. Some states have also provided for the crime of aggression in one form or the other in their criminal codes.[4]

The first part of this chapter will evaluate the national prosecution of the crime of aggression, with an emphasis on the crime of aggression under customary international law. It is not the aim to comprehensively discuss the crime of aggression under domestic law. Rather, selected case studies will be used in order to illustrate the potential and limitations of prosecuting the crime of aggression under domestic law.

The second part of the chapter briefly considers the possibilities and perils of prosecuting the crime of aggression at the regional level.

2. THE RELATIONSHIP BETWEEN INTERNATIONAL (CRIMINAL) LAW AND NATIONAL LAW

In the present chapter it is argued that the success of the system of international criminal law cannot rely solely on prosecutions of individuals before *ad hoc* international tribunals or the International Criminal Court (ICC). For practical,

---

2 Understanding 5, Annex III *infra*.

3 Art 70(4)(a) Rome Statute of the ICC; see further on the implementation of substantive international criminal law, Gerhard Werle and Florian Jessberger (Principles of International Criminal Law) (*supra*) 29–30.

4 For a comprehensive discussion, see in general, Sergey Sayapin *The crime of aggression in international criminal law: historical development, comparative analysis and present state* (2014) Asser Press/Springer, The Hague.

logistical and policy reasons, it is clear that much of the success of the movement against impunity for international crimes depends upon the application of international criminal law in domestic courts.[5]

Certain events shock the whole of humankind. In such contexts domestic prosecutions are of international significance. In the *Eichmann* case, for instance, the Supreme Court of Israel said the following about war crimes and crimes against humanity, as core crimes under international law:

> '[Core crimes] constitute acts which damage vital international interests; they impair the foundations and security of the international community; they violate the universal moral values and humanitarian principles that lie hidden in the criminal law systems adopted by civilised nations ... Those crimes entail individual criminal responsibility because they challenge the foundations of [the] international society and affront the conscience of civilised nations ... [They] involve the perpetration of an international crime which all the nations of the world are interested in preventing.'[6]

The quotation above contains at least three important protected interests: 'humanitarian concerns', 'universal moral values', 'foundations and security of the international community'. The crimes that damage these values are the so-called core crimes prosecuted at Nuremberg and Tokyo (war crimes, crimes against peace, and crimes against humanity). The list of crimes affecting the whole of humanity can be extended to include the post-Nuremberg criminalisation of genocide, as well as crimes of international concern like apartheid and torture.[7]

The history of international criminal law shows that in the absence of an international criminal court, the enforcement in domestic courts of the norms of international criminal law (more specifically the so-called core crimes)[8] gained importance.[9] This possibility (which proved to be quite successful for the prosecution of war crimes and to a certain extent crimes against humanity and

---

5 Chris van den Wyngaert *Strafrecht en Strafprocesrecht* (1999) Maklu, Antwerp, 939–940; Lyal Sunga (Emerging system) (*supra*) 249.

6 *Attorney General of Israel v Eichmann*, 29 May 1962, 36 *ILR* 277, 291–293. For the complete transcripts of the trial (provided by the Nizkor Project) see www.nizkor.org/hweb/people/e/eichmann-adolf/transcripts.

7 Edward Wise and Ellen Podgor *International Criminal Law: Cases and Materials* (2000) Lexis Publishing, New York, 498.

8 War crimes, crimes against humanity, genocide, and aggression. It will be pointed out in this Chapter that aggression, although a serious international crime, was never prosecuted at national level. In fact, since the post-Second World War prosecutions discussed in Ch III *supra*, aggression has never been prosecuted.

9 See also Introduction section 1.1 (*supra*) for more on this aspect of the emerging system of international criminal law.

genocide) was not used for the crime of aggression.[10] Yoram Dinstein submitted the following broad set of reasons for the lack of prosecutions at *national* level for the crime of aggression, or for crimes against peace in general:

> 'The rationale for entrusting an international criminal court with jurisdiction over crimes against peace is palpable. Trials of other international crimes (principally, war crimes and crimes against humanity) have a lot of merit even when conducted before domestic courts. But *the nature of crimes against peace* is such that no domestic proceedings can conceivably dispel doubts regarding the impartiality of the judges. As a matter of law, jurisdiction over crimes against peace is probably universal, although the Joint Separate Opinion of Judges Higgins, Kooijmans and Buergenthal in the 2002 Case Concerning the Arrest Warrant of 11 April 2000 [ICJ] expressed a certain hesitation about the range of application of the exercise of universal jurisdiction. In any event, only enemy (or former enemy) States, rather than neutrals, are likely to convict and sentence offenders charged with crimes against peace. Any panel of judges comprised exclusively of enemy (or former enemy) nationals will be suspected of irrepressible bias. There is no escape from the conclusion that the present state of affairs is lamentable, giving rise as it does to assertions of "victor's justice". The flaw in the system cannot be redressed until the Rome Statute is amended in a satisfactory fashion.'[11]

Indeed, the obstacles to prosecuting individuals in national courts for the crime of aggression do seem (*prima facie*) to prove Dinstein's point that it is best to entrust an *international* court with jurisdiction over the crime of aggression. That indeed is the subtext of the Understandings regarding the amendments to the Rome Statute on the crime of aggression, referred to above. Some of the important theoretical and practical factors affecting the possible prosecution of individuals for the crime of aggression at national level are analysed below.

At present there are no international treaties or instruments *obliging* states *generally* to exercise jurisdiction over individuals for the crime of aggression.[12] States can of course in their domestic legislation provide for the crime of aggression (in various forms).[13] There are at present no reported prosecutions for the crime of aggression on the basis of domestic legislation.[14]

---

10 For a comparative analysis of selective jurisdictions that allow for the prosecution of international crimes in national courts, see Ward Ferdinandusse *Direct Application of International Criminal Law in National Courts* (2006) TMC Asser Press, The Hague, 17–87.

11 Yoram Dinstein (War Aggression Self-Defence) (*supra*) 145 (emphasis added).

12 The same is true for crimes against humanity. See Alexander Zahar and Göran Sluiter *International Criminal Law* (2008) Oxford University Press, Oxford, 498. It was also pointed out above that the Rome Statute also does not require states parties to incorporate the international crimes into domestic substantive law.

13 Apart from Germany and Iraq (see discussion under section 1.3.3 *infra*), further examples of states that provide for the crime of aggression under domestic law in one way or another as part of their penal codes, are: Armenia, the Russian Federation, Uzbekistan, Tajikistan, Ukraine, Republic of Moldova, Bulgaria, Republic of Macedonia, Republic of Montenegro, Latvia. For further comparative discussions, see Sergey Sayapin (The crime of aggression in international criminal law) (*supra*) Chapter 4. See also Christina Villarino Villa 'The Crime of Aggression before the House of Lords' 4 *JICJ* (2006) 866–877, 876.

14 Christina Villarino Villa (Crime of Aggression) (*supra*) 876.

On the assumption that aggression is a crime under *customary international law*,[15] the question is whether the theory of direct application of international criminal law in domestic courts *could* serve as a basis for individual criminal liability for the crime of aggression.

Before the creation of the permanent ICC, the (international) enforcement of the prohibition of crimes under international law depended on *ad hoc* international criminal tribunals like the ICTY and ICTR, and their historical post-Second World War predecessors – the IMT Nuremberg and the IMTFE at Tokyo. International criminal tribunals (including the permanent ICC) do not always have the mandate,[16] or capacity,[17] to enforce the norms of international criminal law to the fullest extent. *National courts* are therefore, generally speaking, very important *complements* to international criminal tribunals.[18] In order to explain the role of national jurisdictions in the context of enforcement of international criminal norms, Jann Kleffner identified two roles: national criminal jurisdictions can function as 'organs of the international community', and as important players in the 'domestic legal order in which they operate'.[19] Regarding the first aspect, Kleffner states as follows:

> 'In enforcing the prohibition of these crimes, national courts … act on behalf of the whole of humanity within the international legal order. In the absence of genuine international enforcement mechanisms, or to the extent that crimes are beyond the reach of such other mechanisms due to their limited mandate or capacity, national suppression of the core crimes is the only way to effectuate their prohibitions.'[20]

The second role referred to above, entails the function of national courts to enforce domestic legal norms, or 'domesticated' international legal norms.[21]

---

15 The basis for this assumption is explained below.

16 For instance, the ICTR's jurisdiction is limited in terms of time, place, and persons (serious violations of international humanitarian law committed in the territory of Rwanda and Rwandan citizens responsible for such violations committed in neighbouring states between 1 Jan 1994 and 31 Dec 1994). See Art 1 ICTR Statute. The ICTY's competence is also limited in terms of time and territory. Art 1 ICTY Statute provides: 'The [ICTY] shall have the power to prosecute persons responsible for serious violations of international humanitarian law committed in the territory of the former Yugoslavia since 1991'.

17 International criminal tribunals often only try the major criminals, based on criteria such as seniority and leadership roles in military and political structures. For an assessment, see Dominic McGoldrick in Dominic McGoldrick, Peter Rowe and Eric Donnelly (eds) *The Permanent International Criminal Court – Legal and Policy Issues* (2004) Hart Publishing, Oxford, 14–25.

18 Jann Kleffner (Complementarity in the Rome Statute) (*supra*) 29–35. On the relationship between international criminal tribunals and national courts, see Zahar and Sluiter (International Criminal Law) (*supra*) 447–476.

19 Jann Kleffner (Complementarity in the Rome Statute) (*supra*) 29–30.

20 Jann Kleffner (Complementarity in the Rome Statute) (*supra*) 30.

21 Jann Kleffner (Complementarity in the Rome Statute) (*supra*) 30–31.

The result of this can be that the original *international* norm is transformed to suit domestic legal purposes. In this context it is necessary to examine the relationship between international and national law generally, and the possibility of implementing international (criminal) law via national courts specifically.

2.1. THE MONISM/DUALISM DEBATE

The role of international law vis-à-vis national legal systems has been the subject of debate.[22] Three[23] distinct theories or schools of thought on the subject emerged: the *monistic doctrine*, advocating the supremacy of domestic law; the *dualist theory*, which acknowledges the existence of two distinct legal orders (international and domestic); and the *second monistic theory*, which maintains the 'unity of the various legal systems and the primacy of international law.'[24]

The first monistic school (dominated by German scholars) viewed national law as supreme. This school in fact regarded international 'rules' not as legal rules, but as guidelines and always subject to the behaviour of powerful states. This doctrine, in the words of Cassese, 'denied the existence of international law as a distinct and autonomous body of law. It clearly reflected the extreme nationalism and authoritarianism of a few great Powers, anxious to protect their respective interests.'[25] The second monistic school (with proponents like Hans Kelsen) advocates the opposite of the first monistic school. This second school regards international law to have primacy over national law. This is based on a hierarchical view of legal systems with international law at the top. An important consequence of this view is that, since international and national law form part of one normative system (with international legal rules at the top), 'transformation' of international law into national law is not necessary. In terms of the application of international law in national legal systems, Cassese states the following about the second (Kelsian) school of monism:

> '[The] sources of international law belong to a legal system that is hierarchically superior to municipal systems, not radically different from them. As a result, international rules can be applied as such by domestic courts, without any need for transformation.'[26]

---

22 On this relationship, see in general Rosalyn Higgins *Problems and Process – International law and how we use it* (1994) Clarendon Press, Oxford, 205–218.

23 John Dugard distinguishes between the *two* main schools – the monist and the dualist schools of thought. See John Dugard (International Law) (*supra*) 47–48. Others, like Antonio Cassese, distinguish further between two different groups within the broader school of monism, plus the dualist school. See discussion *infra*.

24 Antonio Cassese (International Law) (*supra*) 213.

25 Antonio Cassese (International Law) (*supra*) 214.

26 Antonio Cassese (International Law) (*supra*) 215.

Cassese points out that the monistic school allows for certain qualifications in terms of the notion of direct application of international law in national courts:

> 'National constitutions (be they written or unwritten) may require domestic courts to apply only statutes enacted by national legislatures ... Nevertheless, this necessity of transformation is a question of national, not of international law.'[27]

Dualism, the third school of thought, views international law and national legal systems as constituting distinct and separate categories of legal orders.[28] This view of the relationship between international law and national legal systems is dominant in Anglo-American systems. International law may only be applied by national courts if "adopted" by such courts or transformed into local law by legislation.'[29]

The case studies below illustrate the various theoretical problems and possibilities of international (criminal) law applied at domestic level.

2.2. INTERNATIONAL LAW IN SOUTH AFRICA (CONSIDERING ROMAN-DUTCH, ENGLISH AND RECENT CONSTITUTIONAL LAW)

The position in South Africa has to be viewed in terms of the country's Roman-Dutch and English law heritage, as well as constitutional developments since 1994. Some of the most prominent and influential writers on Roman-Dutch law, like Hugo Grotius, regarded international law and domestic law to be part of the same universal legal order (with natural law as common foundation).[30] Dugard points out that the monist–dualist debate (described above) 'postdates the classical period of Roman-Dutch scholarship.'[31] Thus, in terms of South Africa's Roman-Dutch heritage, the position is that international law simply formed part of national law. This position was retained even after the British occupation.[32] English law was, until 1994, an important source of South African public law, including public international law. The recourse to English law confirmed, in the words of Dugard, 'the common-law rule governing the relationship between international law and municipal law.'[33]

---

27 *Ibid.*
28 Antonio Cassese (International Law) (*supra*) 214; John Dugard (International Law) (*supra*) 47.
29 John Dugard (International Law) (*supra*) 47.
30 John Dugard (International Law) (*supra*) 48.
31 *Ibid.*
32 John Dugard (International Law) (*supra*) 49. For a contrary view, see Hercules Booysen 'Is Gewoonteregtelike Volkereg Deel van Ons Reg?' 38 *THRHR* (1975) 315, especially at 316.
33 John Dugard (International Law) (*supra*) 50.

Under common law, customary international law forms part of South African domestic law. In this regard, South African courts 'showed strong support for the monist approach'.[34] Section 232 of the Constitution of South Africa confirms the common law position:

> 'Customary international law is law in the Republic unless it is inconsistent with the Constitution or an Act of Parliament.'

Dugard points out that the common law and judicial decisions 'are now subordinate to customary international law as it is only the Constitution and Acts of Parliament that enjoy greater legal weight.'[35] This view is consistent with the view of some publicists on the doctrine of incorporation in English law. Ian Brownlie points out that the doctrine of incorporation is still the dominant principle in the context of the relationship between customary international law and domestic law in England.[36] Customary rules 'are to be considered part of the law of the land and enforced as such, with the qualification that they are incorporated only so far as is not inconsistent with Acts of Parliament or prior judicial decisions of final authority.'[37] However, Brownlie notes that there is an alternative (but – according to him – unconvincing) view that interprets case law (post-1876) 'in such a way as to displace the doctrine of incorporation by that of transformation'.[38] In terms of the latter doctrine customary international law is part of English domestic law '*only in so far* as the rules have been clearly adopted and made part of the law of England by legislation, judicial decision, or established usage.'[39] This may also be the dominant view in the context of the 'assimilation' of *crimes* under customary international law (including aggression) into the domestic law of England, as illustrated by the opinion of the House of Lords in *R v Jones et al*, discussed below.[40]

From the discussion above it is clear that the monism/dualism debate can at best provide a general background to the question at hand, namely the application of international (criminal) law in domestic courts. Against this background the different ways in which customary international law and treaties become part of domestic law are considered below. The position of *customary international law* vis-à-vis *domestic law* is informed by national jurisprudential and constitutional developments. It is suggested below that a distinction between (general) customary international law and customary international (criminal) law provide

34 John Dugard (International Law) (*supra*) 51.
35 John Dugard (International Law) (*supra*) 56.
36 Ian Brownlie *Principles of Public International Law* 6th (2003) Oxford University Press, Oxford, 41.
37 *Ibid.*
38 Ian Brownlie (Principles of Public International Law) (*supra*) 42.
39 *Ibid.*
40 See section 2.3.6 *infra*.

further nuances relevant for the application of international criminal law in national courts. Apart from customary international law, the position of treaties as a source of law is also briefly addressed below.

2.3. THE APPLICATION OF INTERNATIONAL CRIMINAL LAW IN NATIONAL COURTS

2.3.1. The theoretical framework: Incorporation and transformation of treaties

There are constitutional and other considerations (notably the principle of legality) that have an impact on the application of international (criminal) law at national level. In general, one can distinguish between two methods to implement international law, namely *incorporation* and *transformation*. These two methods are described as follows:

> '*Incorporation* takes place when an international rule is integrated in the national legal order, so that the judiciary can directly apply that rule. This method of incorporation promotes complete implementation of the international rule, as it cannot be modified. *Transformation* denotes the enactment of a national law that mirrors the content of the international rule, thus transforming a rule of international law in a national one. This method of transformation gives the legislature the opportunity to tailor, or even modify, the international rule to fit the peculiarities of the national legal system. Technically speaking, international law is applied not at all after transformation. In these cases, national courts apply national law that reproduces the content of the original international norm.'[41]

It is not always clear what approach is favoured by national systems. Elements of both incorporation and transformation can exist in the domestication of international norms. This often involves different routes of domestication for customary international law and treaty law – as suggested above in the context of the monism/dualism debate.

In South Africa *treaties* ('international agreements') are normally 'incorporated' into national law. Neville Botha described the basic process of incorporation with reference to three broad stages. First, the Cabinet must consent to the submission of the relevant treaty to Parliament. Thereafter a legal-technical stage commences. This stage is obviously important, since the department must draft legislation which will in turn be submitted to the State law advisors to 'ensure its compliance with domestic law'.[42] The legal drafting section of

---

41 Ward Ferdinandusse (Direct Application) (*supra*) 7 [emphasis in the original].

42 NJ Botha 'National treaty law and practice: South Africa' in Duncan Hollis, Merritt Blakeslee and Benjamin Ederington (eds) *National Treaty Law and Practice* (2005) Martinus Nijhoff Publishers, Leiden/Boston, 601.

the Department of Justice is responsible for the formal drafting of the (draft) legislation. Furthermore, the law advisors of the Department of Foreign Affairs have the responsibility to make sure that the draft legislation is 'consistent with international law and with the Republic's international relations and other obligations.'[43] Finally, the draft legislation will have to pass through Parliament, in compliance with Chapter 4 of the Constitution which provides for the national legislative process.[44] The Implementation of the Rome Statute of the International Criminal Court Act 27 of 2002 (ICC Act, 2002) thus 'incorporated' the Rome Statute of the ICC, 1998 (a multilateral treaty to which South Africa is a state party) into South African law. The ICC Act incorporates the definitions of crimes (war crimes, crimes against humanity and genocide) into South African domestic law. In this respect one can say that the ICC Act is an act of *transformation.* Although the definitions of the crimes were not modified, but directly taken from the Rome Statute, the ICC Act also omits some parts of the Rome Statute (notably Article 9 of the Rome Statute on Elements of Crimes). Max du Plessis points out that 'the drafters of the ICC Act have not chosen to expressly adopt Part 3 of the [Rome] Statute on general principles of liability and defences'.[45] Since the drafters of the ICC Act, 2002 have chosen to tailor the Act for South African purposes, Anton Katz[46] is correct to use the term 'act of transformation' to describe the ICC Act, 2002.

Apart from the possibility to incorporate treaties and other international instruments into South African law (making them *part of national law*), courts can also take *judicial notice* of *international law* (including customary international law). Expert testimony to prove international law is inadmissible.[47] It is submitted that the parties should nevertheless be given the opportunity to address the court on the question of judicial notice and application of the content of the rule or norm of international law in question.

South African law does not recognise the crime of aggression. (The question whether aggression as a crime under customary international law is directly applicable in South African courts, will be examined below.) The ICC Act, 2002[48] provides that genocide, crimes against humanity and war crimes are

43 *Ibid.*
44 *Ibid.*
45 Max du Plessis 'South Africa's Implementation of the ICC Statute' 5 *JICJ* (2007) 464.
46 Anton Katz 'An Act of Transformation – The incorporation of the Rome Statute of the ICC into national law in South Africa' 12(4) *African Security Review* (2003) 25–30.
47 See *Inter-Science Research and Development Services (Pty) Ltd v Republica Popular de Mocambique* 1980 2 SA (T) at 124H; *South Atlantic Islands Development Corp v Buchan* 1971 1 SA 234 (C) at 238A-E. See further Schmidt and Rademeyer *Bewysreg* 4th (2000) Butterworths, Durban, 201.
48 27 of 2002. The Act entered into force on 16 Aug 2002. See *GG* No 23761, 16 Aug 2002. For comments on the Act see Max du Plessis 'Bringing the International Criminal Court home

crimes under South African law.[49] Apart from the explicit criminalisation of the three core crimes, Section 2 of the Act provides as follows:

> 'In addition to the Constitution and the law, any competent court in the Republic hearing any matter arising from the application of this Act must also consider and, where appropriate, may apply –
> (a) conventional international law, and in particular the [Rome] Statute;
> (b) customary international law; and
> (c) comparable foreign law.'

Although the Act does not provide for the crime of aggression, the Preamble does refer to 'the crime of aggression' as a crime 'in terms of international law'. The relevant paragraph of the Preamble reads as follows:

> '[T]hroughout the history of human-kind, millions of children, women and men have suffered as a result of atrocities which constitute the crimes of genocide, crimes against humanity, war crimes and the crime of aggression in terms of international law'.

And further:

> '[The] Republic of South Africa is committed to –
> bringing persons who commit such atrocities to justice, either in a court of law of the Republic in terms of its domestic laws where possible, pursuant to its international obligations to do so when the Republic became party to the Rome Statute of the International Criminal Court, or in the event of the national prosecuting authority of the Republic declining or being unable to do so, in line with the principle of complementarity as contemplated in the [Rome] Statute, in the International Criminal Court, created by and functioning in terms of the said Statute'.

The entire Rome Statute of the ICC is attached as an annexure to the ICC Act of 2002. Anton Katz points out that this 'allows South African Courts to have regard to the relevant substantive and procedural provisions [of the Rome Statute]'.[50] Section 1(xix) of the Act provides that 'the ... text of [the Rome Statute] is attached in the Annexure for information'. Schedule 1 of the Act contains the definitions of the crimes within the jurisdiction of the ICC, namely

– the Implementation of the Rome Statute of the International Criminal Court Act 2002' 16 *SACJ* (2003) 1–16; Anton Katz 'An Act of Transformation – The incorporation of the Rome Statute of the ICC into national law in South Africa' 12(4) *African Security Review* (2003) 25–30; Max du Plessis 'South Africa's Implementation of the ICC Statute' 5 *JICJ* (2007) 460–479.

49 See Ch 2, read with Schedule 1 of Act 27 of 2002.

50 Anton Katz 'An Act of Transformation – The incorporation of the Rome Statute of the ICC into national law in South Africa' 12(4) *African Security Review* (2003) 25–30, 27.

genocide, crimes against humanity and war crimes. The definitions are taken from the Rome Statute. By including the definitions of the crimes provided for in the Rome Statute in a Schedule to the ICC Act, the legislature transformed these crimes into South African national law.[51] A legislative amendment will be required in order to transform Article 8*bis* of the Rome Statute (definition of the crime of aggression) into domestic criminal law.

Max du Plessis submitted that this approach of transformation was partly due to the fact that South Africa lacked statutory law defining and criminalising genocide, crimes against humanity and war crimes.[52] It is assumed that the South African Parliament will not draft its own definition of aggression.

2.3.2. In the absence of statutory law on aggression: Possibilities presented by customary international law

Some of the most prominent publicists on the subject of international criminal law view aggression as a crime under international law, with customary status.[53] However, what is the scope of the crime of aggression that is accorded customary status?

Cherif Bassiouni has identified more than fifty instruments relevant to the crime of aggression.[54] It is not the aim here to analyse each and every one of them. However, the path from the Convention for the Pacific Settlement of International Disputes (known as the First Hague Convention) of 1899 to the Rome Statute of the ICC of 1998 points to a chequered history of politics and pragmatism that shows, as a minimum, the international community's opposition to the use of armed force to settle disputes. *At the core of that is the criminality of aggressive war.* Bassiouni has pointed out that most of the instruments referred to above lack the necessary penal characteristics[55] for purposes of criminal liability. The

---

51 For the different methods employed by Parliament to transform treaties into national law, see John Dugard (International Law) (*supra*) 61–62. See further NJ Botha (National treaty law and practice: South Africa) (*supra*) 581–625.

52 Max du Plessis (South Africa's Implementation of the ICC Statute) (*supra*) 463.

53 Cherif Bassiouni (International Criminal Law) (*supra*) 58; Yoram Dinstein (War Aggression Self-Defence) (*supra*) 121–123; Antonio Cassese (International Criminal Law) (*supra*) 113–114; Gerhard Werle and Florian Jessberger (Principles of International Criminal Law) (*supra*) 534.

54 Bassiouni (International Criminal Law) (*supra*) 64–66. The list starts with the Convention for the Pacific Settlement of International Disputes (First Hague Convention) 29 Jul 1899, and ends with the Rome Statute of the ICC, 1998.

55 Cherif Bassiouni (International Criminal Law) (*supra*) 47–48. The author used the following ten penal characteristics to identify proscribed conduct under conventional international law as part of ICL: '(1) Explicit recognition of proscribed conduct as constituting an international crime, or a crime under international law, or a crime; (2) Implicit recognition of the penal nature of the act by establishing a duty to prohibit, prevent, prosecute, punish, or the like;

majority of the instruments are therefore more relevant to a *general* discussion on the use of force in international law. It is clear that the law of Nuremberg (as confirmed by the international community)[56] and a number of international instruments underline the criminality of aggressive war. Yet we do not have any international tribunal *at present* with the necessary jurisdiction to try individuals for the crime of aggression. That leaves us with the possibility of customary international law and the application of customary international law at domestic level.[57] The impact of possible universal jurisdiction over the crime of aggression warrants special attention.

2.3.3. *Proving custom, and the customary status of aggression as a crime under international law*

Customary international law is one of the sources of law provided for in the Statute of the International Court of Justice. The method of proving custom is today well-established and applied by the ICJ. Article 38 of the Statute of the ICJ provides for the law to be applied by the ICJ:

> '(1) The Court, whose function is to decide in accordance with international law such disputes as are submitted to it, shall apply:
> (a) international conventions, whether general or particular, establishing rules expressly recognized by the contesting states;
> (b) international custom, as evidence of a general practice accepted as law;
> (c) the general principles of law recognized by civilized nations;
> (d) subject to the provisions of Article 59, judicial decisions and the teachings of the most highly qualified publicists of the various nations, as subsidiary means for the determination of rules of law.'

The existence of *custom* (a source of law provided for in Article 38(1)(b) of the ICJ Statute)[58] requires the twin elements of state practice, or *usus* (the material element), and a legal conviction that such practice is indeed required or allowed

---

(3) Criminalization of the proscribed conduct; (4) Duty or right to prosecute; (5) Duty or right to punish the proscribed conduct; (6) Duty or right to extradite; (7) Duty or right to cooperate in prosecution, punishment (including judicial assistance in penal proceedings); (8) Establishment of a criminal jurisdictional basis (or theory of criminal jurisdiction or priority in criminal jurisdiction); (9) Reference to the establishment of an international criminal court or an international tribunal with penal characteristics (or prerogatives); (10) Elimination of the defense of superior orders'.

56 UN GA Res 95(I) of 11 Dec 1946 affirms the 'principles of international law recognized by the Charter of the Nuremberg Tribunal and the judgment of the Tribunal.'

57 See Kevin Hopkins 'Can customary international law play a meaningful role in our domestic legal order: A short case study to consider' 30 *SAYIL* (2005) 276–289 for an argument on the progressive application of customary international law in South African domestic law.

58 For an overview of the formation of custom as a source of international law, see Ian Brownlie *The Rule of Law in International Affairs* (1998) Kluwer Law International, The Hague, 18–23.

as a matter of law – the latter referring to the subjective (or psychological) element of custom, namely *opinio juris*.[59]

Regarding the element of *practice*, the ICJ in the past regarded administrative acts, legislation, judicial decisions, and treaties as examples of state practice.[60] Antonio Cassese summarised the progression of the formation of custom, and the relationship between practice and *opinio juris* as constitutive elements thereof, as follows:

> 'It would seem that the two elements [practice and *opinio juris*] need not be both present from the outset. Usually, a practice evolves among certain States under the impulse of economic, political, or military demands. At this stage the practice may thus be regarded as being imposed by social or economic or political needs (*opinio necessitates*). If it does not encounter strong and consistent opposition from other States but is increasingly accepted, or acquiesced in, a customary rule gradually crystallizes. At this later stage it may be held that the practice is dictated by international law (*opinio juris*). In other words, now States begin to believe that they must conform to the practice not so much, or not only, out of economic, political, or military considerations, but because an international rule enjoins them to do so.'[61]

Alain Pellet suggests that the 'collective attitude of states' can be regarded as an important indication of the material element of custom. In this regard the conduct of states at diplomatic conferences,[62] or their conduct as members of international organisations,[63] is also relevant to determine custom. In the context of resolutions adopted by international organisations (like the UN), Pellet argues that in order to ascertain a customary rule of general international law, resolutions adopted by an international organisation belong to 'the manifestation of the *opinio juris*' element.[64] The General Assembly Resolution

59 See Statute of the ICJ, Art 38(1)(b) reproduced in Bruno Simma (The Charter of the United Nations Vol I) (*supra*). See commentary on Art 38 by Alain Pellet 'Article 38' in Andreas Zimmermann, Christian Tomuschat and Karin Oellers-Frahm (eds) *The Statute of the International Court of Justice – A Commentary* (2006) Oxford University Press, Oxford, 677–792. For an exposition of the methodology vis-à-vis proof of custom in international criminal law see *The Prosecutor v Pavle Strugar* (Prosecutor's response to defence brief on interlocutory appeal on jurisdiction) ICTY, Case No IT-01-42-AR72, Response filed on 22 Aug 2002 (copy on file). See further *North Sea Continental Shelf cases*, ICJ Reports (1969), at 43 par 74.

60 See Alain Pellet in Andreas Zimmermann et al (Statute of the ICJ) (*supra*) 750–751.

61 Antonio Cassese (International Law) (*supra*) 157.

62 For instance the statements made by delegations at the UN Diplomatic Conference of Plenipotentiaries on the Establishment of an ICC, Rome 1998. Also of great relevance is the various statements by states at the Kampala Review Conference on the Statute of the ICC, 2010, and as reflected in the travaux prépāratoires.

63 In this regard resolutions of the UN GA are relevant.

64 Alain Pellet in Andreas Zimmermann et al (Statute of the ICJ) (*supra*) 752.

3314 (XXIX) on the Definition of Aggression (1974) (as discussed in Chapter IV[65] above) should, for example, be regarded as a manifestation of *opinio juris* on the notion of aggression.

The Kampala Review Conference on the Statute of the ICC in 2010 should also be regarded as a forum *par excellence* where states had the opportunity to state their views on the various aspects of the definition of aggression and the conditions for the exercise of ICC jurisdiction over the crime of aggression. Indeed, the Kampala Conference was an opportunity where important non-party states with observer status (notably the United States, China, Cuba, Iran, Israel and Russia) made statements relevant to the international community's collective view on the future development of the crime of aggression under international law.[66] It is of course particularly relevant that most of these observer states have significant political and military presence in various regions of the world.

States also had the opportunity to express their views on the domestic criminalisation of the crime of aggression. These views are essentially reflected in the Understandings regarding the amendments to the Rome Statute.

The views of states on the crime of aggression go back to the period following the end of the Second World War, when 'aggressive war' was not an abstract notion. Thus, UN General Assembly Resolution 95(I) of 11 December 1946, in terms of which the criminality of 'waging aggressive war' was 'affirmed', can be viewed as strong evidence of *opinio juris* regarding the crime of aggression. With this resolution the international community 'expressed the view that [the crime of waging of aggressive war] was valid generally, and not merely in regard to the Axis powers'.[67] Furthermore, the Declaration on Principles of International Law Concerning Friendly Relations and Co-operation[68] confirms that 'aggressive war' is a crime against international peace. The ICJ has, in fact, relied in a number of cases (notably in the *Nicaragua* and *Legality of the Threat or Use of Nuclear Weapons* cases) on UN General Assembly Resolutions to prove the existence of *opinio juris*. In the *Nuclear Weapons* case the ICJ stated as follows:

65 See Ch IV sections 2.3, 2.3.1 and 2.3.2 *supra*.

66 Stefan Barriga and Claus Kreß (The travaux préparatoires of the crime of aggression) (*supra*) 814–817.

67 See comments by Gerhard Werle and Florian Jessberger (Principles of International Criminal Law) (*supra*) 536–537.

68 Declaration on Principles of International Law Concerning Friendly Relations and Co-operation among States in Accordance with the Charter of the United Nations, UN Doc A/RES/2625 of 24 Oct 1970.

'The Court notes that General Assembly resolutions, *even if they are not binding*, may sometimes have normative value. They can, in certain circumstances, provide evidence important for establishing the existence of a rule or the emergence of an *opinio juris*.'[69]

In the *Nicaragua* case the ICJ held that the prohibition of the use of force by states is protected under customary international law. The ICJ *in casu* referred to state practice, *opinio juris* and indeed the acceptance of states of the principle as expressed in Article 2(4) of the UN Charter as evidence of the customary status of the prohibition of the use of force.[70] The ICJ *in casu* went further and linked the customary status of the prohibition of the use of force with its status as a principle of *jus cogens* (that is, a superior norm in international law):[71]

'A further confirmation of the validity as customary international law of the principle of the prohibition of the use of force expressed in Art. 2, paragraph 4, of the Charter of the United Nations may be found in the fact that it is frequently referred to in statements by State representatives as being not only a principle of customary international law but also a fundamental or cardinal principle of such law, that is a "principle of *jus cogens*", a position also taken by the ILC and by the contesting States themselves.'[72]

The critical question is whether there is a resemblance between the *opinio juris* of states and actual state behaviour. Dinstein argued persuasively that while 'recourse to force continues to permeate international relations',[73] states are still in the majority of cases at least trying to justify their behaviour in terms of the *jus contra bellum*. He concludes:

'The discrepancy between what States say and what they do may be due to pragmatic reasons, militating in favour of a choice of the line of least exposure to censure. Even so, a disinclination to challenge the validity of a legal norm has a salutary effect in that it shows that the norm is accepted, if only reluctantly, as the rule. There is a common denominator between those who try (even disingenuously) to take

69 *Legality of the Threat or Use of Nuclear Weapons, Advisory Opinion* ICJ Reports 1996, 226, par 70 (emphasis added).

70 *Case Concerning Military and Paramilitary Activities in and against Nicaragua* (*Nicaragua v United States*), Merits, Judgment, ICJ Reports 1986, 14; par 188–190.

71 On occasion the ICJ might label a particular rule or norm as '*erga omnes*', 'peremptory', 'essential', 'inderogable', or 'intransgressible'. Alain Pellet submitted that 'the particular or superior nature of the norms involved can only result from the general belief that these norms are of such a nature'. The ICJ will normally employ the same methodology to determine the existence of a 'peremptory' norm as it would use to determine *opinio juris*. In other words, a peremptory norm, or a norm *erga omnes*, is just an 'intensified *opinio*' of a particular right or obligation. See Alain Pellet in Andreas Zimmermann *et al* (Statute of the ICJ) (*supra*) 759.

72 *Nicaragua v United States* (*supra*) par 190.

73 Yoram Dinstein (War Aggression and Self-Defence) (*supra*) 93.

> advantage of the refinements of the law, and those who rigorously abide by its letter and spirit. They all share a belief in the authority of the law.'[74]

Even though the prohibition of the use of force by states (the *jus contra bellum*) is firmly established under customary international law, it is necessary to determine for purposes of individual criminal liability the extent to which the *crime of aggression* is also established under customary international law.

In Chapter III above the historical processes that led to the criminalisation of aggression are discussed against the background of the development of the modern *jus contra bellum* (as discussed in Chapters I and II above). Criminalisation of aggression as a crime against peace (as at Nuremberg)[75] is the core of the international crime of aggression. To this are added the developments in the second half of the twentieth century (the adoption of various resolutions and draft statutes dealing with various aspects of aggression, referred to above and discussed in Chapter IV).[76] Arguably the most important development since Nuremberg was the adoption of the definition of aggression at the Kampala Review Conference, discussed in Chapter VII.

With this in mind, publicists on international criminal law generally regard the crime of aggression to have customary status.[77] The exact content of this crime under customary international law is contentious, as illustrated by the chequered negotiating history of the definition of aggression leading up to the adoption of Article 8*bis* at the Kampala Review Conference. But there is agreement that the crime of aggression under customary international law has a relatively high threshold of seriousness, in order to distinguish that crime from other acts of aggression.[78] Cassese describes the customary international law notion of the crime of aggression as follows:

> '[The] planning, or organizing, or preparing, or participating in the first use of armed force by a State against the territorial integrity and political independence of another

74 Yoram Dinstein (War Aggression and Self-Defence) (*supra*) 95.
75 See Ch III, in particular section 3 *et seq.*, *supra*.
76 See discussion of the Nuremberg Principles (sections 2.1 and 2.2), as well as the various draft Codes of Crimes against the Peace and Security of Mankind (sections 2.2.1–2.2.3) and the UN GA Def of Aggression (section 2.3), in Ch IV *supra*.
77 Yoram Dinstein (War Aggression Self-Defence) (*supra*) 123; Antonio Cassese (International Criminal Law) (*supra*) 114; Gerhard Werle and Florian Jessberger (Principles of International Criminal Law) (*supra*) 538.
78 Gerhard Werle and Florian Jessberger (Principles of International Criminal Law) (*supra*) 538; Robert Cryer et al *An introduction to international criminal law and procedure* 2nd (2010) Cambridge University Press, Cambridge, 321.

> State in contravention of the UN Charter, provided the acts of aggression concerned have large-scale and serious consequences.'[79]

The above description of the customary law notion of aggression refers to a threshold of seriousness. The description contains the developments in international law from Nuremberg to date. Publicists like Dinstein and Cassese draw a distinction between 'the crime of aggression' and other 'acts of aggression', which are regarded as international wrongful acts, but which do not give rise to individual criminal liability.[80] Thus, the criminalisation of aggression in terms of the Nuremberg Charter, plus the provisions of the international draft codes, some of the provisions of the General Assembly Definition of Aggression of 1974, and, of course, the definition of aggression adopted at the Kampala Review Conference form elements of the international crime of aggression. According to Cassese, the following acts are *not* international crimes, despite being labelled 'acts of aggression':

> '(i) engaging in an armed conflict in violation of international treaties proscribing resort to armed violence, or (ii) participating in a conspiracy to wage aggressive war (that is, planning aggressive war without such planning being followed by action or at least an attempt).'[81]

The above classes of conduct (although provided for in the Charter of the IMT Nuremberg) never became part of customary international law, due to a lack of state practice and *opinio juris*.[82]

Although the ILC's Draft Code of 1954[83] refers to '[a]ny act' of aggression as a crime against peace, later commentaries by the ILC[84] linked individual criminal responsibility for the crime of aggression with the threshold of 'a sufficiently serious violation of the prohibition contained in [Article 2(4)] of the [UN] Charter'.[85] Article 1 of the Rome Statute provides that the ICC 'shall have the power to exercise its jurisdiction over persons for the *most serious crimes of international concern*'. It was pointed out that the threshold qualification in Article 8*bis*(1) is a reflection of this.

---

79 Antonio Cassese (International Criminal Law) (*supra*) 114.

80 Yoram Dinstein (War Aggression Self-Defence) (*supra*) 125 *et seq*; Antonio Cassese (International Criminal Law) (*supra*) 114.

81 Antonio Cassese (International Criminal Law) (*supra*) 114.

82 Antonio Cassese (International Criminal Law) (*supra*) 114; Gerhard Werle and Florian Jessberger (Principles of International Criminal Law) (*supra*) 544.

83 See Ch IV section 2.2.1 *supra*.

84 See Ch IV sections 2.2.2 and 2.2.3 *supra*.

85 Arthur Watts (International Law Commission Vol III) (*supra*) 1739.

Although state practice pertaining to the criminalisation of aggression is relatively scarce[86] and no prosecutions[87] for this crime have occurred since the trials at Nuremberg and Tokyo, the above discussion shows that there is an established *opinio juris* that waging aggressive war is a crime under customary international law. Werle and Jessberger conclude as follows:

---

86 For an overview of the different models of criminalisation of aggression under domestic law, see Sergey Sayapin (The crime of aggression in international criminal law) (*supra*) 199–221. There are a number of states that criminalise aggression (in some form) under domestic law. An example of a state that does provide for the crime of aggression (a domestic variation) in its national criminal law is Germany. The Code of Crimes Against International Law of 2002 (*Völkerstrafgesetzbuch* or *VStGB*) provides for the incorporation of international crimes (notably the core crimes) into German criminal law. The Code of Crimes does not include the crime of aggression, which is understandable, since the Code is aimed at bringing German criminal law in line with the law of the ICC and aggression is not yet a crime effectively within the jurisdiction of the international court. However, section 80 of the German Criminal Code (*Strafgesetzbuch* or *StGB*) provides for the crime of 'preparation of aggressive war'. The crime of preparation of aggressive war is subject to extraterritorial jurisdiction. If the act of preparation of aggressive war (within the meaning of section 80 StGB) occurred in a foreign state, German courts will be able to exercise extraterritorial jurisdiction over the crime. For the position in Germany, see in general Helmut Satzger 'German Criminal Law and the Rome Statute – A critical analysis of the New German Code of Crimes against International Law' 2 *ICLR* (2002) 261–282; Gerhard Werle and Florian Jessberger (Principles of International Criminal Law) (*supra*) 159; Heinrich Wilhelm Laufhütte in Burkhard Jähnke, Heinrich Wilhelm Laufhütte and Wlater Odersky *Strafgesetzbuch – Leipziger Kommentar* Vierter band (2005) De Gruyter Recht, Berlin, 1–30; Nikolaus Schultz 'Was the war on Iraq illegal? – The judgment of the German Federal Administrative Court of 21st June 2005' 7(1) *German Law Journal* (2006) (available at www.germanlawjournal.com/print.php?id=684 25 Jan 2006). Germany ratified the Kampala amendments to the Rome Statute of the ICC in June 2013. There are indications that the crime of aggression as per the Kampala definition will be incorporated into German criminal law. See further Gerhard Werle and Florian Jessberger (Principles of International Criminal Law) (*supra*) 159. Another national jurisdiction that provides for the crime of aggression in some form is Iraq. The IST was established by the American-led Coalition Provisional Authority after the regime of Saddam Hussein was ousted in 2003. In terms of the Statute of the Iraqi Special Tribunal, the IST has jurisdiction over Iraqi nationals or residents for crimes committed since 17 Jul 1968 up until 1 May 2003 in the territory of Iraq or elsewhere, namely the crime of genocide, crimes against humanity, war crimes, and violations of certain Iraqi laws. The latter category of crimes includes: 'The abuse of position and the pursuit of policies that may lead to the threat of war or the use of the armed forces of Iraq against an Arab country, in accordance with Article 1 of Law Number 7 of 1958, as amended.' This particular domestic version of aggression is a downgrade from the Nuremberg Tribunal's treatment of aggression as the 'supreme crime' under international law. Thus, the IST has jurisdiction over an essentially domestic notion of aggression. The provision in the relevant Iraqi legislation of 1958 is not a reference to the *international* crime of aggression as it was formulated by the Nuremberg Tribunal. Thus, it does not incorporate international law; it is simply a particular Iraqi statutory offence. See Claus Kreß 'The Iraqi Special Tribunal and the crime of aggression' 2 *JICJ* (2004) 348. *International* practice (especially via the UN SC) provides evidence of the international community's views on state action that amounts to 'acts of aggression'. See for instance UN SC Res 387 of 31 March 1976, Res 577 of 6 Dec 1985 ('acts of aggression' by South African Defence Force against Angola); UN SC Res 527 of 15 Dec 1982 ('premeditated aggressive act' by South Africa against Lesotho); UN SC Res 568 of 21 Jun 1985 ('acts of aggression' by South Africa against Botswana).

87 Caroline Fournet (International Crimes) (*supra*) 143.

> '[Aggressive] war is criminal under customary international law. The scope of the offence must be determined on the basis of the only precedents to date, the Nuremberg and Tokyo judgments. However, there is no evidence that acts of aggression not reaching the level of intensity of aggressive war are criminal under customary international law.'[88]

It is submitted that aggression as a crime under customary international law ('aggressive war') is relatively narrow in scope. This submission corresponds with the *minimalist view* on the objective elements of the crime of aggression, discussed below. The precedents of Nuremberg and Tokyo (discussed in Chapter III above) and the *opinio juris* that manifested in the second half of the twentieth century (via various resolutions and other documents reflecting the convictions of the international community) confirm the narrow scope of the crime of aggression under customary international law. The elements constituting this crime will be considered below.

2.3.4. *The elements of the crime of aggression under customary international law*

In Chapter III above the history of the criminalisation of aggression is set out against the background of the emergence of the notion of collective security, and the *jus contra bellum* in general. Part of the rationale for the criminalisation of aggression under the Nuremberg Charter (and later the Tokyo Charter) can be found in the view that the aggressive foreign policy of Germany and Japan violated international law, and the prevailing *jus contra bellum*. It must be pointed out, once again, that at the core of the criminalisation of aggression was and is the international community's desire for peace.[89] But the criminalisation of aggressive war rested on more than the illegality of German and Japanese aggressive foreign policy. An additional element – the aggressive aim of the war to subjugate another state – was also added.[90]

For purposes of individual criminal liability for the above described crime of war of aggression (which is essentially the crime of aggression under customary international law),[91] it is necessary to establish the two main elements, namely the subjective element (*mens rea*) and the criminal act(s) or objective element(s) (*actus reus*).[92]

---

88 Gerhard Werle and Florian Jessberger (Principles of International Criminal Law) (*supra*) 538.

89 Antonio Cassese (International Criminal Law) (*supra*) 116.

90 See Ch III section 3.2 *supra* on the aggressive German foreign policy that led to the occupation of other European countries. For the discussion on the Japanese aggressive foreign policy, see Ch III section 4 *supra*.

91 Sergey Sayapin (The crime of aggression in international criminal law) (*supra*) 226 et seq.

92 See also the brief outline of the requirements for individual criminal liability under international criminal law, Introduction section 1.2 *supra*.

In essence, the element of *actus reus* was addressed above with reference to the methods of determining the scope and content of the crime of aggression under customary international law. At least *two (conflicting) views* exist regarding the scope of the objective elements of the customary international law crime of aggression. The *first* (which I call the *minimalist* point of view) suggests that the scope of the crime of aggression under customary international law must be determined with reference to the only judicial precedents – Nuremberg and Tokyo. Other acts of aggression (as for instance listed in Article 3 of the UN General Assembly Definition of 1974, and in the second part of Article 8*bis* of the Rome Statute after the introduction of the Kampala Amendments)[93] are not criminal under customary international law, if they do not reach the intensity and scope of an aggressive war.[94] The second point of view (which I call the *expansive* view) suggests a notion of aggression broader than the precedents of Nuremberg and Tokyo. Antonio Cassese, a proponent of this view, argues that the crime of aggression also includes the acts of aggression listed in Article 3 of the UN General Assembly Definition of Aggression. The fundamental requirement is that these acts must 'have large-scale and serious consequences.'[95] The expansive view on the objective elements of the crime of aggression under customary international law seems at first to be quite progressive, in the sense that it not only relies on the judgments at Nuremberg and Tokyo (and subsequent confirmations of the international validity of these judgments) as bases to determine the *actus reus* of aggression, but also refers to international practice in the form of Security Council resolutions on 'acts of aggression' and the 'opinion' of the international community (especially with the adoption of the General Assembly Definition of 1974).

As far as *mens rea* is concerned, it should be noted that one of the prominent characteristics of the crime of aggression as it developed under customary international law, is the fact that it is a *leadership* crime *par excellence*.[96] It was pointed out in Chapter III above that the aggressive foreign policy of Germany and Japan developed through years of planning by the political leadership of the two countries. However, this should not imply *collective responsibility* of a leadership class, or of all senior government officials.[97] The focus should be on

93 See Ch IV section 2.3.1 *supra*.

94 For this view, see Gerhard Werle and Florian Jessberger (Principles of International Criminal Law) (*supra*) 541.

95 Antonio Cassese (International Criminal Law) (*supra*) 114.

96 Yoram Dinstein (War Aggression Self-Defence) (*supra*) 137; Gerhard Werle and Florian Jessberger (Principles of International Criminal Law) (*supra*) 542–543; see further comments on the crime of aggression at Nuremberg as a 'leadership crime' in Ch III section 3.2.1 *supra*.

97 It has to be pointed out, however, that the trial at Tokyo seemed to focus more on a class of defendants (as representatives of Japanese political leadership) and not on the individual responsibility of the accused to the same extent as the trial at Nuremberg. See comments on this issue in Ch III section 4 *supra*.

the individual's conduct and knowledge. In this regard Yoram Dinstein describes the element of *mens rea* as follows:

> 'The intent to undertake [a] war of aggression may be formed by only one or few individuals at the helm of a State. Others at the policy-making level need not be personally guided by the same intent. The acid test is whether, in assisting the preparations for war, they actually know of the aggressive schemes. If they know that aggression is planned, this may suffice to establish the requisite *mens rea*.'[98]

Some publicists favour *mens rea* in the form of a *special intent*. This approach requires that the individual not only has knowledge of the wrongfulness of his or her actions (for instance planning and waging of a war of aggression), but must also have the additional intent to 'achieve territorial gains, or to obtain economic advantages, or to interfere with the internal affairs'[99] of the victim state. Thus, for instance, a war in contravention of the UN Charter but on humanitarian grounds ('humanitarian intervention')[100] is regarded as illegal state conduct, but does not constitute the crime of aggression with individual criminal liability.[101] This line of argument is controversial, since humanitarian intervention often involves interference with the internal affairs of the victim state. Humanitarian intervention could even involve 'regime change',[102] which certainly amounts to the subjugation of the victim state, and at the very least interference with its internal affairs. Such conduct would satisfy the required *actus reus* of aggressive war, plus the necessary intent (even special intent) to subjugate the victim state. One possibility is to view 'humanitarian intervention' to be the *motive*, which is generally regarded as irrelevant for purposes of determining criminal responsibility. A motive requirement would also not be consistent with the Nuremberg precedent.[103] On the other hand, if one looks at the lack of any specific mental element in the definition of aggression that was adopted at the Kampala Review Conference, the question arises whether a modified *animus aggressionis* would be helpful to differentiate between the objective elements of aggression and the subjective elements. It is clear that under customary international law motive/purpose never formed a part of the

98 Yoram Dinstein (War Aggression Self-Defence) (*supra*) 137.

99 See the views of S Glaser, as quoted in Antonio Cassese (International Criminal Law) (*supra*) 115–116.

100 For a discussion of humanitarian intervention in the context of the *jus contra bellum*, see Ch II section 2.5.2 *supra*.

101 Antonio Cassese (International Criminal Law) (*supra*) 116.

102 See concluding remarks in Ch II section 2.5.1.1 *supra*. The US and UK ultimately presented an argument based on humanitarian grounds ('promotion of freedom and human rights') as rationale for the 2003 invasion of Iraq, and the eventual regime change that followed. It is submitted that the human rights/humanitarian rationale was presented ex post facto, and not the real *casus belli* for the 2003 invasion of Iraq.

103 Gerhard Werle and Florian Jessberger (Principles of International Criminal Law) (*supra*) 544–545.

elements. This makes sense, given the inherent criminal nature of aggressive war. Knowledge of the fulfilment of the objective elements of aggression under customary international law should therefore be enough. In the context of state acts of aggression, which may *prima facie* constitute the objective elements of the crime of aggression in terms of the second part of Article 8*bis*, combined with the threshold and leadership qualifiers in the first part of Article 8*bis*, may not be enough to distinguish between the individual's criminal intent, and lack of criminal intent, perhaps caused by some *bona fide* motivation such as humanitarian intervention. This point was argued in Chapter VII in the context of the crime of aggression under Article 8*bis*. For present purposes it is accepted that motive or purpose does not form part of the subjective element of the crime of aggression under customary international law.

Certain domestic criminal law commentators hold that intent (*dolus*) requires knowledge of the elements of the crime (definition of the crime) as well as knowledge of the unlawfulness of the act. This is sometimes referred to as *dolus malus* ('evil intent').[104] Intent, even *special* intent, is not the same as motive in terms of this view. However laudable the motive (for instance to protect citizens from their abusive and oppressive government), if the individual had the necessary intent in the above sense, the good motive will not absolve the individual from criminal responsibility.[105] To attack another state in order to end mass human rights violations in that state would be regarded as 'aggression', since a war was waged in violation of international law and the aggressor had the intent to subjugate the victim state. The *humanitarian motive* in this context does not take away the intent (*dolus*) of the aggressor. Even if 'political subjugation' would be required as a special intent for the crime of aggression, that would be conceptually different from motive,[106] which does not have a bearing on criminal responsibility. Motive may ultimately be relevant for purposes of punishment after a guilty verdict. The prosecution may also use motive (as circumstantial evidence) in order to establish their case, but it does not form an element of the crime for purposes of criminal responsibility.[107]

The scope and content of the *jus contra bellum* is the subject of debate. Humanitarian intervention[108] and an evolving practice of self-defence[109] (especially in the context of the 'war on terror') indicate that *jus contra bellum* is in flux. Many of the rules concerning the use of force by states, including the

---

104 CR Snyman (Criminal Law) (*supra*) 176.

105 CR Snyman (Criminal Law) (*supra*) 186.

106 For a theoretical analysis of the notion of 'motive' vis-à-vis 'intent', see AP Simester and ATH Smith (eds) *Harm and Culpability* (1996) Clarendon Press, Oxford, 94–98.

107 Glanville Williams *Textbook of Criminal Law* (1978) Stevens & Sons, London, 56.

108 See Ch II section 5.2 *supra*.

109 See Ch II section 5.1 *supra*.

criminality of aggression (at least in the form of 'war of aggression') are well-established. The rule *ignorantia juris non excusat* ('ignorance of the law is no excuse')[110] should in principle apply here. However, some publicists argue that there exists 'relative uncertainty of many rules of international criminal law.'[111] The apparent reason is that international law is a body of law more removed from the daily lives of individuals, who essentially function in a particular domestic legal environment. This may generally speaking be true. However, Dinstein correctly suggests that 'mistake of law may be less potent in the context of crimes against the peace ... since policy-makers are more likely than plain soldiers to be knowledgeable about international law.'[112] In the context of an international system characterised by institutions of collective and regional security, continuous diplomatic interaction through the structures of the UN, and well-publicised condemnations by the Security Council of acts of aggression, it is indeed implausible that individuals in political and military leadership positions can successfully claim ignorance of the law in respect of the prohibition of the use of force. Dinstein goes further than this. He suggests that in situations where the *subjective knowledge of individuals* (in leadership positions) with respect to the norms relating to the use of force and the criminality of aggressive wars 'cannot be ascertained by direct evidence, the task can be facilitated through the use of objective criteria (such as the manifest illegality of the action taken).'[113]

Given the above arguments, a number of submissions can be made relevant to the discussion that follows below (on the prosecution of crimes under customary international law in national courts). Regarding the scope of the crime of aggression under customary international law, and with reference to the objective elements, the minimalist position described above is supported here. From an *international policy perspective*, the more idealistic view of publicists like Cassese (an exponent of the expansive point of view) could certainly be supported. This *aspirational* view of the crime of aggression under customary international law is arguably closer to the overarching rationale for the criminalisation of aggression, namely international peace and security. This view is perhaps also closer to the *substantive justice* approach (as opposed to the strict approach) to legality, referred to below. However, from a *criminal justice point of view*, the expansive notion of the crime of aggression under customary international law cannot be supported. The *minimalist* view stands on firmer ground regarding the methodology to prove custom. This leaves a clearer picture of the elements of the crime. In turn, this could present a better basis for the prosecution in national courts of individuals for the crime of aggression, discussed in the following

110 For a critical discussion of this doctrine (or presumption), see CR Snyman (Criminal Law) (*supra*) 199–204; Gerhard Kemp et al (Criminal Law in South Africa) (*supra*) 225–228.

111 Yoram Dinstein (War Aggression Self-Defence) (*supra*) 138.

112 Yoram Dinstein (War Aggression Self-Defence) (*supra*) 139.

113 *Ibid.*

sections. Other factors, including constitutional considerations, also play a role in this regard. At any rate, if states have the desire to incorporate aggression beyond the minimalist form as per customary international law, they could do no better than to use the definition of aggression as adopted at the Kampala Review Conference. Despite its flaws, Article 8*bis* is the clear alternative to the narrower crime of aggression under customary international law.

2.3.5. Prosecuting crimes under customary international law in South African courts

There exists under South African law the theoretical possibility to prosecute crimes under customary international law through direct application in the courts. No incorporating legislation is in other words required. This is due to section 232 of the Constitution, 1996, which provides: 'Customary international law is law in the Republic unless it is inconsistent with the Constitution or an Act of Parliament.'

In *S v Basson*[114] Judge Sachs in his separate opinion relied on section 232 of the Constitution. He stated that a failure by the Supreme Court of Appeal 'to give sufficient or any weight to the State's obligations under international law, raise constitutional issues'.[115] The accused, Dr Wouter Basson, was initially charged with various offences under South African law, notably in terms of the Riotous Assemblies Act.[116] The facts of the case concerned activities in South Africa and abroad, including conspiracy to commit murder outside the territory of South Africa. Some of the acts could be regarded as possible war crimes against members of the liberation movements who resided in Namibia.[117] All the offences were allegedly committed before 1994. The Constitutional Court was not asked to pronounce on the merits of possible war crimes charges against Basson, who worked for the Civil Co-operation Bureau, a division of the apartheid-era Defence Force. Basson was never charged with war crimes, because of the problem with retroactive application of law. Although South Africa was at the time of the alleged offences a party to the Geneva Conventions of 1949[118] (breaches of which can constitute war crimes), these instruments were not incorporated into national law. The Constitutional Court ultimately chose

114 *S v Basson* 2005 (1) SA 171 (CC).

115 *S v Basson (supra)* separate opinion of Sachs J par 127.

116 17 of 1956.

117 See opinion of Sachs J in *S v Basson* (*supra*) par 121–123.

118 Convention for the Amelioration of the Condition of the Wounded and Sick in Armed Forces in the Field (1949) (Geneva I); Convention for the Amelioration of the Condition of Wounded, Sick and Shipwrecked Members of Armed Forces at Sea (1949) (Geneva II); Convention relative to the Treatment of Prisoners of War (1949) (Geneva III); Convention relative to the Protection of Civilian Persons in the Time of War (1949) (Geneva IV) (reprinted in Christine Van den Wyngaert (International Criminal Law) (*supra*) 445–534.

not to deal with the issue of retroactive application of war crimes; however some of the opinions of the judges in this regard are relevant for present purposes.

Chief Justice Chaskalson, in a separate opinion, pointed to the following:

> 'The objection to the charges under the Riotous Assemblies Act raises an issue of considerable importance. Can a South African court put one of its citizens on trial for conspiring to commit murders and other offences during the period 1981 to 1989 in a territory [Namibia], then under South African administration but beyond the territorial borders of the country? The answer given by the High Court was, no. The reason, so the Court held, was that such matters are not crimes according to South African law. This, despite the fact that the conspiracy is alleged to have been entered into in South Africa, and the crimes, which if proved may amount to war crimes, are alleged to have been committed in the course of a conflict involving the South African armed forces and those fighting against it.'[119]

Importantly, Chief Justice Chaskalson also added that the Constitution alone cannot serve as a basis to prosecute conduct that did not constitute criminal conduct at the time when it occurred. The Chief Justice stated as follows:

> 'If the conduct with which the accused was charged did not constitute an offence under South African law at the time it was committed ... the State cannot contend that it has become an offence because of the provisions of the Constitution.'[120]

In making the above statement, the Chief Justice relied on *Du Plessis and Others v De Klerk and Another*[121] where the Constitutional Court held that the Constitution does not have retroactive operation or impact.[122]

The issue of *retroactivity* aside, it is important to determine whether the Constitution, and in particular section 232, could serve as a basis for prosecutions of crimes under customary international law, where such crimes are not provided for in terms of South African legislation or the common law. This question involves other constitutional issues as well, notably the right to a fair trial.[123]

Having regard to the general principles of South African criminal law, as well as the constitutional right to a fair trial,[124] it is submitted that the Constitution

119 *S v Basson (supra)* separate opinion of Chaskalson CJ par 84.

120 *S v Basson (supra)* separate opinion of Chaskalson CJ par 97.

121 *Du Plessis and Others v De Klerk and Another* 1996 (3) SA 850 (CC). On the non-retrospective rule in South African Constitutional law, see also Iain Currie and Johan de Waal *The Bill of Rights Handbook* 6th (2013) Juta, Cape Town, 53–55.

122 See separate opinion of Chaskalson CJ in *S v Basson (supra)* par 95–96.

123 See comments by Sachs J in *S v Basson (supra)* par 129.

124 Art 35 Constitution of South Africa, 1996.

cannot serve as a basis for the exercise by South African courts of substantive jurisdiction over crimes under international law, including crimes under customary international law. Nico Steytler stated that 'crimes under international law are not *ipso facto* part of South African law.'[125] This is true, not only in terms of the general approach to the application of international law in South Africa as identified above, but in particular because of well-established constitutional and criminal law principles. In terms of the latter, the criminal law principle of legality (*nullum crimen, nulla poena sine lege*) poses an important obstacle in the way of the application of customary international criminal law in South African courts.

2.3.5.1. The legality principle versus the application of customary international (criminal) law in South African courts

Before the principle of legality is discussed from a South African (national) perspective, it is important to briefly refer to the conflicting views of publicists and judges regarding the scope of the principle of legality in the context of international crimes. Publicists generally accept that the principle of legality requires that the criminal behaviour 'be laid down as clearly as possible' but at the same time they also point out that 'this standard is less rigid' than in many domestic legal systems.[126] In terms of the different 'families' of legal systems (notably the civil law/continental European systems and the common law systems) different notions of legality can also be identified. In general, civil law countries (for instance France, Belgium, and Germany) adhere to a strict understanding of legality. One consequence of this view is for instance that criminal offences must be in written law, adopted by parliament. Furthermore, 'rules criminalizing human conduct must be as specific and clear as possible, so as to guide the behaviour of citizens'.[127] Common law systems follow – generally speaking – a less strict approach to the principle of legality. The obvious manifestation of judge-made law is that it may lack the same degree of rigidity or certainty as is the case with written/codified law in civil law systems.[128]

In the context of international criminal law, Cassese has pointed out that (at least initially) international criminal tribunals (like the IMT Nuremberg) followed a less strict approach to the principle of legality.[129] The criminalisation of aggression (crimes against peace) in the Nuremberg Charter and as applied by the IMT Nuremberg, is discussed in Chapter IV above. One pertinent issue that the defence raised at Nuremberg was the issue of legality, in particular the

---

125 Nico Steytler *Constitutional criminal procedure* (1998) Butterworths, Durban, 373.
126 Gerhard Werle and Florian Jessberger (Principles of International Criminal Law) (*supra*) 39.
127 Antonio Cassese (International Criminal Law) (*supra*) 141–142.
128 Antonio Cassese (International Criminal Law) (*supra*) 142.
129 Antonio Cassese (International Criminal Law) (*supra*) 143.

ex post facto criminalisation of crimes against peace. It is not necessary to repeat all the objections here, suffice to say that the approach of the IMT was one of *substantive justice*, where the focus was on the socially harmful conduct, not the question whether the conduct in question had already been criminalised.[130] This approach was also taken by Judge Röling in his dissenting opinion at the IMTFE Tokyo. In particular, the judge concluded that crimes against peace were to be punished 'because of the dangerous character of the individuals who committed them, hence on *security considerations*.' The decisive element, according to Judge Röling, was in other words, 'the danger rather than the guilt.'[131]

More recently, the Special Court for Sierra Leone (SCSL) had the opportunity to address the principle of legality. In *Prosecutor v Sam Hinga Norman*[132] the defence raised a number of points in its submissions in a Preliminary Motion. The following pertained to the principle of legality:

> '(a) The Special Court has no jurisdiction to try the Accused for crimes under Article 4(c) of the Statute ... prohibiting the recruitment of children under 15 "into armed forces or groups or using them to participate actively in hostilities" since the crime of child recruitment was not part of customary international law at the times relevant to the Indictment. (b) Consequently, Article 4(c) of the Special Court Statute violates the principle of *nullum crimen sine lege*.'[133]

To the above the prosecution replied, in part, as follows:

> 'The principle of *nullum crimen sine lege* should not be rigidly applied to an act universally regarded as abhorrent. The question is whether it was foreseeable and accessible to a possible perpetrator that the conduct was punishable.'[134]

The majority of the Court in the *Norman* case favoured (in principle) the less strict approach to legality as described above with reference to the judgments of the IMT and the IMTFE. The Court stated: 'The emphasis on conduct, rather than on the specific description of the offence in substantive criminal law, is of primary relevance.'[135] With reference to the *Tadic* case (ICTY) the Court stated that 'it is not necessary for the *individual criminal responsibility* of the accused to be explicitly stated in a convention for the provisions of the convention to entail individual criminal responsibility under customary international law.'[136]

---

130 Antonio Cassese (International Criminal Law) (*supra*) 139.

131 See discussion by Antonio Cassese (International Criminal Law) (*supra*) 143–144 (emphasis in the original).

132 *Prosecutor v Sam Hinga Norman* (Decision on preliminary motion based on lack of jurisdiction – child recruitment) Case No SCSL-2004-14-AR72 (E) 31 May 2004.

133 *Prosecutor v Sam Hinga Norman* (*supra*) par 1.

134 *Prosecutor v Sam Hinga Norman* (*supra*) par 2.

135 *Prosecutor v Sam Hinga Norman* (*supra*) par 25.

136 *Prosecutor v Sam Hinga Norman* (*supra*) par 38 (emphasis in the original).

The reasoning of the majority of the Court was, all matters considered, less than satisfactory. The Court did not really address the fundamental concern of legality, and how the principle of specificity was addressed – in particular in the context of crimes under customary international law. More elegant was the reasoning of dissenting Judge Robertson. Regarding conduct that shocks the whole of humankind (and for present purposes one could say that this includes the 'most serious crime' of aggression), Judge Robertson warned against convictions based on 'disgust rather than evidence, or of a non-existent crime.'[137] The Judge stated as follows:

> 'The principle of legality, sometimes expressed as a rule against retroactivity, requires that the defendant must at the time of committing the acts alleged to amount to a crime have been in a position to know, or at least readily to establish, that those acts may entail penal consequences. Ignorance of the law is no defence, so long as that law is capable of reasonable ascertainment … The requisite clarity will not necessarily be found in there having been previous successful prosecutions in respect of similar conduct, since there has to be a first prosecution for every crime and we are in the early stages of international criminal law enforcement. Nor is it necessary, at the time of commission, for there to be in existence an international court with the power to punish it, or any foresight that such a court will necessarily be established. In every case, the question is whether the defendant, at the time of conduct which was not clearly outlawed by national law in the place of its commission, could have ascertained … that it was contrary to international criminal law.'[138]

Against the above background, the scope and meaning of the principle of legality in South African law are considered.

Section 35(3)(l) of the Constitution of South Africa provides as follows:

> 'Every accused person has a right to a fair trial, which includes the right – not to be convicted for an act or omission that was not an offence under either national or international law at the time it was committed or omitted'.

This constitutional provision has a number of implications for the application of criminal norms. Snyman commented that this means that any legislation that would criminalise conduct retroactively would be unconstitutional.[139] Section 35(3)(l) actually constitutionalises the *jus praevium* (prohibition of retroactive criminalisation) component of the legality principle in criminal law. The other well-established components are: *jus certum* (clear language[140]); *jus acceptum*

137 Dissenting opinion of Judge Robertson in *Prosecutor v Sam Hinga Norman* (*supra*) par 13.
138 Dissenting opinion of Judge Robertson in *Prosecutor v Sam Hinga Norman* (*supra*) par 13.
139 CR Snyman (Criminal Law) (*supra*) 38. See also Iain Currie and Johan de Waal (Bill of Rights Handbook) 801.
140 *S v Jordan* 2002 2 SACR 499; 2002 (6) SA 642 (CC).

(conduct accepted in law as criminal conduct[141]); and *jus strictum* (narrow or strict interpretation of the definition of a crime[142]).[143]

The legality principle, and in particular the *jus certum* aspect of it, does not mean that there must always be absolute certainty regarding the application of the elements of the crime. The approach of South African courts is, however, that statutory as well as common law offences that are *too vague* will be unconstitutional.[144] Nico Steytler argued that the principle against retroactivity and the prohibition of vaguely defined offences share the same rationale:

> 'A vaguely-defined offence raises the same concerns that underlie the prohibition against retroactive offences. If the definition of an offence is so vague that it cannot give sufficient notification to citizens of the proscribed field of activity, it not only permits the unfair prosecution of an unwitting person, but it also allows the state a wide prosecuting discretion which it may abuse.'[145]

The strict application of the legality principle was confirmed by the Constitutional Court in *Masiya v Director of Public Prosecutions and Others*.[146] In particular, Judge Nkabinde referred to the following aspects of the legality principle:

> 'One of the central tenets underlying the common-law understanding of legality is that of foreseeability – that the rules of criminal law are clear and precise so that an individual may easily behave in a manner that avoids committing crimes.'[147]

And further:

> 'Section 35(3)(l) of the Constitution confirms a long-standing principle of the common law that provides that accused persons may not be convicted of offences where the conduct for which they are charged did not constitute an offence at the time it was committed.'[148]

141 *S v Malgas* 2001 1 SACR 469; 2001 (2) SA 1222 (SCA).

142 *S v Mintoor* 1996 1 SACR 514 (C).

143 For a discussion see CR Snyman (Criminal Law) (*supra*) 37–45.

144 See *S v Friedman* (1) 1996 (1) SACR 181 (W). On the *jus certum* component of legality and the impact of vagueness on the application of criminal law, see *National Coalition for Gay and Lesbian Equality v Minister of Justice* 1998 (2) SACR 102 (W) 117–119.

145 Nico Steytler (Constitutional Criminal Procedure) (*supra*) 374.

146 *Masiya v Director of Public Prosecutions and Others* 2007 (2) SACR 435 (CC). For critical assessments of the case, see Burchell *South African Criminal Law and Procedure Vol I: General Principles of Criminal Law* 4th (2011) Juta, Cape Town, 39–40; CR Snyman (Criminal Law) (*supra*) 45–48. For qualified support of the judgment, see Gerhard Kemp 'Nullum crimen sine lege: Hoe staan dit nou in ons reg?' in Jacques Du Plessis and Gerhard Lubbe (eds) *A Man of Principle – The life and legacy of JC de Wet* (2013) Juta, Cape Town, 387–388.

147 Nkabinde J in *Masiya v DPP* (*supra*) par 52.

148 Nkabinde J in *Masiya v DPP* (*supra*) par 54.

The Constitutional Court also linked the common law and constitutional legality principles to the very *nature* of the constitutional dispensation in South Africa, namely that 'legality is central to the rule of law'.[149]

Considering the writings of publicists and the developing criminal and constitutional law jurisprudence discussed above, a number of submissions regarding the possible prosecution of individuals for the crime of aggression under customary international law are put forward.

First, in the context of the dualist/monist debate, and the impact of the Constitution on the application of international law described in section 2.1.1 *et seq* above, it is submitted that *at present* it will not be possible to prosecute an individual for the crime of aggression in a South African court. In the absence of legislation transforming or incorporating international norms (for instance Article 8*bis* as adopted at the Kampala Review Conference) into crimes under South African law, one cannot simply turn to the Constitution as a basis to prosecute individuals. The Constitution provides that customary international law is law in the Republic, but *other* constitutional and criminal law norms (notably the principle of legality) constitute considerable obstacles in the way of prosecuting individuals on the basis of customary international law. *Secondly*, on the assumption that there is no crime of aggression in South Africa law, the position is that judges cannot rely on international law as a basis to create the crime of aggression for purposes of convicting an individual for this crime in a South African court. The democratic principle is that the legislature is the sole creator of new crimes in South Africa.[150] *Thirdly*, it is submitted that the uncertainty surrounding the elements and scope of the crime of aggression under customary international law provides an additional reason why individuals can at present not be prosecuted for this crime in South African courts. Regardless of whether one supports the minimalist or the expansive view on the elements and scope of the crime of aggression under customary international law, the point is that an accused will be able to raise this uncertainty as a valid constitutional (and criminal law) objection to his or her prosecution. Uncertainty offends the principle that crimes must not be vague. This in turn touches on the element of foreseeability. An accused (even in a leadership position) must be able to foresee that a certain policy decision or act that he authored and had knowledge of will constitute the crime of aggression under customary international law. It was pointed out above that the minimalist view on the elements of aggression under customary international law will probably provide a better basis for

149 Nkabinde J in *Masiya v DPP* (*supra*) par 55. The judge relied on an earlier judgement of the Constitutional Court, in *Veldman v Director of Public Prosecutions* 2006 (2) SACR 319 (CC). The latter concerned the sentencing aspect of the legality principle (*nulla poena sine lege*).

150 For a discussion of this aspect of legality, see CR Snyman (Criminal Law) (*supra*) 39.

the prosecution of individuals for the crime of aggression. Constitutional jurisprudence in South Africa thus far seems to favour criminalisation via legislative incorporation or transformation, rather than direct application of customary international law.

Another case (application of customary international (criminal) law in England) is considered to illustrate the difficulties in applying international criminal law in national courts.

2.3.6. Case study: The application of customary international (criminal) law in English law, with specific reference to the crime of aggression

The 2003 invasion of Iraq and subsequent 'regime change' by the American-led coalition created much debate and animosity. While international lawyers debated the legality of the invasion[151] (which was neither explicitly authorised by the Security Council, nor an apparent act of self-defence under Article 51 of the UN Charter),[152] people all over the world (including people in Britain and America) voiced their opposition to the invasion.[153] Historians and international relations specialists will no doubt analyse the political implications of the 2003 invasion and subsequent occupation of Iraq. From an international law perspective the legality of the invasion will be debated for some time to come. However, for the time being there seems to be no real possibility that any

---

151 It is interesting to note that during the Vietnam conflict a number of individuals raised the issue of the legality of the use of force by the US in US courts. On balance, the cases showed the reluctance of courts to pronounce on matters of foreign policy and 'political' issues. However, some interesting dissenting opinions were delivered. In *Dennis Mora et al v Robert S McNamara, Secretary of Defense et al* 389 US 934, 88 SCt 282, Steward J and Douglas J (dissenting) were willing to accept the possibility that the use of force by the US in Vietnam was illegal. See also an earlier opinion of Douglas J in *David Henry Mitchell III v US* 386 US 972, 87 SCt 1162 at 1163.

152 For comments on the legality of the 2003 invasion of Iraq, see Lori Fisler Damrosch and Bernard H Oxman (eds) *Future Implications of the Iraq Conflict* (2003), ASIL, Washington DC.

153 See George Soros *The Bubble of American Supremacy* (2004), Weidenfeld & Nicolson, London, 22–24 for an argument of how the US-led invasion of Iraq prompted worldwide protests. There exists a vast amount of commentary, analysis and polemical writing on the Iraq-invasion. Some of the early comments referred to the international political implications of the perceived illegality of the invasion. See for instance: Alain Gresh, Maria Ierardi, Olivier Pironet and Philippe Rivière 'The US war on Iraq' (L'empire contre l'Irak) *Le Monde diplomatique*, 2 Sept 2003 (available at http://mondediplo.com/focus/iraq/); 'Casus belli voor Irak smelt weg' *De Standaard*, 11 Jul 2003 (available at www.standaard.be/Misc/print.asp?articleID=DST11072003_024); Paul Krugman 'Who's Accountable?' *The New York Times*, 10 Jun 2003 (available at www.nytimes.com/2003/06/10/opi.../10KRUG.html?pagewanted=print&position); Stanley Hoffmann 'America goes backward' 50(10) *The New York Review of Books*, 12 Jun 2003 (available at www.nybooks.com/articles/16350); 'Bush's America loses hearts and minds' *Mail & Guardian* 4 Jun 2003 (available at http://mg.co.za/Content/13.asp?ao=15196).

(international) criminal law action will be taken against any individuals relating to the invasion of Iraq, and in particular the question whether any individuals can be held liable for the crime of aggression. Indeed, while the international community (including the Security Council) was bitterly divided on the initial question whether the US, the UK and the other members of the coalition had the necessary authority to use force, by May 2003 the Security Council accepted the reality of the occupation and subsequent regime change in Iraq. With Resolution 1483 the Security Council reaffirmed the sovereignty and territorial integrity of Iraq, but at the same time also accepted the presence and role of the American and other coalition forces in Iraq.[154]

Although the above-mentioned political and legal turmoil caused by the 2003 invasion of Iraq will probably never result in any prosecutions of individuals for the crime of aggression (certainly not in the manner and form of international criminal tribunals like the IMT Nuremberg or IMTFE Tokyo),[155] the question whether the invasion should be regarded as aggression under customary international law did come before the courts in England. In *R v Jones et al*[156] the House of Lords considered an appeal[157] that essentially concerned the following assertions: aggression is recognised as a crime under customary international law; customary international law is (without the need for any statute or judicial decision) part of the domestic law of England and Wales; and efforts to prevent the crime of aggression must be seen as legal justifications for what would otherwise be criminal acts.[158]

During February or March 2003 the twenty appellants before the House of Lords committed various criminal acts aimed at disrupting the activities at military facilities in the United Kingdom that were used by the American and

154 SC Res 1483 (22 May 2003), 42 *ILM* 1016 (2003).

155 The former Prosecutor of the ICC, Luis Moreno Ocampo, received more than 200 communications concerning the March 2003 invasion of Iraq. Based on these communications, the Office of the Prosecutor identified the crimes of aggression, crimes against humanity, genocide and war crimes as *prima facie* applicable. In terms of aggression, the Prosecutor pointed out that he cannot proceed with an investigation and prosecution since the Rome Statute lacked a definition and conditions for the exercise of jurisdiction for this crime. Even in the aftermath of the Kampala Resolution on the definition of aggression and conditions for the exercise of ICC jurisdiction over the crime, as we know from the discussion in Ch VII above, the ICC will not be able to exercise jurisdiction retroactively over the invasion of Iraq. For more information see The American Non-Governmental Organization Coalition for the International Criminal Court 'Communications to the ICC regarding the situation in Iraq' 28 Jul 2009 (available at www.amicc.org/docs/Iraq.pdf).

156 *R v Jones et al* (Conjoined Appeals) 29 March 2006, 45 *ILM* 992 (2006).

157 For a comment on the judgment by the Court of Appeal, see R Cryer 'Aggression at the Court of Appeal' 10 *Journal of Conflict and Security Law* (2005) 209–230.

158 See opinion of Lord Bingham of Cornhill in *R v Jones* (*supra*) par 1–36 for an exposition of the propositions made by the appellants.

British armed forces.[159] Their purported justification (to stop the American and British 'crime of aggression against Iraq') was summarised by Lord Bingham of Cornhill as follows:

> 'The appellants acted as they did because they wished to impede, obstruct or disrupt the commission of that crime [aggression], or what they believed would be the commission of that crime, by Her Majesty's Government or the Government of the United States against Iraq in the weeks and days before (as we now know) hostilities began. They accordingly contend, or have contended, that they were legally justified in acting as they did. The House is not asked to rule whether, in preparing to make war against Iraq, the United Kingdom or the United States committed the international law crime of aggression, but it must rule whether, if they may have done, that would justify the appellants' otherwise criminal conduct.'[160]

In determining whether the crime of aggression is a crime under customary international law, Lord Bingham of Cornhill referred to certain milestones on the road to the acceptance of the crime of aggression as part of international law. These milestones include those instruments and cases discussed in previous Chapters of this book, like the instruments from the League of Nations era, the Charter of the United Nations, the trials at Nuremberg and Tokyo (as well as the subsequent trials of individuals for the crime of aggression, especially under the Control Council Laws), the various drafts of the Draft Code of Crimes against Peace and Security of Mankind, the 1974 General Assembly Definition of Aggression and the Rome Statute of the ICC.[161]

Importantly, Lord Bingham of Cornhill referred to the ICJ judgment in *Nicaragua v United States*.[162] He linked the finding of the ICJ that the prohibition on the use of force in Article 2(4) of the UN Charter was accepted as *jus cogens*, to the conclusion of writers like Professor Brownlie that the criminalisation of aggression (as set out in Article 6 of the Nuremberg Charter) has become part of 'general international law'.[163] It was thus accepted by Lord Bingham of Cornhill that the crime of aggression is indeed part of customary international law. The question remained whether the customary international law notion of aggression

159 For instance, Margaret Jones and Paul Milling, two of the appellants, broke into the Royal Air Force Base at Fairfort in Gloucestershire where they caused damage to fuel tankers and bomb trailers. They were charged *inter alia* with counts of conspiracy to cause criminal damage contrary to sec 1(1) of the Criminal Law Act 1977. See *R v Jones* (*supra*) par 3–4.

160 Lord Bingham of Cornhill in *R v Jones* (*supra*) par 2.

161 Lord Bingham of Cornhill in *R v Jones* (*supra*) par 12–17.

162 *Case Concerning Military and Paramilitary Activities in and against Nicaragua* (Merits) (*Nicaragua v United States*) (*supra*).

163 Lord Bingham of Cornhill in *R v Jones* (*supra*) par 18. See further discussion under section 1.3.3 *supra*.

was *specific* enough to serve as a basis for any *criminal* liability. Lord Bingham of Cornhill concluded as follows:

> 'It was suggested, on behalf of the Crown, that the crime of aggression lacked the certainty of definition required of any criminal offence, particularly a crime of this gravity. This submission was based on the requirement in article 5(2) of the Rome statute that the crime of aggression be the subject of definition before the international court [ICC] exercised jurisdiction to try persons accused of that offence. This was an argument which found some favour with the Court of Appeal ... I would not for my part accept it. It is true that some states parties to the Rome statute have sought an extended and more specific definition of aggression. It is also true that there has been protracted discussion of whether a finding of aggression against a state by the Security Council should be a necessary pre-condition of the court's exercise of jurisdiction to try a national of that state accused of committing the crime. I do not, however, think that either of these points undermines the appellants' essential proposition that the core elements of the crime of aggression have been understood, at least since 1945, with sufficient clarity to permit the lawful trial (and, on conviction, punishment) of those accused of this most serious crime. It is unhistorical to suppose that the elements of the crime were clear in 1945 but have since become in any way obscure.'[164]

The next issue for consideration was whether crimes recognised in customary international law are also recognised and enforced by the laws of England and Wales, without the need for domestic statutory incorporation or judicial decisions. Lord Bingham of Cornhill accepted that crimes under customary international law 'may be assimilated into the domestic criminal law' of England and Wales, but this assimilation is not automatic. Lord Bingham of Cornhill favoured the view that new crimes can only be introduced into English law via Parliament. Customary international law may very well be the legal basis or justification for Parliament to legislate on international crimes, for instance the crime of torture (Criminal Justice Act 1988).[165] It is submitted that this view on the need for an act of transformation in English law is consistent with the above espoused view on the application of crimes under (customary) international law in our case study of South African law. Indeed, it is submitted that the ultimate success of the application of international criminal law in national courts will to an important extent depend upon the firm assimilation into national law and legal doctrine, rather than on utopian notions of the direct application of international criminal law in national courts.[166]

---

164 Lord Bingham of Cornhill in *R v Jones* (*supra*) par 19.
165 Lord Bingham of Cornhill in *R v Jones* (*supra*) par 20–23.
166 For further commentary see James Crawford (Public International Law) (*supra*) 67–71.

2.4. PROSECUTING THE CRIME OF AGGRESSION IN NATIONAL COURTS, STATE SOVEREIGNTY AND THE ACT OF STATE DOCTRINE

State sovereignty[167] – perhaps the most important feature of the international system – is 'not unfettered.'[168] While the prosecution of crimes in national courts is a fundamental function (and manifestation) of a sovereign state's ability to conduct its own affairs, there are limits imposed by the 'obligation to respect the sovereignty of other states.'[169] This principle (sometimes expressed by reference to the maxim *par in parem non habet imperium* – 'equals have no jurisdiction over one another'), manifests in a very important limitation on state sovereignty: sovereign immunity. Two important consequences flow from sovereign immunity. First, states 'must not interfere with public acts of foreign sovereign [states] out of respect for their independence.'[170] The second implication concerns the power of national courts over the conduct of foreign sovereign states and over the conduct of foreign affairs by the national government. Here the general approach is that the courts (judicial branch of state) should not interfere.[171] The impact of immunities on the prosecution of crimes under international law will be addressed in section 2.4 below in the context of the exercise of extraterritorial (and more specifically universal) jurisdiction by national courts.

For present purposes it is necessary to highlight two other doctrines in English law that might limit the ability of a national court to pronounce on the conduct of state officials. The *act of state doctrine* (which is not to be confused with the doctrine of sovereign immunity)[172] in general means that the *acts of foreign states* (within their own territories) and the *conduct of foreign affairs of the domestic government* fall beyond judicial scrutiny.[173] The foundational principle here is that the sovereignty and equality of states must be respected.[174] The related concept of 'non-justiciability' (matters essentially within the competence of the executive branch of government) applies to domestic and foreign executive acts.[175] The decision by the executive to go to war is regarded as such a non-

167 See general comments on the notion of state sovereignty in the context of the emerging system of international criminal law, Introduction section 2 *supra*.

168 Antonio Cassese (International Law) (*supra*) 98.

169 *Ibid.*

170 Antonio Cassese (International Law) (*supra*) 99.

171 *Ibid.*

172 See in general Malcolm Shaw *International Law* 3rd (1991) Grotius Publications, Cambridge, 431–433; James Crawford (Public International Law) (*supra*) 72–77.

173 See in general on the development and historical origins of the doctrine Michael Zander 'Act of State Doctrine' 27(5) *The Modern Law Review* (1964) 588–593; for a discussion on the position in South Africa see John Dugard (International Law) (*supra*) 71–79.

174 Malcolm Shaw (International Law) (*supra*) 128.

175 *Ibid.*

justiciable act.[176] The rationale for the doctrine of non-justiciability seems to rest (at least in part) on a policy consideration. For instance, it had been suggested that 'judicial review would not be appropriate in a matter which would have serious international repercussions and which was more properly [within] the sphere of diplomacy.'[177] Others view the doctrine of non-justiciability with some caution. The former President of the Supreme Court of Israel, Aharon Barak, argued that the point of departure should not be 'is this a political question?', but rather the merits of the case as such. He stated: '[The] court should not abdicate its role in a democracy merely because it is uncomfortable or fears tension with the other branches of the state. This tension not only fails to justify dismissing claims, but is even desirable on occasion.'[178] However, Judge Barak recognised the pragmatic foundations of the doctrine, and its use in many national legal systems.[179]

The doctrines of non-justiciability and act of state traditionally held that certain matters were (because of their discretionary nature) beyond the jurisdiction of the courts. Courts thus exercised judicial restraint in these matters. However, *sovereign immunity* (as a jurisdictional immunity) traditionally meant that a national court (which would have substantive jurisdiction over the matter) was simply prevented from exercising jurisdiction because of the immunity.[180]

The following statement by Lord Hoffmann in *R v Jones* (House of Lords) illustrates the constitutional rules and prerogative powers associated with the *act of state* doctrine in English law concerning the conduct of foreign affairs by the British government:

> 'How, consistently with our constitution, is liability for [aggression] to be determined in a domestic court? First, there is the theoretical difficulty of the courts, as the judicial branch of government, holding not merely that some officer of the state has acted unlawfully ... but, as a sine qua non condition, that the state itself, of which the courts form part, has acted unlawfully. Secondly, there is the practical difficulty that the making of war and peace and the disposition of the armed forces has always been regarded as a discretionary power of the Crown into the exercise of which courts will not enquire. I say that it is a practical difficulty because, as Lord Devlin pointed out in *Chandler v Director of Public Prosecutions* [1964] AC 763, 806–812, the reason why the courts cannot enquire is not the technicality that the powers form part of the

---

176 Malcolm Shaw (International Law) (*supra*) 129.

177 See Malcolm Shaw (International Law) (*supra*) 129 and the reference to *R v Secretary of State for Foreign and Commonwealth Affairs, ex parte Pirbai, The Times*, 17 Oct 1985, 4 (Court of Appeal).

178 Aharon Barak 'A judge on judging: The role of a supreme court in a democracy' 116 *Harvard Law Review* (2002) 16, at 97.

179 Aharon Barak (*supra*) 98.

180 Malcolm Shaw (International Law) (*supra*) 431–432.

> royal prerogative. Lord Devlin's view that the prerogative origin of the powers did not in itself exclude judicial control was affirmed by the House in *Council of Civil Service Unions v Minister for the Civil Service* [1985] AC 374. It is because of the discretionary nature of the power itself.'[181]

Lord Hoffmann accordingly held that the 'decision to go to war, whether one thinks it was right or wrong, fell squarely within the discretionary powers of the Crown to defend the realm and conduct its foreign affairs.' Furthermore, the decision to go to war could in the view of Lord Hoffmann also be regarded as a *non-justiciable issue*.[182]

The statements by Lord Hoffmann must be seen in the context of his reasoning. He did not find that the customary international law crime of aggression is not a crime in English law because of vagueness, or lack of definition. He stated:

> 'Of course the definition of a crime so recent and so rarely punished will have uncertainties. But it is true of other crimes as well. If the core elements of the crime are certain enough to have secured convictions at Nuremberg, or to enable everyone to agree that it was committed by the Iraqi invasion of Kuwait [in 1991], then it is in my opinion sufficiently defined to be a crime, whether in international or domestic law.'[183]

Lord Hoffmann identified two reasons why aggression should not be regarded as a crime in English domestic law. First, Parliament alone can create new crimes not previously criminalised under English law.[184] Secondly, Lord Hoffmann stated that, 'in the absence of statutory authority, the prosecution of [aggression] in a domestic court would be *inconsistent with a fundamental principle of our constitution. Aggression is a crime in which the principal is always the state itself. The liability of individuals is in a sense secondary.*'[185] For this emphasis on the conduct by the state Lord Hoffmann relied on the ILC's Draft Code of Crimes Against the Peace and Security of Mankind of 1996.[186]

It is not clear why Lord Hoffmann has chosen to refer to a draft document that preceded more contemporary debates around the definition of aggression and that were accessible at the time of the judgment. The 1996 Draft Code's provision on aggression (discussed in Chapter IV, section 2.2.3 above) must be seen in context. One should be mindful of the fact that the 1996 Draft Code contained a much shorter provision on aggression than the 1991 Draft Code. Indeed, Article 16 of the 1996 Draft Code in essence only *confirms* that individuals can be

181 Lord Hoffmann in *R v Jones* (*supra*) par 65.
182 Lord Hoffmann in *R v Jones* (*supra*) par 66.
183 Lord Hoffmann in *R v Jones* (*supra*) par 59.
184 Lord Hoffmann in *R v Jones* (*supra*) par 60.
185 Lord Hoffmann in *R v Jones* (*supra*) par 63 (emphasis added).
186 For a discussion see Ch IV section 2.2.3 *supra*.

held liable for the crime of aggression. The 'crime of aggression' is not defined at all and according to the commentary on the Draft Code, Article 16 refers to the UN Charter and the judgment of the Nuremberg Tribunal as the main sources of authority with regard to individual criminal responsibility for aggression. To say, as Lord Hoffmann does, that aggression is a crime in which the 'principal is always the state itself', with the liability of individuals 'in a sense secondary', is not correct. It is not correct because it is a very sweeping generalisation, and does not take into account the different ways in which the crime of aggression can come about. States are abstract entities[187] and individuals are indeed necessary to plan and initiate aggressive policies. An individual leader with evil intent (who mobilises and employs the armed forces of a state as part of aggressive foreign policy) can be held liable for aggression without his responsibility resting on a finding of state liability first. This is the legacy of Nuremberg that forms the core of the crime of aggression under customary international law.

Lord Hoffmann's assumption that in the context of aggression 'the principal is always the state' led him to consider the impact of the *act of state* doctrine and the *non-justiciability* of the decision to go to war (referred to above), on the question of whether liability for aggression can be determined by a domestic court in England. Lord Hoffmann held that the 'discretionary nature or non-justiciability of the power to make war is … simply one of the reasons why aggression is not a crime in domestic law.'[188] This way of reasoning precludes a first finding whether aggression is a *crime* in English law and then to consider whether the issues which the crime raises (notably individual liability) are at all justiciable. Indeed, the logic of Lord Hoffmann's argument is that the very nature of the powers necessary to deploy the armed forces of the state is discretionary in nature. This is the reason why aggression is not a crime under domestic English law – not for reasons of vagueness of definition. It is unfortunate that Lord Hoffmann simply accepted that state liability is a condition *sine qua non* for individual liability for aggression.[189]

Vagueness of the crime of aggression (under customary international law) is arguably a far better reason to state that it cannot be applied in domestic courts. Indeed, this was also one of the main criticisms against the 1991 Draft Code of Crimes Against the Peace and Security of Mankind.[190] This reason, plus the argument that only Parliament can create new crimes (even when crimes under customary international law served as legal basis for such legislation) are better grounds to state that the crime of aggression is not part of English law. Instead of stating that state liability is a condition *sine qua non* to determine aggression, the

---

187 See criticism from an international criminal law perspective of the 1996 Draft Code in Ch IV section 2.2.3 *supra*.

188 Lord Hoffmann in *R v Jones* (*supra*) par 67.

189 Lord Hoffmann in *R v Jones* (*supra*) par 65.

190 See discussion in Ch IV section 2.2.2 *supra*.

better position is that a conclusion that a state has committed aggression (and in this regard a finding by the Security Council would be particularly relevant) could make it easier for a national court to find that aggression was perpetrated and whether any individuals can be held liable for the crime.[191]

Another reason for a national court to refuse to exercise jurisdiction could also have been where *sovereign immunity* was an issue. This aspect is dealt with in section 4 below. But sovereign immunity (as jurisdictional immunity) is not the same as saying that, because of the nature of the crime of aggression, a court cannot determine whether the crime is actually a crime under national law. It is submitted that the application of the doctrines of act of state and non-justiciability are not appropriate in the context of crimes under international law. Indeed, judicial restraint in this area of the law seems to be misplaced – given the movement against impunity for crimes that affect the whole of humanity.

In South African case law it was held that the decision to go to war must be regarded as falling within the power of government to conduct foreign affairs.[192] The question is whether the South African courts will also regard the government's decision to go to war as an act of state; a non-justiciable matter. Before the new constitutional dispensation of 1994, South African courts followed English law when considering the application of international law in South Africa. Dugard pointed out that the notion of 'prerogative powers' of the executive and other constitutional matters impacting on a court's ability to pronounce on acts of state, derived from English law.[193] After the adoption of the Interim Constitution in 1994 and thereafter the Constitution of 1996, the 'principles of executive accountability and transparency'[194] started to feature prominently.[195] The position in South Africa now seems somewhat different from that of England, as discussed above. Dugard observed that while 'the executive retains its discretionary non-statutory powers to enable it to conduct foreign relations, these powers are no longer beyond the reach of judicial review.'[196] The fundamental difference between Lord Hoffmann's understanding of the act of state doctrine and the non-justiciability of discretionary decisions of the state, on the one hand, and the position in South Africa under the present Constitution of 1996, on the other hand, seems to be the following: South African courts may apply rules of customary international law (to the extent that the rules are not

---

191 See argument by Antonio Cassese (International Criminal Law) (*supra*) 117.

192 *Minister of Home Affairs v Bickle* 1984 (2) SA 439 (ZS) at 450H. See further discussion by John Dugard (International Law) (*supra*) 71.

193 John Dugard (International Law) (*supra*) 71.

194 *Ibid.*

195 See in this regard *President of the Republic of South Africa v Hugo* 1997 (4) SA 1 (CC) on the reviewability of the President's 'prerogative powers'. The Constitutional Court rejected the argument that certain presidential powers were not subject to review.

196 John Dugard (International Law) (*supra*) 72.

inconsistent with the Constitution itself, or with an Act of Parliament). The implication is that a court can apply a rule of customary international law – even when it is contrary to an executive decision[197] (including what would be regarded as an 'an act of state'). The absolutist position under English law (apparently favoured by Lord Hoffmann) was summarised by the publicist JG Starke, as follows:

> 'Acts of State by the Executive, for example a declaration of war, or an annexation of territory, may not be questioned by British municipal Courts, notwithstanding that a breach of international law may have been involved.'[198]

Such an absolutist position seems not to be applicable to South African courts. The nature of aggression as involving the state (and I have already pointed out above that one should not view the responsibility of the state as a condition *sine qua non* for individual liability) cannot bar a court from enquiring whether the conduct of an individual amounts to the crime of aggression. The correct inquiry is whether the crime of aggression is indeed a crime under customary international and national law. This involves the issue of legality (and the concern of vagueness, also discussed in the South African context above) more than questions about the applicability of the act of state doctrine. And if one assumes that the crime of aggression is indeed part of domestic law (even on the basis of customary international law), questions of *enforcement* and *jurisdiction* will come into play. In turn, the impact of immunities (including state immunities) is also relevant in this context. These issues are addressed below.

3. APPLICATION OF INTERNATIONAL CRIMINAL LAW IN THE CONTEXT OF THE UNIVERSALITY PRINCIPLE, OR UNIVERSAL JURISDICTION

3.1. PROSECUTION OF INTERNATIONAL CRIMES ON THE BASIS OF UNIVERSAL JURISDICTION

3.1.1. Case study: The Belgian universal jurisdiction law: Principles, practice and politics

Belgium's Act on the Punishment of Serious Violations of International Humanitarian Law of 1993, as amended in 1999, (the 'Genocide Act')[199] provided

197 John Dugard (International Law) (*supra*) 73.

198 JG Starke *An Introduction to International Law* 7th (1972) Butterworths, London.

199 Wet 16 juni 1993 betreffende de bestraffing van ernstige schendingen van het international humanitair recht, gew wet 10 februari 1999, *BS* 23 maart 1999. For a discussion see Chris

for the criminalisation and punishment of war crimes,[200] genocide, and crimes against humanity.[201] After the amendment in 1999, the Genocide Act was one of the most progressive (and controversial) legislative instruments in the world, providing for *unlimited* universal jurisdiction over the crimes referred to above. None of the traditional jurisdictional links (like personality or territoriality) with Belgium was necessary for a Belgian court to exercise jurisdiction over an individual accused. The Act also provided that the official status of the individual accused would not bar a prosecution.

The unlimited universality of the Genocide Act led to a number of high-profile investigations for serious violations of international humanitarian law against a number of foreign Heads of State and Government, including the former President of Chile, General Augusto Pinochet, the former Minister of Foreign Affairs of the Democratic Republic of Congo, Abdulaye Yerodia Ndombasi,[202] the (former) Prime Minister of Israel, Ariel Sharon, and – perhaps most controversially from a political perspective – against a number of American leaders and officials: Former President George HW Bush, former Secretary of State Colin Powell (in relation with the Gulf War of 1991), and former President George W Bush, former Defence Secretary Donald Rumsfeld, and General Tommy Franks (in relation with the Iraq War of 2003).[203] There were also investigations of a number of companies. One high-profile example is the investigation against the multinational oil giant Total-Elf Aquitaine, in relation with allegations of slave-labour in Myanmar (Burma).[204]

None of the investigations (except against Pinochet and Yerodia) progressed beyond the initial, investigatory stages. The investigations against Pinochet and Yerodia led to arrest warrants against them.[205] It is the latter arrest warrant that prompted the Democratic Republic of Congo (of which Yerodia was a former Minister of Foreign Affairs) to institute proceedings against Belgium in the ICJ.[206] This case is discussed below. A criminal case that resulted from the

---

van den Wyngaert *Strafrecht, Strafprocesrecht & Internationaal Strafrecht* 5th (2003) Vol II, Maklu, Antwerp/Apeldoorn, 1110–1116.

200 The 1993 Act provided only for war crimes (violations of the Geneva Conventions of 1949) and the two additional Protocols to the Conventions, of 1977.

201 After the adoption of the Rome Statute of the ICC of 1998, the Act of 1993 was amended in 1999 to include the crimes of genocide and crimes against humanity. See further Chris van den Wyngaert (Strafrecht) (*supra*) 1110–1111.

202 This criminal investigation led to the ICJ case of *DRC v Belgium*, discussed *infra*.

203 Others included the former President of Chad, Hissen Habré, the former Iraqi President Saddam Hussein, and President Fidel Castro of Cuba. For further detail see Chris van Den Wyngaert (Strafrecht) (*supra*) 1111.

204 Chris van den Wyngaert (Strafrecht) (*supra*) 1111.

205 Chris van den Wyngaert (Strafrecht) (*supra*) 1111–1112.

206 See discussion of *Case Concerning the Arrest Warrant of 11 April 2000 (Democratic Republic of Congo v Belgium)* ICJ 14 Feb 2002 (*infra*).

investigations in terms of the Genocide Act is the so-called 'Four of Butare' case of 2001 (relating to the 1994 genocide in Rwanda). The accused in this case were eventually convicted.[207]

Under considerable pressure from the United States, Israel and other nations, as well as some Belgian politicians,[208] the wide-reaching Genocide Act was amended in 2003[209] to restrict its scope and application.[210] However, this proved not to have gone far enough, and in August 2003 the Genocide Act was repealed. The criminalisation provisions (on war crimes, genocide and crimes against humanity) of the Act were transferred to the general Criminal Code (*Strafwetboek*) of Belgium and the controversial section on universal jurisdiction was replaced by a much stricter provision on extraterritorial jurisdiction in the Code on Criminal Procedure (*Wetboek van Strafvordering*).[211] The latter provides for a very limited extraterritorial application of the Belgian criminal law on war crimes, crimes against humanity and genocide. The universal jurisdiction of the controversial Genocide Act was thus replaced by a jurisdiction regime based on active and passive personality.[212] In addition to the strict provisions on extraterritorial jurisdiction, the new position in Belgian law is that only the Federal Prosecutor has the competency to initiate a prosecution for war crimes, crimes against humanity and genocide, committed abroad.[213]

The controversies surrounding the universal jurisdiction provision of the Genocide Act coincided with a period of political tension following the American-led invasion of Iraq in 2003. Belgium, like many other countries, was vocal in its opposition to the war. When a prosecutor in Belgium proceeded to investigate possible war crimes charges against senior American officials (including the President) the Genocide Act's provision on universal jurisdiction became the eye of a transatlantic political storm. The (international) political

207 Chris van den Wyngaert (Strafrecht) (*supra*) 1112.

208 See Chris van den Wyngaert (Strafrecht) (*supra*) 1112–1113 for a description of the economic, political and diplomatic pressure on Belgium that eventually contributed to the amendment of the Genocide Act and the abolition of the far-reaching provisions on universal jurisdiction.

209 For the English text, see 'Belgium's amendment to the Law of June 15, 1993 (As amended by the Law of February 10, 1999) Concerning the Punishment of Grave Breaches of Humanitarian Law [April 23, 2003], 42 *ILM* 749 (2003).

210 For a comment on the controversies surrounding the Belgian Genocide Act, see Steven Ratner 'Belgium's War Crimes Statute: A postmortem' 97 *AJIL* (2003) 888–897. For a discussion of the scope of the universal jurisdiction provisions *before* the 2003 amendment, see Luc Reydams 'Universal jurisdiction: The Belgian State of Affairs' 11 *Criminal Law Forum* (2000) 813–216.

211 Chris van den Wyngaert (Strafrecht) (*supra*) 1113.

212 The accused must be a Belgian national, or must have his/her principal place of residence in Belgium; or, jurisdiction can be exercised by a Belgian court if the victim is a Belgian national, or a person effectively, ordinarily and legally living in Belgium for at least three years. See discussion by Chris van den Wyngaert (Strafrecht) (*supra*) 1113.

213 See discussion of the relevant provisions by Chris van den Wyngaert (Strafrecht) (*supra*) 1114.

conditions were simply not conducive to rational appreciation of the legal principles contained in the Act. The legal principles underlying the Genocide Act were derived from international instruments like the Geneva Conventions of 1949 – which urge the international community to cast a wide net to end impunity for the worst crimes under international law.[214] Ultimately, the Belgian Genocide Act was perhaps also too idealistic and the application a bit cavalier – even irresponsible. One can certainly agree with Christine van den Wyngaert's lament that the political and policy conditions of the time caused good legal principles to be sacrificed.[215] Belgium and the progress of international criminal law are all the poorer as a result. The nadir in the saga of the Genocide Act came with the ICJ case *DRC v Belgium*. This case put the focus on the tension between the *ideals* of international criminal law and the *realities* of the international political and legal order.

3.1.2. The Arrest Warrant case (DRC v Belgium) before the ICJ

It was pointed out above that one of the investigations in terms of the Belgian Genocide Act led to an international arrest warrant (issued by a Belgian investigating judge) against Abdulaye Yerodia Ndombasi, the former Minister of Foreign Affairs of the Democratic Republic of Congo (DRC). In terms of this warrant Belgium sought the provisional detention of Yerodia (pending a request for his extradition to Belgium) for alleged serious violations of international humanitarian law, committed by him in the DRC. The DRC subsequently brought the matter before the ICJ[216] in order to obtain a finding by the Court

---

214 See for instance Art 49 of the Convention for the Amelioration of the Condition of the Wounded and Sick in Armed Forces in the Field, 1949 (Geneva Convention I): 'The High Contracting Parties undertake to enact any legislation necessary to provide effective penal sanctions for persons committing, or ordering to be committed, any of the grave breaches of the present Convention defined in the following Article. Each High Contracting Party shall be under the obligation to search for persons alleged to have committed, or to have ordered to be committed, such grave breaches, and shall bring such persons, regardless of their nationality, before its own courts. It may also, if it prefers, and in accordance with the provisions of its own legislation, hand such persons over for trial to another High Contracting Party concerned provided such High Contracting Party has made out a *prima facie* case. Each High Contracting Party shall take measures necessary for the suppression of all acts contrary to the provisions of the present Convention other than the grave breaches, defined in the following Article. In all circumstances, the accused persons shall benefit by safeguards of proper trial and defence, which shall not be less favourable than those provided by Article 105 and those following of the Geneva Convention relative to the Treatment of Prisoners of War of 12 August 1949.' This provision provides for the so-called *aut dedere aut judicare* enforcement system in international criminal law. See further Richard van Elst 'Implementing universal jurisdiction over grave breaches of the Geneva Conventions' 13 *LJIL* (2000) 815–854.

215 Chris van den Wyngaert (Strafrecht) (*supra*) 1114–1115.

216 *Case Concerning the Arrest Warrant of 11 April 2000 (Democratic Republic of Congo v Belgium)* ICJ 14 Feb 2002; 41 *ILM* 536 (2002) (henceforth '*DRC v Belgium*').

that the arrest warrant violated international law. While the issue before the ICJ evidently stemmed from Belgium's exercise of universal jurisdiction over serious crimes under international law, the approach of the DRC was to focus on the issue of diplomatic immunity of Ministers of Foreign Affairs. Thus, the notion of universal jurisdiction turned out to be a secondary issue in the case between the DRC and Belgium. However, the ICJ had the opportunity to consider this very important (and contentious) issue in international criminal law.[217]

On the question of the exercise of jurisdiction over serious crimes under international law, the ICJ held as follows:

> 'It should ... be noted that the rules governing the jurisdiction of national courts must be carefully distinguished from those governing jurisdictional immunities: jurisdiction does not imply absence of immunity, while absence of immunity does not imply jurisdiction. Thus, although various international conventions on the prevention and punishment of certain serious crimes impose on States obligations of prosecution or extradition, thereby requiring them to extend their criminal jurisdiction, such extension of jurisdiction in no way affects immunities under customary international law, including those of Ministers for Foreign Affairs. These remain opposable before the courts of a foreign State, even where those courts exercise such a jurisdiction under these conventions.'[218]

Judge *ad hoc* Van den Wyngaert stated in her dissenting opinion the following regarding the concept of universal jurisdiction:

> 'There is no generally accepted definition of universal jurisdiction in conventional or customary international law. States that have incorporated the principle in their domestic legislation have done so in very different ways. Although there are many examples of States exercising extraterritorial jurisdiction for international crimes such as war crimes and crimes against humanity and torture, it may often be on other jurisdictional grounds such as the nationality of the victim. A prominent example was the Eichmann case which was in fact based, not on universal jurisdiction but on passive personality. In the Spanish Pinochet case, an important connecting factor was the Spanish nationality of some of the victims.'[219]

---

217 *DRC v Belgium* (*supra*) par 42: 'The Congo, for its part, states that its interest in bringing these proceedings is to obtain a finding by the Court that it has been the victim of an internationally wrongful act, the question whether this case involves the "exercise of an excessive universal jurisdiction" being in this connection only a secondary consideration. The Congo asserts that any consideration by the Court of the issues of international law raised by universal jurisdiction would be undertaken not at the request of the Congo but, rather, by virtue of the defence strategy adopted by Belgium, which appears to maintain that the exercise of such jurisdiction can "represent a valid counterweight to the observance of immunities".'

218 *DRC v Belgium* (*supra*) par 59.

219 Van den Wyngaert J in *DRC v Belgium* (*supra*) par 44.

The issue of universal jurisdiction and the judges' treatment of this subject also attracted academic commentary, especially from international criminal lawyers.[220] Roger O'Keefe commented as follows on Judge Van den Wyngaert's statements on universal jurisdiction:

> '[One] might fairly question whether treaty or custom could be expected to provide such a definition [of universal jurisdiction], rather than just permissive or prohibitive rules regarding a phenomenon defined doctrinally. One might query, also, the genuineness or seriousness of the alleged debate over the meaning of universal jurisdiction. And, one might, with reason, point out that the absence of a customary or conventional definition and the supposed plurality of doctrinal definitions do not mean that no single soundest definition of universal jurisdiction cannot be given.'[221]

Following on his critical comments concerning Judge van den Wyngaert's treatment of the definition (or lack thereof) of universal jurisdiction, O'Keefe suggested the following definition:

> '[Universal] jurisdiction can be defined as prescriptive jurisdiction over offences committed abroad by persons who, at the time of commission, are non-resident aliens, where such offences are not deemed to constitute threats to the fundamental interests of the prescribing state or, in appropriate cases, to give rise to effects within its territory.'[222]

3.1.3. *The notion of universal jurisdiction in the wake of DRC v Belgium*

Roger O'Keefe criticised[223] the judges in *DRC v Belgium* for not being specific enough in the way they had dealt with the issue of universal jurisdiction. The result was a muddled understanding of universal jurisdiction. Other commentators criticised the inconsistent methodology employed by most of the judges when determining the existence of universal jurisdiction under international law. In this regard, Claus Kreß pointed out that the judgment reflected a schizophrenic approach to the question of universal jurisdiction: while the majority of the judges had no problem employing a methodology of 'principled extension' to extend customary immunity *ratione personae* to (acting) Foreign Ministers, the judgment reflects 'an orthodox approach regarding the determination of the customary law on universal jurisdiction'.[224]

---

220 See for instance Kevin Hopkins 'The international court of justice and sovereign immunity: why the Yerodia case is an unfortunate ruling for the development of public international law' 27 *SAYIL* (2002) 256; Max du Plessis and Shannon Bosch 'Immunities and universal jurisdiction – the world court steps in (or on?)' 28 *SAYIL* (2003) 246.

221 Roger O'Keefe 'Universal Jurisdiction – Clarifying the basic concept' 2 *JICJ* (2004) 744–745.

222 Roger O'Keefe (Universal Jurisdiction) (*supra*) 745.

223 Roger O'Keefe (Universal jurisdiction) (*supra*) 735–760.

224 Claus Kreß 'Universal jurisdiction over international crimes and the Institut de Droit international' 4 *JICJ* (2006) 561–585, 574.

Judges Higgins, Kooijmans and Buergenthal framed their understanding of universal jurisdiction with reference to the following facts of the case:

> 'As Mr Yerodia [the DRC's former Foreign Affairs Minister] was a non-national of Belgium and the alleged offences described in the arrest warrant occurred outside of the territory over which Belgium has jurisdiction, the victims being non-Belgians, the arrest warrant was necessarily predicated on a universal jurisdiction. Indeed, both it and the enabling legislation of 1993 and 1999 expressly say so. Moreover, Mr. Yerodia himself was outside of Belgium at the time the warrant was issued.'[225]

The above statement proved, according to O'Keefe, the fusion of the *prescriptive* and *enforcement* elements of jurisdiction by the three judges. Judges Higgins, Kooijmans and Buergenthal looked at various national legal systems (for instance the Australian War Crimes Act 1945, the United Kingdom War Crimes Act 1991, and the Criminal Code of Canada 1985)[226] and compared them with the Belgian statute. The judges concluded:

> 'All of these illustrate the trend to provide for the trial and punishment under international law of certain crimes that have been committed extraterritorially. But none of them, nor the many others that have been studied by the Court, represent a classical assertion of a universal jurisdiction over particular offences committed elsewhere by persons having no relationship or connection with the forum State.'[227]

Apart from the references to national legislation and national case law (notably the *Bouterse* case in the Netherlands[228] and a German genocide case[229]), Judges Higgins, Kooijmans and Buergenthal also put the issue of universal jurisdiction

225 Joint Separate Opinion of Higgins, Kooijmans and Buergenthal JJ in *DRC v Belgium* (*supra*) par 6.

226 See references to national legislation in Joint Separate Opinion of Higgins, Kooijmans and Buergenthal JJ in *DRC v Belgium* (*supra*) par 20.

227 Joint Separate Opinion of Higgins, Kooijmans and Buergenthal JJ in *DRC v Belgium* (*supra*) par 21.

228 The *Bouterse* case concerned the prosecution of an individual who tortured and murdered a number of persons in Paramaribo (Suriname) in Dec 1982. Regarding the question of extraterritorial or universal jurisdiction, the court in Amsterdam (which agreed with the expert opinion of Prof John Dugard) concluded that torture is a crime against humanity and that a state (any state) can – on the basis of customary international law – exercise extraterritorial (universal) jurisdiction over an individual accused of crimes against humanity. See *Beschikking Hof Amsterdam* 3 maart 2000, *NJ* 2000, 266, r.o. 2.2. (copy of summary on file). Later the *Hoge Raad* (Supreme Court) did attach certain conditions (notably nationality or presence on Dutch territory) to the extraterritorial application of jurisdiction. The Supreme Court furthermore held that a prosecution based on the direct application of crimes under customary international law (which were not criminalised under Dutch national law) violated the principle of legality, as protected in the Dutch constitution and in the Dutch Penal Code. See judgment of Dutch Supreme Court *In re Bouterse* 18 Sept 2001, *NJ* 2002/559. For an English translation see 32 *NYIL* (2001) 282–296.

229 No further particulars were given by the judges. See Joint Separate Opinion of Higgins, Kooijmans and Buergenthal JJ in *DRC v Belgium* (*supra*) par 24. The German case concerned

in the context of certain relevant international instruments. With reference to the Geneva Conventions of 1949 and Additional Protocol I of 1977, the judges concluded that the grave breaches provisions of these instruments provide for States parties to search for persons alleged to have committed grave breaches, and furthermore that such states have the obligation to bring such persons (regardless of nationality) before their courts. The judges stated that this scheme suggests a 'true universality principle'. However, the judges also pointed to the *Pictet Commentary* on the First Geneva Convention 'which contends that this obligation was understood as being an obligation upon States parties to search for offenders who may be on their territory.'[230] The judges asked: 'Is [this] a true example of universality, if the obligation to search is restricted to the own territory? Does the obligation to search imply a permission to prosecute *in absentia*, if the search had no result?'[231] Having considered national legislation and case law, the provisions of relevant international instruments and academic writings, Judges Higgins, Kooijmans and Buergenthal concluded:

> 'That there is no established practice in which States exercise universal jurisdiction, properly so called, is undeniable. As we have seen, virtually all national legislation envisages links of some sort to the forum State; and no case law exists in which pure universal jurisdiction has formed the basis of jurisdiction. This does not necessarily indicate, however, that such an exercise would be unlawful. In the first place, national legislation reflects the circumstances in which a State provides in its own law the ability to exercise jurisdiction. But a State is not required to legislate up to the full scope of the jurisdiction allowed by international law. ... Moreover, while none of the national case law to which we have referred happens to be based on the exercise of a universal jurisdiction properly so called, there is equally nothing in this case law which evidences an *opinio juris* on the illegality of such a jurisdiction. In short, national legislation and case law, – that is, State practice – is neutral as to exercise of universal jurisdiction.'[232]

The conclusion of Judges Higgins, Kooijmans and Buergenthal (that state practice is neutral as to the exercise of universal jurisdiction) was criticised by O'Keefe on the basis that the terminological distinctions drawn by the judges '[were] less than sound'.[233] Thus, the state practice that the judges refer to is in fact manifestations of universal jurisdiction (universal jurisdiction to *prescribe*). Whether a state would in any given case be in a position to enforce the jurisdiction with regard to the particular accused, is another matter. What is certain, is the meaning of universal jurisdiction with reference to the conduct concerned, and with reference to the individual accused concerned: '[Universal

a trial at the Bavarian Higher Regional Court 'in respect of a prosecution for genocide (the accused in this case being arrested in Germany).'

230 Higgins, Kooijmans and Buergenthal JJ in *DRC v Belgium* (*supra*) par 31.
231 Higgins, Kooijmans and Buergenthal JJ in *DRC v Belgium* (*supra*) par 31.
232 Higgins, Kooijmans and Buergenthal JJ in *DRC v Belgium* (*supra*) par 45.
233 Roger O'Keefe (Universal jurisdiction) (*supra*) 754.

jurisdiction] applies irrespective of whether this prescriptive jurisdiction is exercised *in personam* or *in absentia*'.[234]

While Judges Higgins, Kooijmans and Buergenthal could not find state practice supporting the exercise of universal jurisdiction 'properly so called', they also stated that the exercise of universal jurisdiction would not be unlawful *per se*. In her dissenting opinion Judge *ad hoc* Van den Wyngaert also stated that the exercise of universal jurisdiction by a state is not illegal under international law. She stated that the only real obstacles to the exercise of universal jurisdiction are political or foreign relations limitations:

> 'It may be *politically* inconvenient to have such a wide jurisdiction because it is not conducive to international relations and national public opinion may not approve of trials against foreigners for crimes committed abroad. This does not, however, make such trials illegal under international law.'[235]

Judge *ad hoc* Van den Wyngaert also referred to certain practical or pragmatic reasons why states would not be inclined to exercise universal jurisdiction:

> 'A *practical* consideration may be the difficulty in obtaining evidence in trials of extraterritorial crimes. Another practical reason may be that States are afraid of overburdening their court system … The concern for a linkage with the national order thus seems to be more of a pragmatic than of a juridical nature. It is not, therefore, necessarily the expression of an *opinio juris* to the effect that this form of universal jurisdiction is contrary to international law.'[236]

Indeed, as was pointed out above, the political ramifications of the application of Belgium's law of 1999 did prove to be so severe that the legislation was amended in 2003 in order to make it much more restrictive in terms of the *application* of the law.[237] Roger O'Keefe also pointed out that other jurisdictions (for instance Scotland) thought it wise when the relevant legislation was debated in parliament to consider the political consequences of universal jurisdiction over crimes under international law.[238]

From the judgment in *DRC v Belgium* and the various comments on the opinions of the judges, a very complex picture regarding the application of international criminal law through domestic legal systems (on the basis of the universality

234 Roger O'Keefe (Universal jurisdiction) (*supra*) 755.
235 Dissenting opinion of Van den Wyngaert J in *DRC v Belgium* (*supra*) par 56 (emphasis in the original).
236 *Ibid.*
237 See comments by Steven Ratner (Belgium's War Crimes Statute) (*supra*).
238 Roger O'Keefe (Universal jurisdiction) (*supra*) 758. The author referred to the International Criminal Court (Scotland) Act 2001.

principle) emerges. It is clear that not only the ICJ's treatment of diplomatic immunity (the central issue in the case), but also the issue of *universal jurisdiction*, sparked debate and led to more uncertainty instead of providing clear and satisfactory answers. Insofar as states would want to rely on universal jurisdiction to prosecute crimes under international law, the debate was certainly not terminated by the judgment in *DRC v Belgium*. Furthermore, despite the political fall-out caused by some of the high-profile investigations in Belgium under the (previous) Belgian universal jurisdiction law (the Genocide Act),[239] that certainly did not stop other states from exercising extraterritorial jurisdiction (based on the universality principle) to prosecute crimes under international law.

Apart from the chilling effect caused by political and practical limitations on the exercise of universal jurisdiction by states, there are also certain doctrinal reasons for domestic courts to be careful when confronted with a prosecution for a crime under international law. Claus Kreß warned: '[The] criminalization of certain conduct under *international* law does not necessarily coincide with the existence of a right of states to universal jurisdiction; the latter must still be proven with respect to each crime under international law concerned.'[240]

In her dissenting opinion in *DRC v Belgium*, Judge *ad hoc* Van den Wyngaert made it clear that the exercise by a state of universal jurisdiction (prescriptive jurisdiction) over crimes under international law is not contrary to international law. She stated:

> 'International law does not prohibit States from asserting prescriptive jurisdiction of this kind. On the contrary, international law permits and even encourages States to assert this form of jurisdiction in order to ensure that suspects of war crimes and crimes against humanity do not find safe havens.'[241]

A critical examination of the way national courts deal with domestic prosecutions (based on universal jurisdiction) for crimes under international law, is necessary. In other words, to follow on from Claus Kreß's warning referred to above, what elements should be present to enable a national court to exercise jurisdiction over a crime under international law on the basis of universality?

The authors of the Princeton Principles on Universal Jurisdiction[242] described the notion of universal jurisdiction in terms of the *lack of traditional jurisdictional links* between the offender and the forum state:

239 See discussion section 3.1.1 (*supra*).

240 Claus Kreß (Universal jurisdiction over international crimes) (*supra*) 571–572.

241 Dissenting opinion of Van den Wyngaert J in *DRC v Belgium* (*supra*) par 67.

242 The Princeton Principles on Universal Jurisdiction, 23 Jul 2001 (available at www.princeton.edu/~lapa/unive_jur.pdf). The Principles were authored by a number of prominent international law and politics scholars, aimed at the study of the many problems raised by

> 'A nation's courts exercise jurisdiction over crimes committed in its territory and proceed against those crimes committed abroad by its nationals, or against its nationals, or against its national interests. When these and other connections are absent, national courts may nevertheless exercise jurisdiction under international law over crimes of such exceptional gravity that they affect the fundamental interests of the international community as a whole. This is universal jurisdiction: it is jurisdiction based solely on the nature of the crime.'[243]

In terms of the further development and application of international law in domestic legal systems, the authors of the Princeton Principles thus proposed the following definition of universal jurisdiction:

> 'For purposes of these Principles, universal jurisdiction is criminal jurisdiction based solely on the nature of the crime, without regard to where the crime was committed, the nationality of the alleged or convicted perpetrator, the nationality of the victim, or any other connection to the state exercising such jurisdiction.'[244]

The Princeton Principles proposed that states may exercise universal jurisdiction in order to try individuals, accused of committing 'serious crimes under international law'.[245] For the purposes of the Principles, serious crimes under international law include '(1) piracy; (2) slavery; (3) war crimes; (4) crimes against peace; (5) crimes against humanity; (6) genocide; and (7) torture.'[246] In their commentary on the Principles the authors stated that the list of 'serious crimes under international law' was ordered on the basis of 'historical progression' and not in terms of a ranking based on gravity.[247]

One of the potentially far-reaching proposals contained in the Princeton Principles is Principle 3: reliance on universal jurisdiction in the absence of national legislation:

> 'With respect to serious crimes under international law … national judicial organs may rely on universal jurisdiction even if their national legislation does not specifically provide for it.'[248]

universal jurisdiction and to produce a set of principles on this notion (see Preface by Stephen Macedo), Princeton Principles (*supra*) 11–12. In her dissenting opinion in *DRC v Belgium* (*supra*) Judge Van den Wyngaert observed that projects like the Princeton Principles can 'be seen as the opinion of *civil society*, an opinion that cannot be completely discounted in the formation of customary international law today.' See Van den Wyngaert J in *DRC v Belgium* (*supra*) par 27.

243 Princeton Principles (*supra*) 23.

244 Princeton Principles, Principle 1(1) (*supra*) 28.

245 Princeton Principles, Principle 1(2) (*supra*) 28.

246 Princeton Principles, Principle 2(1) (*supra*) 29.

247 Princeton Principles, Commentary (*supra*) 45.

248 Princeton Principles, Principle 3 (*supra*) 30.

For present purposes it is assumed that the essence of the theory of universal jurisdiction lies in the fact that the *nature of the crime* triggers the exercising of jurisdiction of a state over the said crime, and it does so in the absence of any other jurisdictional nexus like territory or nationality.

Roger O'Keefe analysed the meaning of universal jurisdiction with reference to some general observations on the different elements or components of jurisdiction. Firstly, O'Keefe pointed to the fact that jurisdiction 'is not a unitary concept.'[249] There are two distinct aspects to jurisdiction relevant for present purposes, namely *jurisdiction to prescribe* and *jurisdiction to enforce*. The first of the two concepts refers to 'a state's authority under international law to assert the applicability of its criminal law to given conduct, whether by primary or subordinate legislation, executive decree or, in certain circumstances, judicial ruling.'[250] Jurisdiction to enforce, however, 'refers to a state's authority under international law actually to apply its criminal law, through police and other executive action, and through the courts.'[251] Thus, the aspect of jurisdiction known as 'prescriptive jurisdiction' clearly refers to the ability or authority of a state to criminalise certain conduct, while enforcement jurisdiction refers to actions by the state like the arrest, prosecution and punishment of individuals for conduct criminalised in terms of the state's law. O'Keefe observed that universal jurisdiction 'is a species of jurisdiction to prescribe'.[252] Obviously, in practice, as O'Keefe further noted, the 'act of prescription and the act of enforcement are … intertwined.'[253] It is submitted that the judgment of the ICJ in *DRC v Belgium* have important implications for the 'act of enforcement' of international criminal law. In this sense, although the primary question before the ICJ was on immunities, the judgment also affected the notion (and practice) of universal jurisdiction. In fact, the judgment was one of the factors that caused Belgium to eventually repeal the Genocide Act that provided for universal jurisdiction.[254] However, regardless of the actual or potential impact of the judgment in *DRC v Belgium*, there is a definite need to have clarity on the theory and practice of universal jurisdiction. Indeed, Claus Kreß's submission on the adoption of an international convention on universal jurisdiction[255] seems to be the best way forward.

---

249 Roger O'Keefe (Universal jurisdiction) (*supra*) 736.

250 Roger O'Keefe (Universal jurisdiction) (*supra*) 736.

251 Roger O'Keefe (Universal jurisdiction) (*supra*) 736.

252 Roger O'Keefe (Universal jurisdiction) (*supra*) 737.

253 Roger O'Keefe (Universal jurisdiction) (*supra*) 741.

254 Christine van den Wyngaert (Strafrecht) (*supra*) 1115. The author stated that the absolute low point for the Genocide Act was the ICJ's ruling against Belgium in *DRC v Belgium* (*supra*).

255 Claus Kreß (Universal jurisdiction over international crimes) (*supra*) 584–585.

3.1.4. Case study: Universal jurisdiction in Spain: Law and legality

An example from case law illustrating many of the difficulties with states' assertion of universal jurisdiction, is the judgement of the Spanish *Audiencia Nacional* (National Court, AN) in the *Scilingo* case.[256] This case concerned the arrest and prosecution and eventual conviction in the AN in Spain of Adolfo Scilingo for crimes against humanity committed in Argentina during the reign of the Military Junta (1976–1983).[257] Although Scilingo was initially charged with genocide, terrorism and torture, the AN convicted him for crimes against humanity. Crimes against humanity was only introduced into Spanish law in 2004, but the AN held that the conviction was not a violation of the *nullum crimen nulla poena sine lege* principle. The court reasoned that crimes against humanity existed in customary international law at the time of the alleged acts of torture and the other acts that constituted crimes against humanity.[258] The AN in particular asserted its jurisdiction on the basis of universal jurisdiction, regardless of the fact that the relevant Spanish law did not provide for universal jurisdiction over crimes against humanity, and, as Alicia Gil Gil has pointed out, 'no obligation of universal prosecution of the crimes at issue [crimes against humanity] is stipulated in any international treaty.'[259] The assertion by the court of universal jurisdiction over crimes against humanity came in for criticism.

Christian Tomuschat, in his analysis of the *Scilingo* case, employed the following notion of universal jurisdiction (as exercised by states) as opposed to the jurisdiction of international criminal tribunals:

> 'Universal jurisdiction means the right of national tribunals unilaterally to prosecute grave crimes, while international tribunals discharge a mandate that has been entrusted to them by the international community.'[260]

The author accepted that crimes against humanity are indeed recognised as crimes under international law and that individuals can incur criminal liability for this crime. However, this still does not imply the necessary authority for a national court to exercise universal jurisdiction over an individual who allegedly committed crimes against humanity in a foreign state. Tomuschat writes:

---

256 For a discussion of the case, see Christian Tomuschat 'Issues of universal jurisdiction in the *Scilingo* case' 3 *JICJ* (2005) 1074–1081; Alicia Gil Gil 'The flaws of the *Scilingo* judgment' 3 *JICJ* (2005) 1082–1091; Giulia Pinzauti 'An instance of reasonable universality' 3 *JICJ* (2005) 1092–1105.

257 Christian Tomuschat (Universal jurisdiction) (*supra*) 1074–1075; Alicia Gil Gil (Scilingo judgment) (*supra*) 1082–1083.

258 Alicia Gil Gil (Scilingo judgment) (*supra*) 1083.

259 *Ibid.*

260 Christian Tomuschat (Universal jurisdiction) (*supra*) 1079.

> 'Even before attempting to show in a detailed analysis that universal jurisdiction exists for crimes against humanity, the AN pre-emptively claims that this is the case. It is of the view that individual criminal responsibility and universal jurisdiction go hand in hand, and that a twofold consequence derives from the categorization of a crime as a crime against humanity, namely on the level of substantive criminal responsibility as well as on the level of procedure.'[261]

Two questions remain: Did the judgment of the AN in *Scilingo* satisfy the legality principle (*nullum crimen nulla poena sine lege*), which is accepted as a fundamental principle of not only all major legal systems of the world, but also of international criminal law generally?[262] How exactly did the court derive its jurisdiction from international law?

With regard to the first question, Alicia Gil Gil concluded that the *Scilingo* judgment can be faulted because the court relied on customary international law 'to justify the retroactive use of a legislative provision'.[263] With reference to the Spanish Constitution, Alicia Gil Gil stated the following: 'In my opinion, our legal system [Spain], which includes a strict principle of legality, precludes criminal tribunals from directly applying customary international law, since it does not meet the formal and material requirements that our legal system ascribes to the principle of legality.'[264] Regarding the nature of crimes against humanity under customary international law, Gil Gil stated emphatically: 'It is obvious that international custom does not comply with the principle of specificity as far as crimes against humanity are concerned. Their definition has evolved notably since Nuremberg until the present day'.[265]

Regarding the second question referred to above, Alicia Gil Gil, like Tomuschat and other commentators, objected to the creative but wrong manner in which the AN employed the notion of universal jurisdiction to assert its jurisdiction over crimes against humanity. Gil Gil also pointed out that the AN disregarded the fact that 'the obligation of universal prosecution of the crimes at issue [crimes against humanity] is not stipulated in any international treaty.'[266] On this point, Giulia Pinzauti objected to the AN's reasoning. The author summarised the AN's approach as follows:

---

261 Christian Tomuschat (Universal jurisdiction) (*supra*) 1078.

262 See Introduction section 1.3 (*supra*).

263 Alicia Gil Gil (Scilingo judgment) (*supra*) 1085.

264 Alicia Gil Gil (Scilingo judgment) (*supra*) 1085.

265 Alicia Gil Gil (Scilingo judgment) (*supra*) 1086. Not only national jurisprudence, but also the case law of the *ad hoc* tribunals ICTR and ICTY contributed to the development of the notion of crimes against humanity.

266 Alicia Gil Gil (Scilingo judgment) (*supra*) 1088–1089.

'[The] international rules prohibiting crimes against humanity are peremptory norms (*jus cogens*) which impose *erga omnes* obligations; it follows that the international community as a whole is injured by their violation, with the consequence that there arises a universal claim to the repression of such violations. The exercise of jurisdiction by the courts of a state other than the territorial one is also warranted, for the AN, by the unique nature of crimes against humanity: as they are normally perpetrated by state officials, or at least with their connivance or acquiescence, it is indeed difficult for them to be prosecuted by the territorial state.'[267]

3.1.5. *South Africa and universal jurisdiction*

A number of legislative frameworks provide for the prosecution of crimes under international law in South African courts. These are the frameworks under the Implementation of the International Criminal Court Act 27 of 2002 (the ICC Act); the Implementation of the Geneva Conventions Act 8 of 2012 (the Geneva Conventions Act); the Prevention and Combating of Torture of Persons Act 13 of 2013; and the direct application of customary international law, as discussed above. The most important for present purposes is the ICC Act.

The ICC Act, which was adopted in 2002, provides for cooperation with the ICC. It also incorporates the crimes of genocide, war crimes and crimes against humanity into South African domestic criminal law. The ICC Act provides for a comprehensive jurisdictional regime: territorial jurisdiction, nationality, active personality and universal jurisdiction. Nationality and active personality jurisdiction may be founded on citizenship or if the person concerned (either the perpetrator or victim respectively) is 'ordinarily resident in the Republic.'[268] Universal jurisdiction is provided for in the following terms:

'In order to secure the jurisdiction of a South African court for purposes of this Chapter, any person who commits [an ICC] crime outside the territory of the Republic, is deemed to have committed that crime within the territory of the Republic if –

that person, after the commission of the crime, is present in the territory of the Republic.'[269]

Universal jurisdiction as expressed in section 4 of the ICC Act recognises that South Africa cannot hold trials *in absentia*. It thus confirms the limits of South Africa's enforcement jurisdiction. As far as prescriptive jurisdiction is concerned, the ICC Act provides for full universal jurisdiction over the crimes of genocide, war crimes and crimes against humanity.[270] It does not provide

267 Giulia Pinzauti 'An instance of reasonable universality' 3 *JICJ* (2005) 1095–1096.
268 Sections 4(3)(b) and (d) of the ICC Act.
269 Section 4(3)(c) of the ICC Act.
270 Chris Gevers in Gerhard Kemp et al (Criminal Law in South Africa) (*supra*) 561.

for universal jurisdiction over the crime of aggression. The crime of aggression under Article 8*bis* of the Rome Statute will thus have to be incorporated via the ICC Act. That is assuming South Africa ratifies and incorporates the crime without any declarations or reservations.

The implications of universal jurisdictions under the ICC Act were considered by the Constitutional Court.[271] However, the focus of the judgment was the question of whether the presence of a suspect was a requirement for the initiation of an investigation into an alleged crime under the ICC Act (in this instance the crime of torture as a crime against humanity, allegedly committed in Zimbabwe). The Court also made some important observations about the ambit of universal jurisdiction under the ICC Act. In general, the Constitutional Court noted the following guiding principles when exercising universal jurisdiction:

- the existence of a substantial and *bona fide* connection between the subject-matter and the source of the jurisdiction;
- the principle of non-intervention in the domestic or territorial jurisdiction of other states; and
- elements of accommodation, mutuality and proportionality.

The Constitutional Court noted that there is an international treaty law obligation to prosecute torture.[272] Furthermore, the Prevention and Combating of Torture of Persons Act 13 of 2013, which came into operation on 29 July 2013, gave effect to South Africa's obligations in terms of this Convention. It was pointed out that torture as a crime against humanity was criminalised under section 232 of the Constitution (the customary international law incorporation), the Prevention of Torture Act and the ICC Act. South Africa is thus required, where appropriate, to exercise universal jurisdiction in relation to torture.[273] The same would be true of the other crimes under the ICC Act.

For purposes of determining the ambit of universal jurisdiction, the Constitutional Court distinguished between presence when being tried and absence during the investigation. Presence at trial is a constitutional fair trial imperative, whereas the exercise of universal jurisdiction for purposes of the *investigation* of an international crime committed outside South African territory, may take place even if the suspect is not in South Africa. The Constitutional Court reasoned as follows:

---

271 *National Commissioner of the South African Police Service v Southern African Human Rights Litigation Centre and Another* 2015 (1) SA 315 (CC).

272 Convention against Torture and Other Cruel, Inhuman or Degrading Treatment or Punishment, adopted by the General Assembly of the United Nations on 10 December 1984 and ratified by South Africa on 10 December 1998.

273 *National Commissioner of the South African Police Service v Southern African Human Rights Litigation Centre (supra)* par 40.

> 'This approach is to be followed for several valid reasons. Requiring presence for an investigation would render nugatory the object of combating crimes against humanity. If a suspect were to enter and remain briefly in the territory of a state party, without a certain level of prior investigation, it would not be practicable to initiate charges and prosecution. An anticipatory investigation does not violate fair trial rights of the suspect or accused person. A determination of presence or anticipated presence requires an investigation in the first instance. Ascertaining a current or anticipated location of a suspect could not occur otherwise. Furthermore, any possible next step that could arise as a result of an investigation such as a prosecution or an extradition request, requires an assessment of information which can only be attained through an investigation. By way of example, it is only once a docket has been completed and handed to a prosecutor that there can be an assessment as to whether or not to prosecute.'[274]

The Constitutional Court thus dismissed the contention by the South African Police Service that it could not investigate crimes under international law without a suspect's presence in the country. Indeed, the South African Police Service not only has the *power* to investigate alleged international crimes, it has under South African law a *duty* to do so.[275] The Constitutional Court went further and held that the obligation to investigate international crimes 'is most pressing in instances where those crimes are committed ... within the territory of countries that are not parties to the Rome Statute, because to do otherwise would permit impunity'.[276]

The Constitutional Court articulated certain qualifiers that would assist the South African authorities in dealing with the investigation and possible prosecution of international crimes, flowing from the duties imposed by the ICC Act. The Court held that 'the universal jurisdiction to investigate international crimes is not absolute', and proceeded to set out two limitations in this regard. The first 'limiting principle'[277] consists of two distinct principles: 'subsidiarity' and 'non-intervention'. The principle of subsidiarity 'requires that ordinarily there must be a substantial and true connection between the subject-matter and the source of the jurisdiction'.[278] Under the principle of non-intervention, investigating international crimes committed abroad is permissible only if the state with jurisdiction is unwilling or unable to prosecute and only if the

274 *National Commissioner of the South African Police Service v Southern African Human Rights Litigation Centre* (*supra*) par 48.

275 *National Commissioner of the South African Police Service v Southern African Human Rights Litigation Centre* (*supra*) par 55.

276 *National Commissioner of the South African Police Service v Southern African Human Rights Litigation Centre* (*supra*) par 32.

277 *National Commissioner of the South African Police Service v Southern African Human Rights Litigation Centre* (*supra*) par 63.

278 *National Commissioner of the South African Police Service v Southern African Human Rights Litigation Centre* (*supra*) par 61.

investigation is confined to the territory of the investigating state.[279] The second 'limiting principle' is a practical consideration. The state should 'consider whether embarking on an investigation into an international crime committed elsewhere is reasonable and practicable in the circumstances of each particular case'.[280] According to the Constitutional Court, this would require the following: (i) whether the investigation is likely to lead to a prosecution and accordingly whether the alleged perpetrators are likely to be present in South Africa on their own or through an extradition request; (ii) the geographical proximity of South Africa to the place of the crime and the likelihood of the suspects being arrested for the purpose of prosecution; (iii) the prospects of gathering evidence which is needed to satisfy the elements of a crime; and (iv) the nature and the extent of the resources required for an effective investigation.[281]

3.1.6. *The impact of immunities on the application of international criminal law in national courts*

The South African ICC Act provides for the applicability of head of state and other official immunities under international law in the following terms:

> '[Notwithstanding any] other law to the contrary, including customary and conventional international law, the fact that a person ... is or was a head of State or government, a member of a government or parliament, an elected representative or a government official ... is neither – (i) a defence to a crime; nor (ii) a ground for any possible reduction of sentence once a person has been convicted of a crime.[282]

A first interpretation of this provision is that it removes personal immunity of heads of state and government and diplomatic immunity, notwithstanding customary international law and the ICJ decision in the *Arrest Warrant* case (*DRC v Belgium*). In this case the ICJ considered the scope of personal immunities under customary international law. This first interpretation emphasises that section 232 of the Constitution makes customary international law part of South African law; but it does so only to the extent that it is not 'inconsistent with the Constitution or *an Act of Parliament*'. So if the ICC Act is interpreted as removing immunity *ratione personae* then it would do so notwithstanding the customary international law obligations on South Africa to observe it.[283]

---

279 *National Commissioner of the South African Police Service v Southern African Human Rights Litigation Centre* (*supra*) par 61.

280 *National Commissioner of the South African Police Service v Southern African Human Rights Litigation Centre* (*supra*) par 61.

281 *National Commissioner of the South African Police Service v Southern African Human Rights Litigation Centre* (*supra*) par 64.

282 Section 4(2)(a) ICC Act.

283 Chris Gevers in Gerhard Kemp et al (Criminal Law in South Africa) (*supra*) 588.

A second, alternative interpretation is that section 4(2)(a) of the ICC Act is modelled on Article 27(1) of the Rome Statute. The latter deals with the irrelevance of official capacity as a defence or as a ground for the reduction of sentence. The argument goes that section 4(2)(a) is not modelled on Article 27(2) of the Rome Statute, which deals with *personal* immunity.[284] Consequently, section 4(2)(a) of the ICC Act effectively removes *functional* immunity of persons, but leaves *personal* immunity intact.[285] This interpretation can also find support in the interpretive presumption contained in section 233 of the Constitution, which states: 'When interpreting any legislation, every court must prefer any reasonable interpretation of the legislation that is consistent with international law over any alternative interpretation that is inconsistent with international law'.[286]

In *DRC v Belgium* the ICJ stated that under international law it is firmly established that certain individuals (holders of high-ranking office of State) enjoy immunity from jurisdiction (civil and criminal) in other states.[287] The majority of the ICJ seems to draw no distinction between the individual's official and private capacities. The judges stated:

> 'That immunity and that inviolability protect the individual concerned against any act of authority of another State which would hinder him or her in the performance of his or her duties.'[288]

And further, on the scope of the immunity:

> 'In this respect, no distinction can be drawn between acts performed by a Minister for Foreign Affairs in an "official" capacity, and those claimed to have been performed in a "private capacity", or, for that matter, between acts performed before the person concerned assumed office as Minister for Foreign Affairs and acts committed during the period of office. Thus, if a Minister for Foreign Affairs is arrested in another State on a criminal charge, he or she is clearly thereby prevented from exercising the functions of his or her office. The consequences of such impediment to the exercise of those official functions are equally serious, regardless of whether the Minister for Foreign Affairs was, at the time of arrest, present in the territory of the arresting State on an "official" visit or a "private" visit, regardless of whether the arrest relates to acts

284 Article 27(2) of the Rome Statute of the ICC states: 'Immunities or special procedural rules which may attach to the official capacity of a person, whether under national or international law, shall not bar the Court from exercising its jurisdiction over such a person.'

285 See further Chris Gevers 'Immunity and the implementation legislation of South Africa, Uganda and Kenya' in Kai Ambos and Ottilia Maunganidze (eds) *Power and Prosecution: Challenges and Opportunities for International Criminal Justice in Sub-Saharan Africa* (2013) Universitätsverlag Göttingen, Göttingen, 85–118.

286 Chris Gevers in Gerhard Kemp et al (Criminal Law in South Africa) (*supra*) 588.

287 *DRC v Belgium* (*supra*) par 51.

288 *DRC v Belgium* (*supra*) par 54.

> allegedly performed before the person became the Minister for Foreign Affairs or to acts performed while in office, and regardless of whether the arrest relates to alleged acts performed in an "official" capacity or a "private" capacity.'[289]

The above statements by the ICJ are indeed unfortunate. The ICJ *in casu* should have drawn a clearer distinction between immunity *ratione personae* (relating to the individual's office, status or position) and immunity *ratione materiae* (referring to acts performed in an official capacity). Immunity *ratione personae* will typically apply to heads of state, heads of government or senior ministers of state. This immunity will protect them against criminal prosecution in a foreign state for the duration of their period in office.[290] Although immunity *ratione materiae* used to be a kind of blanket immunity, covering all official acts performed by senior state officials, the House of Lords judgment in *Pinochet*[291] provided progressive new perspectives on the scope of immunity *ratione materiae*. It is submitted that in light of the *Pinochet* judgment (and developments in international criminal law in general) immunity *ratione materiae* cannot be applied when an individual (for instance a former head of state) is charged with serious crimes under international law. This should especially be the case when the crime in question concerns a violation of *jus cogens* norms.[292] In the context of international crimes (in particular the most serious crimes, namely aggression, war crimes, genocide and crimes against humanity), Salvatore Zappalà argued that functional immunity does not apply to these crimes.[293] Thus, the act of a state (constituting an international crime like aggression) is not merely attributed to the state. The state official also bears responsibility under international law. The state official is thus criminally liable and cannot (according to Zappalà) claim functional (or *ratione materiae*) immunity before a foreign court.[294]

The nature of the crime in question is another aspect of the debate on immunities. In her dissenting opinion in *DRC v Belgium*, Judge *ad hoc* Van den Wyngaert criticised the majority judgment for not taking into account the *nature of the crimes* when considering immunity from criminal prosecutions. She held:

---

289 *DRC v Belgium* (*supra*) par 55.

290 For a discussion of this immunity, see Salvatore Zappalà 'Do heads of state in office enjoy immunity from jurisdiction for international crimes? The *Ghaddafi* case before the French *Cour de Cassation*' *EJIL* (2001) 595.

291 *R v Bow Street Metropolitan Stipendiary Magistrate: Ex Parte Pinochet Ugarte* (No 3) 1999 2 *All ER* 97 (HL).

292 See in general Powell and Pillay 'Revisiting Pinochet: The development of customary international criminal law' *SAJHR* (2001) 477.

293 Salvatore Zappalà 'The German Federal Prosecutor's decision not to prosecute a former Uzbek minister' 4 *JICJ* (2006) 602–622.

294 Salvatore Zappalà (The German Federal Prosecutor's decision) (*supra*) 613–614.

> 'In a more principled way, the case was about how far States can or must go when implementing modern international criminal law. It was about the question what international law requires or allows States to do as 'agents' of the international community when they are confronted with complaints of victims of such crimes, given the fact that international criminal courts will not be able to judge *all* international crimes.'[295]

Subsequent to the judgment in *DRC v Belgium* (and considering other developments in international criminal law, for instance the judgment in *Pinochet*) the position seems that state officials (including the head of state and other senior government officials) may not claim immunity from jurisdiction (or functional immunity) for crimes under international law. However, senior state officials (including the head of state and senior officials like ministers of foreign affairs) are still entitled to personal immunities (based on comity and in order to prevent possible abuse of process) '*as long as they hold office*'.[296]

It is furthermore clear that for purposes of prosecution of individuals at *international level* (at international tribunals or the ICC) the official status of an individual is irrelevant. Article 27 of the Rome Statute of the ICC excludes immunities for state officials. Head of state immunity and diplomatic immunity[297] will however still apply for purposes of prosecutions in national courts.[298]

4. REGIONAL COURTS AND THE PROSECUTION OF THE CRIME OF AGGRESSION

4.1. THE CRIMINAL JURISDICTION OF THE AFRICAN COURT ON JUSTICE AND HUMAN RIGHTS

The Protocol on Amendments to the Protocol on the Statute of the African Court of Justice and Human Rights (also known as the Malabo Protocol)[299] vests the African Court on Human and Peoples' Rights with international criminal jurisdiction. The existing regional human rights court's jurisdiction is thus extended. The Protocol does not create a separate institution, but for ease of

---

295 *DRC v Belgium* (*supra*) dissenting opinion of Judge *ad hoc* Van den Wyngaert par 5 (emphasis in the original).

296 Antonio Cassese (International Law) (*supra*) 113.

297 See judgment in *DRC v Belgium* (*supra*) par 61.

298 See comments by Iain Cameron in Dominic McGoldrick, Peter Rowe and Eric Donnelly (eds) *The Permanent International Criminal Court* (2004) Hart Publishing, Oxford, 73–74.

299 Protocol on Amendments to the Protocol on the Statute of the African Court of Justice and Human Rights (available at www.au.int/en/content/protocol-amendments-protocol-statute-african-court-justice-and-human-rights). Known as the Malabo Protocol, named after the capital of Equatorial Guinea in West Africa, where the Protocol was adopted in July 2014.

reference and for purposes of the discussion here, the term 'African Criminal Court' (ACC) will be used.

The initial decision to pursue the possibility to extend the jurisdiction of the Human Rights Court to include international criminal jurisdiction was taken at the African Union (AU) summit of February 2009.[300] The Malabo Protocol was adopted in July 2014.

Some view the establishment of the ACC as primarily politically motivated and in reaction to the supposed 'targeting' by the International Criminal Court of African cases, and in the context of the souring relations between the AU and the ICC.[301] Objectively speaking it is true, at least at the time of writing, that all the cases before the ICC are from Africa. Of course, some of these cases came before the ICC as a result of referrals by African states (for instance Uganda and the Democratic Republic of Congo) and by Security Council referral (for instance Sudan). In the Kenya situation it was the Prosecutor who took *proprio motu* action. According to some, the event that triggered the AU decision to create a regional criminal court (as alternative to the ICC) was the indictment and warrant for the arrest of President Omar Al Bashir of Sudan for charges of crimes against humanity and war crimes; later also genocide. This simplistic reduction of the AU rationale for a regional criminal justice mechanism to a single event is rejected by knowledgeable commentators.[302] The more plausible rationale is that the prosecution of African heads of state before the ICC provided a political climate conducive for the accelerated drafting and eventual adoption of the Malabo Protocol. The inclusion of the immunity provision in the Protocol is perhaps the clearest evidence of the possible political impact of the prosecution of African Heads of States before the ICC.[303]

The Protocol provides[304] for an ambitious list of crimes within its jurisdiction, namely:

(1) Genocide
(2) Crimes against humanity

---

300 Assembly/AU/Dec. 213 (XII). For background see Chacha Bhoke Murungu 'Towards a Criminal Chamber in the African Court of Justice and Human Rights' 9 *Journal of International Criminal Justice* (2011) 1067–1088; A Abass 'The Proposed Criminal Jurisdiction for the African Court: Some problematic aspects' 60 *Netherlands International Law Review* (2013) 27–50.

301 For more on this issue, see Gerhard Werle, Lovell Fernandez and Moritz Vormbaum (eds) *Africa and the International Criminal Court* (2014) Asser Press/Springer, The Hague.

302 A Abass 'Prosecuting international crimes in Africa: Rationale, prospects and challenges' 24 *European Journal of International Law* (2013) 933–946.

303 Dire Tladi 'The immunity provision in the AU Amendment Protocol' 13 *Journal of International Criminal Justice* (2015) 3–17, 4.

304 Malabo Protocol, Article 28A.

(3) War crimes
(4) The crime of unconstitutional change of government
(5) Piracy
(6) Terrorism
(7) Mercenarism
(8) Corruption
(9) Money laundering
(10) Trafficking in persons
(11) Trafficking in drugs
(12) Trafficking in hazardous wastes
(13) Illicit exploitation of natural resources
(14) The crime of aggression

The substantive criminal jurisdiction of the ACC will thus extend beyond the core crimes.

The Malabo Protocol provides for individual criminal responsibility.[305] Unlike the Rome Statute of the ICC, the Protocol provides for corporate criminal liability (with the exclusion of state liability)[306] in addition to liability of natural persons. Jurisdiction over persons who were under the age of eighteen at the time of the alleged commission of the offence is excluded.[307]

4.2. JURISDICTION OVER THE CRIME OF AGGRESSION

The Malabo Protocol provides for the following definition of the crime of aggression:

> 'Article 28M
> Crime of aggression
>
> A. For the purpose of this Statute, "Crime of Aggression" means the planning, preparation, initiation or execution, by a person in a position effectively to exercise control over or to direct the political or military action of a state or organization, whether connected to the state or not of an act of aggression which, by its character, gravity and scale, constitutes a manifest violation of the Charter of the United Nations or the Constitutive Act of the African Union and with regard to the territorial integrity and human security of the population of a State Party.

305 Article 46B.
306 Article 46C.
307 Article 46D.

B. The following shall constitute acts of aggression, regardless of a declaration of war by a State, group of States, organizations of States, or non-State actor(s) or by any foreign entity:

a) The use of armed forces against the sovereignty, territorial integrity and political independence of any state, or any other act inconsistent with the provisions of the Constitutive Act of the African Union and the Charter of the United Nations.
b) The invasion or attack by armed forces against the territory of a State, or military occupation however temporary, resulting from such an invasion or attack, or any annexation by the use of force of the territory of a State or part thereof.
c) The bombardment by the armed forces of a State against the territory of another State or the use of any weapons by a State against the territory of another State.
d) The blockade of the ports, coasts or airspace of a State by the armed forces of another State.
e) The attack by the armed forces of a State on the land, sea or air forces, or marine and fleets of another State.
f) The use of the armed forces of one State which are within the territory of another State with the agreement of the receiving State, in contravention of the conditions provided for in the African Union Non-Aggression and Common Defence Pact or any extension of their presence in such territory beyond the termination of the agreement.
g) The action of a State in allowing its territory, which it has placed at the disposal of another State to be used by another State for perpetrating an act of aggression against a third State.
h) The sending or materially supporting by or on behalf of a State of armed bands, groups, irregulars or mercenaries, which carry out acts of armed force against another State of such gravity as to amount to the acts listed above, or its substantial involvement therein.'

It is evident from the text of Article 28M that it follows the same basic structure as Article 8*bis* of the Rome Statute. Article 28M (A) provides for the *crime of aggression* and the various *acts of aggression* are provided for in Article 28M (B). While the same structure is followed, it is also obvious that there are elements in the definition contained in Article 28M that are not provided for under Article 8*bis*.

The threshold in Article 28M (A), like the threshold in the first part of Article 8*bis*, refers to a manifest violation of the UN Charter. The disjunctive in Article 28M (A) appears to create a second, discreet threshold. Could an act of aggression be a manifest violation of the Constitutive Act of the African Union without being a manifest violation of the UN Charter? The combined effect of the disjunctive in Article 28M (A), read with the acts listed in (B) and the inclusion of acts committed by 'non-State actors' or by 'any foreign entity' clearly and radically depart from the definition of aggression under Article 8*bis* of the Rome Statute of the ICC. Article 28M provides for a different crime of aggression; a regional version of the international crime.

The inclusion of non-state actors and the (somewhat ambiguous) 'any foreign entities' is presumably aimed at the role of non-state armed groups in conflicts in Africa. Human security on the continent is indeed affected by this phenomenon and the role of non-state armed groups is pervasive.[308] In this sense the crime created in Article 28M seems to be an African solution for an African problem. There may even be lessons for international criminal law generally. But there are elements of the crime that are vague and the lack of *travaux préparatoires* makes the definition harder to understand in terms of its proper foundations.

The underlying protected interests still seem to be in line with those protected by the 1974 General Assembly Definition of Aggression, which explicitly forms the basis of the second part of Article 8*bis* of the Rome Statute of the ICC and implicitly of Article 28M (B). The threshold of seriousness is qualified now also with reference to the Constitutive Act of the African Union, which provides for a regional collective security regime, as pointed out in Chapter I above.[309]

4.3. THE IMPACT OF IMMUNITIES

The crime of aggression is a leadership crime, as pointed out throughout this book. Both Article 8*bis*(1) of the Rome Statute and Article 28M (A) of the Malabo Protocol underscore this. The Rome Statute of the ICC provides for the irrelevance of official capacity and of immunities for purposes of ICC jurisdiction over individuals, including Heads of State. The Malabo Protocol departs from this development in international criminal law, and provides as follows:

> 'Immunities
> No charges shall be commenced or continued before the Court against any serving AU Head of State or Government, or anybody acting or entitled to act in such capacity, or other senior state officials based on their functions, during their tenure of office.'[310]

It is hard to reconcile, on any *bona fide* reading of the relevant provisions of the Protocol, the criminalisation of aggression as a *leadership* crime on the one hand,

308 For background, also from an African perspective, see Noemi Gal-Or, Cedric Ryngaert and Math Noortmann (eds) *Responsibilities of the non-state actor in armed conflict and the market place* (2015) Brill, Leiden, Ch 13–17.

309 See Ch I section 4.3.3 *supra*. The African Union Non-Aggression and Common Defence Pact provides for a definition of aggression which is different from the definition contained in the Malabo Protocol. The list of acts of aggression in the Malabo Protocol is shorter and more closely aligned with the 1974 UN Definition. The 2005 AU Non-Aggression and Common Defence Pact is reproduced in Christine van den Wyngaert (International Criminal Law) (*supra*) 399–402.

310 Article 46A *bis*. For a nuanced analysis of Article 46A *bis*, see Dire Tladi 'The immunity provision in the AU Amendment Protocol' 13 *Journal of International Criminal Justice* (2015) 3–17.

with the immunities provision contained in Article 46A *bis* on the other hand. Of course Article 46A *bis* is not an impunity clause; the Head of State or other person in a leadership position covered by immunity can be prosecuted when he or she steps down from office. But in Africa that can take a long time, even a couple of decades. That is the unfortunate reality in many African states.[311] It is also true that the leaders of non-state actors responsible for acts of aggression can be prosecuted under Article 28M. Such individuals will normally not be covered by any immunity. So the immunity clause is not destructive, but it is problematic in terms of the effective criminalisation and prosecution of the crime of aggression before the African Court. It is perhaps not unreasonable to conclude that the criminalisation of aggression under Article 28M is primarily aimed at non-state actors and 'foreign entities' and not so much the leaders of states.

5. CONCLUDING REMARKS

The complementarity imperative is supposed to make the application of international criminal law before domestic courts the default option of the international criminal justice project. The crime of aggression poses legal and political complexities that put it in a different category than the other core crimes. Its nature as a leadership crime, and the conduct element that is reliant on state conduct, invoke rules and principles of international law that makes prosecution of the crime of aggression before domestic courts difficult. The lack of actual prosecutions at the national level is proof of this.

From a normative perspective there is no harm in stopping the impunity gap. Not all states are parties to the International Criminal Court. There is also the need to preserve the crime of aggression at least in its customary international law form. In this sense criminalisation and the potential of prosecution of the crime of aggression at the national level is normatively justifiable.

The criminalisation of aggression at the regional level, for instance via the Protocol on Amendments to the Protocol on the Statute of the African Court of Justice and Human Rights, provides for the protection of regional interests. However, it is submitted that regional modifications of the crime of aggression, progressive as it may be, should not undermine this achievement by *de facto* impunity for individuals in leadership positions as a result of the application of immunities. Aggression is after all a leadership crime.

311 Zimbabwe, for instance, has had the same Head of State/Government ininterrupted since independence in 1980. The Protocol also provides for the crime of 'Unconstitutional Change of Government' which is aimed at criminalising coups and the practice of presidents who refuse to leave office, even after losing in democratic elections. See Article 28E of the African Protocol.

PART VI

ANNEXES

ANNEX I

AMENDMENTS TO THE ROME STATUTE OF THE INTERNATIONAL CRIMINAL COURT ON THE CRIME OF AGGRESSION*

1. Article 5, paragraph 2, of the Statute is deleted.

2. The following text is inserted after article 8 of the Statute:

Article 8 *bis*
Crime of aggression
1. For the purpose of this Statute, "crime of aggression" means the planning, preparation, initiation or execution, by a person in a position effectively to exercise control over or to direct the political or military action of a State, of an act of aggression which, by its character, gravity and scale, constitutes a manifest violation of the Charter of the United Nations.

2. For the purpose of paragraph 1, "act of aggression" means the use of armed force by a State against the sovereignty, territorial integrity or political independence of another State, or in any other manner inconsistent with the Charter of the United Nations. Any of the following acts, regardless of a declaration of war, shall, in accordance with United Nations General Assembly resolution 3314 (XXIX) of 14 December 1974, qualify as an act of aggression:

a) The invasion or attack by the armed forces of a State of the territory of another State, or any military occupation, however temporary, resulting from such invasion or attack, or any annexation by the use of force of the territory of another State or part thereof;

---

* The Amendments to the Rome Statute of the International Criminal Court on the Crime of Aggression, was adopted on 11 June 2010, at the Review Conference of the Rome Statute, held in Kampala, Uganda, from 31 May to 11 June 2010. The Parties adopted, in accordance with article 121, paragraph 3, of the Rome Statute of the International Criminal Court, amendments on the crime of aggression to the Rome Statute by Resolution RC/Res.6. The text is available at www.icc-cpi.int/iccdocs/asp_docs/RC2010/AMENDMENTS/CN.651.2010-ENG-CoA.pdf (last visited 25 August 2015.) The text is also reproduced in Stefan Barriga and Claus Kreß (eds) *The travaux préparatoires of the crime of aggression* (2012) Cambridge University Press, Cambridge, 102–104.

b) Bombardment by the armed forces of a State against the territory of another State or the use of any weapons by a State against the territory of another State;
c) The blockade of the ports or coasts of a State by the armed forces of another State;
d) An attack by the armed forces of a State on the land, sea or air forces, or marine and air fleets of another State;
e) The use of armed forces of one State which are within the territory of another State with the agreement of the receiving State, in contravention of the conditions provided for in the agreement or any extension of their presence in such territory beyond the termination of the agreement;
f) The action of a State in allowing its territory, which it has placed at the disposal of another State, to be used by that other State for perpetrating an act of aggression against a third State;
g) The sending by or on behalf of a State of armed bands, groups, irregulars or mercenaries, which carry out acts of armed force against another State of such gravity as to amount to the acts listed above, or its substantial involvement therein.

3. *The following text is inserted after article 15 of the Statute:*

Article 15 *bis*
Exercise of jurisdiction over the crime of aggression
(State referral, proprio motu)

1. The Court may exercise jurisdiction over the crime of aggression in accordance with article 13, paragraphs (a) and (c), subject to the provisions of this article.

2. The Court may exercise jurisdiction only with respect to crimes of aggression committed one year after the ratification or acceptance of the amendments by thirty States Parties.

3. The Court shall exercise jurisdiction over the crime of aggression in accordance with this article, subject to a decision to be taken after 1 January 2017 by the same majority of States Parties as is required for the adoption of an amendment to the Statute.

4. The Court may, in accordance with article 12, exercise jurisdiction over a crime of aggression, arising from an act of aggression committed by a State Party, unless that State Party has previously declared that it does not accept such jurisdiction by lodging a declaration with the Registrar. The withdrawal of such a declaration may be effected at any time and shall be considered by the State Party within three years.

5. In respect of a State that is not a party to this Statute, the Court shall not exercise its jurisdiction over the crime of aggression when committed by that State's nationals or on its territory.

6. Where the Prosecutor concludes that there is a reasonable basis to proceed with an investigation in respect of a crime of aggression, he or she shall first ascertain whether the Security Council has made a determination of an act of aggression committed by the

State concerned. The Prosecutor shall notify the Secretary-General of the United Nations of the situation before the Court, including any relevant information and documents.

7. Where the Security Council has made such a determination, the Prosecutor may proceed with the investigation in respect of a crime of aggression.

8. Where no such determination is made within six months after the date of notification, the Prosecutor may proceed with the investigation in respect of a crime of aggression, provided that the Pre-Trial Division has authorized the commencement of the investigation in respect of a crime of aggression in accordance with the procedure contained in article 15, and the Security Council has not decided otherwise in accordance with article 16.

9. A determination of an act of aggression by an organ outside the Court shall be without prejudice to the Court's own findings under this Statute.

10. This article is without prejudice to the provisions relating to the exercise of jurisdiction with respect to other crimes referred to in article 5.

4. The following text is inserted after article 15 bis of the Statute:

Article 15 *ter*
Exercise of jurisdiction over the crime of aggression
(Security Council referral)

1. The Court may exercise jurisdiction over the crime of aggression in accordance with article 13, paragraph (b), subject to the provisions of this article.

2. The Court may exercise jurisdiction only with respect to crimes of aggression committed one year after the ratification or acceptance of the amendments by thirty States Parties.

3. The Court shall exercise jurisdiction over the crime of aggression in accordance with this article, subject to a decision to be taken after 1 January 2017 by the same majority of States Parties as is required for the adoption of an amendment to the Statute.

4. A determination of an act of aggression by an organ outside the Court shall be without prejudice to the Court's own findings under this Statute.

5. This article is without prejudice to the provisions relating to the exercise of jurisdiction with respect to other crimes referred to in article 5.

5. The following text is inserted after article 25, paragraph 3, of the Statute:

3 *bis*.
In respect of the crime of aggression, the provisions of this article shall apply only to persons in a position effectively to exercise control over or to direct the political or military action of a State.

6. The first sentence of article 9, paragraph 1, of the Statute is replaced by the following sentence:

1. Elements of Crimes shall assist the Court in the interpretation and application of articles 6, 7, 8 and 8 *bis*.

7. The chapeau of article 20, paragraph 3, of the Statute is replaced by the following paragraph; the rest of the paragraph remains unchanged:

3. No person who has been tried by another court for conduct also proscribed under article 6, 7, 8 or 8 *bis* shall be tried by the Court with respect to the same conduct unless the proceedings in the other court:

ANNEX II

AMENDMENTS TO THE ELEMENTS OF CRIMES, ROME STATUTE OF THE INTERNATIONAL CRIMINAL COURT*

Article 8 *bis*
Crime of aggression

Introduction

1. It is understood that any of the acts referred to in article 8 bis, paragraph 2, qualify as an act of aggression.
2. There is no requirement to prove that the perpetrator has made a legal evaluation as to whether the use of armed force was inconsistent with the Charter of the United Nations.
3. The term "manifest" is an objective qualification.
4. There is no requirement to prove that the perpetrator has made a legal evaluation as to the "manifest" nature of the violation of the Charter of the United Nations.

Elements

1. The perpetrator planned, prepared, initiated or executed an act of aggression.
2. The perpetrator was a person[1] in a position effectively to exercise control over or to direct the political or military action of the State which committed the act of aggression.
3. The act of aggression – the use of armed force by a State against the sovereignty, territorial integrity or political independence of another State, or in any other manner inconsistent with the Charter of the United Nations – was committed.
4. The perpetrator was aware of the factual circumstances that established that such a use of armed force was inconsistent with the Charter of the United Nations.
5. The act of aggression, by its character, gravity and scale, constituted a manifest violation of the Charter of the United Nations.
6. The perpetrator was aware of the factual circumstances that established such a manifest violation of the Charter of the United Nations.

---

* Reproduced in Barriga and Kreß *The travaux préparatoires of the crime of aggression* (*supra*) 105.

1 With respect to an act of aggression, more than one person may be in a position that meets these criteria.

ANNEX III

UNDERSTANDINGS REGARDING THE AMENDMENTS TO THE ROME STATUTE OF THE INTERNATIONAL CRIMINAL COURT ON THE CRIME OF AGGRESSION*

Referrals by the Security Council

1. It is understood that the Court may exercise jurisdiction on the basis of a Security Council referral in accordance with article 13, paragraph (b), of the Statute only with respect to crimes of aggression committed after a decision in accordance with article 15 *ter*, paragraph 3, is taken, and one year after the ratification or acceptance of the amendments by thirty States Parties, whichever is later.
2. It is understood that the Court shall exercise jurisdiction over the crime of aggression on the basis of a Security Council referral in accordance with article 13, paragraph (b), of the Statute irrespective of whether the State concerned has accepted the Court's jurisdiction in this regard.

Jurisdiction *ratione temporis*

3. It is understood that in case of article 13, paragraph (a) or (c), the Court may exercise its jurisdiction only with respect to crimes of aggression committed after a decision in accordance with article 15 *bis*, paragraph 3, is taken, and one year after the ratification or acceptance of the amendments by thirty States Parties, whichever is later.

Domestic jurisdiction over the crime of aggression

4. It is understood that the amendments that address the definition of the act of aggression and the crime of aggression do so for the purpose of this Statute only. The amendments shall, in accordance with article 10 of the Rome Statute, not be interpreted as limiting or prejudicing in any way existing or developing rules of international law for purposes other than this Statute.
5. It is understood that the amendments shall not be interpreted as creating the right or obligation to exercise domestic jurisdiction with respect to an act of aggression committed by another State.

* Reproduced in Barriga and Kreß *The travaux préparatoires of the crime of aggression* (*supra*) 106–107.

Other understandings

6. It is understood that aggression is the most serious and dangerous form of the illegal use of force; and that a determination whether an act of aggression has been committed requires consideration of all the circumstances of each particular case, including the gravity of the acts concerned and their consequences in accordance with the Charter of the United Nations.
7. It is understood that in establishing whether an act of aggression constitutes a manifest violation of the Charter of the United Nations, the three components of character, gravity and scale must be sufficient to justify a "manifest" determination. No one component can be significant enough to satisfy the manifest standard by itself.

CASE REGISTER

GERMANY

BverwG, 2 WS 12.04, 21 Jun 2005 (www.bundesverwaltungsgericht.de)

INTERNATIONAL COURT OF JUSTICE

Case Concerning the Arrest Warrant of 11 April 2000 (Democratic Republic of Congo v Belgium) ICJ 14 Feb 2002; 41 ILM 536 (2002)

Case concerning armed activities on the territory of the Congo (Democratic Republic of Congo v Uganda) 45 ILM 271 (2006)

Case concerning military and paramilitary activities in and against Nicaragua (Nicaragua v United States of America) Merits, Judgment, ICJ Reports 1986, 14; 25 ILM 1023 (1986)

Case concerning military and paramilitary activities in and against Nicaragua (Nicaragua v United States of America) Judgment on jurisdiction, ICJ Reports 1984, 392; 24 ILM 59 (1985)

Legal Consequences of the Construction of a Wall in the Occupied Palestinian Territory (Advisory Opinion) 9 Jul 2004 ICJ Reports 2004, 136

Legality of the Threat or Use of Nuclear Weapons, Advisory Opinion ICJ Reports (1996) 226

North Sea Continental Shelf cases (Federal Republic of Germany/Denmark; Federal Republic of Germany/Netherlands), *ICJ Reports* (1969) 43; 8 *ILM* 340 (1969)

INTERNATIONAL CRIMINAL TRIBUNAL FOR THE FORMER YUGOSLAVIA

Prosecutor v Blaskic (Judgment on the request of the Republic of Croatia for a review of the Decision of Trial Chamber II of 18 Jul 1997) Case No IT-95-14-AR 108*bis* (1997) 110 *ILR* 688

Prosecutor v Pavle Strugar (Prosecutor's response to defence brief on interlocutory appeal on jurisdiction) Case No IT-01-42-AR72

Prosecutor v Dusko Tadic (Appeals Chamber) Case No IT-94-1-A, 15 Jul 1999

Prosecutor v Dusko Tadic (Decision on the Defence Motion for interlocutory appeal on jurisdiction) Case No IT-94-1-AR72, 2 Oct 1995

INTERNATIONAL CRIMINAL TRIBUNAL FOR RWANDA

Prosecutor v Jean Paul Akayesu Case No ICTR-96-4-T, 2 Sept 1998

INTERNATIONAL MILITARY TRIBUNAL AT NUREMBERG

Nuremberg Judgment of Oct 1, 1946, International Military Tribunal Judgment and Sentences, IMT 171; 41 *AJIL* 172 – 333 (1947)

ISRAEL

Attorney-General of Israel v Eichmann 29 May 1962, 36 ILR 277

NETHERLANDS

In re Bouterse 18 Sept 2001, *NJ* 2002/559

SOUTH AFRICA

Du Plessis and Others v De Klerk and Another 1996 (3) SA 850 (CC)
Inter-Science Research and Development Services (Pty) Ltd v Republica Popular de Mocambique 1980 (2) SA 111 (T)
Masiya v Director of Public Prosecutions and Others Case CCT 54/06, 10 May 2007
National Coalition for Gay and Lesbian Equality v Minister of Justice 1998 (2) SACR 102 (W)
National Commissioner of the South African Police Service v Southern African Human Rights Litigation Centre and Another 2015 (1) SA 315 (CC)
Pan American World Airways Inc v SA Fire and Accident Fire Insurance Company Ltd 1965 (3) SA 150 (A)
President of the Republic of South Africa v Hugo 1997 (4) SA 1 (CC)
South Atlantic Islands Development Corp v Buchan 1971 (1) SA 234 (C)
S v Basson 2005 (1) SA 171 (CC)
S v Friedman (1) 1996 (1) SACR 181 (W)
S v Jordan 2002 2 SACR 499; 2002 (6) SA 642 (CC)
S v Malgas 2001 1 SACR 469; 2001 (2) SA 1222 (SCA)
S v Mintoor 1996 1 SACR 514 (C)
Veldman v Director of Public Prosecutions 2006 (2) SACR 319 (CC)

SPECIAL COURT FOR SIERRA LEONE

Prosecutor v Sam Hinga Norman (Decision on Preliminary Motion based on lack of jurisdiction – Child Recruitment) Case No SCSL-2004–14-AR72 (E) 31 May 2004

UNITED KINGDOM

Driefontein Consolidated Gold Mines v Janson [1900] 2 QB 339
R v Bow Street Metropolitan Stipendiary Magistrate: Ex Parte Pinochet Ugarte (No 3) 1999 2 All ER 97 (HL)
R v Jones et al (Conjoined Appeals) 29 March 2006 45 International Legal Materials 992 (2006)

UNITED STATES OF AMERICA

Coronally v General Construction Company 296 US 385, 391 (1926)
David Henry Mitchell III v US 386 US 972, 87 SCt 1162 (1967)
Dennis Mora et al v Robert S McNamara, Secretary of Defense et al 389 US 934, 88 SCt 282 (1967)

UNITED STATES MILITARY TRIBUNAL AT NUREMBERG

The Ministries Case, Military Tribunal IV, Case 11, *The United States of America v Weizsaeker et al*, Vol XII, XIII, Trials of War Criminals, Nuremberg Military Tribunals
The United States of America v Wilhelm von Leeb and Others, US Military Tribunal at Nuremberg, 28 Oct 1948

BIBLIOGRAPHY

ARTICLES IN JOURNALS

Abass, A 'Prosecuting international crimes in Africa: Rationale, prospects and challenges' 24 *European Journal of International Law* (2013) 933–946

Abass, A 'The Proposed Criminal Jurisdiction for the African Court: Some problematic aspects' 60 *Netherlands International Law Review* (2013) 27–50

Abraham, Garth and Hopkins, Kevin 'Bombing for humanity: The American response to the 11 September attacks and the plea of self-defence' 119(4) *South African Law Journal* (2002) 783–801

Anderson, Perry 'Arms and Rights – Rawls, Habermas and Bobbio in an Age of War' 31 *New Left Review* (2005) 5–40

Appiah-Mensah, CDR Seth 'AU's critical assignment in Darfur' 14(2) *African Security Review* (2005) 7–21

Barak, Aharon 'A judge on judging: The role of a supreme court in a democracy' 116 *Harvard Law Review* (2002) 16

Barnidge, Robert 'The United Nations and the African Union: Assessing a partnership for peace in Darfur' 14(1) *Journal of Conflict & Security Law* (2009) 93–113

Barrie, G 'Forcible intervention and international law: legal theory and realities' 116(4) *South African Law Journal* (1999) 791–809

Bertram, Christopher 'Afghanistan: A just intervention' 6(2) *Imprints* (2002) (http://bris.ac.uk/~plcdib/imprints/bertram.html)

Boas, Gideon 'Comparing the ICTY and the ICC: Some procedural and substantive issues' *Netherlands International Law Review* (2000) 267–292

Bolton, John 'Courting Danger: What's wrong with the International Criminal Court' *The National Interest* (1998/1999) 60–66

Booysen, Hercules 'Is Gewoonteregtelike Volkereg deel van ons reg?' 38 *Tydskrif vir Hedendaags Romeins-Hollandse Reg* (1975) 315

Bouvier, Antoine 'Assesing the relationship between jus in bello and jus ad bellum: An "Orthodox" view' *ASIL Proceedings* (2006) 109–112

Brunnée, Jutta and Toope, Stephen J 'Slouching towards new 'Just' Wars: International law and the use of force after September 11th' *Netherlands International Law Review* (2004) 363–392

Burke-White, William 'Proactive complementarity: The International Criminal Court and national courts in the Rome system of international justice' 49 *Harvard International Law Journal* (2008) 53

Bush, Jonathan A '"The Supreme... Crime" and its origins: The lost legislative history of the crime of aggressive war' 102(8) *Columbia Law Review* (2002) 2324–2424

Byford, Grenville 'The wrong war' *Foreign Affairs* Jul/Aug 2002 (www.foreignaffairs.org/Sea.../printable_fulltext.asp?i=20020701FAEssay8518.xm)

Caron, David 'Framing political theory of international courts and tribunals: Reflections at the Centennial' *ASIL Proceedings* (2006) 56

Carr, Comyns AS 'The judgment of the International Military Tribunal for the Far East' 34 *Transactions of the Grotius Society, Problems of Public and Private International Law, Transactions of the Year 1948* (1948) 141–151

Cassese, Antonio 'Reflections on International Criminal Justice' 61 *Modern Law Review* (1998) 1–10

Condorelli, Luigi and Ciampi, Annalisa 'Comments on the Security Council referral of the situation in Darfur to the ICC' 3 *Journal of International Criminal Justice* (2005) 590–599

Cowling, Michael 'The African Union – an evaluation' 27 *South African Yearbook of International law* (2002) 193–205

Cowling, Michael 'The relationship between the Security Council and the General Assembly with particular reference to the ICJ Advisory Opinion in the "Israeli Wall" case' (2005) 30 *South African Yearbook of International Law* 50–81

Cryer, R 'Aggression at the Court of Appeal' 10 *Journal of Conflict and Security Law* (2005) 209–230

Danner, Allison Marston 'Beyond the Geneva Conventions: Lessons from the Tokyo Tribunal in prosecuting war and terrorism' 46 *Virginia Journal of International Law* (2005) 83–130

Danner, Allison Marston 'The Nuremberg Industrialist prosecutions and aggressive war' 46 *Virginia Journal of International Law* (2006) 651–676

Dascalopoulou-Livada, Phani 'The crime of aggression: making operative the jurisdiction of the ICC – Tendencies in the PrepCom' *ASIL Proceedings* (2002) American Society of International Law, Washington DC

Delmas-Marty, Mireille 'The contribution of comparative law to a pluralist conception of International Criminal Law' 1 *Journal of International Criminal Justice* (2003) 13–25

Delmas-Marty, Mireille 'The Paradigm of the War on Crime – Legitimating inhuman treatment?' 5 *Journal of International Criminal Justice* (2007) 584–598

Delmas-Marty, Mireille 'Violence and massacres – Toward a criminal law of inhumanity?' 7 (1) *Journal of International Criminal Justice* (2009) 5–16

Du Plessis, Max 'Bringing the International Criminal Court home – the Implementation of the Rome Statute of the International Criminal Court Act 2002' 16 *South African Journal on Criminal Justice* (2003) 1–16

Du Plessis, Max 'South Africa's Implementation of the ICC Statute' 5 *Journal of International Criminal Justice* (2007) 460–479

Du Plessis, Max and Bosch, Shannon 'Immunities and universal jurisdiction – the world court steps in (or on?)' 28 *South African Yearbook of International Law* (2003) 246–262

Edlin, Douglas 'The anxiety of sovereignty: Britain, the United States and the International Criminal Court' 29(1) *Boston College International and Comparative Law Review*

Erasmus, Gerhard and Kemp, Gerhard 'The application of international criminal law before domestic courts in the light of recent developments in international and constitutional law' 27 *South African Yearbook of International Law* (2002) 64–81

Ferencz, Benjamin 'Ending impunity for the crime of aggression' 41 *Case Western Reserve Journal of International Law* (2009) 281

Fletcher, George and Ohlin, Jens David 'Reclaiming fundamental principles of criminal law in the Darfur case' 3 *Journal of International Criminal Justice* (2005) 539–561

Gallavin, Chris 'Article 53 of the Rome Statute of the International Criminal Court: In the interests of justice?' 14(2) *King's Law Journal* (2003) 179–198

Gil Gil, Alicia 'The flaws of the *Scilingo* judgment' 3 *Journal of International Criminal Justice* (2005) 1082–1091

Gross, Leo 'The criminality of aggressive war' 41(2) *The American Political Science Review* (1947) 205–225

Gross, Leo 'The Peace of Westphalia, 1648–1948' 42 *American Journal of International Law* (1948) 20–41

Habermas, Jürgen 'Interpreting the fall of a monument' 4(7) *German Law Journal* (2003) 701–708

Hoffmann, Stanley 'America goes backward' 50(10) *The New York Review of Books* 12 Jun 2003 (www.nybooks.com/articles/16350)

Hogan-Doran, Justin and Van Ginkel, Bibi T 'Aggression as a crime under international law and the prosecution of individuals by the proposed International Criminal Court' (1996) *Netherlands International Law Review* 321–351

Hopkins, Kevin 'Can customary international law play a meaningful role in our domestic legal order: A short case study to consider' 30 *South African Yearbook of International Law* (2005) 276–289

Hopkins, Kevin 'The International Court of Justice and sovereign immunity: why the Yerodia case is an unfortunate ruling for the development of public international law' 27 *South African Yearbook of International Law* 256–263

Jescheck, Hans-Heinrich 'The General Principles of International Criminal Law set out in Nuremberg, as mirrored in the ICC Statute' 2 *Journal of International Criminal Justice* (2004) 38–55

Jessup, Philip C 'The crime of aggression and the future of international law' 62(1) *Political Science Quarterly* (1947) 1–10

Katz, Anton 'An Act of transformation – The incorporation of the Rome Statute of the ICC into national law in South Africa' 12(4) *African Security Review* (2003) 25–30

Kelsen, Hans 'Collective security and collective self-defense under the Charter of the United Nations' 42 *American Journal of International Law* (1948) 783–796

Kemp, Gerhard 'Constitutionalization and the International Criminal Court: Whither individual criminal liability for aggression?' 4 *South African Law Journal* (2008) 694–714.

Kemp, Gerhard 'Foreign relations, international co-operation in criminal matters and the position of the individual' 16(3) *South African Journal of Criminal Justice* (2003) 370–392

Kemp, Gerhard 'Mission Impossible? "Humanitarian intervention" and the new paradigm of international criminal law' 3 *Stellenbosch Law Review* (2002) 460–472

Kemp, Gerhard 'The United Nations Convention Against Transnational Organized Crime: A milestone in international criminal law' 2 *South African Journal of Criminal Justice* (2001) 152–167

Khanna, Parag 'Terrorism as War' 121 *Policy Review* (2003) (www.policyreview.org/oct03/khanna_print.html)

Kirsch, Phillipe and Holmes, John 'The birth of the International Criminal Court: The 1998 Rome Conference' 36 *Canadian Yearbook of International Law* 3–39

Kleffner, Jann 'The impact of complementarity on national implementation of substantive international criminal law' 1 *Journal of International Criminal Justice* (2003) 86–113

Klingebiel, Stephan 'Africa's new peace and security architecture' 14(2) *African Security Review* (2005) 35–44

Komarow, Gary 'Individual responsibility under international law: The Nuremberg Principles in domestic legal systems' 29(1) *The International and Comparative Law Quarterly* (1980) 21–37

Kopelman, E 'Ideology and International law: the dissent of the Indian Justice at the Tokyo War Crimes Tribunal' 23 *New York University Journal of International Law and Politics* (1991) 373

Krasner, Stephen D 'Realist views of international law' *ASIL Proceedings* (2002) 265

Kreß, Claus 'The Iraqi Special Tribunal and the crime of aggression' 2 *Journal of International Criminal Justice* (2004) 347–352

Kreß, Claus 'Universal jurisdiction over international crimes and the Institut de Droit internationale' 4 *Journal of International Criminal Justice* (2006) 561–585

Kreß, Claus & Von Holtzendorff, Leonie 'The Kampala compromise on the crime of aggression' 8 *Journal of International Criminal Justice* (2010) 1179–1217

Leclerc-Gagné, Elise & Byers, Michael 'A question of intent: The crime of aggression and unilateral humanitarian intervention' 41 *Case Western Reserve Journal of International Law* (2009) 379–390.

Leonhardt, Hans 'The Nuremberg trial: A legal analysis' 11(4) *The Review of Politics* (1949) 449–476

Lynch, Colum 'They just stood watching' *Foreign Policy* 7 April 2014 (www.foreignpolicy.com/2014/04/07/they-just-stood-watching-2/)

Mancini, Marina 'A brand new definition for the crime of aggression: The Kampala outcome' 81 *Nordic Journal of International Law* (2012) 227–248

Marks, Stephen PM 'Branding the "War on Terrorism": Is there a "New Paradigm" of International Law?' 14(1) *Michigan State Journal of International Law* (2006) 71–119

McCormack, Timothy and Simpson, Gerry 'The International Law Commission's Draft Code of Crimes against Peace and Security of Mankind: An Appraisal of the substantive provisions' 5(1) *Criminal Law Forum* (1994) 1–55

Mertus, Julie 'The danger of conflating jus ad bellum and jus in bello' *ASIL Proceedings* (2006) 114–117

Moellendorf, Darrel 'Is the War in Afghanistan just?' 6(2) *Imprints* (2002) (http://info.bris.ac.uk/~plcdib/imprints/moellendorf.html)

Mundis, D 'The Assembly of States Parties and the Institutional Framework of the International Criminal Court' 97 *American Journal of International Law* (2003) 132–147

Murungu, Chacha Bhoke 'Towards a Criminal Chamber in the African Court of Justice and Human Rights' 9 *Journal of International Criminal Justice* (2011) 1067–1088

Nsereko, Daniel 'Bringing aggressors to justice: From Nuremberg to Rome' *University of Botswana Law Journal* 2 (2005) 5–32

Oeter, Stefan 'International law and General Systems Theory' 44 *German Yearbook of International Law* (2001) 77

O'Keefe, Roger 'Universal jurisdiction – Clarifying the basic concept' 2 *Journal of International Criminal Justice* (2004) 735–760

O'Shea, Andreas 'The Statute of the International Criminal Court' 116 *South African Law Journal* (1999) 243–261

Peters, Anne 'There is nothing more practical than a good theory: An overview of contemporary approaches to international law' 44 *German Yearbook of International Law* (2001) 25–37

Pinzauti, Giulia 'An instance of reasonable universality' 3 *Journal of International Criminal Justice* (2005) 1092–1105

Powell, C and Pillay, N 'Revisiting Pinochet: The development of customary international criminal law' *South African Journal on Human Rights* (2001) 477–502

Ratner, Steven 'Belgium's War Crimes Statute: A postmortem' 97 *The American Journal of International Law* (2003) 888–897

Reisman, Michael 'Aftershocks: Reflections on the implications of September 11' 6 *Yale Human Rights & Development Law Journal* (2003) 81–102

Reisman, Michael 'Introduction: The definition of aggression and the ICC' *ASIL Proceedings* (2002) American Society of International Law, Washington DC

Reisman, Michael 'Stopping wars and making peace: reflections on the ideology and practice of conflict termination in contemporary world politics' 6 *Tulane Journal of International and Comparative Law* (1998) 48

Reydams, Luc 'Universal jurisdiction: The Belgian state of affairs' 11 *Criminal Law Forum* (2000) 183–216

Ryngaert, Cedric 'Applying the Rome Statute's complementarity principle: Drawing lessons from the prosecution of core crimes by states acting under the universality principle' 19 *Criminal Law Forum* (2008) 153

Sarooshi, D 'Aspects of the relationship between the International Criminal Court and the United Nations' XXXII *Netherlands Yearbook of International Law* (2001) 27–53

Satzger, Helmut 'German Criminal Law and the Rome Statute – A critical analysis of the New German Code of Crimes against International Law' 2 *International Criminal Law Review* (2002) 261–282

Schabas, William 'Conjoined twins of transitional justice? – The Sierra Leone Truth and Reconciliation Commission and the Special Court' 2 *Journal of International Criminal Justice* (2004) 1082–1099

Schick, Franz B 'Crimes against peace' 38(5) *Journal of Criminal Law and Criminology* (1948) 445–465

Schick, FB 'The Nuremberg Trial and the International Law of the Future' 41 *American Journal of International Law* (1947) 770–794

Schultz, Nikolaus 'Was the war on Iraq illegal? – The judgment of the German Federal Administrative Court of 21st June 2005' 7(1) *German Law Journal* (2006) (www.germanlawjournal.com/print.php?id=684 25 Jan 2006)

Schwarzenberger, Georg 'The problem of an international criminal law' 3 *Current Legal Problems* (1950) 263–296

Sriram, Chandra L 'Wrong-sizing international justice? The hybrid tribunal in Sierra Leone' 29 *Fordham International Law Journal* 472–506

Stahn, Carsten '"Jus ad bellum, "Jus in bello," "Jus post bellum?" Rethinking the conception of the law of armed force' *ASIL Proceedings* (2006) 158–160

Stahn, Carsten 'Syria and the semantics of intervention, aggression and punishment' 11 *Journal of International Criminal Justice* (2013) 955–977

Steinberg, Richard 'Overview: Realism in International Law' *ASIL Proceedings* (2002) 260–262

Sterio, Milena 'Creating and building a "state": international law and Kosovo' *ASIL Proceedings* (2010) 361–365

Stone, Julius 'Hopes and loopholes in the 1974 Definition of Aggression' 71 *The American Journal of International Law* (1977) 224–246

Strydom, Hennie 'Peace and Security under the African Union' 28 *South African Yearbook of International Law* (2003) 59–81

Swart, Mia 'Legality as inhibitor: The special place of nullum crimen sine lege in the jurisprudence of international criminal tribunals' 30 *South African Yearbook of International Law* (2005) 33–49

Talmon, Stefan 'The Security Council as World Legislature' 99 *The American Journal of International Law* (2005) 175–193

Taylor, Telford 'The Nuremberg Trials' 55(4) *Columbia Law Review* (1955) 488–525

Tladi, Dire 'The immunity provision in the AU Amendment Protocol' 13 *Journal of International Criminal Justice* (2015) 3–17

Tomuschat, Christian 'Issues of universal jurisdiction in the *Scilingo* case' 3 *Journal of International Criminal Justice* (2005) 1074–1081

Van As, Francois 'African Peacekeeping: Past practices, future prospects and its contribution to international law' 45 *Revue de Droit Militaire et de Droit de la Guerre* (2006) 329–354

Van der Vyver, Johan '*Ius contra bellum* and American foreign policy' 28 *South African Yearbook of International Law* (2003) 1–28

Van den Wyngaert, Christine 'The criminal justice systems facing the challenge of organised crime' 70 *Revue Internationale de Droit Penal* (1999) 136–221

Van Elst, Richard 'Implementing universal jurisdiction over grave breaches of the Geneva Conventions' 13 (2000) *Leiden Journal of International Law* 815–854

Villarino Villa, Christina 'The crime of aggression before the House of Lords' 4 *Journal of International Criminal Justice* (2006) 866–877

Wedgwood, Ruth 'The fall of Saddam Hussein: Security Council mandates and Preemptive self-defense' 97 *American Journal of International Law* (2003) 576–585

Weigend, Thomas 'Foreword' 8 *Journal of International Criminal Justice* (2010) 1177–1178

Wenaweser, Christian 'Reaching the Kampala compromise on aggression: The Chair's perspective' 23 *Leiden Journal of International Law* (2010) 883–887

Werner, Wouter 'Constitutionalisation, fragmentation, politicisation, the constitutionalisation of international law as a janus-faced phenomenon' 8(2) *Griffin's View on International and Comparative Law* (2007) 17–30

Williamson, Cécile Aptel 'Justice empowered or justice hampered: The International Criminal Court in Darfur' 15(1) *African Security Review* (2006) 20–31

Williamson, Edwin D 'Realism versus legalism in international relations' *ASIL Proceedings* (2002) 262–265

Wright, Quincy 'The law of the Nuremberg Trial' 41(1) *The American Journal of International Law* (1947) 38–72

Zander, Michael 'Act of State Doctrine' 27(5) *The Modern Law Review* (1964) 588–593

Zappalà, Salvatore 'Do heads of state in office enjoy immunity from jurisdiction for international crimes? The *Ghaddafi* case before the French Cour de Cassation' 2001 *European Journal on International Law* 595

Zappalà, Salvatore 'The German Federal Prosecutor's decision not to prosecute a former Uzbek minister' 4 *Journal of International Criminal Justice* (2006) 602–622

Zimmermann, Andreas 'Amending the Amendment Provisions of the Rome Statute: The Kampala compromise on the crime of aggression and the law of treaties' 10 *Journal of International Criminal Justice* (2012) 209–227

Zolo, Danilo 'Peace through Criminal Law?' 2 *Journal of International Criminal Justice* (2004) 727–734

Zwanenburg, Marten 'The Statute for an International Criminal Court and the United States: Peacekeepers under fire?' 10 *European Journal of International Law* (1999) 124–143

BOOKS AND MONOGRAPHS

Abiew, Francis Kofi *The evolution of the doctrine and practice of humanitarian intervention* (1999) Kluwer Law International, The Hague

Alexandrov, SA *Self-Defense against the Use of Force in International Law* (1996) Kluwer Law International, The Hague

Ambos, Kai and Maunganidze, Ottilia (eds) *Power and Prosecution: Challenges and Opportunities for International Criminal Justice in Sub-Saharan Africa* (2013) Universitätsverlag Göttingen, Göttingen

Ambrose, Stephen E *Rise to Globalism – American foreign policy since 1938* 7th (1993) Penguin Books, New York

Bachmann, Klaus and Lyubashenko, Igor (eds) *The Maidan Uprising, separatism and foreign intervention* (2014) Peter Lang, Frankfurt am Main

Bakircioglu, Onder *Self-defence in international and criminal law* (2011) Routledge, Oxford

Barker, Craig *International law and international relations* (2000) Continuum, London and New York

Barriga, Stefan and Kreß, Claus (eds) *The travaux préparatoires of the crime of aggression* (2012) Cambridge University Press, Cambridge

Bassiouni, Cherif *International Criminal Law Conventions and their penal provisions* (1997) Transnational Publishers, New York

Bassiouni, Cherif *International Criminal Law* 2nd Vol I (1999) Transnational Publishers, New York

Bassiouni, Cherif *The legislative history of the International Criminal Court* Vol I (2005) Transnational Publishers, New York

Bassiouni, Cherif *The legislative history of the International Criminal Court* Vol 2 (2005) Transnational Publishers, New York

Bassiouni, Cherif *The legislative history of the International Criminal Court* Vol 3 (2005) Transnational Publishers, New York

Bassiouni, Cherif 'Preface' in *International Criminal Law Quo Vadis?* (2004) Association Internationale de Droit Penal, Ramonville Saint-Agne

Bassiouni, Cherif *The legislative history of the International Criminal Court*: Vol I Introduction, Analysis and Integrated Text (2005) Transnational Publishers, New York

Broomhall, Bruce *International Justice & The International Criminal Court – Between Sovereignty and the Rule of Law* (2003) Oxford University Press, Oxford

Brownlie, Ian *International Law and the use of force by states* (1963) Clarendon Press, Oxford

Brownlie, Ian *Principles of Public International Law* 6th (2003) Oxford University Press, Oxford

Brownlie, Ian *The rule of law in international affairs* (1998) Martinus Nijhoff Publishers, The Hague

Burchell, Jonathan *Principles of Criminal Law* 3rd (2005) Juta, Cape Town

Burchell, Jonathan *South African Criminal Law and Procedure Vol I: General Principles of Criminal Law* 4th (2011) Juta, Cape Town

Cannizzaro, Enzo and Palchetti, Paolo *Customary international law on the use of force – A methodological approach* (2005) Martinus Nijhoff Publishers, Leiden

Cassese, Antonio *International Criminal Law* (2003) Oxford University Press, Oxford

Cassese, Antonio *International Law* 2nd (2005) Oxford University Press, Oxford

Cassese, Antonio *International law in a divided world* (1986) Oxford University Press, Oxford

Claude, Inis L *Swords into plowshares* 4th (1971) Random House, New York

Crawford, James *Brownlie's Principles of Public International Law* 8th (2012) Oxford University Press, Oxford

Cryer, Robert, et al *An introduction to international criminal law and procedure* 2nd (2010) Cambridge University Press, Cambridge

Currie, Iain and De Waal, Johan *The Bill of Rights Handbook* 6th (2013) Juta, Cape Town

Damrosch, Lori F and Oxman, Bernard H (eds) *Future Implications of the Iraq Conflict* (2003) The American Society of International Law, Washington DC

De Wet, Erika *The Chapter VII Powers of the United Nations Security Council* (2004) Hart Publishing, Portland

Dinniss, Heather Harrison *Cyber warfare and the Laws of War* (2012) Cambridge University Press, Cambridge

Dinstein, Yoram *War Aggression and Self-Defence* 4th (2005) Cambridge University Press, Cambridge

Dinstein, Yoram and Tabory, Mala *War crimes in international law* (1996) Kluwer law International, The Hague

Dugard, John *International Law – A South African Perspective* 4th (2011) Juta, Cape Town

Du Plessis, Jacques and Lubbe, Gerhard (eds) *A Man of Principle – The life and legacy of JC de Wet* (2013) Juta, Cape Town

Ferdinandusse, Ward *Direct application of International Criminal Law in National Courts* (2006) TMC Asser Press, The Hague

Ferguson, Niall *The War of the World* (2006) Penguin Books, London

Fleck, Dieter (ed) *The Handbook of Humanitarian Law in Armed Conflicts* (1995) Oxford University Press, Oxford

Fournet, Caroline *International crimes: Theories, Practice and Evolution* (2006) Cameron May Ltd, London

Fox, Hazel (ed) *The changing constitution of the United Nations* (1998) British Inst of Int & Comp Law, London

Gal-Or, Noemi, Ryngaert, Cedric and Noortmann, Math (eds) *Responsibilities of the non-state actor in armed conflict and the market place* (2015) Brill, Leiden

Gray, Christine *International law and the use of force* (2000) Oxford University Press, Oxford

Green, Leslie *The Contemporary law of armed conflict* 2nd (2000) Manchester University Press, Manchester

Grotius, Hugo *Prolegomena to the Law of War and Peace*, translated by Francis W Kelsey (1957) The Bobbs-Merill Company, New York

Henckaerts, Jean-Marie and Doswald-Beck, Louise *Customary International Humanitarian Law Vol I: Rules* (2005) Cambridge University Press, Cambridge

Higgins, Pearce (ed) *Hall's A Treatise on International Law* 8th (1924) Clarendon Press, Oxford

Higgins, Rosalyn *Problems and Process – International law and how we use it* (1994) Clarendon Press, Oxford

Hilaire, Max *International law and the United States military intervention in the Western Hemisphere* (1997) Kluwer Law International, The Hague

Hollis, Duncan, Blakeslee, Merritt and Ederington, Benjamin (eds) *National Treaty Law and Practice* (2005) Martinus Nijhoff Publishers, Leiden/Boston

Ignatieff, Michael *Virtual War – Kosovo and beyond* (2000) Chatto & Windus, London

Jähnke, Burkhard, Laufhütte, Heinrich W and Odersky, Walter *Strafgesetzbuch – Leipziger Kommentar* Vierter Band (2005) De Gruyter Recht, Berlin

Joyner, Christopher (ed) *The United Nations and International Law* (1997) Cambridge University Press, Cambridge

Karns, Margaret P and Mingst, Karen A *International organizations – The politics and processes of global governance* (2004) Lynne Rienner Publishers, London

Kaul, Inge, Grunberg, Isabelle and Stern, Marc (eds) *Global Public Goods – International cooperation in the 21st century* (1999) Oxford University Press, Oxford

Kemp, Gerhard et al *Criminal Law in South Africa* (2012) Oxford University Press, Cape Town

Kennedy, Paul *The Parliament of Man: The past, present and future of the United Nations* (2006) Random House, New York

Kissinger, Henry *Diplomacy* (1994) Touchstone, New York

Kissinger, Henry *World Order - Reflections on the character of nations and the course of history* (2014) Allen Lane, New York

Kittichaisaree, Kriangsak *International Criminal Law* (2001) Oxford University Press, Oxford

Kleffner, Jann *Complementarity in the Rome Statute and National Criminal Jurisdiction* (2007) Unpublished doctoral dissertation, University of Amsterdam

Klip, Andre and Sluiter, Göran (eds) *Annotated Leading Cases of International Criminal Tribunals - Student Ed* (2005) Intersentia, Antwerp

Knoops, Geert-Jan *Defenses in Contemporary International Criminal Law* (2001) Transnational Publishers, New York

Langsam, Walter C *Historic Documents of World War II* (1958) Greenwood Press Publishers, Westport (Connecticut)

Lee, Roy (ed) *The International Criminal Court - The making of the Rome Statute* (1999) Kluwer Law International, The Hague

Levitt, Jeremy *Africa: Mapping new boundaries in international law* (2008) Bloomsbury, London

Lindley-French, Julian *The North Atlantic Treaty Organization - The enduring alliance* (2007) Routledge, Oxford

Malekian, Farhad *The monopolization of international criminal law in the United Nations* (1993) Almqvist & Wiksell International, Uppsala

McDougall, Carrie *The crime of aggression under the Rome Statute of the International Criminal Court* (2013) Cambridge University Press, Cambridge

McGoldrick, Dominic, Rowe, Peter and Donnelly, Eric *The Permanent International Criminal Court - Legal and Policy Issues* (2004) Hart Publishing, Oxford

McNair *The Law of Treaties* (1961) Clarendon Press, Oxford

Melikan, RA (ed) *Domestic and International Trials, 1700–2000, The Trial in History* Vol II (2003) Manchester University Press, Manchester

Murithi, Timothy *The African Union - Pan-Africanism, Peacebuilding and Development* (2005) Ashgate Publishing, Aldershot

Nouwen, Sarah *Complementarity in the line of fire: The catalysing effect of the International Criminal Court in Uganda and Sudan (*2013) Cambridge University Press, Cambridge

Orakhelashvili, Alexander *Peremptory Norms in International Law* (2006) Oxford University Press, Oxford

Packer, HL *The limits of the criminal sanction* (1968) Stanford University Press, Stanford

Politi, Mauro and Nesi, Guiseppi (eds) *The International Criminal Court and the Crime of Aggression* (2004) Ashgate, Aldershot

Rabie, MA and Strauss, SA *Punishment: An introduction to principles* 5th (1994) Lex Patria, Durban

Ratner, Steven and Abrams, Jason *Accountability for human rights atrocities in International Law* 2nd (2001) Oxford University Press, Oxford

Report of the Independent International Commission on Kosovo (2000) Oxford University Press, Oxford

Robertson, Geoffrey *Crimes against humanity - The struggle for global justice* (1999) The New Press, New York

Rodin, David *War & Self-Defense* (2002) Clarendon Press, Oxford

Röling, BVA *International law and the Grotian Heritage* (1985) TMC Asser Institute, The Hague

Röling, BVA and Cassese, A *The Tokyo trial and beyond: Reflections of a peacemaker* (1993) Polity Press, Cambridge

Sadat, Leila N *The International Criminal Court and the transformation of International Law: Justice for the New Millennium* (2002) Transnational Publishers, New York

Sarooshi, Danesh *The United Nations and the Development of collective security – The delegation by the UN Security Council of its Chapter VII powers* (1999) Oxford University Press, Oxford

Sayapin, Sergey *The crime of aggression in international criminal law: historical development, comparative analysis and present state* (2014) Asser Press/Springer, The Hague

Schmidt and Rademeyer *Bewysreg* 4th (2000) Butterworths, Durban

Segall, Anna *Punishing violations of International Humanitarian Law at the national level* (2001) International Committee of the Red Cross, Geneva

Sewall, Sarah and Kaysen, Carl *The United States and the International Criminal Court* (2000) Rowman & Littlefield Publishers, Lanham (Maryland)

Shaw, Malcolm *International Law* 3rd (1991) Grotius Publications, Cambridge

Simester, AP and Smith, ATH *Harm and Culpability* (1996) Clarendon Press, Oxford

Simma, Bruno (ed) *The Charter of the United Nations – A commentary* 2nd Vol I (2002), CH Beck Verlag/Oxford University Press, Oxford

Snyman, CR *Strafreg* 5th (2006) LexisNexis Butterworths, Durban

Stahn, Carsten and Sluiter, Göran (eds) *The emerging practice of the International Criminal Court* (2009) Martinus Nijhoff, The Hague

Starke, JG *An Introduction to International Law* 7th (1972) Butterworths, London

Steytler, Nico *Constitutional criminal procedure* (1998) Butterworths, Durban

Sunga, Lyle *The emerging system of International Criminal Law – Developments in Codification and Implementation* (1997) Kluwer Law International, The Hague

Triffterer, Otto (ed) *Commentary on the Rome Statute of the International Criminal Court* (1999) Nomos Verlagsgesellschaft, Baden-Baden

Tuck, Richard *The Rights of War and Peace – Political thought and the International Order from Grotius to Kant* (1999) Oxford University Press, Oxford

Van den Wyngaert, Christine (ed) *International Criminal Law – A collection of International and European Instruments* 4th (2011) Martinus Nijhoff Publishers, Leiden

Van den Wyngaert, Chris *Strafrecht en Strafprocesrecht* (1999) Maklu, Antwerp

Van den Wyngaert, Chris *Strafrecht, Strafprocesrecht & Internationaal Strafrecht* 5th Vol II (2003) Maklu, Antwerp/Apeldoorn

Von Hebel, Herman, Lammers, Johan and Schukking, Jolien (eds) *Reflections on the International Criminal Court – Essays in Honour of Adriaan Bos* (1999) TMC Asser Press, The Hague

Watts, Arthur Sir *The International Law Commission 1949–1998* Vol I (1999) Oxford University Press, Oxford

Watts, Arthur Sir *The International Law Commission 1949–1998* Vol II (1999) Oxford University Press, Oxford

Watts, Arthur Sir *The International Law Commission 1949–1998* Vol III (1999) Oxford University Press, Oxford
Weller, Marc *The crisis in Kosovo 1989–1999* Vol I (1999) Documents & Analysis Publishing Ltd, Cambridge
Weller, Marc *Contested Statehood: Kosovo's struggle for independence* (2009) Oxford University Press, Oxford
Werle, Gerhard and Jessberger, Florian *Principles of International Criminal Law* 3rd (2014) Oxford University Press, Oxford
Werle, Gerhard, Fernandez, Lovell and Vormbaum, Moritz (eds) *Africa and the International Criminal Court* (2014) Asser Press/Springer, The Hague
Williams, Glanville *Textbook of Criminal Law* (1978) Stevens & Sons, London
Wise, Edward M and Podgor, Ellen S *International Criminal Law: Cases and Materials* (2000) Lexis Publishing, New York
Woodward, Bob *Plan of Attack* (2004) Simon & Schuster, New York
Zahar, Alexander and Sluiter, Göran *International Criminal Law* (2008) Oxford University Press, Oxford
Zimmermann, Andreas, Tomuschat, Christian and Oellers-Frahm, Karin (eds) *The Statute of the International Court of Justice – A Commentary* (2006) Oxford University Press, Oxford

INTERNATIONAL AND REGIONAL INSTRUMENTS AND TREATIES

Charter of the United Nations, 26 Jun 1945, UNCIO XV, 335
Charter of the IMT Nuremberg (1945) UN Treaty Series, vol 82, 279
Charter of the IMTFE Tokyo (1946) Special Proclamation by the Supreme Commander for the Allied Powers, as amended 26 April 1946, TIAS No 1589
Convention on the Prevention and Suppression of the Crime of Genocide (1948) UN Treaty Series, vol 78, 227
Convention for the Amelioration of the Condition of the Wounded and Sick in Armed Forces in the Field (Geneva Convention I) (1949) UN Treaty Series, vol 75, 31
Convention for the Amelioration of the Condition of Wounded, Sick and Shipwrecked Members of Armed Forces at Sea (Geneva Convention II) (1949) UN Treaty Series, vol 75, 85
Convention on the Elimination of All Forms of Discrimination against Women, Dec 18, 1979, UN GAOR, 34th Sess, Supp No 21, UN Doc A/Res/34/180
Convention relative to the Protection of Civilian Persons in Time of War (Geneva Convention IV) (1949) UN Treaty Series, vol 75, 287
Convention relative to the Treatment of Prisoners of War (Geneva Convention III) (1949) UN Treaty Series, vol 75, 135
Definition of Aggression, GA Res 3314 (xxix), 29 UN GAOR Supp No 31, 142 UN Doc A/9631 (1974)
General Treaty for Renunciation of War as an Instrument of National Policy (Kellogg-Briand Pact) 27 Aug 1928, Treaty Series 29 (1929), Cmd 3410

International Convention on the Suppression and Punishment of the Crime of Apartheid (1973) *ILM* 50
International Covenant on Civil and Political Rights, 16 Dec 1966, 999 UNTS 171 (1966)
International Covenant on Economic, Social and Cultural Rights, 16 Dec 1966, 999 UNTS 3 (1966)
Law of the Sea Convention of 1982 (1982) 21 *ILM* 1261
Multilateral Treaty banning Nuclear Weapons Tests in the Atmosphere, in Outer Space, and Under Water, 5 Aug 1963, 480 UNTS 43 (1963)
Nuremberg Principles, 29 Jul 1950, UNGAOR, 5th Session, Supp No 12, UN Doc A/1316 (1950)
Protocol Additional to the Geneva Conventions of 12 Aug 1949, and relating to the Protection of Victims of International Armed Conflicts (Protocol I) (1977) UNGA A/32/144, 15 Aug 1977
Protocol Additional to the Geneva Conventions of 12 Aug 1949, and relating to the Protection of Victims of Non-international Armed Conflicts (Protocol II) (1977) UNGA A/32/144, 15 Aug 1977
Protocol Relating to the Establishment of the Peace and Security Council of the African Union 9 Jul 2002
Protocol on Amendments to the Protocol on the Statute of the African Court of Justice and Human Rights, Jul 2014
Rome Statute of the International Criminal Court (1998) UN Doc A/CONF.183/9 (1998) *ILM*, 999
Statute of the Special Court for Sierra Leone (2002) 16 Jan 2002 (www.sc-sl.org)
Statute of the International Criminal Tribunal for Rwanda (1994) *ILM*, 1598
Statute of the International Criminal Tribunal for the Former Yugoslavia (1993) *ILM*, 1192
Statute of the Office of the UN High Commissioner for Refugees, GA 428 (V) (Annex) 14 Dec 1950
The North Atlantic Treaty of 4 April 1949 (www.nato.int/docu/basictxt/treaty.htm)
Treaty of Peace between the Allied and Associated Powers and Germany (Treaty of Versailles) 28 Jun 1919, 11 Martens Nouveau Recueil (3) 323
Treaty on Principles Governing the Activities of States in the Exploration and Use of Outer Space, Including the Moon and other celestial bodies, GA Res 2222 (XXI) Dec 19, 1966, 610 UNTS 205
Universal Declaration of Human Rights, GA Res 217A (III) UN Doc A/810 (1948)
UN Environment Programme (UNEP) UN Doc A/8730 (1972)
Uniting for Peace Resolution adopted by the UN General Assembly 3 Nov 1950, GA Res 337 (V) Do A/1775 (1951)
UN GA Res 95(I) (1946) (Affirmation of the Principles of International Law recognized by the Charter of the Nurnberg Tribunal)
UN SC Res 82 (1950) (Complaint of Aggression upon the Republic of Korea)
UN SC Res 83 (1950) (Complaint of Aggression upon the Republic of Korea)
UN SC Res 387 (1976) (Angola-South Africa)
UN SC Res 527 (1982) (Lesotho-South Africa)
UN SC Res 568 (1985) (Botswana-South Africa)
UN SC Res 577 (1985) (Angola-South Africa)

UN SC Res 1368 (2001) (Threats to international peace and security caused by terrorist acts)
UN SC Res 1373 (2001) (Threats to international peace and security caused by terrorist acts)
UN SC Res 1377 (2001) (Threats to international peace and security caused by terrorist acts)
UN SC Res 1483 (2003) (The situation between Iraq and Kuwait)
UN SC Res 1593 (2005) (Reports of the Secretary-General on the Sudan)
UN SC Res 1769 (2007) (reports of the Secretary-General on the Sudan)

NATIONAL LEGISLATION

Implementation of the Rome Statute of the International Criminal Court Act 27 of 2002 (South Africa)
International Criminal Court Act 2001 c.17 [2001] 1 Law Reports: Statutes 1367 (England and Wales)
Riotous Assemblies Act 17 of 1956 (South Africa)
Statute of the Iraqi Special Tribunal, 10 Dec 2003, Coalition Provisional Authority (www.cpa-iraq.org/cgi-bin/prfriendly.cgi) (Iraq)
Strafgesetzbuch (StGB) (Germany)
Völkerstrafgesetzbuch (VStGB) 26 Jun 2002, *BGB* 1 2002 I, 2254 (www.juris.de) (Germany)
Wet 16 juni 1993 betreffende de bestraffing van ernstige schendingen van het internationaal humanitair recht, gew wet 10 februari 1999, *BS* 23 maart 1999 (Belgium)

MISCELLANEOUS

Belgium's amendment to the Law of June 15, 1993 (As amended by the Law of February 10, 1999) Concerning the Punishment of Grave Breaches of Humanitarian Law [April 23, 2003] 42 *ILM* 749 (2003)
'Bush's America loses hearts and minds' *Mail & Guardian* 4 Jun 2003 (http://mg.co.za/Content/13.asp?ao=15196)
'Casus belli voor Iraq smelt weg' *De Standaard* 11 Jul 2003 (www.standaard.be/Misc/print.asp?articleID=DST11072003_024)
Control Council Law No 10 (1945) *Official Gazette* Control Council for Germany No 3, Berlin, 31 Jan 1946 50 *et seq*
Delegations to the Review Conference of the Rome Statute of the International Criminal Court 26 Aug 2010 (RC/INF.1) (www.icc-cpi.int/iccdocs/asp_docs/RC2010/RC-INF.1-reissued-ENG-FRA-SPA.pdf)
Discussion paper proposed by the Chairman, Assembly of States Parties, Resumed 5th Session 29 Jan-1 Feb 2007 Annex II, Report of the Special Working Group on the Crime of Aggression, ICC-ASP/5/35 (www.icc-cpi.org)

Discussion paper proposed by the Chairman (Special Working Group) ICC-ASP/5/SWGCA/2 (16 Jan 2007) (www.icc-cpi.int)

Draft Code of Offences against the Peace and Security of Mankind (1954) YILC, 1954, 151; UN Doc A/2693 (1954)

Draft Code of Crimes against the Peace and Security of Mankind (1991) Report of the ILC, 43rd Session, UNGAOR, 46th Session, Supp No 10, A/46/10 (1991)

Draft Code of Crimes against the Peace and Security of Mankind (1996) YILC, 1996, vol II(2); (www.un.org/law/ilc/texts/dcodefra.htm)

GA Res ES-10/14 8 Dec 2003

GA Res A/Res/63/308 14 Sept 2009

Hoffmann, Stanley 'America goes backward' 50(10) *The New York Review of Books* 12 Jun 2003 (www.nybooks.com/articles/16350)

Iraq's Weapons of Mass Destruction – The Assessment of the British Government ID 114567 9/2002 776073, The Stationary Office (www.official-documents.co.uk)

Julian Brett 'The interrelationship between the African peace and security architecture, the global peace and security architecture and regional initiatives' 24 October 2013 (www.um.dk/en/~/media/UM/English-site/Documents/Danida/About-Danida/Danidatransparency/Documents/Grantcommittee/2013/Extdoc/02aAnnexAAPSA study.pdf)

Kosovo Declaration of Independence (17 February 2008) (www.assembly-kosova.org/?cid=2,128,1635)

Press Conference by Chairman of Working Group on Crime of Aggression' 31 Jan 2007 (www.un.org/News/briefings/docs/2007/070131_Wenaweser.doc.htm)

Report on the General Assembly Plenary Debate on the responsibility to Protect 15 Sept 2009 (www.responsibilitytoprotect.org)

Report of the Informal inter-sessional meeting of the Special Working Group on the Crime of Aggression, 8–11 Jun 2006 (www.icc-cpi.int/library/asp/ASP_Advancecopy_Aggression200629jun.pdf)

Report of the International Commission of Inquiry on Darfur to the Secretary General Pursuant to SC Res 1564, 18 Sept 2004 (www.un.org/News/dh/sudan/com_inq_darfur.pdf)

Report of the International Law Commission, 46th Sess, 2 May-22 Jul 1994, UN GAOR, 49th Sess, Supp No 10, UN Doc A/49/10 (1994)

Report of the Secretary-General's High-level Panel on Threats, Challenges and Change' UN Doc A/59/565, 1 Dec 2004

Report of the Seventy-Second Conference of the ILA (Toronto 2006), ILA, London

Report of the Special Working Group on the Crime of Aggression ICC-ASP/5/35 Annex II, 9 (www.icc-cpi.int/asp)

Righter, Rosemary 'What use the UN?' *Timesonline* 5 Dec 2006 (http://tls.timesonline.co.uk)

'Russia accused of unleashing cyberwar to disable Estonia' *The Guardian* 17 May 2007 (www.guardian.co.uk/print/0,,329864981–103610,00.html)

Simone Haysom 'Security and humanitarian crisis in Mali – the role of regional organisations' (March 2014) Humanitarian Policy Group (www.odi.org/sites/odi.org.uk/files/odi-assets/publications-opinion-files/8829.pdf)

Situation on Registered Vessels of the Union of the Comoros, the Hellenic Republic of Greece and the Kingdom of Cambodia,ICC-01/13, 29 January 2015, Public Redacted Version with Confidential Annexes 1, 2 and 3, Application for Review pursuant to Article 53(3)(a) of the Prosecutor's Decision of 6 November 2014 not to initiate an investigation in the Situation (available at www.icc-cpi.int/iccdocs/doc/doc1910341.pdf)

State of the Union Address by US Pres George W Bush, *The New York Times* 29 Jan 2003 (www.nytimes.com/2003/01/29)

Statement by the European Union on the creation of special criminal chambers in Kosovo (3 August 2015) (www.europa.eu/statements-eeas/2015/150803_01_en.htm)

The National Security Strategy of the United States of America, Sept 2002

The National Security Strategy of the United States of America, March 2006

The Princeton Principles on Universal Jurisdiction 23 Jul 2001 (www.princeton.edu/~lapa/unive_jur.pdf)

UN General Assembly Declaration on Friendly Relations and Co-operation among States GA Res 2625 (XXV) 24 Oct 1970

Van den Wyngaert, Christine 'De bijdrage van de internationale straftribunalen tot de ontwikkeling van het straf(process)recht vanuit internationaal en Belgisch perspektief' Paper delivered at Delva cyclus, Gent, Belgium, 17 March 2006

'Who's accountable?' *The New York Times* 10 Jun 2003 (www.nytimes.com/2003/06/10/opi.../10KRUG.html?pagewanted=print&position)

www.ingramcontent.com/pod-product-compliance
Ingram Content Group UK Ltd.
Pitfield, Milton Keynes, MK11 3LW, UK
UKHW051926100926
8556IPUK00022B/1395